Birds For Dummies

Getting Your Bird Off to a Good Start

Buying a bird and setting him up in a new, happy home can be a big investment, but you don't need to purchase much of the gear some retailers suggest. Some of the products out there are more than unnecessary — they're dangerous. One thing not to cut corners on: Start with a healthy, well-socialized bird from a reputable breeder or bird shop.

What you absolutely need

- Examination by an avian veterinarian, including a baseline laboratory workup.
- A well-designed, safe cage of appropriate size for the species. (A good rule: Choose one size bigger than the label suggests; for example, choose a small parrot cage for a cockatiel.)
- A diet appropriate to the species. For most birds, a pellet diet supplemented by fresh vegetables and fruit.
- Stainless steel or crockery (with a nontoxic glaze) bowls.
- Perches: wooden, rope, natural branches (such as manzanita or citrus), and cement.
- Sturdy toys for amusement and exercise.
- Squirt bottle, for misting your bird.
- Nail trimmer (dog or cat variety) or Dremmel tool for blunting nails, plus styptic powder to halt any bleeding.
- First aid kit (buy one ready-made or see our list of suggested contents in Chapter 10).
- Travel cage or carrier.
- Cleaning supplies.

Things you shouldn't buy (but may be told to get anyway)

- Over-the-counter medications, including antibiotics, feather-picking "cures," vitamins, or parasite controls
- Sandpaper perches
- Seed-exclusive diets
- Plastic toys that can be swallowed
- Grit
- Nesting boxes (except for a breeding bird)

Things that are nice to have — for you and your bird

- Air filter and humidifier
- Handheld vacuum
- Play gym
- Cage skirt to catch food and other messes
- Identification, either microchip or leg band

...For Dummies®: Bestselling Book Series for Beginners

Birds For Dummies®

Cheat Sheet

Signs of a Healthy Bird

In the wild, the very survival of a bird depends on his ability to look and act healthy, because predators target those who show signs of vulnerability. In pet birds, this survival behavior doesn't work quite so well. Too often, bird-owners fail to notice early clues of illness because their pets are particularly skilled at hiding these signs. You can find out plenty about your bird's health in Part III. At the very least, though, you need to know what's normal for your bird so that you can spot changes that mean illness — and call your veterinarian! A healthy bird

- Behaves normally, perching without problems, moving with coordination, using the full body without favoring one side or the other.
- Bears weight evenly, all four toes present on each foot and in proper position.
- Is alert and responsive.
- Breathes easily, with no sign of laboring or tail-bobbing.
- Has eyes, ears, and nostrils that are free of debris.
- Has healthy plumage. Feathers have normal color and structure, with no signs of improper development or excessive wear. No evidence of damage from feather-picking, improper housing, or other trauma.
- Consistently produces droppings that are normal in appearance. No pasting of waste on the fanny.
- Has a well-muscled body of appropriate weight, not obese. Skin smooth and translucent without excessive amounts of fat showing underneath or excessive flakiness or crustiness.

Schedule of Routine Care to Ensure Good Health

Putting yourself on a schedule is a great way to make sure your bird's basic needs are covered. While your avian veterinarian may have specific recommendations for your bird, here's a general outline of a good routine:

- Daily (or even more frequently!): Clean food and water dishes and refill them; change cage papers. Most important: Provide attention and interaction, keeping an eye out for changes in behavior, routine, or appearance.
- Weekly: Scrub cage where feces have accumulated. Rotate toys for variety, if your bird is comfortable with changes.
- Monthly: Blunt toenails; check wings for new feathers that need to be trimmed. Check toys; replace any worn ones. Get a feel for body mass — has your bird gained or lost weight or muscle tone? Scrub and disinfect entire cage.
- Annually: Schedule a "well-bird" exam by an avian veterinarian, possibly including some baseline laboratory tests.

Cheat Sheet $2.95 value. Item 5139-6.
For more information about IDG Books, call 1-800-762-2974.

...For Dummies®: Bestselling Book Series for Beginners

Praise for Birds For Dummies

"Gina Spadafori and Dr. Brian Speer have done a remarkable job on *Birds For Dummies*. I found the book to be everything I hoped it would be. The information contained in it is first-rate and helpful to anyone with an interest or love for pet birds. I highly recommend it for everyone who reads the ...*For Dummies* series. You will not be disappointed. This endorsement comes from a board certified pet avian specialist with over 30 years of practice experience who feels educating clients is his number one priority."

— Walter J. Rosskopf, Jr., DVM, Dipl. ABVP (Avian Practice)

"At last — A book that contains more than just pretty bird pictures. This was fun to read. It is clear, concise, factual, useful, and understandable. Truly a book worth reading for new and old Avian Addicts. As a bird store owner, I would recommend it to first-time bird-owners as a basic survival tool, changing that first week together from "Fearful" to "Fantastic." For us old-timers, the book provides tons of new insights and often forgotten techniques, along with how to get modern-day resources for even more knowledge on any given subject."

— Linda Biggi, Bird Gardens, Owner

"Squawk about this! This is one light-hearted, easy-reading, and thoroughly informative book about the care and maintenance of our fine-feathered friends. A must-have for every bird owner."

— Gary A. Gallerstein, DVM, author of *The Complete Bird Owner's Handbook* and *First Aid for Birds*

"An excellent book for bird beginners and novices alike. This book is filled with the information every bird owner (or person contemplating purchasing a bird) needs to keep their pet bird healthy and happy."

— Joel Murphy, DVM, Dipl. ABVP (Avian Practice), author of *How to Care for Your Pet Bird*

"It's refreshing to finally see a book available to pet bird lovers that gives accurate information taken from reputable sources such as Dr. Speer and Gina Spadafori. Unlike many other publications currently on the market today, *Birds For Dummies* is not based on personal opinion that oftentimes lacks a factual foundation, nor does it contain conflicting information. I feel it's a great resource for any pet bird lover. I personally recommend it to anyone who wishes to gain a better understanding of these amazing companions we invite into our lives."

— Debbie Schluter, Bird Lady Productions

"Birds are not for everybody. With that said, *Birds For Dummies* is the most complete discussion of the pros and cons of pet bird ownership that I have seen. If more people read this book before they bought a bird, I would see fewer sick, maladjusted, and behavior-problem birds. If you own a bird, you should read this book; if you are thinking about owning a bird, you MUST read this book."

— Michael J. Murray, DVM

TM

References for the Rest of Us!™

BESTSELLING BOOK SERIES

Do you find that traditional reference books are overloaded with technical details and advice you'll never use? Do you postpone important life decisions because you just don't want to deal with them? Then our *...For Dummies®* business and general reference book series is for you.

...For Dummies business and general reference books are written for those frustrated and hard-working souls who know they aren't dumb, but find that the myriad of personal and business issues and the accompanying horror stories make them feel helpless. *...For Dummies* books use a lighthearted approach, a down-to-earth style, and even cartoons and humorous icons to dispel fears and build confidence. Lighthearted but not lightweight, these books are perfect survival guides to solve your everyday personal and business problems.

"More than a publishing phenomenon, 'Dummies' is a sign of the times."

— The New York Times

"A world of detailed and authoritative information is packed into them..."

— U.S. News and World Report

"...you won't go wrong buying them."

— Walter Mossberg, Wall Street Journal, on IDG Books' ...For Dummies books

Already, millions of satisfied readers agree. They have made *...For Dummies* the #1 introductory level computer book series and a best-selling business book series. They have written asking for more. So, if you're looking for the best and easiest way to learn about business and other general reference topics, look to *...For Dummies* to give you a helping hand.

1/99

Birds FOR DUMMIES®

by Gina Spadafori and
Brian L. Speer, DVM

Foreword by Joe Carvalho

IDG Books Worldwide, Inc.
An International Data Group Company

Foster City, CA ◆ Chicago, IL ◆ Indianapolis, IN ◆ New York, NY

Birds For Dummies®

Published by
IDG Books Worldwide, Inc.
An International Data Group Company
919 E. Hillsdale Blvd.
Suite 400
Foster City, CA 94404
www.idgbooks.com (IDG Books Worldwide Web site)
www.dummies.com (Dummies Press Web site)

Library of Congress Catalog Card No.: 99-65976

ISBN: 0-7645-5139-6

Printed in the United States of America

10 9 8 7 6 5 4 3 2 1

1B/RQ/QZ/ZZ/IN

Distributed in the United States by IDG Books Worldwide, Inc.

Distributed by CDG Books Canada Inc. for Canada; by Transworld Publishers Limited in the United Kingdom; by IDG Norge Books for Norway; by IDG Sweden Books for Sweden; by IDG Books Australia Publishing Corporation Pty. Ltd. for Australia and New Zealand; by TransQuest Publishers Pte Ltd. for Singapore, Malaysia, Thailand, Indonesia, and Hong Kong; by Gotop Information Inc. for Taiwan; by ICG Muse, Inc. for Japan; by Intersoft for South Africa; by Eyrolles for France; by International Thomson Publishing for Germany, Austria and Switzerland; by Distribuidora Cuspide for Argentina; by LR International for Brazil; by Galileo Libros for Chile; by Ediciones ZETA S.C.R. Ltda. for Peru; by WS Computer Publishing Corporation, Inc., for the Philippines; by Contemporanea de Ediciones for Venezuela; by Express Computer Distributors for the Caribbean and West Indies; by Micronesia Media Distributor, Inc. for Micronesia; by Chips Computadoras S.A. de C.V. for Mexico; by Editorial Norma de Panama S.A. for Panama; by American Bookshops for Finland.

For general information on IDG Books Worldwide's books in the U.S., please call our Consumer Customer Service department at 800-762-2974. For reseller information, including discounts and premium sales, please call our Reseller Customer Service department at 800-434-3422.

For information on where to purchase IDG Books Worldwide's books outside the U.S., please contact our International Sales department at 317-596-5530 or fax 317-596-5692.

For consumer information on foreign language translations, please contact our Customer Service department at 1-800-434-3422, fax 317-596-5692, or e-mail rights@idgbooks.com.

For information on licensing foreign or domestic rights, please phone +1-650-655-3109.

For sales inquiries and special prices for bulk quantities, please contact our Sales department at 650-655-3200 or write to the address above.

For information on using IDG Books Worldwide's books in the classroom or for ordering examination copies, please contact our Educational Sales department at 800-434-2086 or fax 317-596-5499.

For press review copies, author interviews, or other publicity information, please contact our Public Relations department at 650-655-3000 or fax 650-655-3299.

For authorization to photocopy items for corporate, personal, or educational use, please contact Copyright Clearance Center, 222 Rosewood Drive, Danvers, MA 01923, or fax 978-750-4470.

About the Authors

Gina Spadafori is an award-winning author with two top-selling pet care books to her credit: *Dogs For Dummies* and *Cats For Dummies* (the latter co-authored with Paul D. Pion, DVM, Dipl. ACVIM). Her weekly Pet Connection column is offered through the Universal Press Syndicate and appears in some of the major newspapers in the country, as well as in the Pet Care Forum of America Online. Gina is a contributing editor and essayist for Pets.com, the leading pet store on the Internet, and she has also written extensively about pets for both pet-related and mainstream magazines.

The Dog Writers Association of America presented *Dogs For Dummies* with the President's Award for the best writing on dogs and the Maxwell Medallion for best general reference book. The Cat Writers Association hailed *Cats For Dummies* as the Best Work on Responsible Cat Care, Best Work on Feline Nutrition, and Best Work on Feline Behavior.

Gina lives in Sacramento, California, with Patrick, a Senegal parrot; Andy, a Shetland sheepdog; and two flat-coated retrievers, Heather and Benjamin.

Brian L. Speer, DVM, Dipl. ABVP (Avian Practice), ECAMS, is one of only a handful of veterinarians certified as an avian specialist in both the United States and in Europe. His specialty practice, The Medical Center for Birds, draws its clientele from all over Northern California, and he consults on cases around the globe.

A graduate of the University of California, Davis, School of Veterinary Medicine, Dr. Speer has limited his practice to birds since 1989, treating everything from budgies and cockatiels to storks and condors. Dr. Speer has lectured in the United States, Canada, and Australia to both veterinary and avicultural audiences. He is the author of many articles in both the academic and mainstream press and serves as an expert legal witness on avian matters. Active in the Association of Avian Veterinarians, he has served as chair of the aviculture committee, as a member of the board of directors, and is currently serving as the group's president. He is an avian-medicine consultant to the Veterinary Information Network.

Dr. Speer lives on the fringes of the San Francisco Bay Area on a two-acre "bird ranch" populated with everything from a turkey named Margie to an ostrich named Bart Junior (BJ), with parrots, chickens, geese, emus, and more filling out the flock. He and his incredibly understanding wife, Denise, have two children, Robin and Cody, both of whom find birds quite boring but tolerate dad and his flock very well, all things considered.

ABOUT IDG BOOKS WORLDWIDE

Welcome to the world of IDG Books Worldwide.

IDG Books Worldwide, Inc., is a subsidiary of International Data Group, the world's largest publisher of computer-related information and the leading global provider of information services on information technology. IDG was founded more than 30 years ago by Patrick J. McGovern and now employs more than 9,000 people worldwide. IDG publishes more than 290 computer publications in over 75 countries. More than 90 million people read one or more IDG publications each month.

Launched in 1990, IDG Books Worldwide is today the #1 publisher of best-selling computer books in the United States. We are proud to have received eight awards from the Computer Press Association in recognition of editorial excellence and three from Computer Currents' First Annual Readers' Choice Awards. Our best-selling *...For Dummies®* series has more than 50 million copies in print with translations in 31 languages. IDG Books Worldwide, through a joint venture with IDG's Hi-Tech Beijing, became the first U.S. publisher to publish a computer book in the People's Republic of China. In record time, IDG Books Worldwide has become the first choice for millions of readers around the world who want to learn how to better manage their businesses.

Our mission is simple: Every one of our books is designed to bring extra value and skill-building instructions to the reader. Our books are written by experts who understand and care about our readers. The knowledge base of our editorial staff comes from years of experience in publishing, education, and journalism — experience we use to produce books to carry us into the new millennium. In short, we care about books, so we attract the best people. We devote special attention to details such as audience, interior design, use of icons, and illustrations. And because we use an efficient process of authoring, editing, and desktop publishing our books electronically, we can spend more time ensuring superior content and less time on the technicalities of making books.

You can count on our commitment to deliver high-quality books at competitive prices on topics you want to read about. At IDG Books Worldwide, we continue in the IDG tradition of delivering quality for more than 30 years. You'll find no better book on a subject than one from IDG Books Worldwide.

John Kilcullen
Chairman and CEO
IDG Books Worldwide, Inc.

Steven Berkowitz
President and Publisher
IDG Books Worldwide, Inc.

Eighth Annual Computer Press Awards 1992

Ninth Annual Computer Press Awards 1993

Tenth Annual Computer Press Awards 1994

Eleventh Annual Computer Press Awards 1995

IDG is the world's leading IT media, research and exposition company. Founded in 1964, IDG had 1997 revenues of $2.05 billion and has more than 9,000 employees worldwide. IDG offers the widest range of media options that reach IT buyers in 75 countries representing 95% of worldwide IT spending. IDG's diverse product and services portfolio spans six key areas including print publishing, online publishing, expositions and conferences, market research, education and training, and global marketing services. More than 90 million people read one or more of IDG's 290 magazines and newspapers, including IDG's leading global brands — Computerworld, PC World, Network World, Macworld and the Channel World family of publications. IDG Books Worldwide is one of the fastest-growing computer book publishers in the world, with more than 700 titles in 36 languages. The "...For Dummies®" series alone has more than 50 million copies in print. IDG offers online users the largest network of technology-specific Web sites around the world through IDG.net (http://www.idg.net), which comprises more than 225 targeted Web sites in 55 countries worldwide. International Data Corporation (IDC) is the world's largest provider of information technology data, analysis and consulting, with research centers in over 41 countries and more than 400 research analysts worldwide. IDG World Expo is a leading producer of more than 168 globally branded conferences and expositions in 35 countries including E3 (Electronic Entertainment Expo), Macworld Expo, ComNet, Windows World Expo, ICE (Internet Commerce Expo), Agenda, DEMO, and Spotlight. IDG's training subsidiary, ExecuTrain, is the world's largest computer training company, with more than 230 locations worldwide and 785 training courses. IDG Marketing Services helps industry-leading IT companies build international brand recognition by developing global integrated marketing programs via IDG's print, online and exposition products worldwide. Further information about the company can be found at www.idg.com.

1/24/99

Dedication

Gina: To the amazing Margarets, Peggy Conway and Peg Gavel, true animal-lovers and even better friends, and to Patrick, the Senegal parrot who is my adored little muse.

Brian: To my wife, Denise, and our children, Robin and Cody, because so much of what I am and what I do is because they have made me whole in so many ways. To my parents, my instructors and mentors, my patients, and my clients — all of whom have taught me so well over the years and continue to do so every day. And to my first bird, Toby, a blue-and-gold macaw who showed me how cool birds are, and truly opened up my mind and heart to them.

Publisher's Acknowledgments

We're proud of this book; please register your comments through our IDG Books Worldwide Online Registration Form located at `http://my2cents.dummies.com`.

Some of the people who helped bring this book to market include the following:

Acquisitions and Editorial

Project Editors: Christine Meloy Beck, Jennifer Ehrlich

Acquisitions Editor: Stacy S. Collins

Copy Editors: Linda S. Stark, Elizabeth Netedu Kuball

Technical Editor: William G. Porte, MBA, DVM

Editorial Coordinator: Maureen F. Kelly

Associate Permissions Editor: Carmen Krikorian

Editorial Managers: Mary C. Corder, Jennifer Ehrlich

Editorial Assistant: Alison Walthall

Production

Project Coordinator: Maridee V. Ennis

Layout and Graphics: Amy A. Adrian, Angela F. Hunckler, Kate Jenkins, Barry Offringa, Jill Piscitelli, Douglas L. Rollison, Brent Savage, Janet Seib, Maggie Ubertini, Mary Jo Weis, Dan Whetstine

Proofreaders: Joanne Keaton, Melissa Martin, Nancy Price, Marianne Santy, Toni Settle

Indexer: Christine Spina Karpeles

Special Help

Illustrator: Jay Gavron

General and Administrative

IDG Books Worldwide, Inc.: John Kilcullen, CEO; Steven Berkowitz, President and Publisher

IDG Books Technology Publishing Group: Richard Swadley, Senior Vice President and Publisher; Walter Bruce III, Vice President and Associate Publisher; Steven Sayre, Associate Publisher; Joseph Wikert, Associate Publisher; Mary Bednarek, Branded Product Development Director; Mary Corder, Editorial Director

IDG Books Consumer Publishing Group: Roland Elgey, Senior Vice President and Publisher; Kathleen A. Welton, Vice President and Publisher; Kevin Thornton, Acquisitions Manager; Kristin A. Cocks, Editorial Director

IDG Books Internet Publishing Group: Brenda McLaughlin, Senior Vice President and Publisher; Diane Graves Steele, Vice President and Associate Publisher; Sofia Marchant, Online Marketing Manager

IDG Books Production for Dummies Press: Michael R. Britton, Vice President of Production; Debbie Stailey, Associate Director of Production; Cindy L. Phipps, Manager of Project Coordination, Production Proofreading, and Indexing; Tony Augsburger, Manager of Prepress, Reprints, and Systems; Laura Carpenter, Production Control Manager; Shelley Lea, Supervisor of Graphics and Design; Debbie J. Gates, Production Systems Specialist; Robert Springer, Supervisor of Proofreading; Kathie Schutte, Production Supervisor

Dummies Packaging and Book Design: Patty Page, Manager, Promotions Marketing

◆

The publisher would like to give special thanks to Patrick J. McGovern, without whom this book would not have been possible.

◆

Authors' Acknowledgments

Our first words of gratitude have to go to Paul D. Pion, DVM, Dipl. ACVIM (Cardiology), a brilliant and pioneering veterinarian, co-founder and CEO of the Veterinary Information Network and Gina's co-author on *Cats For Dummies.* Paul decided that we would be a good team as co-authors, and he was right. Every day, in every way, Paul works to push veterinary medicine forward, and the lives of countless animals and people are healthier and happier for his efforts.

Thanks also to our technical reviewer, William G. Porte, MBA, DVM, of Sacramento Veterinary Surgical Services, who also served on the team of *Dogs For Dummies* and *Cats For Dummies.* He epitomizes the qualities of cutting-edge knowledge and compassion that all good veterinarians possess. Thanks also to Christine Eckerman-Ross, who helped in the proofing of the manuscript.

We are again pleased to bring Jay Gavron's outstanding illustrations to such a wide audience. Thanks also to Sharon Garsee of The Bird Shop in Sacramento, Julie Murad of The Gabriel Foundation, Dr. Michael J. Murray of the Avian and Exotic Clinic of the Monterey Peninsula, as well as to Laurella Desborough, Joe Carvalho, Cerise Duran, and Dr. Christine Sellers-Stalie.

The folks at IDG Books Worldwide are an author's dream and deserve to take a bow: Kathy Welton, Stacy Collins, Christy Beck, Jennifer Ehrlich, Linda Stark, and Elizabeth Kuball.

A very heartfelt thank-you to Brian's staff at the Oakley Veterinary Medical Center, who made it possible for him to have time to write this book and maintain a busy travel schedule. Special thanks to veterinarians Scott Echols, Carla Weinberg, Julie Martin, Martin Orr, Diane Mitchell, and Susan Choy, all of whom came to learn from Brian and in so doing also taught him. Thanks to Drs. James Harris, Walter Rosskopf, Greg Harrison, Bob Altman, Branson Ritchie, David Phalen, Susan Clubb, Susan Orosz, Alan Fudge, Kevin Flammer, and Chuck Galvin. As Brian says, "You have directly mentored and molded my 'bird brain' over the years. It is truly an honor to have you all as colleagues in a profession and specialty that we love with such a passion as we do."

Gina would like to acknowledge the contributions of Joan Frazzini, Jan Haag, J.R. Taylor, Tonya Machen, Pam Silva, KT Jorgensen, Christie Keith, Linda Batson, and Ginger Sanders. Literary attorney Patricia Crown of Coblence and Warner in New York City deserves special thanks for her kindness and her skill. Thanks, too, to editors Greg Melvin and Alan McDermott of the Universal Press

Syndicate. Gina would also like to acknowledge the support of her family: Parents Louise and Nino, brothers Joe and Pete, Pete's wife, Sally, and their children, Katharine and Steven.

As always, Bruce Rubin cannot be thanked enough for his business advice and encouragement. And finally, a special word of gratitude to a wonderful veterinarian, Dr. Carla Weinberg, who refused to euthanize a feather-picked little mess of a Senegal parrot when he was brought to her, believing she could make him healthy and find him a good new home. The home she found was Gina's, and the bird is now Patrick, Gina's cherished avian companion.

Contents at a Glance

Foreword xxvii

Introduction 1

Part I: Which Bird For You? 9

Chapter 1: Birds and Humans: It's Only Natural! 11
Chapter 2: Narrowing the Choices 23
Chapter 3: A Bird of Your Own 47

Part II: Caring for Your Bird Properly 63

Chapter 4: All the Right Stuff 65
Chapter 5: Starting Your Bird Off Right 83
Chapter 6: The New Art, Science, and Fun of Feeding Birds Right 99
Chapter 7: Beyond Food and Water: Bird Basics 115

Part III: Keeping Your Bird Healthy 137

Chapter 8: How Birds Work: The Short Course 139
Chapter 9: A Preventive Care Approach to Your Bird's Health 157
Chapter 10: Your Bird in Sickness — and Back to Health 173
Chapter 11: Lifelong Care for Your Bird 193

Part IV: Living Happily with Your Bird 207

Chapter 12: Getting to "Good Bird!": Dealing with Behavior Problems 209
Chapter 13: Living in a Multiple-Bird Household 223

Part V: The Part of Tens 239

Chapter 14: Ten Bird Myths — Debunked! 241
Chapter 15: Ten Steps to a Healthy Bird 249
Chapter 16: Ten Questions to Ask When Buying a Bird 257
Chapter 17: Ten Must-See Avian Web Sites 265
Chapter 18: Ten Best Birds for Beginners 275
Chapter 19: Ten Common Dangers to Your Bird's Life 283
Chapter 20: Ten Disaster-Planning Tips for Bird-Lovers 293
Chapter 21: Ten Classic Bird Jokes (Just the Clean Ones) 299
Appendix: Additional Resources 303

Index 309
Book Registration Information........................*Back of Book*

Cartoons at a Glance

By Rich Tennant

page 9

The 5th Wave By Rich Tennant

"He loves his ball and string, but once in a while he'll pick up the trombone and play 'Under Paris Skies' over and over again."

page 63

"It's Feathers; I think she's taking steroids."

page 137

"Listen McKenzie–those are my sheep in your living room! Now, either you do something about keeping your Border canary locked up, or I WILL!!"

page 207

"Of course I'm jittery. I'm here alone, the lights went out, and now I can't find the bird."

page 239

Fax: 978-546-7747 • E-mail: the5wave@tiac.net

Table of Contents

Foreword .... *xxvii*

Introduction *1*

Approaching Bird Ownership Realistically 1
How This Book Is Organized 2
Part I: Which Bird for You? 2
Part II: Caring for Your Bird Properly 3
Part III: Keeping Your Bird Healthy 3
Part IV: Living Happily with Your Bird 4
Part V: The Part of Tens 4
When it comes to birds, you need color! 5
Icons Used In This Book 5
Some Final Words on Pronouns and Your Pets 6
How to Reach Us 6

Part I: Which Bird For You? *9*

Chapter 1: Birds and Humans: It's Only Natural! 11

Don't Know Much about History? Read On! 12
Food, feathers, and (finally!) friendship 12
Our enduring involvement 13
Are You Really Ready for a Bird? 16
Putting in the time . . . and time again 16
Shelling out the bucks 17
Dealing with the noise and mess 18
Exploring Avian Cyberspace 19

Chapter 2: Narrowing the Choices 23

What Are You Looking For in a Bird? 24
Judging interactivity 24
Considering size 24
Mess and more mess 25
Bring in da noise 25
Talking ability 26
How much is that birdie in the window? 26

Considering the Species 27
The hands-off color and song birds 28
Small parrots 30
Medium-sized parrots 35
Large parrots 38
Toucans, mynahs, and some others 43
Chickens, ducks, geese, peafowl, and turkeys 43

Chapter 3: A Bird of Your Own 47

Considering Wild-Caught versus Captive-Raised 48
Telling the Girls from the Guys 49
Checking Up on a Bird's Good Health 50
Making Mature Decisions about Age 51
Weighing the pros and cons of baby birds 52
Considering the prospects of older birds 54
Finding a Reputable Source 55
Pet shops 56
Breeders 59
Private parties 59
Protecting Your Rights 60

Part II: Caring for Your Bird Properly 63

Chapter 4: All the Right Stuff 65

A Cage to Call Her Own 66
Bigger is better 66
Wood you buy metal, please? 67
A checklist for cage quality 67
The time-out cage 69
Cage to go 70
Perch Perfect 71
Playstands and Gyms 74
Dishes and Waterers 74
Toys? Keep 'em Coming 75
Clearing the Air 77
Cleanups Made Easy 78
Basic cleaning supplies 78
Preventing messes 79
The Best of the Rest Accessory-Wise 81

Chapter 5: Starting Your Bird Off Right 83

Starting the Relationship Right 84
Setting Up the Cage 84
Traveling Home Safely and Sanely 86
Settling In 86

Managing Introductions 87
Kids 87
Cats 87
Dogs 88
Other birds 89
Building Trust through Training 90
Rules for you 91
Teaching the step-up command 92
Taming the wild ones 93
Keeping Things Clean: A Basic Regimen 94
Setting up for cleaning 95
Everyday cleanups 96
The big clean 98

Chapter 6: The New Art, Science, and Fun of Feeding Birds Right 99

Raising Generations of Junk-Food Junkies 100
Enter the Pelleted Diet 100
Chicken feed? It isn't that easy! 102
The revolution moves slowly 102
Nutrition — the Short Course 103
Protein 103
Carbohydrates 104
Fats 105
Water 105
Vitamins 106
Minerals 106
What Your Bird Should Be Eating 106
Pellet diets 107
Fruits and vegetables 107
Food for people and other pets 109
Nuts 110
Seeds 110
What about vitamin and mineral supplements? 110
Practical Plans for Converting Your Bird's Diet 111
Birds of a (Slightly) Different Feather 113

Chapter 7: Beyond Food and Water: Bird Basics 115

Translating Bird Body Language 116
The eyes have it 116
Say what? 117
Beak bulletins 118
Wing things 120
Tail tales 121
Posture primer 122

Getting a Handle on Your Bird 124
Restraining by hand: The "parrot popsicle" 124
Meet "Mr. Towel" 125
Practicing Good Grooming 127
Trimming nails 127
Clipping wings 128
Raining down with showers, baths, and misting 130
Bird Care When You Can't 132
Pet-sitters 132
Boarding 133
Can your bird go with you? 134

Part III: Keeping Your Bird Healthy 137

Chapter 8: How Birds Work: The Short Course 139

The Outside: More than Just Beautiful 140
Built for versatility: The beak 140
A bird's eye view 144
The better to ear you with 144
Beautiful, functional feathers 145
A leg to stand on, times two 149
Finding Your Inner Bird 150
Them bones, them bones 150
Live and breathe: The cardiopulmonary system 152
Ya gotta eat: The gastrointestinal system 152

Chapter 9: A Preventive Care Approach to Your Bird's Health 157

Preventive Care Is the Best Care 158
What your bird won't tell you — and why 158
More arguments for preventive care 159
A Three-Part Plan for Preventive Care 161
Starting with a healthy bird 162
Proper care and nutrition 163
Working with the pros 164
Finding the Right Veterinarian 165
Why "any veterinarian" may not be right for your bird 165
Special care for a special pet 167
Who's out there, and what are they offering? 169

Chapter 10: Your Bird in Sickness — and Back to Health 173

Birds Are Birds — Not People, Not Dogs 174
Home Care Fallacies 176
First Aid Basics 177
So what's an emergency? 177
Whom to call, where to go 178
What to do, in what order 179
Emergency! The veterinarian's role 183

Infectious Diseases That Panic Parrot-Lovers 184
Tiny beings, big problems 184
Psittacine Beak and Feather Disease 185
Pacheco's parrot disease 186
Avian polyomavirus 187
Proventricular dilation disease 187
Psittacosis 187
Aspergillosis and candidiasis 188
Supportive Care 189
The hospital stay 189
Home care 190
Giving medication 191

Chapter 11: Lifelong Care for Your Bird 193

Why Birds Are Living Longer 194
Domestically raised versus wild-caught 194
New views on nutrition 195
The veterinary contribution 196
Health and the Older Bird 197
Chronic malnutrition 197
Cataracts 200
Arthritis 200
Heart disease 200
Knowing When It's "Time" 200
Euthanasia options 201
Dealing with loss 203
What If You Go First? 205

Part IV: Living Happily with Your Bird 207

Chapter 12: Getting to "Good Bird!": Dealing with Behavior Problems 209

A Framework for Good Behavior 210
Ensure Your Bird's Health 211
Be Fair to Your Bird 211
Create a suitable environment 213
Spend time in positive interaction 213
Get that bird a job! 214
Be Firm with Your Bird — but Gently 214
Becoming top bird 215
Why punishment doesn't work 217
Problem-Solving Troublesome Behaviors 217
Feather-picking 218
Biting and other forms of aggression 219
Screaming 220
What If You Can't Fix the Problem? 221

Chapter 13: Living in a Multiple-Bird Household 223
Companion Birds or Breeders? 224
The more the merrier 224
Are you breeder material? 225
Closed Aviary Concept: Rules to Live By 226
Choosing Compatible Pets 227
Species and gender issues 228
Size and temperament issues 228
The Joy and Challenges of Breeding 229
Pair bonding: 'Til death do us part 230
Setting up your love birds 231
The Awesome Egg 232
Natural incubation 233
Artificial incubation 233
Raising the Babies 234
Hand-feeding and socializing 235
Weaning and fledging 237

Part V: The Part of Tens 239

Chapter 14: Ten Bird Myths — Debunked! 241
Birds Are Low-Maintenance Pets 241
Birds Are High-Maintenance Pets 242
Birds Are Fragile 243
A Hand-Fed Bird Makes a Better Pet 243
Seed Is the Best Diet for Birds 244
Birds Get Mites Easily 244
Birds Catch Colds from People 245
A Sick Bird Is a Dead Bird 245
Lovebirds Will Die of Loneliness If Not Kept in Pairs 246
All Parrots Talk 246

Chapter 15: Ten Steps to a Healthy Bird 249
The Physical Examination 250
Caging and Husbandry Review 251
Food for Thought: The Right Nutrition 252
Behavioral Check-Up 252
Guideline for Multi-Bird Households 253
Testing the Blood 253
Screening for Bacteria 253
A Couple More Diseases — Maybe 254
For the Record: What and Who Are You? 254
A Shot for Birdy? 255

Chapter 16: Ten Questions to Ask When Buying a Bird 257
Where Do You Get Your Birds? ...257
How Many Birds Do You Sell a Year? ...258
What Are the Terms of the Sales Contract and Post-Purchase Warranty? ...259
What Are Your References? ...260
How Old Is This Bird? ...260
Does This Bird Have Any Medical Problems, Past or Current? ...261
Does This Bird Have Any Behavioral Problems? ...262
How Have You Socialized This Bird? ...263
What Have You Been Feeding This Bird? ...263
May I Visit and Get to Know the Bird Before Buying? ...264

Chapter 17: Ten Must-See Avian Web Sites 265
Fun for Kids — and Adults, Too ...266
Behavior Help and Then Some ...267
Enrapt over Raptors ...267
Help Us Get Home ...268
Meet Alex, the Star ...269
It's Academic ...269
Birds of a Feather, Flocking Together ...270
The Source for Health ...270
Remembering Birds in Need ...271
And a Flock of Others ...272

Chapter 18: Ten Best Birds for Beginners 275
Canaries ...276
Finches ...277
Budgies (Parakeets) ...278
Cockatiels ...278
Quaker Parakeets ...279
Poicephalus Parrots and Parrotlets ...280
Pionus Parrots ...280
Pyrrhura Conures ...281
Amazon Parrots ...281
Peach-Faced Lovebirds ...282

Chapter 19: Ten Common Dangers to Your Bird's Life 283
Yum-Yum Little Birdy ...284
Flying Is for the Birds ...285
Bird on the Loose ...286
Inhalant Dangers ...286
Plants Not for Nibbling ...287
Foods That Shouldn't Be Shared ...289

Metals That Are, Like, Heavy, Man 289
Maybe Some Medicine Will Help? 290
Watch Where You Step 290
A Shocking Surprise 291

Chapter 20: Ten Disaster-Planning Tips for Bird-Lovers 293

Consider the Possibilities 294
Make a Contact List 294
Make Sure Your Bird Carries an ID 295
Make and Trade Bird-Care Files 295
Collect Food and Supplies 296
Keep a First Aid Kit Fully Stocked 296
Plan, Plan, Plan, and Practice 297
Keep Your Bird Secure — and Separate 297
Keep a "Lost Bird" Kit Ready 297
Be Prepared to Help Others 298

Chapter 21: Ten Classic Bird Jokes (Just the Clean Ones) 299

What Would We Do without the Guy Who Walks into the Pet Store? ...299
Will We Ever Get Out of the Pet Store? 300
Oh, This One Is Punny 300
If You Thought That One Was Silly 300
And Back to the Pet Store 300
Take a Cruise with Us 301
It's Always Good to Pray 301
A Little Respect, Please 302
Elementary, My Dear Watson 302
Enough Parrots! 302

Appendix: Additional Resources 303

Supplies 303
Periodicals 304
Veterinary and Aviculture Groups 305
Conservation Groups 305
Rescue and Adoption Organizations 306

Index....................309

Book Registration Information ....Back of Book

Foreword

Falling in love with a bird can change your life. No one knows this better than I do.

I never figured when I was growing up that I'd end up as a bird-trainer, putting on shows all over the world and appearing with my birds on *Late Night With David Letterman* and *The Tonight Show With Jay Leno*. But life takes funny turns sometimes, from teaching behaviors to my pet parrots to a TV appearance on *The Gong Show* to a phone call from Knott's Berry Farm asking me to set up a show to where I am now, living a life dedicated to entertaining and educating bird-lovers of all ages.

My life is full of hard work and challenges, but it never lacks for excitement. And I owe a lot of the credit to my birds, my beautiful, inspiring partners. Time with them is always well-spent and always a pleasure.

Birds are wonderful companions, I'll be the first to tell you, but too many people don't know how to care for them properly or how to handle them. And too many birds suffer as a result.

That's why I was excited to hear about *Birds For Dummies*. Talk about a dream team! How could you beat the pairing of one of the world's top avian veterinarians with a talented and experienced pet writer?

The book you hold in your hand is the wonderful result of their collaboration, and reading it will provide you with the knowledge you need to realize the full potential of your relationship with your bird.

All that's left to do is fall in love. And that part's the easiest. Believe me, I know.

Joe Carvalho
President, Friends of a Feather
Danville, California

Introduction

Welcome to *Birds For Dummies,* the only book you need to turn your admiration and appreciation of birds into a lasting, loving relationship with an avian companion.

This book is a labor of love for both of us. Brian is a pioneering veterinarian — one of only a few dozen full-time avian specialists in the world. He realized his interest in birds before he even entered veterinary school. While working for a large-animal veterinarian, he found himself being reprimanded for paying attention to peacocks and other farm birds instead of holding the horses for his boss.

As a veterinarian, he took a big risk after a few years in traditional practice and decided to focus solely on birds. Some of his clients disagreed with his stand, to the point that one family even taped chicken feathers to their dog in a lighthearted effort to get him to treat the animal — to no avail. Brian's love is birds, and he has treated a great many of them, from pet parrots to barnyard fowl to exotics such as flamingos and cassowaries.

Other than a couple of cats who are very aware of their minority status, you can find no animals except birds on his Northern California mini-ranch. And what birds they are! Brian's avian family includes not only chickens, geese, turkeys, and ducks, but also several pairs of beautiful macaws, emus, and ostriches.

Gina's flock is limited to one bird, a Senegal parrot named Patrick with whom she shares her office, her life, and her heart. Patrick sat on the desk (and sometimes on the keyboard) during the writing of this book, checking the words on the screen, looking down his beak at Gina's three dogs, and occasionally demanding a snuggle.

As you can tell, we love birds, and we can think of few better ways to show it than with a book to help others adore them, too.

Approaching Bird Ownership Realistically

A big problem with pet ownership originates not with the animal but with the animal caretaker. No one wins when someone picks a pet for the wrong reasons or harbors odd ideas about what it takes to properly care for the new family member. Although you may think that folks are inclined to do some homework before dropping up to a couple thousand dollars on an exotic bird, we've seen enough to know that common sense is all too often neither common nor sense. People purchase birds for their status, for their beauty, for their song — and even for how well they match the furniture.

But birds aren't simple creatures. They have needs and desires (some call them demands!), and many are highly affectionate and social. Some can also test your tolerance when it comes to noise and mess. You need to know all this going in, along with which bird to buy, where to buy one, and how to deal with the inevitable behavior problems that challenge nearly every bird-owner from time to time.

Successful bird-lovers are knowledgeable, realistic, flexible, and possessed of a good sense of humor. For their efforts, they share their lives with a marvelous companion. We want you to be among the successful ones, and every line in this book is part of our heartfelt effort to help you.

How This Book Is Organized

Birds For Dummies is divided into five parts. If you've never had a bird in your life and are just starting to entertain the idea of adding one, you may want to start at the beginning. If you already have a bird, you can skip around, checking out the chapters that address your needs at any given time. Is your bird eating as well as he should? Want to add another bird? Thinking about getting into breeding? We have it all covered, along with what you need to know to deal with health and behavior problems.

We've packed so much information into *Birds For Dummies* that we're guessing you're probably going to want to read every page eventually, in any order that pleases you. After all, you do want to make the most of your relationship with your bird, right?

No matter where you choose to start, jump to, or pause within this book, here are the basics of what you can expect to find in *Birds For Dummies*.

Part I: Which Bird for You?

Everyone seems to fall in love with those flashy macaws and handsome cockatoos, but is either of those really the right bird for you and your lifestyle? We help you sort it all out, explaining why people are drawn to birds and exactly what you're getting into when you decide to bring any particular member of the species into your life. Time and money factor into your decision, but there's more — and we share it all, because we know an educated buyer has the best chance at being a successful bird-owner.

After you decide that you're a Bird Person, what sort of bird is right for you? A colorful canary, with his lovely song? Bright and active finches? Affectionate little parrots, such as budgies and cockatiels? Or are you destined for such lovelies as the eclectus or sun conure, or the clever Amazons and African greys? You can find dozens of birds to choose from, including a few lessor-known species that we think make fantastic pets.

You need to know more than what kind of bird you want: You also have to know where to find a healthy, well-socialized companion. We walk you through the minefield of buying a bird and tell you how to find that one perfect pet.

Finally, something you can't find in any other bird book: an exclusive *...For Dummies* guide to avian Internet resources — how to get the most out of your online experience while avoiding the inaccurate, misguided, and even deadly information.

Part II: Caring for Your Bird Properly

What kind of cage is right for your new pet? What about bowls, perches, carriers, and toys? What do you really need, what's nice to have, and what isn't worth spending money on? Part II is where you find all that good information. What about your bird's first veterinary examination? And how should you introduce your new pet to your kids, other birds, or pet cats or dogs?

Part II also helps you to bond with your bird and understand how to handle him in a way that prevents behavior problems as he settles in as a family member. Good husbandry gets its share of attention here, too, with detailed instructions on how to groom your bird and keep her environment clean and safe.

You also find one of the more important chapters in Part II, on good nutrition. Here's a hint: Forget the seeds! Dispensing with the myths, we provide a cutting-edge course on how to feed your pet bird, along with timesaving tips.

Part III: Keeping Your Bird Healthy

Avian medicine has come a long way in a comparatively very short time, leaving many bird-lovers (and some veterinarians, sadly) in the dust. In this part, we provide you with a short course in keeping your bird healthy, from identifying signs of illness to finding and working with a good veterinarian. We tell you what you need to know about anatomy and what's normal for your bird, and we familiarize you with the tools your veterinarian uses to diagnose and treat illness.

We cover common diseases, too, along with nursing skills, giving you the information you need to medicate and otherwise care for a recuperating bird.

Finally, although no one likes to think about such things, we cover pet loss, offering practical help for grief and related problems. Of course, your bird may outlive you, and you can find no-nonsense advice on how to prepare for that situation, too.

Part IV: Living Happily with Your Bird

What can you do about biting? About screaming? About a bird who chews off all his beautiful plumage? In Part IV, the emphasis shifts to developing a relationship with your bird that will last for life, starting with help for the behavior problems that drive owners crazy — and make some birds homeless.

After you experience life with one bird, you may fall prey to what some bird-lovers call "NEB disease" — Never Enough Birds. If you find yourself afflicted, we can help you deal with it via advice on compatibility issues, on caging and aviaries, and on health concerns for multi-bird households.

And if you get the urge to try your hand at breeding, we can help you there, too, with information on breeding birds and raising babies. You don't want your precious youngsters sold to just anyone, so we share with you tips on how to find good homes for your birds.

Part V: The Part of Tens

A little bit of everything here — some chapters just for fun, and others dead serious. In The Part of Tens, we tell you what questions to ask when buying a bird, as well as the ten best birds for beginners. Take a tour of the World (Wide Web) without ever leaving home — we tracked down some fabulous stops on the Information Superhighway that any bird-lover is bound to enjoy. Avoiding common household dangers is another chapter within this part, as is an explanation of common diagnostic tests your veterinarian may suggest.

We top off the book with a bit of whimsy, with jokes about birds. Our Additional Resources appendix provides you with the information to find everything you need for your bird, along with references to bird clubs and charities you may want to contact.

When it comes to birds, you need color!

The beauty of birds can't be appreciated without color, which is why we're pleased to bring you a full-color section in the center of this book. In it, we give you a basic lesson in bird anatomy and show you how to choose and equip a cage for your bird. The rest of the section consists of pictures of various popular species, along with information to help you make an intelligent choice for your avian companion.

Icons Used In This Book

Every *...For Dummies* book has little pictures in the margins — we call them icons — to help you navigate through the book, and *Birds For Dummies* is no different in that respect. A little twist on the norm, though: Many of our icons are unique to this book, and they celebrate our feathered companions to boot! Here's a rundown on what each icon means:

You don't *have* to read the information next to our *...For Dummies* guy, but we really think you should anyway. You see a lot of him in the health sections especially, where we give you in-depth information, but we also offer you the chance to skip over him and still manage a good grasp of the basic concepts.

If you're in a hurry, give him a pass. But come back, please, for that little bit of extra information. We think you're going to find it's worthwhile.

This icon flags especially useful clues to making life with your bird easier or making your pet happier and healthier. It highlights time- and money-savers, too!

Your bird wants you to read very carefully every word next to this icon, because it marks some of the best products or services available for birds — and for those who love them.

We put information that's especially amusing or intriguing in a lot of places, and we use this little symbol to point out that neat stuff for you so you're sure not to miss it.

For related information or for more detailed coverage of a topic or a similar subject, you want to heed this icon's advice and visit another section of the book.

If we think something's so important that it deserves restating or summarizing, this icon appears to make sure that you don't jump over that vital information. If you see this little flag, know that it marks some rich and rewarding wisdom that we think is worth reading more than once.

This icon denotes some common mistakes bird-owners make, along with tips for avoiding them. Pay heed! Some of these errors can be deadly to your pet.

Some Final Words on Pronouns and Your Pets

In addition to advising people about their pets, Gina has made her living as an editor, so she's pretty fussy about the "correct" use of language. In one little area, however, she disagrees with the experts: the use of the pronoun "it" for referring to animals.

We don't like the use of "it" to describe our animal companions — and what's more, we refuse to use it!

Although many bird-owners don't even know the gender of their birds — you find out why in Chapter 3 — we think using "it" for any living being sets up an association that's just not right. A chair is an "it." A bird cage is an "it." But animals are not "things." They are living, thinking, loving beings: "hims" and "hers," even if we don't know which is which. And so are they alternately described in this book.

The use of "him" or "her" in any given reference applies to both genders, unless specifically noted otherwise.

How to Reach Us

We invite you to tell us about *your* bird and your tales of living with an avian companion. You can read the exploits of Gina's animals — as well as up-to-date information on animal health and behavior — as part of her weekly column, “Pet Connection,” which is provided to newspapers by the Universal Press Syndicate and also appears every week in the America Online *Pet Care Forum*. (The keyword PET CARE takes you there if you’re an AOL subscriber.) She also writes a weekly essay for Pets.com. You can e-mail us at `WriteToGina@yourpetplace.com`, but snail mail is just as nice to get, at the following address:

Gina Spadafori/Dr. Brian L. Speer
PMB 211
5714 Folsom Blvd.
Sacramento, CA 95819

Part I
Which Bird For You?

In this part . . .

This part gives you the information you simply must have to make an intelligent and lasting choice of an avian companion. The relationship humankind has had with birds goes back thousands of years and was largely based on an appreciation of the beauty and song of these fascinating creatures. Nowadays people are realizing that pet birds, especially parrots, are intelligent, affectionate, and rewarding companions. When it comes to selecting your own bird, we tell you the good and the not-so of the many species available as pets, and we also tell you what to look for in a reputable seller — and what to avoid at all cost. After all, you can expect to have your bird for a long time, so starting out right is very important.

Chapter 1

Birds and Humans: It's Only Natural!

In This Chapter

- Witnessing a creature of myth and magic
- Beauty, mimicry, intelligence — and more!
- Meeting the challenges of bird-keeping
- Taking a flight through avian cyberspace

Who among us hasn't looked up with awe and even envy at the sight of a soaring hawk or the V-formation of migratory waterfowl? Who hasn't smiled at the clever capering of chickadees or the luminescent colors of a hovering hummingbird? And what about the sweet song of the canary or the clever mimicry of the parrot? For as long as our collective consciousness can remember, we have shared our environment with birds, creatures of myth and magic, soaring sprits who remind us always of a dimension beyond our own. Look up, they remind us, and in so doing we gain both perspective and inspiration.

Perhaps we have always wondered what it would be like to bring birds closer to us, out of the heavens and into our lives. And in response to the immense and primeval appeal of these flighted creatures, we have done exactly that, enjoying their song and their beauty in our homes. The ancient civilizations in China, Egypt, and Rome, among others, found pleasure in bird-keeping, a joy that follows us to modern times as more people than ever discover the benefits of sharing their lives with avian companions.

But have we done birds any favors by taking them under our wings? Clipped and caged, often admired more for their ornamental presentation than for their companion qualities, these marvelous creatures are too often sold short. When we treat them with less respect than they warrant, we make our pets miserable and sick, and we deny ourselves the full pleasure of their company. Even worse, through greed and ignorance, we decimate their numbers in the wild, driving some incredible species to extinction in our quest for their uniqueness and their habitat.

Are things darkest before the dawn? The phrase may fit when it comes to pet birds. Knowledge of how to care for them properly — physically *and* emotionally — has grown in the last couple of decades, thanks to pioneering avian veterinarians, researchers, breeders, and to bird-lovers themselves who are no longer satisfied to allow birds to be second-class compared to pet dogs or cats. All of us are part of an evolving society that increasingly appreciates the creatures with which we share our world.

The changing times are exciting, and by buying this book you're claiming your interest in becoming part of the new and improved perspective on pet birds. Finding out how to care for them properly is a wonderful first step on the road to bird-keeping. But first steps can lead to lots of new territory, and in this chapter we help you explore a promising trail of information.

As with all pets, doing your homework is essential to success as a bird parent. You need to know what you're getting into and where to find the bird of your dreams. And you need to know how to care for your pet and what to do when things go wrong (and they will, sometimes!). So don't rush. Enjoy discovering details about birds, and you can expect to be better prepared for the time you bring home a bird of your own.

Don't Know Much about History? Read On!

Birds For Dummies isn't a history book, and neither one of us is an historian. And we're certainly not looking to bore you. But we think some historical perspective is both important and interesting. And besides, sometimes looking back helps clear the vision of what's ahead. So read on! We promise: no pop quiz.

Because birds have been a big part of our lives and culture for so long, many of the words we use when we talk about our feathered fellows are ancient in origin, derived from *avis,* the Latin word for *bird.* Count in this group the words *avian* (having to do with birds), *aviculture* (the keeping of birds, especially for breeding purposes), and *aviary* (a place to house birds). And what about *aviation, aviator,* and *avionics*? You got it: When you see the letters *a-v-i* at the beginning of a word, you can figure a connection to birds or to one of their most notable qualities — flight!

Food, feathers, and (finally!) friendship

Our earliest ancestors didn't have the luxury of enjoying birds as pets — they needed them for food, and they hunted birds and collected eggs to meet their most basic sustenance needs. Before long, though, humankind started to realize the benefits of domestication — adopting and changing wild creatures so that they may better serve us as food, as helpers, and as companions. These changes began 10,000 to 12,000 years ago and haven't stopped since. The worldwide growth of fried-chicken fast-food chains is but a modern milestone on the road that began in the jungles of Asia, where people first discovered the tasty ancestor of domestic chickens, the red jungle fowl.

Such close proximity did not breed contempt, though. Domestic fowl were admired and worshipped for their fertility, their courage, and even their role as the earliest alarm clocks. With so much going for them, birds rather quickly graduated to a place of honor for their nonmeat attributes — their beauty became reason enough to keep them.

Although many of the world's cultures are horrified at the very idea of eating dogs and cats, the use of birds for food is nearly universally accepted (with the exception of individuals who abstain for philosophical or religious reasons). Why is it that some birds are prized as family members and others are best appreciated when served with orange sauce? We certainly don't know, but we can perhaps surprise you in Chapter 2 with how some of the birds we routinely consider as "food" really have decent pet potential.

Our enduring involvement

People keep birds today for many of the same reasons the Egyptian pharaohs or ancient Romans captured them — for beauty — and for some reasons the bird fanciers of times past probably never gave much thought to. Figuring out what attracts you to birds can give you an understanding of the trade-offs you can live with (and those you cannot!). And those realizations are bound to set you up for success in choosing your avian companion.

The beauty of birds

Let's face it: Humans are plain. Oh sure, we have some different skin tones and different hair and eye colors, but put us next to birds, and we have to admit to being pretty dull. Which is probably one reason why we appreciate the beauty of birds and why our history with them in close company spans hundreds of years — we just want to be able to gaze upon (or wear) their glorious feathers.

Is it any surprise, do you suppose, that some of the more popular pet birds are also the flashiest? The beautiful macaws — the scarlet (see Figure 1-1), the blue-and-gold, and the giant blue hyacinth — are breathtaking to behold, as are their glorious smaller relatives, such as the dazzling sun conure, with a beautiful complement of sun-yellow feathers. Even smaller birds are prized for their plumage. From a simple singer discovered on a far island, the canary has been bred into all kinds of fancy feathered forms.

Figure 1-1: Birds such as this scarlet macaw are prized as much for their companionship as for their beauty.

Photo by Dr. Brian L. Speer

The lust for beauty spelled extinction for more than a few species of birds, ruthlessly slaughtered for feathers to adorn ladies' hats in the last century — as many as five million a year died for their plumage. Among the victims: one of the United States' only two native parrot species, the Carolina parakeet. By the turn of the century, groups such as the Audubon Society were working to stop the killings. Too late for the Carolina parakeet, though: The last one died in the Cincinnati Zoo in 1918.

How beautiful do humans consider birds? So much that if you're trying to attract attention to a product or service, a picture of a bird typically works wonders. The eye-catching potential of birds makes them popular with the folks in the advertising and marketing businesses. Brian — who always has his eye out for birds — has noticed that about a quarter of the booths at veterinary conferences use birds in their displays, even if birds can't use the product!

Of song and speech

Birds use song and mimicry to protect their territory, warn of danger, and attract mates, and throughout history, their fascinating music has also engaged a human audience. Such birds as the canary and the singing greenfinch have long been prized for their song, and the members of the *psittacine* family — otherwise known as parrots — are so well known for their vocal talents that they've inspired a figure of speech. (To *parrot* something means to repeat it, of course, whether you're a bird or a human being.) Even finches such as the ones shown in Figure 1-2 keep up a companionable twittering.

Figure 1-2: The lively noises and antics of little birds like these diamond finches add to their wide appeal.

Photo by Dr. Michael J. Murray

The breeding of canaries dates back to the 16th century, and our relationship with wild-caught parrots is traceable to even earlier times. The Greeks and Romans fell in love with parrots, so much so that a trained one was considered more valuable than the slave who trained him. A favorite phrase to teach a Roman parrot? Why, "Hail the Emperor!" of course.

Recent research strongly suggests that birds don't, in fact, merely "parrot," or repeat, what they hear — some understand the words they're saying. The work of Dr. Irene Pepperberg and her African grey, Alex, has changed everyone's understanding of the intelligence of birds. Alex doesn't just talk — he listens and understands. We recommend that you make Dr. Pepperberg's Web page your first and foremost stop as you tour the must-see avian sites we list in Chapter 17.

A charming companion

Although birds have lived as part of the human family for tens of thousands of years, the here and now may be the best time to enjoy an avian companion. Laws enacted to conserve birds in the wild and to stymie the worst sins of the importation trade (in which thousands upon thousands of birds died, either in transit or after entering the public realm as pet birds) have put the focus on breeding. The birds that come out of the best breeding programs make the very best quality pets, better than any a Roman Caesar could have known.

Socialized since infancy to see humans as part of their "flock," many of today's pet birds have companionship potential that can amaze anyone who believes the old stereotypes about wild-caught birds. Every bit as beautiful as their wild relatives, breeder-raised babies are loving and intelligent, and improvements in what we know about their care keep them healthier than ever before. Our newfound knowledge, combined with centuries of experience and perspective, means that if you educate yourself to care for your pet, you can expect a phenomenal relationship — better than you may have imagined when you decided to become a bird-owner.

Are You Really Ready for a Bird?

Let us sing the praises of birds for those of you still sitting on the fence between bird-admiring and bird-keeping. Pet birds bring so much into the lives they share — color, song, speech, and a relationship that, at its best, approaches what you would find with a mate or a child. (And at its worst, approaches what you would find with a mate or a child.) And there, for some people, is the problem. Birds give as good as they get. Sometimes birds are a joy to live with, and other times . . . they're a big pain in the tail feathers.

For your own sanity, and for the health of the bird you hope to introduce to your world, you need to ask yourself whether you're really up to the challenge. Forewarned is forearmed, after all.

Putting in the time . . . and time again

Forget any notion you ever had about birds being low-maintenance pets. Although canaries and finches can fall loosely into that category, the same cannot be said of all the other birds we love as pets. From budgies to cockatiels to the flashiest of macaws, birds can be — how shall we say this politely? — demanding. You can't just put them in a cage, change the papers, add food and water, and ignore them. They won't let you.

Most of the birds we keep as pets are highly intelligent and very social. We deny them the company of their own kind and the stimulation of the environment they belong in. We ask them to be happy with us, and they can be, but not without effort on our part. And effort takes time. If you're not prepared to spend that time in working with your bird, in training your bird, in snuggling with your bird, and in allowing your bird plenty of supervised out-of-cage time to enjoy, you're going to have an unhappy bird. A biter. A screamer. A feather-picker.

Cared for properly, birds can be as time-consuming as dogs. Really. They need to be loved, handled, trained, fed, and cleaned up after — a lot! If you don't have that kind of time and energy, be sure the bird you choose is a finch or a canary. Or maybe a tank of fish.

Parakeetis Tyrannosaurus?

One of the more unusual aspects to consider when taking a bird into your life: This association is likely to be the closest you'll ever get to sharing space with a dinosaur. Although scientists once figured that reptiles were next of kin to dinosaurs, they now believe that birds are even closer. Birds are descended from a small meat-eating dinosaur that walked on two legs. The link between the two was made with the discovery of *Archaeopteryx,* a Jurassic period fossil of a creature that was part bird and part dinosaur.

If you have a hard time making the leap between birds and dinosaurs (the word means "terrible *lizards,*" after all, not "terrible *birds*"), check out the foot of a ostrich sometime — but not closely. Their claws alone may give you Jurassic Park jitters.

With any relationship, the more you put into it, the more you get out of it. The same is true when it comes to birds. The more time you spend with your bird, the more loving and socialized she will be — and the more time you'll want to spend with your bird as a result!

Another aspect of time that you need to consider when it comes to birds: longevity, yours and theirs. Healthy pet parrots can live for *decades,* which requires a major commitment to such companionship. Can you imagine spending most of your life with a pet? Are you able to plan for the pet who outlives you? These issues are very real for bird-owners, and you need to factor them into your decision-making.

Improvements in avian medicine are evident in Brian's practice, where birds in their 20s and beyond are increasingly common. The champion at Brian's practice in the longevity department has to go to a scarlet macaw named Mac, imported to the United States as a wild-caught young adult in 1922. Sadly, he passed away while we were writing this book, but he won't be forgotten.

For help in understanding an older bird and in keeping him healthy, check out Chapter 11.

Shelling out the bucks

We talk more about the costs involved in keeping a bird in Chapter 2, where we cover individual species of birds, but we need to point out here and now that birds are expensive to care for properly, much more so than most people anticipate. The price of acquiring the bird itself can run from the downright inexpensive — and, we advise, better avoided — loss-leader price for finches, canaries, and budgies to the monthly-salary figures that some of us are willing to shell out for large, flashy parrots.

And that's just the beginning.

Safe, roomy caging isn't cheap, nor is a proper diet. Preventive veterinary care to keep your pet healthy is a pricey must, and if your pet gets really sick, be prepared to dig deep. All of these factors must be figured in, along with such necessities as toys, which a large parrot can go through with awesome efficiency. It all adds up.

We take every opportunity throughout this book to note places where you can cut corners without cheating your bird. A good place to start is when you choose a bird. Although people are drawn to the largest and most colorful of parrots, some of the other species available are less expensive to acquire and maintain. We highlight these alternatives both in Chapter 2 and in our best birds for beginners list, in Chapter 18.

Dealing with the noise and mess

To hear some people tell it, the best tools for anyone who wants to keep a bird are earplugs and a handheld cordless vacuum. And it's true some birds can give a rowdy rock band a run for their money when it comes to decibel levels and the ability to trash a room.

Some of the problems are natural and normal, and some are caused by humans, but either way, the potential for noise and mess is an important consideration when you're thinking about a bird.

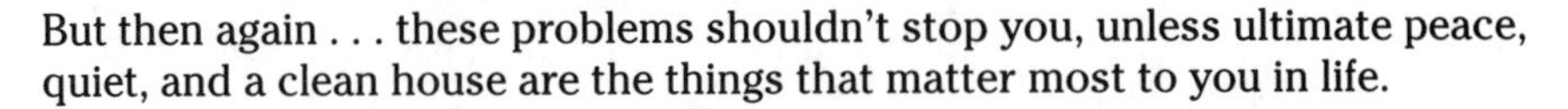

But then again . . . these problems shouldn't stop you, unless ultimate peace, quiet, and a clean house are the things that matter most to you in life.

For a better handle on which birds are noisiest, see Chapter 2. For ways to minimize mess, see our cage and cage setup coverage in Chapter 4.

We're not trying to put you off bird-keeping. But we believe in the importance of understanding potential problems before you take the plunge. The best attributes a bird-lover can have are the same as a good parent — love, patience, structure, and a good sense of humor. You'll need them all! But the payoff . . . oh, it's grand. (And unlike being a parent to a human child, you don't have to save for a college fund.)

Exploring Avian Cyberspace

A great place to research anything is cyberspace, and birds are no exception. Bird-lovers have taken to the Internet eagerly, filling the online world with bird information, stories, and pictures. You can find bird-related e-mail lists, newsgroups, chat, and Web sites on the Internet, as well as active online communities on commercial services such as America Online.

You can also find us! Gina's weekly pet care column, "Gina Spadafori's Pet Connection," runs in its own section of the Pet Care Forum, at AOL keyword PET CARE, and Brian answers bird-health question in the Pet Care Forum's Veterinary Hospital, as well as serving as an avian medicine consultant for the owner of the Pet Care Forum, the Veterinary Information Network (`www.vin.com`). Gina also writes a weekly essay for Pets.com.

What's so amazing about the Internet is the generosity of the people who contribute to making the online world decidedly bird-friendly. These people put in an astonishing amount of work to provide bird-lovers with solid information on birds and their care.

Cyberspace may be your ticket to education and entertainment, especially if you take the time to share with other bird-lovers — and learn from their experiences, too.

All the good intentions in the world don't guarantee good information. The Internet is strictly a "reader beware" world when it comes to finding information on birds. Out-of-date information — even of the deadly variety — gets trotted out time and time again. Just because the communication vehicle is the most modern of technologies doesn't mean you can count on the most current or accurate information! Rumors, too, fly through cyberspace quickly, assuming a level of legitimacy and urgency they rarely deserve. Enjoy your time on the Net, but be careful out there: Check out what you read against known sources of reliable information, such as this book or an avian veterinarian.

The online world has more to offer than research. Some of the most clever and amusing sites on the World Wide Web are bird-related and well worth a visit. For a sampling of some of the better sites, see Chapter 17.

You can locate online information on birds in many ways. Here's the rundown:

- **FAQs:** Short for *Frequently Asked Questions*, these bird-related documents on the Net range from such broad topics as choosing a bird and understanding health care to specific descriptions of particular species and detailed insights into different behaviors. Some FAQs are lists of other Internet resources, such as e-mail lists, Web pages, online publications, and pet product suppliers. The Up At Six Web site has a great collection, at `www.upatsix.com/faq`.

- **E-mail lists:** For those who like a full mailbox, you can't find anything that quite compares with joining an e-mail list. Some are overwhelming, with hundreds of pieces of mail collected every day from members and distributed to everyone on the list, which may range from a couple dozen people to several hundred. The best e-mail lists develop a sense of community, with people united by a common interest — such as a particular species of bird — sharing helpful tips and warm stories of their avian companions. If you have a particular bird in mind but aren't sure what they're like to live with, a couple of months on an e-mail list should paint you an accurate picture — and may help you find the right source, if you decide to go ahead.

  You can subscribe to lists in several ways. For some, you need only to send a note to a host computer. With other lists, subscriptions are handled manually by the list owner, also called a *moderator*. Some lists have numerical limits on their memberships; others screen members to keep out people who may prove disruptive.

  After you join an e-mail list, read it for a couple of days to develop a feel for the discussion before jumping in with a flurry of postings. This practice is part of what's called *netiquette,* but it's also known as good common sense. You don't know who's out there reading, and you don't want to get off on the wrong foot with people who could help expand your knowledge. So wait, watch, and then, if you're comfortable, post a low-key introduction. After you gain some sense of rapport with the group, jump in!

  Some e-mail lists generate an astonishing volume of mail — up to hundreds of pieces hitting your e-mail box on a daily basis! Because of this overload problem, many lists offer a "digest" format, in which letters are bunched together several times a day. You receive the same material, but in fewer, larger packages. Some people find this method easier to deal with. We recommend that you try both ways and see which suits you better.

  The best list of avian e-mail groups and sign-up information is again at Up At Six. To get started, point your Web browser to the following URL:

  ```
  www.upatsix.com/faq
  ```

  When you get to the FAQs page, click on the mailing lists window.

- **Newsgroups:** A newsgroup is sort of like an e-mail list, except that anyone in the whole world can post to it, and the information doesn't come to your mailbox — you must go get it.

  Because newsgroups are open to anyone — including anonymous twits who like to cause trouble — you have less of a sense of community than you do with an e-mail list and less reason to be civil, because the threat of being thrown off the subscriber list doesn't exist. The wide-open nature of newsgroups means that some people are more likely to post outrageous items — and engage in annoying *flame wars,* which are similar to the squabbles of children and just as entertaining.

We like e-mail lists better — they stay on the subject, and annoying people aren't tolerated for long — but for more general information, newsgroups are worth exploring. Just take them with a grain of salt.

The `rec.pet.birds` newsgroup is a good place to start. Also check out `alt.pets.parrots.african-grey`, `alt.pets.parrots.amazons`, `alt.pet.parrots.cockatiels`, and `alt.pet.parrots.jardines`.

Newsgroups aren't the same as Web sites. Your Internet service provider should have a way for you to access newsgroups — on America Online, for example, you can find them by clicking on the Internet icon on the top toolbar. When you get to the newsgroups, you typically subscribe to one by typing in the name of the group; you can then check for new posts periodically.

- **Web sites:** Web sites are probably the best-known and most frequently used category of information delivery on the Internet, and their popularity is due mostly to graphics and pictures — they look pretty! Hundreds of avian-related Web sites exist, from ones dedicated to individual species to ones devoted to pictures or shopping. Most Web sites are either an individual's labor of love or a profit-minded commercial venture, so content and quality vary widely.

  For a list of bird-related Web sites, point your Web browser to

  ```
  www.upatsix.com
  ```

Don't forget to make use of your Web browser's *bookmark* feature to remember the location of sites you're likely to visit again. Sometimes when you're Web browsing, clicking links here and there, you can lose track of how you maneuvered somewhere — and how you can find your way back!

- **Web rings:** If you enjoy not knowing what will turn up next, why not hook in to a *Web ring* — a group of Web sites unified by a single theme, such as "Amazons" or "canaries." Look over any Web page that you're on, especially toward the bottom. If the page is part of a Web ring, it will mention it and ask you to click to go to the next page or to bring up a random page in the ring. Usually, you're also able to click on a page that displays all the sites in the ring, so you can pick and choose what you want to see. Our advice: Just do it! Click on "Next" or "Random" and see where it goes. You can end up finding some really great Web pages that way. A good place to start is the Bird Hotline's collection of Web rings at `www.birdhotline.com/ring.htm`.

Chapter 2

Narrowing the Choices

In This Chapter

- Deciding what you can live with and what you can't
- Considering size, noise, and messiness
- Hands-off or hands-on?
- Taking a look at some common pet birds
- A few unusual choices

You may find it an easy decision to bring a bird into your life. But what kind? That call can be the hardest of all. So many choices, so much stunning beauty, cleverness, and personality. How can you choose? We say: Choose carefully!

We know people who've chosen birds based on some really awful criteria, like which bird best matches new carpeting — a parrot to coordinate with just the right shade of blue. Other people choose birds for status — some rare birds can set a buyer back thousands, even tens of thousands of dollars. A decision based on such terms can be a disaster. The buyer may miss out on one of the big benefits of bird ownership — the company and closeness of the new family member — and the mess and noise delivered by the decorative status object aren't likely to win any adoring coos. Vanity can be a pretty expensive lesson, too, when a bird who isn't getting the care and attention he needs becomes sick or dies.

How can you avoid such a scenario? Through research and insight, develop an understanding of what birds really are about and what they need, and a realization of what you can and can't live with. Far from being a dangerous thing, even a little knowledge can be good — and more facts, even better!

We're not saying a bird can't be chosen strictly for its aesthetics. Some pet birds, such as the finches and canaries, are very content to live with as little human contact as possible, spending their days delighting our lives with song, color, and playful antics in their cages. But to expect a larger and more social parrot to adapt to such a situation isn't a good idea. We want you to realize that the variety of pet birds available is quite remarkable, and the bird you're naturally drawn to may or may not be the right one for you in the long run. You need to consider your lifestyle, your personal tolerances for noise and mess, and the amount of time you have for your pet bird. With this information at hand, you have the best chance at pairing up with the particular species that suits you.

Although we feature many varieties of pet birds in this chapter — including a few the vast majority of bird-lovers are best off avoiding — we offer a list of the ten best birds for beginners in Chapter 18. Don't forget, too, to visit the color pages of this book to see what many of these birds look like in all their glory.

What Are You Looking for in a Bird?

If you can't just fall in love with the look of a bird, what are the characteristics worth considering? In the following sections, we describe the traits most people love or hate, so you can develop your own standards and compare them to the various species.

Judging interactivity

Bird species range in friendliness from the "don't touch me" attitude of most finches to the Velcro-like manner of some cockatoos. Do you want a bird in the hand or one in the cage? Even within the highly intelligent and social parrot species you can find differences in the amount of attention a bird wants — or demands, in some cases.

Are you comfortable with being the center of another being's life, or are you likely to find the demands for attention from such a bird to be tedious or entrapping after a while? The answer to this question can take you a step closer to one group of birds or another — and responding too casually to the question can lead both to your own unhappiness and your bird's. So think about it.

Considering size

No matter how friendly, larger birds scare some people. Their flappy wings and impressive beaks have only a distant appeal to the person whose idea of the perfect pet bird is a budgie who can balance easily on a single finger. Other folks love the dramatic presence the larger birds command.

You can find charming personality types in all sizes. If you like a social bird in a small package, parrotlets, lovebirds, and budgies can fill the bill. You don't have to buy a big parrot to get a big personality!

Size counts for more than presence, however. Large birds require larger, more expensive cages, plus they go through big amounts of food, toys, and perches even faster than their smaller counterparts and generally make a much larger mess than their smaller relatives. The initial price of a large bird is often more, too.

Mess and more mess

Logically, larger birds make larger messes, but some birds really are over the top when it comes to covering every available surface with feces, feathers, and food. Top of the list: The lories and lorikeets, lively and colorful nectar eaters with the ability to shoot their runny droppings for some remarkable distances. This trait limits their pet appeal for many people, but some folks take these talents in stride, figuring the extra work is worth the companionship of these charmers.

While the lories and lorikeets may be the messiest, no bird can be considered truly neat. Well-designed cages, plenty of newspaper, a hand-vacuum, and towels of both the cloth and paper variety can keep things under control, for the most part. Again, it's all a matter of preference, tolerance, and mutual compatibility.

You can train many different kinds of birds to eliminate on command, allowing you to hold them over a wastebasket or other container to capture the mess. For help in accomplishing this nifty feat, see Chapter 7.

Bring in da noise

No bird is perfectly quiet. Finches keep up a constant chatter, and canaries have been encouraged through centuries of breeding to sing. Some birds, however, can make you yearn for the relative quiet that a house next to a major airport offers. Birds use their voices to communicate their feelings — of loneliness, of boredom, of isolation, or of just being alive. Some pet birds are noisy only at certain times, such as early morning or at dusk, while others can start up at any time. You need to figure out your tolerance levels, and balance them with the bird you are considering. If peace and quiet is of paramount importance to you, no bird may fit into your life, and even more forbearing souls may discover that the real screamers are going to try their patience at one time or another.

Consider, too, your living situation — apartment, attached house, suburban dwelling, or acreage. The walls of an apartment building or attached house do little to muffle the sounds of the loudest birds, and that could lead to trouble with the neighbors — or even get you evicted.

Sometimes bird-lovers make matters worse by their reactions to screaming birds. For tips on what to do — and what not to do — with a screamer, see Chapter 12.

Talking ability

The ability to mimic sounds is one of the things that makes parrots so popular, but the skill and ability of mimicry isn't found equally in all parrots. With patience and work, many parrot species can utter a few words or phrases, but if you're really looking for the gift of gab, be sure to choose a yellow-naped or double-yellow-headed Amazon parrot or an African grey parrot, all species especially known for their speaking ability. Even then, realize you can't be sure you're getting a bird who will talk unless he was talking when you bought him. (The same thing, incidentally, goes for the singing skill of canaries. Make sure you hear singing before you buy, if that's what's important to you.)

For tips on teaching a bird to talk, see Chapter 7. Chapter 12 is the place to go for hints about how to coax your pet to be quiet for a while!

How much is that birdie in the window?

The price of a pet bird can be considerable, starting from less than $20 for some small budgies or finches and climbing rapidly into the hundreds of dollars for some of the large common parrots and into the thousands and tens of thousands for species that are especially rare, large, or difficult to breed in captivity.

Bargain-hunting is usually a bad idea when it comes to birds, however. Raising healthy, well-socialized birds is time-consuming and expensive, and the prices for these birds reflect the labor that goes into their raising. You have to wonder what kind of corners were cut when you find a price that's out of line with what's normal for a particular species in a particular area. Is the bird a medical time-bomb just waiting to explode with the stress of a new home? A simmering behavior problem waiting to develop? Too often the answer is "Yes" to one or both questions.

Figure out the price you can afford to pay and then shop for the best bird possible for that money. Don't fret over the bird you can't afford, because you can find many wonderful and underappreciated species in every price

Pet preference: Cuddle-bug, "wild" thing, or breeder?

Most of the birds commonly available as pets today are valued as much for their companionship as anything else. Socialized, hand-raised babies grow up thinking humans are pretty cool, and they want us to be a member of their flock. We become their family!

The new emphasis on companionship of the pet bird reflects a change in the way many people interact with their pet birds. Some folks, though, still want birds more to look at than to cuddle, and those people are likely to be happier with birds who are content to live in an aviary with little or no human contact. Although these preferred pets are domestically raised birds, to be sure, they're typically as little interested in us as their wild-born relatives might be.

A third group, the hobby or professional breeder, has a different goal altogether — the production of more birds. A breeder's objective may be to develop new colors or varieties, win prizes at shows, make money (or at least pay the costs of production), provide the intense joy and satisfaction that comes from successfully breeding them, or all of the above.

So, what are you looking for in a bird? We talk about the joys, as well as the challenges, of breeding and raising birds in Chapter 13, and you can find plenty on both the hands-off and hands-on species later in this chapter. But you are the one who has to consider what relationship you're looking for with your bird, because your decision affects the kind of bird you choose — not just the species, but in many cases the individual bird itself.

range, and all of them make wonderful pets. We'd rather see you spend what may seem initially to be an "outrageous" $50 on a healthy, well-socialized budgie with great pet potential than $20 on a mass-produced budgie of unknown genetics or health, or $300 on a sick or emotionally crippled parrot of a species that usually retails for considerably more. You're better off with the well-raised and socialized budgie, trust us. Budgies are cool.

The cost of a bird is only part of the hit you take when you bring home a feathered companion. Cages, perches, toys, and more are expensive, and so is that post-purchase veterinary examination, but they all need to be factored in to keep your pet bird healthy and happy. For more on bird gear — what you need, what you don't, and more — see Chapter 4.

Considering the Species

After you figure out what you want in your feathered companion, you can realistically look at what's out there and start matching the species that connect with your personality and lifestyle. Don't feel restricted! The variety of species and types of pet birds available today is so broad that all except the most dedicated quiet-and-neatness types can find more than one species to fit the bill — and probably several!

We put our observations on the record here to let you know what each species is really like, both the good and the not-so-good qualities. Nobody's perfect — not you, not us, and not any single bird. But getting the match as close as possible is your best bet for a long, happy, and healthy relationship.

Make no mistake: The qualities we're talking about in this chapter refer to truly healthy pet birds acquired from reputable sources — and in the case of the parrot species, well-socialized birds to boot. Brian's experience confirms that a healthy, well-cared-for bird can live twice as long as the generic life spans published in most of the older reference works. You'll never find a better testimonial to good preventive care. For information on choosing a reputable bird source, see Chapter 3. And don't forget that a good start is *only a start:* Explore the latest on avian nutrition in Chapter 6 and on preventive care in Chapter 9.

The hands-off color and song birds

Finches — and canaries are finches, too — have been popular for centuries, and with good reason. They're attractive, active, and fill our world with sound, including the sweet songs canaries are known for. Well-suited to life in a cage or aviary, these canaries and other finches — we show a handful in Figure 2-1 — are perfect for people who don't want a lot of physical interaction with their pet birds. If you keep the cage or aviary clean and make sure your pets are healthy and well-fed, they're quite content to keep you on the periphery, sharing their lives with you from afar. These small charmers can also be interesting to breed, without the time-consuming hand-feeding that parrots may require.

Finches

Relatively inexpensive with a couple of very hardy species in the group, finches make a good first bird, a child's pet, or charming aviary residents for both experienced or beginner-level bird-keepers. Best bets: Society or zebra finches, which are very common, inexpensive (less than $20, usually), and fairly resistant to the mistakes beginners often make.

Beyond these two species is a world of exotic and lovely finches, such as the multicolored Gouldians or the Fischer's, with its long tail plumes. The more unusual finches are much more expensive than the society or zebra finches, and they're also more difficult to keep. Easily chilled and quickly stressed, many of the more unusual finches are really best left in the hands of experienced bird-lovers.

Figure 2-1: Canaries and other finches delight with color and song, but they'd generally rather not be handled.

The society and zebra finches, though, are a definite best bet for anyone looking to bring the zest of these little guys into their lives. Easy-keepers both, a pair or handful of zebras or societies can comfortably keep themselves amused while you're at work.

The life span is around 3 to 6 years for a "typical" pet, but a healthy bird from a reputable source, cared for properly, can hit the 20-year mark. Finches are fine for almost any living situation, from studio apartment to outdoor aviary.

The classic finch noise is a constant peepy-chatter, but at least one species goes one better — with sweet song. The singing greenfinch can give some of his canary cousins a run for their money!

More finches . . . canaries, actually

The Sinatras of the pet bird world, canaries have enjoyed a long run of popularity — and a fair amount of fame, too. Consider the classic Warner Brothers cartoon character, Tweety Bird, who has done plenty to promote his real-life counterparts. (We won't quibble with the fact that Tweety doesn't seem to sing much at all, since his uncharacteristic gift of conversational skills makes up for the deficit.)

Canaries have been bred for centuries and, as a result, come in a wide variety of colors, shapes, and feather patterns. The yellow border fancy is perhaps the one who looks the most like Tweety, a clear, vibrant burst of sunshine in any room. Borders are available in other colors, too, including white, blue, and green. Canaries also come in a dramatic red-orange and a cinnamon color. Fancy feathers were the aim of other breeders, who've produced frilled versions with elegant feather puffs or fringes over the eyes.

Red canaries need a little human help to maintain their breathtakingly vibrant color. People who exhibit their birds add special ingredients — color foods — to their red canaries' diets to help them become just the right hue.

When it comes to what canaries are best known for — song — the green roller takes the prize. The roller is more humble in appearance, perhaps, but eagerly sought out for the complexity and length of his song. (And we do mean "his," because in canaries, the girls leave the singing to the boys.)

Canaries can start at prices not much higher than the common finches, but if you're really looking for great singing or distinctive colors or feather patterns, you can easily shell out $300 to $400 or more in some cases. Ordinary life span for most canaries is roughly 8 to 16 years, but 20- and 30-year-olds who enjoy good care turn up fairly regularly. The canary is another fine bird for any living situation, from small apartment to outdoor aviary.

Small parrots

Quieter, neater, and, of course, smaller than their larger relations, the parrots we group together in this section include what may be the world's most popular pet bird, the budgerigar, and others with loads of fans, too, such as the cockatiel. And don't forget one other little one who's coming up in popularity, the parrotlet. Don't let their size fool you: Some of these small parrots have plenty of personality, make affectionate companions, and offer surprising talking ability. Most are very reasonably priced, as well.

Five varieties of small parrots are shown in Figure 2-2: the English budgerigar, the American budgerigar, the lovebird, the celestial parrotlet, and the cockatiel. You can read about them in the following sections.

Parakeets

When Americans think "parakeet," they're usually picturing what the rest of the world calls a *budgerigar*, or *budgie*. A budgie is a parakeet, but to believe that it's the only parakeet sadly ignores some of the more magnificent pet birds available. Most popular among these birds are the Asiatic parakeets — ring-neckeds, Alexandrians, derbians, plum-headeds, and mustached parakeets. As a group, they're known for flashy, vibrant color and long, elegant tails.

Figure 2-2: Don't dismiss the little parrots; they're packed with personality and love to be part of your life.

Largely considered hands-off aviary birds, Asiatic parakeets are gradually gaining ground as more up-close-and-personal pets. When captive-raised and well-socialized, some of these birds have great potential as affectionate companions and even great talkers — one of the better talkers Brian has ever met is a blue ring-necked parakeet named Sid. These species are gorgeous in an aviary, however, and seem to be happy there, too. An attractive feature with most Asiatic parakeets — either in the home or the aviary — is that they're not very loud, and many have a very pleasant and soothing call.

Most Asiatic parakeets are relatively quiet, making them acceptable in any living situation. Prices start at $200 to $300 for the blue or green ring-necked variety and climb according to color or species rarity. Life spans for well-cared-for birds run from 20 to 40 years.

The Asiastics aren't the only parakeets around. One popular parakeet native to South America is the Quaker, also called the Monk. Quakers are so adept at establishing themselves in the wild in places where they don't belong, however, that some states and countries don't allow them to be kept as pets. If your part of the world doesn't have a regulation against ownership, though, these parakeets can be a pet. (Check for the latest restrictions with your local agriculture department.) Although most states allow Quakers to be owned by the public, California does not.

Quakers are a handsome green-and-silver bird with decent talking potential and an affectionate nature, when raised and handled properly. Prices are reasonable for these charmers, around $300 or less.

The brotogeris gang are also parakeets of South American origin. These little guys love riding in pockets, are pretty quiet, and aren't very messy. Primarily green in color with small, contrasting markings, brotogeris are big guys in little bodies — some even like to pick fights with much bigger birds! The canary-winged parakeet — green with bright yellow under the wings — and grey-cheeked are two of the more commonly available brotogeris parakeets. A little more expensive than some other parakeets, well-socialized individuals can start at $400 and up.

Budgerigar

When budgies were discovered by Europeans in Australia in the mid-1800s, they created quite a stir back home in Europe. They had everything going for them — bright color, affectionate nature, and a real facility for talking. These same traits make this awesome little bird the world's most popular today. You just can't top a nice budgie — they have it all!

In some ways, the popularity of budgies has led many people to dismiss them, more so in recent years. Too common, too cheap, too ordinary, these lovely pets are too often considered just a "starter" bird, especially for children. And that idea opens the doors to mass breeding to fill public demand for low-cost sources of budgerigars, which further reinforces any perception of the budgie as a "throwaway pet." What a waste!

Budgies are remarkable pets, for children, adults, beginners, and experienced bird-lovers alike.

To assure the best experience with a budgie as a pet, skip the under-$20 mass-produced specimens (which are often a bit of a gamble because of uncertain health, background, and pet potential) and search out a hand-raised baby. You can usually tame a parent-raised bird into an acceptable companion, but such a bird is rarely as interested in you as one who has known humans from the beginning.

Budgies come in many colors and patterns and two basic body types. The American style of budgie is slender and long compared to the husky, almost bulldog look of the English budgie. Personalities are the same, though, so color or body type is strictly a matter of personal preference.

Parent-raised birds can be fine as hands-off cage or aviary pets, but we think you can enjoy the greatest rewards from your relationship if you choose a bird you can become friends with. In any case, these versatile pets are suitable for any living situation. Prices range from under $20 for what are typically mass-produced birds to around $100 for more unusual colors in hand-raised birds. You can probably find a hand-raised American type for around $40, and we say that's a good deal. Although eight years is the common forecast on life span, a well-cared-for budgie can make it well into the teens and beyond.

A talking budgie possesses the charm to make a statue break out in a smile. Their lispy little high-pitched voices are adorable! And some are incredibly good talkers, learning up to 300 words or phrases. If you listen carefully, you may figure out why we think these little guys are equipped to give the better known big-parrot talkers a run for their money! In our minds, that tiny hand-raised budgie that you can carry around in your shirt pocket is worth his weight in gold!

Lovebirds

Another parrot who owes much of the variety in plumage color to human genetic meddling, the lovebird is a small, sweet companion who comes in a rainbow array of colors. Natural-born snugglers, lovebirds adore holing up in a pocket or other warm, hidden place. Not great talkers, but some can learn a few words and phrases if you have the time and patience to work with them.

For a pet, a single lovebird is best; otherwise your pair will only have eyes for each other, not for you. Forget that old myth about them dying of loneliness — it just isn't true. One healthy, well-socialized lovebird is plenty enough to be your contented pal.

Lovebirds are also popular as aviary pets and breeders, and many hobbyists are working hard to increase the available varieties of these lovely birds.

Fine for almost any living situation, lovebirds have life spans of 8 to 14 years, and well-cared-for birds over 20 years old are out there. Costs run from $40 to $80 for the basic peach-faced variety, more for rare species or new color variations.

Parrotlets

The tiny parrotlet can fit in your hand, but anyone who owns one can tell you they have as much attitude as any macaw, more proof that good — no, make that *great* — things can certainly come in small packages. These vibrant green or blue wonders pack the potential to be more popular than they are — and we predict more people will give these terrific little guys a shot. Parrotlets generally have minimal talking ability, but they are great fun to handle and to watch. And, in many ways, they demonstrate how they are just big parrots trapped in a little parrot body!

Reasonably priced, starting at $80, parrotlets can and should enjoy a life span of up to 20 years.

Cockatiels

Like the budgie, the cockatiel is one of the world's more popular pet birds. Indeed, both of these wonders from Down Under made their European debut at about the same time, midway through the 19th century. With crests reminiscent of the larger cockatoo, these birds were for a while known as "cockatoo parrots" until the modern coinage of *cockatiel,* from the Portuguese word "cacatilho" — little cockatoo.

Cockatiels justly deserve their legions of fans. Handsome and affectionate, the cockatiel is a perfect fit with any living situation, and a relatively easy breeder for anyone who wants to give that hobby a try. Many people have enjoyed the adventure of breeding cockatiels over the years, producing lovely varieties of colors and patterns, from the naturally occurring grey to the pale yellow lutino, the *pied* (blotches of two or more colors), cinnamon, pearl, and albino. Prices can start at under $20 for some of the mass-produced birds, but most pet cockatiels run between $40 and $120, with hand-raised babies and the rarer colors and patterns at the higher end of the scale. Life spans for most cockatiels are often quoted to run 10 to 14 years, but again, a bird who starts healthy and is well cared for can live well into the 20s.

As interesting as the many variations of cockatiels can be, some health problems have slipped into the mix. Some varieties, such as the white-faced and cinnamon, may develop kidney problems on certain formulated diets. Talk to a veterinarian who is qualified and experienced in avian medicine to determine how to best keep these birds in optimum health and how to detect or avoid early problems.

Pet birds and children

Birds can be wonderful companions for children, but sometimes the reverse isn't so true. Children who are too young or unable to understand the importance of gentle, respectful handling can end up with a dead bird pretty quickly — truly a tragedy for all involved.

The look-don't-touch birds such as canaries and other finches are best for very young children. From the age of 8 or so, a child can begin to understand instructions in correctly handling smaller parrots, making budgies and cockatiels a good match for these older children. When kids enter their teens, almost any bird that fits the family's lifestyle can be a good match.

Remember, though, that taking proper care of any pet is the parent's responsibility, and lead by example. Don't make the pet the focus of a tug-of-war between you and your child. The lesson of responsibility is a good one to draw from a relationship with a pet, but so, too, are the lessons of compassion, caring, and respect for another living being.

Males are usually better at vocalizing, with whistling a specialty. Cockatiels are generally not the best talkers, but the males can pick up a few words or phrases. Don't let the lack of verbosity dissuade you, though: The gentle cockatiel is about as fine an avian companion as you can imagine.

As with budgies, you can find plenty of mass-produced cockatiels with price tags that may seem irresistible. If you're looking for a healthy, long-term companion, however, the hand-raised bird is a much better bet, even if the price is higher.

Medium-sized parrots

Pricier and less commonly available than budgies and cockatiels — and generally less flashy and colorful than their larger relatives — the medium-sized parrots are often overlooked and underappreciated. And that's a shame, because in this group you can find some wonderful companions — handsome birds that are relatively neat and quiet (with a couple notable exceptions) and reasonably priced to attain and care for. A great bunch!

Poicephalus

The Senegal is probably the most popular of the class of smaller African parrots species known collectively under the genus *poicephalus*. The Senegal parrot is also the most reasonably priced, at around $300 to $400 for a hand-fed baby. Senegals are neat and quiet as parrots go, and handsome in a somewhat unspectacular way — green feathers on the back, a mango-colored breast, and a gray head. (We feature them in Figure 2-3 as the best of the "easy-keepers," along with the larger pionus.) Personable and affectionate, Senegals are capable of picking up a few words and phrases, but they're not generally known for their talking ability. Good for any living situation, small apartments included, Senegal parrots have much to offer as companion birds for many people.

The others in this group — including the red-bellied, Meyer's, and Jardine's parrots — are comparatively harder to find and notably more expensive (up to $800 or so) than the Senegal parrot but are well worth seeking out. The life span of a healthy, well-cared-for poicephalus can range from 20 to 40 years.

Lories and lorikeets

You see a lot of lories and lorikeets in zoos and commercial aviaries — their fantastic good looks and clownish personalities are undeniable attractions. They're a delight to watch, a rainbow of intense, vibrant color. The lory-feeding exhibits in many zoos and wildlife parks are popular draws for thousands of people worldwide. (One such exhibit, in fact, is pictured on our cover!)

Figure 2-3: Quieter and more easy-going than many other parrots, the pionus and Senegal are good choices for first-time bird-buyers.

As household pets, though, these guys have one decided drawback — they're incredibly messy. Unlike most of the birds available as pets, most lories and lorikeets don't eat hard food, for the most part, but instead consume more liquid rations — in the wild they're nectar-eaters. This sticky diet is harder to keep up with than that of other commonly kept birds, and that's not the only problem. Their diet results in oodles of watery droppings, which the birds seem to delight in shooting as far from their cages as possible.

If you can overlook the mess — and many people cope just fine — lories are fine pets. The spectacular rainbow lory, in particular, is a good choice in this group, goofy and fun to be around. Lories aren't suited for close-quartered living, however, because of some decidedly high decibel noise. Prices of lories are moderate: $200 and up, depending on the species.

The difference between lories and lorikeets is generally the length of their tails. Lorikeets, like parakeets, have longer tail feathers.

Conures

The rap on conures is that they ought to be sold along with earplugs for everyone around them — neighbors very much included. Some conures well deserve this reputation for noisiness — those vociferous sorts may be more closely related to macaws — but not all conures can take credit (or blame) for a noisy nature.

We include conures with the medium parrots because most of the common ones, such as the sun conure, aren't all that large. As a group, though, conures display a wide range of size, with species such as the mitred really qualifying as a large parrot.

The conures of the aratinga genus are usually the real noisemakers — the sun, jenday, golden-capped, mitred, red-fronted, dusky, and white-eyed, to name a few. Although not of the aratinga genus, the nanday and the Patagonian conures are other conures with a well-earned reputation for noise.

Conures have formidable abilities when it comes to shrieking and frequently have little hesitation to share their talents. Of these, the sun conure is probably the most attractive, enticing people to figure they can live with the noise just to enjoy the beauty and antics of these clever parrots.

The bottom line with these birds is the same hard truth you have to face with any winged pet: knowing what you can live with. You can't change the nature of a bird; the best you can do is live with the traits that are challenging, to say the least. If the appearance and liveliness of a sun conure overwhelms any doubts you have about the noise, then maybe you're meant to have one. (As long as you're not living with close-by neighbors, that is.)

All conures aren't the noisemakers the aratingas are known for. The species of the pyrrhura genus — such as the maroon-belly, green-cheeked, and black-cap — don't have nearly the volume, and they're smaller and less expensive as well. The pyrrhura conures fall into our underappreciated category — well worth seeking out.

Conures range in price from $200 or so for some of the pyrrhuras to considerably more for the flashier or rarer varieties. Life spans for healthy, well-cared-for birds can run from the 20s to 40s.

Caiques and hawkheads

We group the caiques (pronounced ki-EEKS) and hawkheads together for no other reason than their size. Of the two, the caiques are the more common and more reasonably priced than the rarer hawkhead.

Caiques are commonly available in two species, either the white-bellied or black-capped. The names are a tad deceiving, for both kinds have white fronts. The black caps have . . . oh, can you guess? Caiques are lively, busy birds, highly entertaining as companions, and real clowns. Their popularity appears to be on the rise, and for good reason.

Hawkheads are relatively quiet birds named for their distinctive bird-of-prey-looking heads. A gorgeous bird and a good pet, albeit somewhat pricey.

Like most of the medium-sized parrots, life spans range from the 20s up for healthy, well-cared-for birds. You can find the more common caiques available at around $400 to $500, and you can expect to pay hundreds more for a hawkhead — if you can find one. The hawkhead is fine for any living situation, but the caique may be a little noisy for those with close neighbors.

Large parrots

Flashy, colorful, noisy, intelligent, and talkative, the large parrots shown in Figure 2-4 are the ones folks usually visualize when they hear the word "parrot," partially because some of these guys can really talk! You can find some excellent companions among these birds — and some challenging ones, too. But don't expect to ever run across one that isn't a parade-stopper — these birds have star status, without a doubt!

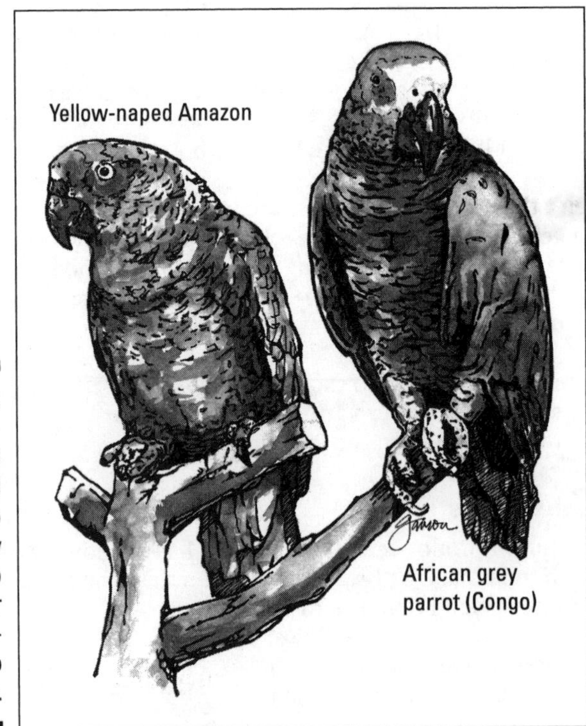

Figure 2-4: The yellow-naped Amazon and the Congo African grey are two species for whom talking seems to come easily.

Amazons

Clever, colorful, talkative, and often bratty, Amazon parrots are sometimes considered a handful — but within the group you can find some species that defy commonly held beliefs.

First, the characters: The yellow-naped and double-yellow-headeds are vastly popular and generally good talkers, but they can be loud and demanding as pets, and they possess the potential to become a "one-person bird." You need to know about the possibility before you start out with an Amazon. Some people like their in-your-face attitude, some don't. Amazons definitely command a presence, no matter how you feel about them.

Other Amazons are easier to live with, among them the lilac-crowns, red-lored, and white-fronted. These smaller species are less likely to push, are generally quieter, and are all-around easy to handle. The trade-off: Their talking ability is usually not as good as the yellow-naped or double-yellow-headed.

Life spans can match the longest among pet birds; more than a hundred years is possible, particularly because we now better understand what it takes to keep these birds healthy. Unfortunately, poor diets and lousy care limit the life expectancy potential of many birds; most of the pet population is gone long before the age of 50, with geriatric problems showing up in birds as young as 20 years old. Prices range from $300 to $1,200.

A common health problem seen in Amazons is obesity! If you have an Amazon, make sure you offer him a healthy diet and plenty of exercise, or else these natural perch potatoes will go to . . . er, seed, rather easily.

African greys

Introducing the undisputed Einsteins of the parrot world! African greys — both the more common Congo and the smaller Timneh — are marvelous talkers who have demonstrated that they actually understand what they're saying.

The greys do need an attentive owner, however. They need to be kept engaged and challenged. Without a good relationship with a human caretaker, the birds can become phobic, sullen, or even aggressive. Boredom and a lack of variety and intellectual stimulation makes for a miserable life for these clever pets. Because of their vocal volume, African greys are not suited for close-quartered living or easily annoyed neighbors.

Most African greys kept as pets are of the Congo variety — larger and more vividly colored than the Timneh. In terms of personality, though, there's little difference. Although there used to be a big price difference between the two, the prices of hand-raised Timneh greys is now approaching that of the Congo — around $1,000. The secret's out: Timneh greys are pretty cool, too!

Cockatoos

Cockatoos have a reputation as "love sponges" — birds who, in the words of animal behaviorist Chris Davis, would choose to be "surgically grafted" onto their human companion. That's only half the story, though. In fact, cockatoos come in two basic behavioral types, which we call the "love sponges" and the "hyperactive children."

Umbrellas and Moluccans, both shown in Figure 2-5, are in the first group. These flashy birds are easily spoiled and can be a pain in the fanny, demanding attention 28 hours a day. If denied what they see as their due, they can develop behavior problems such as unstoppable screaming and feather-picking.

Figure 2-5: Some cockatoos, like these two species, are born to snuggle. Other cockatoos species are natural clowns and clever escape artists.

The "hyperactive children" are best represented by the Goffin's and bare-eyed cockatoos. Not always so keen on snuggling, these clowns never met a toy (or cage door) they couldn't figure out and take apart. Some of these birds have to have padlocks on their cages to keep them from escaping — and not combination locks, either! The Goffin's and bare-eyeds learn trick behaviors quickly and perform them with great enthusiasm.

Keeping a cockatoo means never a dull moment in your household, that's for sure. Prices range from $400 for some of the smaller species, such as the Goffin's cockatoos, to $2,000 for Moluccans. Rare species such as some of the black cockatoos can run as high as $20,000. Life spans can hit 100, with most cockatoos currently being quoted at a generic 20 to 40 years. Most can and should live longer through better care and nutrition.

We recommend that people with allergies (particularly to feathers or feather dust) steer clear of cockatoos as pets. Cockatoos are among the dustiest of birds, distributing lots of feather dust and dander.

Eclectus

One of the more interesting pet birds and certainly among the most beautiful, eclectus have a few characteristics that make them less than suitable for beginners. They can be more sensitive to their environment than many other parrots, and you may need to feed them a higher percentage of fresh fruits and vegetables to keep them healthy. Seed-exclusive diets are particularly hard for the eclectus parrot to survive on for long, one of the reasons why the eclectus rarely did well in captivity until the evolution of better diets.

Unlike many pet birds, in the eclectus the female is often the more dominant — and certainly the more beautiful (if you like red). Four common subspecies of eclectus parrots are available for the pet trade — the red-sided, vosmaeri, grand, and Solomon Island. Prices start at around $1,000 for these showstoppers.

Pionus

The pionus could be the poster child for the underappreciated parrots. Relatively quiet and easygoing, these birds are among the very best choices when it comes to pet parrots. They're not necessarily the best talkers, but they're quite capable of picking up a few words and phrases. Because of their gentle nature, the pionus parrots, including the blue-head, white-cap, dusky, and bronze-wing, are ideal for any living situation.

Why are these fabulous pets overlooked? Probably because their coloration isn't as striking as other parrots' — you could even call them plain. Don't overlook them, though: The pionus parrots have fantastic potential to become wonderful companions. You can purchase these birds in the $400 to $800 range; in most settings of good nutrition, husbandry, and love, their life expectancy can reach 30 to 40 years.

An interesting characteristic of the pionus is the "pionus snarfle," which sometimes frightens new owners, and even some veterinarians who've never heard the noise, into believing that some sort of serious respiratory problem is present. When under stress, the birds occasionally wheeze noisily in and out of their nostrils until they calm down. We don't really know why they do this, but the pionus snarfle is nothing to worry about, and actually is often the subject of a good laugh!

Macaws

Macaws are among the most sought-after pet birds, treasured for their stunning looks and, increasingly, for their companionship potential. You can find a range of personality types and prices within the collection of birds known as macaws. The large macaws can live up to 80 or even 100 years, while the "minis" can hit 40 years — a long time to have a pet. No macaw is particularly suited for apartment living — their caging requirements take up a lot of space, and they're not quiet. Here's the breakdown on these popular pets:

- **Blue-and-gold:** Most popular pet among the macaws, the blue-and-gold shares with his relatives the desire to periodically test his human family, just in case he stands a chance of rearranging the dominance hierarchy in his favor. Blue-and-golds are fine for educated beginners, as long as the owner understands the occasional social-climbing drives these birds attempt and knows how to deal properly with the situation. In the right hands, blue-and-golds make beautiful and enjoyable companions. The price range for blue-and-golds runs $800 to $1,200.
- **Scarlet:** Popular in show-biz as well as pet homes for their stunning looks, scarlet macaws sport a long tail and red, yellow, and blue feathers (primarily red, hence the name). Like the blue-and-gold, the scarlet will not hesitate to place his owners below him in the social hierarchy, if possible. Give a scarlet macaw an inch, and he often tries to take a yard. Scarlets have a reputation for becoming "nippy," but this behavior is actually seen most commonly in those birds who believe they have a greater-than-reality position of dominance in their homes. Probably not the best bird for beginners but a fine companion for an experienced bird-lover. Prices range from $1,200 to $2,000.
- **Military:** Overshadowed by the popularity of the blue-and-gold and the scarlet, military macaws are, in our opinion, underrated and under-appreciated for their value as pets. Slightly smaller than their blue-and-gold counterparts, these birds seem to be much more active, busier little guys, and they can make wonderful pet birds. If allowed, the military macaw certainly tries to test his owners and home situation also, attempting to climb up that social-dominance hierarchy ladder as much as possible. Prices range typically from $600 to $800 or even higher in some parts of the country.
- **Green-winged:** These birds are the second largest of the ara genus macaws. (All of the common macaws, except the hyacinth, belong to the genus ara). The green-winged macaw can be a somewhat stubborn and head-strong individual, usually resistant to changing bad behaviors back into more acceptable ones if he has learned what he can get away with. For the experienced bird-lover, though, green-winged macaws, like most other macaw species, can be wonderfully rewarding pets. Prices range from $1,200 to $1,800.

- **Hyacinth:** So special, this guy's in a class of his own — in scientific classification as well as price. The domestically raised pet hyacinth macaw is often known as the "gentle blue giant" and is the largest of all commonly available pet parrots. In spite of their immense size, these birds are dramatically gentle and easily handled by most people. The birds can be quite noisy, however, and have a major destructive potential with their huge beaks. The price? Are you sitting down? $8,000 to $12,000.
- **Minis:** The mini macaws include the yellow-collared, Hahn's, noble, red-bellied, severe, and Illiger's. Smaller versions of the larger counterparts discussed in this section, these macaws can be quite enjoyable as pets — they're pretty similar in all ways except size. Prices range from a very reasonable $400 to about $1,000.

In addition to his work on this book, Brian is a co-author of the definitive work on macaws, *The Large Macaws: Their Care, Breeding and Conservation* (Raintree Publications).

Toucans, mynahs, and some others

Toucans and mynahs are two species that took a big hit when laws banning importations were passed. They don't breed well in captivity (at least not at the present time), so their available numbers in the pet world have fallen steadily. And the decline is probably not bad news for would-be owners, because many birds among those that do breed well in captivity have greater pet potential than either of these species.

The mynah's main claim to fame is mimicry, and they're good at it. (One horrible myth that seems to follow them is that you have to split their tongues for them to talk — not true!)

Toucans can't talk and largely are kept as attractive aviary species because of their striking looks.

Chickens, ducks, geese, peafowl, and turkeys

Although many people may raise their eyes at the idea of a pet chicken, common (and not-so-common) barnyard fowl can be absolutely charming, ideal for the person with a bit of land. Chickens and ducks, especially, come in some very striking varieties, and chickens can provide you with the extra benefit of fresh eggs! Geese can be outstanding watch-birds, and even turkeys can be beautiful and affectionate.

The dinosaur birds: Ostriches and emus

To look at the feet of an ostrich or emu is to believe the link between birds and dinosaurs. These massive, flightless birds have a small but devoted core of fanciers. Should you be among them? That depends.

The larger of the species, the ostriches, are popular as breeders and suppliers of meat, hide, and feathers, but now and then you can find people who keep them as pets. Female ostriches are often manageable, but the males can be extremely difficult to control and flat-out intimidating to many people. They're really not for most people.

Emus, on the other hand, are potentially interesting pets. Baby emus are really cute, marked with their own little "racing stripes" that fade as the bird matures. If you're able to locate an emu that has been raised to see humans as "family," you're likely to have one who thinks he's a person. These friendly birds love to be hugged and are wonderful at pest-control in your yard. Still, they're not for the timid — full-grown birds are 5 feet tall and 80 to 100 pounds.

If you ever run into an ostrich or emu (or, even rarer, a cassowary), don't be as concerned about their heads as their feet. These forward-kicking birds can really pack a wallop, enough to knock the breath from you — or worse. Their beaks can hurt, too.

Brian has ostriches and emus and clients with cassowaries. He's experienced in handling them, and he's always careful to keep an eye on their movements. Gina, however, is content to watch these interesting birds from the other side of a very solid fence.

Photo by Dr. Brian L. Speer

Although none of these birds are known for their intelligence, many are kept and enjoyed as companion animals. Brian has clients with pet chickens, ducks, and geese who come when they're called and seek out their owners for affection. On his own happy birdstead, he has a turkey named Margie who adores him and follows him like a shadow.

Chickens, ducks, and geese can be kept comfortable on a large suburban lot (if your community's zoning allows it, of course), but the same can't be said of the glorious peacock. Prized for their fantastic plumage, peacocks (the female is a *peahen,* and both are *peafowl*) can get you in trouble with the neighbors in short order for their amazingly high-decibel calls at night. These lovely creatures are best suited to houses on large acreages — or to places with deaf neighbors.

Chapter 3

A Bird of Your Own

In This Chapter

- The importance of savvy shopping
- Male? Female? Does it matter? Can you tell?
- Choosing between bird babies or adults
- Knowing the pros and cons of pet stores, breeders, and more

From all the plumed possibilities, you now have in mind your pick of potential pet birds — hands-on or hands-off, small or large, noisy or relatively quiet. Your homework complete, you're moving marvelously closer to sharing your home with the bird of your choice.

Where do you find that special bird?

Perhaps you believe the selection process is simple, a matter of going to the nearest pet shop or opening the classified section of your local paper. If only choosing wisely were that easy! Unfortunately, Brian sees evidence to the contrary in his practice every day — birds too sick, too young, or too wild to be good pets. Some of them pay with their lives for the poor choices their owners make, or suffer from illness or become unwanted because they weren't the pets their owners expected.

What can you take away from other people's sad mistakes? Two words to remember: *Buyer beware!*

All sellers are *not* the same, which is why you need to arm yourself with knowledge and take your time before plunking down your cash, whether the outlay is a few dollars for a budgie or several thousand for a more exotic bird. The shopping experience offers all the security of a minefield. Take our hands, and we can walk you through it, safe and sound.

Don't forget to review Chapter 2 for our evaluation of each of the popular pet bird species — and some of the more unusual ones, too. If you're just starting out, you may want to explore Chapter 18, which features our picks of the ten best birds for beginners. And no matter whether this is your first bird or you're an experienced bird-keeper, check out Chapter 16 for a quick rundown of the right questions to ask when you buy a bird.

Did we hear a "Yes, but"?

For all we say about the best way to choose and buy a bird, we know of people who did the opposite and everything worked out fine. These exceptions usually take the form of "Yes, buts," if you will, as in "Yes, but we didn't do that and our bird is great." And it's true, some folks have bought birds from less-than-ideal sources, or bought them too young, or bought birds others couldn't handle, and the situation worked.

To all of those folks we have a "Yes, but" of our own: "Yes, but you were *lucky.*"

Everything you read in this chapter is about minimizing risk, about avoiding the most common ways people end up with birds who break their hearts and their budgets. Don't rely on luck: Approach bird-buying sensibly and get the healthiest and best pet-quality bird you can. You can find plenty of time later for falling deeply and irretrievably in love.

Considering Wild-Caught versus Captive-Raised

The Wild Bird Conservation Act of 1992 changed the pet bird landscape dramatically in the United States, virtually eliminating the flow of wild-caught birds into the country for the pet trade. The bill was a victory to animal activists who documented problems in the import trade, where birds often died before ever coming close to a caring home.

The shift toward the captive breeding of pet birds has provided an unintended benefit: the improved availability of better pet birds, from both a health and a temperament perspective. Caring, informed breeders stepped up to produce pet birds who see humans as friends and who aren't damaged by the stresses of capture and transportation.

Other countries besides the United States also prohibit the importation of pet birds, but even if yours does not, we feel strongly that your better choice for a pet bird is one who has been captive-raised. We also believe that choosing a captive-raised bird as your pet delivers benefits to the wild counterparts out there, too — the wild birds can stay in the wild, the place they call home.

The reduction in the demand for wild-caught birds for the pet bird trade hasn't ended the threats to the survival of parrot species in the wild. Habitat destruction is proving to be just as damaging, if not more so, to many bird species. Groups such as the World Parrot Trust are fighting to preserve birds in the wild. We encourage you to support them; you can find their contact numbers in the Additional Resources appendix at the back of the book.

Telling the Girls from the Guys

Which do you prefer — a male bird or a female? Does gender really matter? How can you tell the he's from the she's, anyway?

Selection of one sex or the other depends on the qualities you're seeking in your new family addition. If you're buying a canary and you want a singer, a male is your choice. (And still, you need to hear the bird sing before you buy him.) Male cockatiels are usually better whistlers than are females, and the red and blue female eclectus parrot is considered the real looker of her kind — much flashier than her green and red mate, although he's not that bad-looking, either. In terms of health, females sometimes have obstetric problems, such as *egg-binding,* where eggs get trapped inside, especially in smaller parrot species such as budgies, cockatiels, or lovebirds. And of course, the folks who breed birds have preferences: They don't want to end up with all males or all females!

In many cases, though, not only does gender make no difference in terms of pet potential, but you also won't even know whether a bird's a male or female when you buy. (If you really have to know, your veterinarian can find out for you through either surgical sexing — going inside to identify the sexual parts — or through DNA testing, done by drawing a blood sample for testing. More on that later in this chapter.)

The term for males and females who don't look alike is *sexual dimorphism,* and many species of birds don't exhibit any differences, at least not as far as we mere humans can tell. Birds themselves can tell the difference, of course, although we don't always understand how.

Some species do have gender identities that are obvious to our eyes. The eclectus is certainly one of the more extreme examples — the male and female are so different that folks once believed the two genders were separate species — but other, more subtle differences exist in many species. An experienced seller can usually tell the girls from the boys in adult budgies, cockatiels, and some of the other parrot species where the colors are the same but the marking pattern is just a wee bit different, such as in the Senegal parrot.

In their quest for birds that are different, bird breeders have added another element of confusion to the identification of some species. The classic example is the cockatiel. The common grey cockatiel is easy to sex: The males are grey, with bright orange cheeks and no white on the underneath side of their wing feathers. Females have grey heads with duller-colored orange cheeks.

Simple? Sure, but what about all the new color mutations among cockatiels? It's anybody's guess. In varieties such as the cinnamon, the white-faced, and the albino, telling male from female can be very difficult, if not impossible.

Do you really need to know whether any bird is a boy or a girl? In general, both males and females make equally fine pets, so determining gender is not a necessity — unless, of course, you plan to breed your bird. Give your pet a nice non-gender-specific name like Jan and go on with your life. Some folks, though, can't leave it at that. They have to know. Enter DNA testing, where a blood sample is sent off to a special lab for gender determination. The cost: Usually around $30 to $60 or so — a rather big investment in a $60 cockatiel, perhaps, but a relative drop in the bucket when the bird's a $10,000 hyacinth macaw. Birds can also be surgically sexed, a procedure in which a veterinarian examines the animal under anesthesia in order to determine gender.

The outcome of a sex determination is usually documented in writing. If you're considering buying a bird represented as either male or female (in species where the difference isn't visible to the eye), ask to see the documentation. Don't just take the seller's word for it. Birds who have been surgically sexed typically have a tattoo under their right or left wing webs; males are right, females are left. Chromosomal or DNA sexing results also are recorded on a certificate that correlates to the identification number of the bird's leg band, if she has one, or microchip number. (You can find more information on identification in Chapter 4.) Again, a word of buyer beware: If there's no ID to match with the sexing result, you can't be sure you have the same bird, can you?

Checking Up on a Bird's Good Health

In the wild, a big part of a bird's survival depends on not presenting a tempting target to predators, who actively seek out the sick, old, and weak. Even in birds who are in little danger from predators — generally safe souls such as our own pet birds — the genetic imperative to hide illness still holds.

Some signs of sickness often are visible, however, and you need to look for these tip-offs as you form an overall impression of good health. Remember, though, that a bird can be a big investment, and one of the better ways to protect that investment is to have your new pet thoroughly examined by a veterinarian who's experienced and qualified in the field of avian medicine before your warranty period expires. (More on warranties in "Protecting Your Rights," later in this chapter.)

Any pet bird you consider buying ought to display the following characteristics:

- Behaves normally — perching without problems, moving with coordination, and using the full body without favoring one side or the other. The bird should bear weight evenly, all four toes present on each foot and in proper position — two toes forward, two backward, in the case of parrots.
- Is alert and responsive.
- Breathes easily, with no sign of laboring to move air and no tail-bobbing, which is another indicator of breathing problems.
- Has eyes, ears, and nostrils (nares) that are clean and free of debris and discharge.
- Has healthy-appearing plumage. Feathers should have normal color and structure, showing no signs of *stress bars* (horizontal lines indicating problems with feather development) or excessive wear. Look for evidence of damage from feather-picking, improper housing, or other trauma.
- Consistently produces droppings that are normal in appearance and have all three components in evidence in normal appearance and quantity — urine (liquid), feces (solids), and urates (white semi-solids). Check for pasting of waste around the fanny. (For the complete scoop on poop, see Chapter 8.)
- Has a well-muscled body of appropriate weight, with no signs of obesity. Skin should be smooth and translucent, without excessive amounts of fat showing underneath, nor excessive flakiness, scabs, areas of damaged skin, or crustiness.

A bird who's showing even some of these general signs of illness may be gravely ill and may die even with veterinary intervention. Spare yourself the expense and heartache such a bird represents. Suggest to the seller that the bird needs help, but think twice before taking on the project of nursing the bird yourself.

Making Mature Decisions about Age

Many species of pet birds live for decades with proper care, even to the point of outliving their original owners, which means that birds for sale or adoption are available in a wide spectrum of ages. Most people are probably best off with a fully weaned baby bird, and you may be among them. But we recommend that you consider all the possibilities nonetheless.

Weighing the pros and cons of baby birds

The appeal of babies is obvious. First, they're adorable. Second, they're a pretty clean slate, should have no bad habits that you will have to deal with, and are ready to bond with you and grow into a perfect lifelong companion. Still, problems can surface even with baby birds.

The problem with unweaned birds

In this sense, babies come in two varieties: weaned and unweaned. *Weaned* is a term for a bird who can eat on his own, instead of relying on parent birds or human surrogates to feed him. (When humans assume the duties of parent birds, they're *hand-feeding.*)

We *do not* recommend you buy an unweaned bird. Some folks believe that bringing an unweaned bird into your heart and home is the best way to end up with a strongly bonded pet. Others push the economic aspect of such a purchase: Because the buyer takes over the round-the-clock work of hand-feeding, the cost of an unweaned bird is usually less. To put it bluntly: A dead or dying baby bird can't bond with you, making him something less than a bargain. Too many things can go wrong when novices attempt to hand-raise a bird.

Take the typical blue-and-gold macaw baby, who crawls out of the egg weighing less than an ounce. That baby gains more than 30 times her body weight in the first eight weeks if properly fed and cared for. And "properly fed and cared for" usually means feeding *every two hours,* especially during the first couple of weeks of life. Experienced hand-raisers can feed on auto-pilot. They fall out of bed, warm the formula, feed the babies, and go back to bed without ever really waking up.

When a novice tries hand-feeding while half-asleep, however, the lack of experience can really hurt. Formula can be overheated, burning the baby bird's food-storage organ, called the *crop.* Formula can be fed too fast, flooding down the windpipe and into the bird's lungs. The brooder where he's kept can be too cold or too hot for the true needs of the baby — weakening him and setting the stage for other problems to develop.

A baby can die, very easily, from your mistakes, leaving you at 2 a.m. feeling like the biggest bird-murderer in the world, all alone with no one to call for help. Don't put yourself through the pain, and please try not to put any baby bird through the torture. Brian all too often performs autopsies on baby birds from these settings to pinpoint the reason they died. We strongly suggest that you leave the baby-raising to folks who know what they're doing.

If, after having birds for a while, you decide that you want to go the breeder route, you certainly need to learn how to hand-feed babies. See Chapter 13 to discover more about the joys and challenges of being a bird-breeder and the thrills and chills of hand-raising bird babies of your own. Although Brian admits that the excitement, satisfaction, and fulfillment of successfully raising baby birds is immense, he also warns that the endeavor of bird breeding is not an easy one and is certainly not for everyone.

Socialization — not hand-feeding — is everything

A hand-raised bird has the best pet potential in those species that we enjoy interacting with — the parrots, from budgies and cockatiels all the way through to the giant hyacinth macaw. As we build our knowledge of raising birds in captivity, though, we repeatedly find that it's not the hand-feeding so much as the social contact with humans (really just a by-product of hand-feeding) that increases the pet potential of birds.

A recent study, in fact, tested this theory by letting orange-winged Amazons raise their own babies, who were handled regularly by humans during the preweaning period. The results? The human-socialized, parent-raised babies made fine pets.

The study's results make good sense, considering what we know about other companion animals. For example, experts recognize the importance of a puppy being fed by his mother and of the lessons he can learn from his mother and siblings. We don't hand-raise puppies or kittens (unless they're orphaned, of course), but we do understand the significance of socializing them. The best breeders of dogs and cats make sure their babies are gently handled from the time they're born and are exposed to the sights, sounds, and smells of human existence. Logically, the same rules apply to birds. And yet, hand-feeding is still the gold standard when it comes to raising and socializing baby birds. We think the time is right to change that definition: Successful raising of baby birds may rely on hand-feeding, but proper socialization is the key to pet quality in many ways. The two do not necessarily have to go together (and often don't).

Although the situation may change in years to come, the practical reality for now is that if you want a baby bird who has been lovingly handled, you're likely to buy a hand-fed animal. And that's fine — they make outstanding pets. But ask the seller about socialization — have the babies been handled regularly and gently? If you run into a breeder who lets parent birds do the feeding but still makes sure the babies are socialized, you're probably in good hands.

Considering the prospects of older birds

When you start looking for birds, you can expect to find a fair number for sale who are past — and in some cases, long past — their adorable baby stage. They become available for all the reasons other pets do — their owners died, moved, divorced, became bored with their birds, or couldn't deal with their pet's behavior problems. Are older birds eligible for your consideration? Yes! But you need to look at each candidate individually, because the details of every situation — such as behavior patterns reinforced over the years — are going to vary.

Before the age of sexual maturity

Young birds who are between the baby stage and the age of sexual maturity are often better candidates for settling in with a new owner. You're more likely to be able to alter behavioral problems, and your chances are greater for successfully converting a young bird to a healthier diet (if he isn't on one already).

The onset of sexual maturity varies from species to species. Budgerigars and lovebirds become sexually mature rather quickly, at the age of 6 to 12 months or so. Other birds can take years before becoming sexually mature; for example, the hyacinth macaw often turns 7 years old before becoming interested in a mate.

After the age of sexual maturity

Birds who are beyond the age of sexual maturity are among the riskiest purchases you can make. Like people, grown-up birds are often set in their ways, and if their ways include some bad behaviors, you can expect a harder time making any changes. Some birds also become available *because* they're sexually mature. Like human teenagers, birds can drive you crazy because of the hormones that are driving them crazy. Some birds change from Jekyll to Hyde seemingly overnight, and owners who don't understand or know how to cope often give up their pets in frustration. Sometimes such birds pass from home to home to home, sold and sold again (because they still command a price), becoming a bigger problem at each stop. These birds are not necessarily good pet candidates; realistically, they're rehabilitation projects at best and may be suited only for experienced bird-keepers. Nonetheless, those birds do deserve a good home — but it needs to be the right home, with a loving and experienced owner.

With that word to the wise in mind, know that even among older birds some real gems become available — birds with good manners and good health, loving, well-socialized birds who are fully capable of bonding with a new owner. Move with all due caution, but if you find such a bird, buy her. She's a good deal and a good deed, all rolled into one.

As the popularity of pet birds continues to grow, so, too, do the numbers of birds given up by their owners. The typical dog-and-cat-oriented animal shelter isn't really equipped to accept and rehome birds (although some do, of course). A variety of groups now operate to fill the gap, serving solely to rescue, rehabilitate, and rehome pet birds. Some of these groups provide careful screening and extensive education of prospective owners to increase a bird's chances of sticking in a new home. These organizations can be an excellent source of pet birds. To find one, talk to veterinarians, bird shops, and shelters in your area. We list a few in the Additional Resources appendix at the back of this book.

Finding a Reputable Source

Two factors are arguably more important than any others when it comes to buying the right bird with pet potential.

The first factor is species selection: Have you chosen the right kind of bird for what you want in a pet? Have you looked beyond the flash and feathers and selected the bird with the level of care, interactivity, and noise that you can live with? (If you can't answer, back up to Chapter 2 for a look at pet bird species, or visit Chapter 18 for our list of best birds for beginners.)

The second factor: finding a reputable source for a healthy, well-socialized pet. If you choose a species that's right for you and then go to the wrong source to purchase your bird, you may be in store for a disaster as big as, if not bigger than, picking the wrong kind of bird in the first place.

The interesting thing about bird sellers is that retail outlets are not only the most popular places to get a pet bird but also one of the better sources for a winged pet. This situation runs counter to what experts advise when people look for puppies and kittens. Reputable dog and cat breeders *do not* sell to pet stores (in fact, many a breed club's code of ethics forbids it). Pet-store puppies and kittens too often come from breeding operations where animals are mass-produced with no consideration for health or temperament, often under unspeakably cruel conditions. Others come from casual local breeders with "oops" litters to get rid of — puppies that add to the problem of overpopulation.

The bird world is different. While sickly, mass-produced birds are also a problem in the pet bird trade, many pet stores either breed their own birds or contract exclusively with reputable local breeders. (Some retailers handle the hand-feeding, while others buy only fully weaned babies.)

For the bird-buyer, putting pet stores into the mix means you don't have to deal directly with a breeder to get a great pet bird. Sometimes you can't go straight to the breeder — they work through pet stores because they want no contact with the public.

The avian veterinarian as a bird-buying resource

If you're fortunate to have an experienced and qualified avian veterinarian in your area, consider tapping into his or her knowledge of bird-sellers in your vicinity. Veterinarians see and hear it all — the healthy birds and the sick ones, the good advice people get from reliable sources and the counsel so poor that the vet has to struggle to keep his jaw off the floor. And over time, any good veterinarian makes sense of trends — good birds and good advice from some sources, and the opposite from others.

Don't expect a veterinarian to trash-talk any particular source, though. Aside from demonstrating a lack of professionalism, the veterinarian who issues negative comments leaves himself vulnerable to accusations of violating the doctor-client relationship and to possible litigation. But any good veterinarian is happy to steer you toward shops and breeders that consistently sell healthy, well-socialized pet birds and dispense up-to-date advice. Just ask.

Why do many bird breeders steer clear of selling directly to the public? In truth, the reasons are as varied as the breeders themselves, but one of the more common explanations involves privacy and security. As any police officer can tell you, inviting strangers into your home is risky. And the exposure increases when you have an aviary full of breeding birds whose potential worth runs into thousands of dollars each. Easily stolen, these birds can be sold through ads or at flea markets, netting the thief a few hundred quick dollars for not much effort. (Another reason for thinking twice before buying a "bargain" bird — he could be stolen!)

Reputable sources show themselves by their actions and their words. So leave your credit card and checkbook at home — you're going shopping. The buying comes later.

Pet shops

A retail pet store has to have a lot on the ball to make it in a competitive marketplace. Before you even consider making a purchase, check to make sure all aspects of the business are up to par. The key areas to check out include the following.

The staff

People working in a pet store ought to know what kinds of birds they have and be able to discuss the characteristics of each species. If you're dealing with salespeople who can't tell you the difference between a yellow-naped Amazon and an African grey (beyond the fact that they're colored differently), you have to wonder what else they don't know about birds, like proper care, nutrition, and preventive health care of the animals in their charge.

And speaking of proper nutrition, a qualified staff can talk to you in an educated manner about proper diets such as formulated feeds. A staffer who staunchly defends an all-seed diet and wants to sell you birds trained into this dietary approach is, at the very least, not current on the latest nutritional knowledge. Look and listen for a store staff who can also recommend proper cages, toys, and other bird gear.

Pet-store staff need to know their limits. Medical advice is best left to a qualified veterinarian — avoid any pet store where the staff is eager to recommend and sell you useless over-the-counter products.

Expect the staff of a reputable store to truly care about any available birds (after all, they are not "merchandise" for sale, but rather "babies" for proper placement). A conscientious operation really wants to make sure that you're the right person for the role of bird companion and that you're going to take good care of your pet. Listen for it — a caring and sometimes detailed inquisition is a very good sign.

A first-rate pet store employs a staff that's clearly interested in and knowledgeable about birds and who understands the importance of a good working relationship with veterinarians and bird behaviorists, as well. The emphasis, always, should be on prevention of problems through the education of the customer — you.

The store

First thing to notice: how clean and odor-free the pet store seems when you enter and wander through the shop (see Figure 3-1). But before you find any operation guilty of unsanitary surroundings, consider the difficulty of maintaining a single bird, much less a shop full of them. So cut the staff some slack if a bird has made poop soup in her water dish or if the food-scattering antics have made the floor a little cluttered. Temporary untidiness is to be expected, especially if you come in several hours after the store opens.

What's not acceptable, however, is evidence of long-term sanitation problems — a 3-inch pile of feces underneath the perches, for example.

Consider, too, how well the shop attends to its pets. Confirm that birds are kept in a controlled situation, where staff can oversee any interaction between them and the customers. Note whether the birds are placed near other stress-provoking pets.

Look, too, for a variety of appropriate cages, toys, and perches. A selection of good reference books and magazines is another plus. Very important: pelleted diets on the shelves — and in the food dishes. Seeds, nuts, and other foodstuffs are fine, as long as the store clearly recommends a balanced, basic diet. Ideally, a good pet store avoids unproven or dangerous products such as over-the-counter antibiotics or mite treatment products. (And make sure the staff doesn't use these questionable remedies on the birds in the shop!)

Figure 3-1: Clean and well-lit, a good bird shop is a wonderful place to familiarize yourself with the various birds before you buy.

Photo by Dr. Brian L. Speer

A store that operates safely and sensibly keeps grooming and boarding services in a completely separate part of the establishment, to protect its birds from the introduction of disease.

As you develop an overall impression of a pet shop, look carefully at the birds themselves. Consider how healthy and well-cared-for they appear. Pay attention to tell-tale details such as appropriate cages, and toys and perches to keep them happy. The potential pets should be interested in people and want to be held (some species more than others, of course — not all birds are born to be love sponges). If the store is hand-feeding babies, you may be able to see them through a window, but beware of any store that invites you in to handle these young birds, at least not without requesting that you wash your hands and put on some protective clothing.

You can glean the most from these reconnaissance runs by being friendly and open. Being opinionated is one thing, but you won't get very far being judgmental. Watch, listen, and learn.

More than anything else, you're looking for evidence of current knowledge, progressive thinking, and a willingness to share information. A cage label that clearly identifies a bird's age and indicates that the bird has been started off right with a high-quality food (see Figure 3-2) is one example of that kind of evidence. Proper care, including proper diets, is the sign of a store whose owner, manager, and staff (who may all be the same person) are in the business because they love birds.

Figure 3-2: Look for a willingness to share information and an emphasis on nutrition.

Photo by Dr. Brian L. Speer

Breeders

Some breeders do sell directly to the public, and to evaluate them, you need to use many of the same criteria as you apply to pet stores. Evidence of current, accurate information is probably the most important sign that you're dealing with someone of merit. The odds are greater that their birds will be, too.

Good breeders, like good pet stores, don't want to place their babies, so lovingly raised, into a home where they won't be cherished. Don't be offended if you're asked lots of questions — it's the sign of a caring seller. Expect to be asked about your living circumstances, how long you're away from home every day, if you've ever had birds before, how many birds you have now, and so on. A good seller refuses to place a bird with a person who's looking for a bird to match the color of the carpet. Folks with character and integrity want their babies to match your heart.

Private parties

A person selling a single bird can be the hardest of all to get a read on. Of course, the first question you need to ask is "Why is this bird for sale?" A "good" answer might be "The owner died." A response such as "It bit the heck out of my husband" warrants a little eyebrow-raising.

In the same way you check out a bird in a shop, you look for signs of quality care and good health in a pet being offered by an individual. We think everyone deserves a second chance (or third, or fourth), and birds are no exception. If only we could put every one of the unwanteds back into the rain forest! But because that dream is unrealistic, we promote the importance of connecting with the kind of human care these animals so richly deserve.

Sticker shock

Don't bargain-hunt when it comes to birds. Raising healthy birds to be good pets is expensive, time-consuming work, and if you find a "bargain," you really need to stop and ask yourself what corners may have been cut in the nurturing process. The bird may come from a mass-production type of origin that made little or no socialization effort, or the animal may be ill or in unknown health. In either case, the bird's potential for becoming a good pet is greatly reduced. He's no bargain, at any price!

If cost poses a problem to your personal finances, you're better off choosing a less-expensive species than trying to get a "bargain" on a more expensive bird. You can purchase some of the smaller parrots, for example, for a fraction of the price of their larger cousins. Better to spend $100 on a healthy, well-socialized cockatiel than $100 on a sick Amazon with behavior problems — even if the Amazon's price is touted as the "sale of the century." A sick or unmanagable bird is no bargain. Consider price as one factor, but not the primary one.

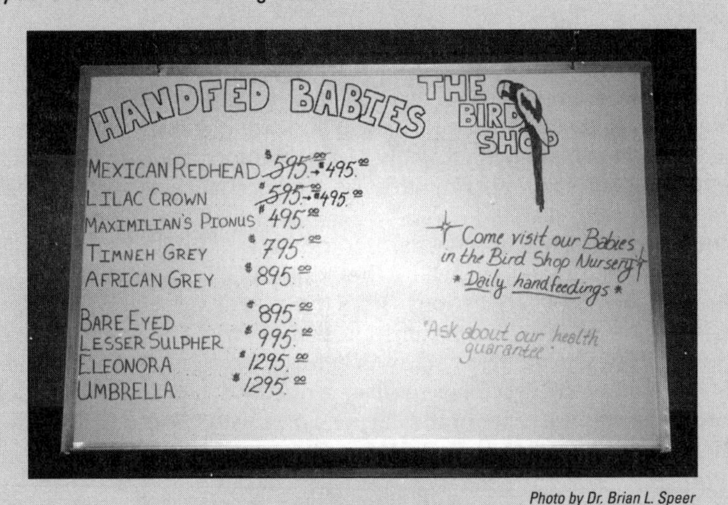

Photo by Dr. Brian L. Speer

Don't let your altruism override your common sense, though. Go into any purchase with your eyes wide open — especially when you're dealing with a bird someone else is dying to get rid of.

Protecting Your Rights

No matter where or from whom you buy a bird, don't even consider proceeding without a written sales contract and warranty — for your protection, and for the seller's as well.

Commonly, a decent warranty strongly recommends an examination by a veterinarian, usually within 48 to 72 hours of purchase but sometimes within as many as 14 days. The warranty ought to spell out what will happen if your new pet is found to be ill or have a pre-existing medical problem — although the agreement may require a second opinion to confirm the problem. Compensation for medical expenses to treat a sick bird may be limited or nonexistent.

As a buyer, you may have some responsibilities set forth in the contract, too. For example, the sales contract may require you to keep your new bird separate from other birds in your home so that a returned bird won't pose a hazard to others in the breeder's aviary or nursery or to the avian residents of the bird shop.

Serious problems are usually dealt with by replacement, not refund of the purchase price (particularly in the cases of the more costly species), in the terms of most contracts.

A sales contract is a good thing for all parties involved. As with all other legal documents, though, read it carefully and make sure you're comfortable with the terms before closing the deal.

Part II
Caring for Your Bird Properly

"He loves his ball and string, but once in a while he'll pick up the trombone and play 'Under Paris Skies' over and over again."

In this part . . .

A bird in hand is worth . . . the best care and consideration you can possibly provide, and once you've chosen your avian companion, you want to make sure you set your pet up with all the right stuff for a long and happy life with you. In this part, we tell you everything you need to know about cages, dishes, perches, toys, and even microchips, and we steer you away from money-wasting products that are good for neither your bird nor your budget. You want to feed your bird properly, and we tell you how. Good food isn't hard to figure out, and you may find that the choices you make can lead to a healthier diet for you, too. We also tell you how to handle your bird, trim wings and nails, and use gentle techniques to avoid behavior problems — all for the benefit of your bird companion and his new family.

Chapter 4

All the Right Stuff

In This Chapter

- Choosing the right cage
- Picking perfect perches for your pal
- Toys, toys, toys
- Bird-cleaning tools of the trade

Love to shop? Need a reason to? You're in the right place at the right time. Your bird needs some gear; you want to shop — a perfect match, so read on.

If you like to spend money on your pets, you're certainly not alone. The pet-supplies industry is huge, a multibillion-dollar dynamo that thrives through boom times and recessions alike. From Mom-and-Pop pet stores to mail-order catalogs to superstores to online shopping, a whole lot of spending's going on — and, for the most part, our birds end up much better off for the investment we make in their comfort, amusement, and safe-keeping.

But not always.

You can find unsafe or unnecessary products anywhere pet supplies are sold. Some are just a waste of your money, but others can be a risk to your bird's health. And you can't always rely on the advice of a pet-store owner or employee to help you sort out the good from the bad. Although most sales personnel are well-meaning, many may not have up-to-date information on the best products for your pet. Some inadvertently pass on very outdated and even dangerous information.

The good news is you can find correct and current information right here, right now. This chapter shares the knowledge you need to buy safe and reasonably priced cages, perches, toys, and all the other necessary paraphernalia that goes with bringing a bird into your life.

Although the situation is improving, plenty of outdated advice about avian nutrition still exists — and much of it is shared in pet stores and by other bird retailers or even veterinarians. These folks are often the same people who may give you bum advice on bird gear. Make sure you're offering the best food to your pet by checking out Chapter 6 for current advice on appropriate diet.

A Cage to Call Her Own

No purchase is more important than your bird's cage. The cage is where your pet will spend time when you're not home, when the family is sleeping, or when you're doing other things and can't pay attention to your pet. Some birds — we call them the "hands-off" varieties — almost never leave their cages. A cage is security and protection, a place to play, and a place to rest. For all these reasons and more, it pays to shop carefully. The cage is a big-ticket item, in some cases costing more than the bird himself.

If you stay alert to the possibilities offered by classified ads and tag sales, you can save some serious change by buying a cage secondhand. Be sure the cage is high-quality, and then make your best deal. Plan to scrub the used residence before introducing your bird to it, though. An easy way to clean a cage: Take it to a do-it-yourself car wash and use the high-pressure hose on it. Just be sure to rinse all the soap off well when you're done. After cleaning a secondhand cage thoroughly, play it safe by disinfecting it, too. Use diluted bleach, at about one-half cup per gallon of water, and then let the cage air-dry.

How to set up your cage and make sense of all the other goodies you end up with is in Chapter 5.

Bigger is better

The first rule of caging: Buy the biggest cage you can afford. Forget the generic categorization you'll find in pet stores of "finch cage," "budgie cage," "small parrot cage," and so on. Those descriptions represent the *minimum* size to consider — a better bet is at least one size bigger.

No matter how much attention we're able to devote to our birds, they still spend a lot of time cooped up — almost all their lives, in the case of canaries and other finches. Give your pet a break, right from the start, and buy a cage that will allow her as much freedom of movement as possible.

The only problem with buying a cage larger than commonly recommended is that the bar spacing may be the wrong size for your pet. Before you buy any cage, check to see that your bird can't put his head through the bars. Some pets accidentally catch themselves this way — with injuries or even death as the result! Fortunately, many manufacturers of high-quality cages offer different bar-spacing options on their models, so you can secure a large cage of the dimensions that are best for your individual bird's needs and provide safe surroundings for your pet. The basic bar spacing for cockatiels is about ¾-inch. Finches require smaller bar spacing, and Amazons and macaws need larger.

Wood you buy metal, please?

Metal is the best material for cage construction. Wood is too hard to clean and usually won't stand up to the abuse parrots can give out. Some manufacturers are experimenting with acrylics, but while these components can make attractive housing for your pet, they may not offer enough social interaction and ventilation to keep a bird happy. (Acrylics do make some of the best toys, though.)

Metal cages are made of stainless steel, brass, aluminum, galvanized wire, or iron and come in all kinds of designs, with or without paint. Choose a model without fussiness — an embellished lodging may look good in the store, but you're apt to regret the purchase every time you try to clean poop out of the decorative elements. Make sure you think and shop from a practical, as well as safe, standpoint for your bird.

Cages are often lacking in an important dimension: width. Those tall and narrow circular cages may look nice, but they force birds to fly more like a helicopter than in the style that comes naturally for them. Remember to consider the way the birds move. Finches and canaries usually prefer to fly horizontally, not vertically. Parrot species like to fly horizontally as well as climb up and down in their cages.

Galvanized metal is fine — at least it won't rust — but look for galvanizing material that's electroplated on, not dipped. The latter process too often leaves beads of material that parrots can chip off and swallow, putting them at risk of zinc or lead poisoning or both. Powder-coating is popular in many decorator colors and is fine for most birds. (Some dedicated chewers can remove the paint, though, and some paints can contain risky levels of zinc, lead, or other heavy metals.)

A checklist for cage quality

With so many cages on the market (or available as secondhand), how can you be sure you're buying one of high quality? Here are a few points to consider:

- **Design:** You want a cage to be attractive, but even more importantly, it should be workable for your bird. Fortunately, if you shop well you can find a cage that's both well-designed and good-looking. Look for features such as a bird-proof latch (especially if you have an escape artist like the Goffin's cockatoo), dishes that are easy to move, remove, and clean, and a droppings tray that takes standard-sized newspapers. Make sure that you can easily reach in and make contact with your bird, wherever she may be within the cage. In some emergencies, easy access is a critical concern. Make sure the food and water sources provide no "traps" to catch and injure toes, heads, wings, and so on. Mess-catchers can be helpful, too — they look like an inverted metal skirt around the base of the cage. The best position for the slide-out droppings tray at the bottom of the cage is under a grid so your bird can't access it. High-impact, durable plastic or metal is a good choice for a droppings tray — no matter what the material, the tray ought to slide out smoothly and be easy to clean.

Check your bird's ability to move freely and comfortably in his cage without bumping into some obstruction. Too many perches, bowls, toys, or corners within the cage actually can lead to a loss of freedom of movement and a reduction of quality of life, if you're not careful.

Most people prefer vertical bars with the idea they're easier on long tail feathers. Horizontal bars are easier to climb for some birds, though. In reality, either kind is fine, and some cages even mix them up, with vertical bars on some sides and horizontal on others.

- **Sturdiness:** You're going to have your bird and the cage for a very long time, so you need to make sure the construction is solid. Check seams, welds, and places where wires and corners meet — is everything all smooth and sturdy, with nothing for a bird to chip off and chew? Beware chipping or flaking paint.
- **Convenience:** A stand is great, especially with cages designed for smaller birds. You and your bird are likely to appreciate having the cage off the ground — in your case, for ease of access; for hers, visual perspective. Some stands come with shelves, handy for storing newspapers, food, and other supplies. Casters are a blessing, too, because you can easily move the cage and stand out from the wall to clean behind it.

Placing a cage directly on the ground puts your bird in a very vulnerable "low altitude position" — one that is stressful and psychologically undesirable for most birds. Ideally, a cage, perch, and stand combination that enables the bird to perch comfortably at about mid-chest height (yours, not his) is a great goal. Watch out, though. If you have middle- to larger-sized parrots, and you allow them to get outside their cages and onto the tops — especially to a higher position than your heart — you may set the stage for a bit of a "superiority complex" attitude problem. Too high can be as bad, if not worse, as too low. For more on behavior problems, see Chapter 12.

Most cages come in one or two solid pieces — typically the cage part and the base, in the two-part variety — but you can buy some models that ship flat and require reassembly. These cages, called *knockdowns,* are held together with nuts and bolts, and a well-designed one has these fasteners in places where a busy bird is less likely to find them. Knockdowns are fine, but you have to remember to check the nuts and bolts from time to time to be sure they're still tight. Parrots are really good at undoing your best efforts to keep nuts and bolts fastened.

Although largely inadequate for the needs of our pet birds as we know them today, some antique bird cages are beautiful, ornate works of art, meant to mimic temples, mansions, and other examples of architectural splendor, created from the finest woods and jewels (see Figure 4-1). One of the better places to eyeball these interesting creations is Vogelbauer Museum, located near Dortmund, Germany, and dedicated to bird cages and other paraphernalia related to the keeping of birds. Although antique cages provide a poor living arrangement for your pet bird, houseplants look great in these delightful relics!

Figure 4-1: Ornate older cages may be beautiful, but they're usually not suited for housing birds.

The time-out cage

Some parrot-owners may benefit from the purchase of a smaller *time-out* cage for use when your bird is driving you crazy (it happens in the best of families, believe us!). The cage doesn't have to be elaborate — sturdy and just large enough to fit your bird comfortably, and portable enough to allow him to chill for a while — out of the traffic flow in the home. The time-out cage can also do double duty as your bird's travel cage and can even do triple duty as an outside "shower cage," too, when set under a fine mister outdoors.

If you've ever seen how happy birds are at a bird bath, it'll come as no surprise to you that your pet bird will enjoy getting wet from time to time. And it's good for her, too! For more on showers, see Chapter 7.

Although you never need a cage cover to keep your bird warm in a heated home, sometimes this tool is useful in handling an out-of-control bird. For more on the use of cage covers, see Chapter 12.

Cage to go

Small birds such as finches are able to travel fine in the cage they live in every day (and usually more comfortably, too), but that's not an option for bigger birds whose bigger cages aren't made to move much. For larger birds, a separate cage is well worth the investment for those traveling times.

A small travel cage is fine, but so, too, are carriers designed for cats or small dogs (see Figure 4-2), the kind made of high-impact plastic with vents on the side and a grid door on the front or top. For short trips, no perch is necessary — just put down a clean towel to give your bird solid footing. For longer trips or for your bird's increased comfort even with short trips, however, fasten a perch dowel near the base of the carrier with two screws placed through the walls and into the ends of the perch, as shown in Figure 4-2.

Figure 4-2: A dog or cat carrier works well as a travel cage for your bird.

Travel cages and carriers are important for reasons beyond the occasional trip to the veterinarian. In times of disaster, these transportable homes make it far easier to evacuate your pet and keep him safe until conditions improve.

Although you can carry a small bird in a paper bag, the benefits of owning and using a safe carrier far outweigh the modest price of acquiring one.

Perch Perfect

Gravity being what it is, even a creature made for flying spends a lot of time on his feet. And considering the need to keep wings trimmed for safety — we explain how in Chapter 7 — pet birds spend even more time on their feet than their wild relatives do. Which makes what's under those feet — *perches* — very important. Perches give our birds something to stand on, something to chew on, something to rub and groom their beaks on, a vantage point from which to survey their domain, and a secure home base to rest on.

Three things to remember when it comes to perches: safety, variety, and destructibility. Safety because . . . well, that's kind of obvious. Variety because a wide array of shapes, sizes, and material can go far in keeping your bird's feet healthy as well as helping him stay busy, fit, and free of boredom. Destructibility? Perches, in particular, are appropriate targets for demolition. The need to rip the snot out of something is of paramount importance, and besides, it's only natural!

And now for an illustration of the importance of destructibility: When Brian was in Australia a few years ago, he watched in awe as a flock of about 20 red-tailed black cockatoos (birds that retail for up to $20,000 each in the United States, if you can even find one!) landed into a small stand of pine trees — and proceeded to rip the trees apart. Limbs, bark, and pulp rained down, as nature's pruning service did their work. How does this story relate to your pet bird? By making you remember: Buy cages and dishes that are bird-proof (or as near to indestructible as possible), but make sure that everything else is chewable, shreddable, and totally and completely destroyable. It's good for your bird!

An ideal perch is not too smooth, not too hard, not too soft. Excessively smooth perches may be hard to maintain balance on — and in a wing-clipped bird, that lack of traction may result in a bad fall. Perches that are too hard are difficult to chew up and have fun with, and perches that are too soft get destroyed too fast.

Here's what's out there in the perch world:

- **Wood:** Plain pine perches come standard with nearly every cage, and there's nothing wrong with them per se, except . . . you can do better for your bird. One way is to harvest your own wood for perches (see the sidebar "Perches au naturel"), and another is to vary the sizes and shapes of the perches you buy. Some ready-made dowels are available in different diameters along the length of the perch, and these at least add some variation on the boring old theme. If you don't want to or can't find tree branches like the one shown in Figure 4-3, a good bird store probably offers a supply of these perch prospects, too.

Figure 4-3: This eclectus is enjoying his wooden perch.

Photo by Dr. Brian L. Speer

Rope: Great foot feel! Rope perches give your bird something decent to hold on to and also provide some boredom relief because they're a good plaything. The neat thing about rope perches is that you can just throw them in the washing machine or dishwasher when they get dirty. The downside to rope is the possibility of your pet catching a toe in a worn and frayed part of the perch. Also, your bird may chew and swallow strands of the rope, which can cause problems as well. You have to watch closely and discard the perch when the rope gets stringy.

Rope perches can be really expensive if you buy them ready-made for use with birds. You don't have to, though. Check out untreated cotton rope at a boating-supply outlet and make your own perches. By exercising your creativity, you can save money, have fun, and "do right" by your bird!

One kind of rope perch rates our complete endorsement: the stiff rope coil. These perches combine the best elements of rope, a swing, and a bungee cord, all of which provide exercise for your bird. Absolutely fantastic for overweight birds!

- **Mineral:** Almost every bird should have one mineral perch, also called a *concrete* or *cement perch.* The rough texture feels good underfoot, and the surface is great for helping to keep nails blunt and beaks clean and well-groomed (birds like to wipe their beaks against the rough surface). Make sure the size of perch you select is large enough to allow normal weight-bearing and provide some abrasion of the nail tips at the same time. A concrete perch that is too small will not necessarily help blunt nails, unless it meets the tips of those nails. Some birds with particularly strong wills and jaws may decide to chew up, destroy, and eat the concrete, though, and those characters should not have this particular perch.

Don't confuse a mineral or concrete perch with those covered with sandpaper. If you have a sandpaper-covered perch (some cages do come with them), toss it and replace it with a mineral one. Sandpaper coverings on perches can cause more problems than they're worth, giving some birds foot problems, on top of providing no real benefit for the health of the nails or feet of the birds. Would you want to stand on sandpaper in your bare feet? Neither does your bird.

Perches au naturel

If you're looking for a real bargain in bird equipment, search no further than the perch. No, not that plain pine dowel that came with the cage or that you can find by the scores at any pet-supply store. Some of the best perches around are free and easy to find. They grow on trees, you could say.

Tree branches make great perches. They add variety to your bird's environment, help him maintain healthy feet and legs, and give him something else to rip up for entertainment. Most fruit and nut trees (almond, apple, prune, and all citrus) are fine to use, as are ash, elm, dogwood, and magnolia. If you can get your pruners on some manzanita, go for it — it's a hard wood that can stand up to a lot of abuse. Try grapevines, too. And leave the bark on for your bird to peel off.

Cut the branches to a length to fit in your cage, scrub and clean them well with detergent, rinse, and dry in the sun. Check for insect egg pods, and if you find them, just break them off and discard before putting the branch in your pet's cage. (If you don't, you may find a zillion little buglets thinking it's spring in your home.)

You can also use scrap lumber to keep bigger parrots entertained. Brian's macaws have been shredding the remains of an old deck for months. Just be sure that you know the source of the wood and that you're not offering your pet pressure-treated lumber or wood that may be coated with preservatives or other potential toxins.

Think of perches as replaceable cage furnishings: When your bird rips them up, that's great! That means that he likes them! Replace them with more of the same when those are gone. The extra labor and cost involved in replacing those perches is another strong hint that you're doing a great job in your bird's eyes.

- **Plastics:** Two kinds here, acrylic and PVC, both popular because of their sturdiness and relative ease of cleaning. We're not real keen on either kind, although of the two, acrylic is a better choice because it's virtually indestructible. Remember, though, that having a perch to chew up is important to most parrots. If you use plastics, add other chewable perch options to your bird's environment. PVC too often and too easily ends up in pieces in a bird's stomach and can cause some medical problems, as well as slippery footing and boredom. Plastic perches are often too slippery to be comfortable (particularly for heavy-bodied and wing-clipped birds), although some manufacturers compensate for this problem by abrading the surface of the perch. You can do the same with a little sandpaper if you want to offer a plastic perch.

For tips on how to place perches in the cage, see Chapter 5.

Playstands and Gyms

Most pet parrots — from budgies on up in size — need time out of their cages to explore, exercise, and socialize (the exceptions are canaries and other finches, who are happy to be left alone in roomy cages). You can allow your parrots to explore, taste, chew, and destroy your furniture, or you can offer them an alternative — a playstand or gym.

These accessories come in two varieties, for the most part: large, freestanding models or those designed to rest on a table. The freestanding models are fit for the largest parrots.

Any size stand or gym offers a variety of perches, swings, and ladders, places to attach toys, and usually a container for food and water. They can be made of natural material such as grapevine or manzanita branches or of turned pine dowels or hard plastics. A skirt or tray incorporated into the design helps capture mess and thrown food.

When choosing a playstand or gym, look for a model that combines entertainment for your bird with easy clean-up for you. Turned pine or abraded hard plastic is fine, but more natural pieces of wood are likely easier on your bird's feet.

Some cage designs feature a play gym on top, or they're flat-topped to accommodate the addition of a separately purchased set-up. Although a gym on top of your bird's cage may be okay, many behaviorists caution against their use if a bird feels that he is dominant over family members. Height equals might and right in the bird world, and the uppity attitude of some birds can be remedied by making sure their heads are never higher than their owners' shoulders. Cage-top play gyms are a no-no for these terrorists. In a respectful pet bird relationship, however, where your position of authority is not questioned or challenged, your bird can enjoy the height of some lofty perching opportunities. (For more on avian behavior problems, see Chapter 12.)

Dishes and Waterers

Your cage probably came with bowls for food and water, and these containers are likely to be perfectly fine for your pet's dining pleasure. Look for construction of stainless steel, crockery, or high-impact plastic — and dishwasher-safe, because you're going to be running them through the hot cycle, a lot. We don't recommend galvanized crocks or bowls — they can oxidize, are harder to clean, and pose some toxic risks to your birds.

Dishes seem to inspire a lot of creativity on the part of manufacturers, who do their best to come up with designs to minimize mess, stand up to the abuse some parrots can dish out, and retain an attractive appearance and washability. Experiment with these all you like until you find the combination that works best for you and your bird.

The workhorse of the cage is always going to be the plain dish, and we encourage you to keep a few of these on hand so your bird isn't without food and water when you're cleaning the replacements. With larger parrots, make sure that these dishes are not easily up-ended, picked up, thrown, or broken. Although "bowl-tossing" may be a lot of fun from a bird's point of view, a few damaged crocks can be frustrating and costly to you.

Birds can drink water from a dish or from a water bottle the way guinea pigs and rabbits do. If you choose to use a water bottle, make sure your bird knows how to use it, and check the spout frequently with a touch of your finger to ensure that water is still flowing. Dehydration from water deprivation can deal a lethal blow to birds quite rapidly.

Some bird-keepers prefer bottles because it's harder for their pets to foul the supply of water — some birds actually poop in their water dishes, or they love to make "soup" by carefully carrying their food over and dumping it into their water bowls. Don't let the relative convenience of the water bottle give you an excuse to change it less frequently than you would a water dish. Water bottles need to be cleaned out daily and refilled with fresh water. (Keep a bottle brush handy for cleaning.)

Toys? Keep 'em Coming

Toys are not optional when it comes to pet birds. A constant variety of interesting and destructible toys is essential to your bird's mental and physical well-being. They give your pet something to do with both his mind and his body, keep him fit, and stave off boredom. A bored bird is one at high risk for behavioral and health problems, such as feather-picking.

Food as entertainment

Don't underestimate food as a way to keep your bird busy and amused. Check out food holders designed to make eating a challenge. These holders have skewers or nooks to hold foods such as fruits or nuts and are meant to make a game out of getting to these treats. One of our particular favorites is an acrylic tube you load up with nuts in their shells, with holes to insert plain wooden pegs. To get the nuts out, the bird has to figure out how to pull the plugs. Ingenious!

Look for these kinds of accessories in a good bird shop. You can also visit a bird show or check out a catalog or Web site from our list in the Additional Resources appendix at the back of this book.

Fortunately, toys are fun — to buy, to give to your bird, and to watch her enjoy. Knock yourself out, and know that your bird appreciates the effort. Try toys your pet can hold, toys that hang from the top and sides of the cage, and toys that really serve as perches, like swings. Twirlies, holdies, chewies, puzzles, bright colors, and noisemakers all can provide your bird with plenty to keep her occupied.

Do you know the saying, "He who dies with the most toys wins"? Although a large number and variety of toys is important, you can go overboard. Sort of. If your bird's entire treasury of perches, dishes, and toys is stuffed in his cage, you may be limiting his movement and reducing his quality of life. Instead of giving your bird everything, get in the habit of rotating toys through his life. Rotation every month not only keeps up your bird's interest but also helps you spot toys that need to be cleaned or replaced from wear.

Toys come in an almost unimaginable array, and many of them are lovingly handmade. Some basic rules apply, though, when shopping for toys to ensure they are suitable for your bird and, of course, safe. Look for the following things when you're in the market for toys:

- **Materials:** Like perches, toys are subject to your bird's destructive nature — and safety in the rack and ruin process is a must. Wood, rawhide, plastic or steel chain, rope, cloth, and hard plastic are among the more popular construction materials. Importantly, consider toys that can break down but not into splinters or other pieces that can be swallowed. (Clappers on bells, for example, often require removal.)
- **Construction:** Challenging toys, the best choice for busy birds, feature pieces combined in ways that make it hard for birds to pull the whole product apart — but not too hard. Indestructible toys are not appropriate for most birds, because the fun of ripping the gadget apart is missing.
- **Size:** Little toys for little birds, big toys for big birds. A big bird can catch and lose a toe in a toy made for a smaller bird, and small birds can get their heads trapped in toys made for larger relatives.
- **Connectors:** The best is probably a simple key ring, available from any hardware store (if the toy isn't already equipped with a connector). Other good ways to connect toys to cage bars are shown in Figure 4-4 and include "C" clamps and balls that rest on top of the cage with a hook hanging down for attaching a toy. You can also tie toys in place with pieces of rope or rawhide, but they won't stay put very long.

What toy is bound to light up your bird's face? Unfortunately, no clear-cut answer exists. Toys are a trial-and-error endeavor, a matter of individual preference where only your bird has a vote. Watch your bird. Look for trends in the kind of toys she prefers; those clues can guide you when you're shopping for new ones.

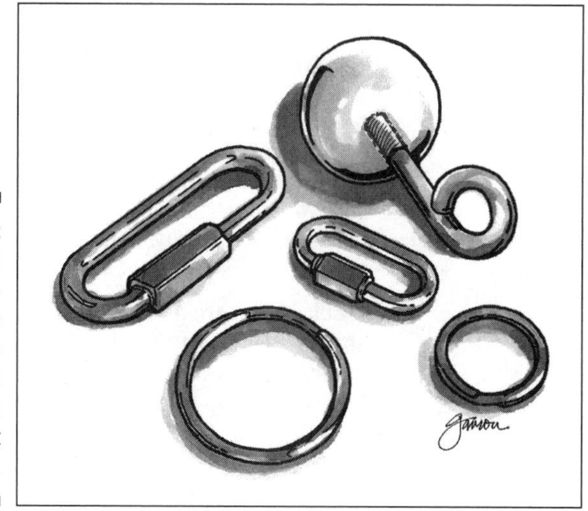

Figure 4-4: Safe and sturdy fasteners help keep cage toys from endangering your pet bird.

Some birds are apprehensive of new toys. If yours is one of them, try to set the toy outside the cage (but within eye range) for a day or two and then put it on the floor of the cage for another day or two. If your bird starts to play with the toy, you can hang it up.

Clearing the Air

Depending on where you live and what kind and how many birds you keep, you may want to add an air-cleaner or humidifier (or both!) to your must-buy list. Paying attention to air quality is good for your bird and good for you, too.

First, the pitch on humidifiers: Our climate-controlled houses are often too dry for our birds, many of whom represent species most at home in tropical rain forests. Daily misting is a great idea — and we talk about it more in Chapter 7 — but so, too, is keeping the moisture content of the air up with a humidifier. If you live in Hawaii or South Florida or another tropical environment, lack of humidity isn't a concern. In other parts of the country, however, dry air is a problem. Remember, too, that when it gets cold outside and the heater is turned on inside the home, the relative humidity of your home drops.

As for air cleaners, the decision whether you need one depends on a couple of factors. Some species of pet birds — the cockatoo is perhaps the best example — give off a lot of *feather dust,* a powdery natural grooming material that originates from the powderdown feathers over the flank and hip areas. (The dust factor is why we don't recommend cockatoos for people with allergies — other particularly dusty species are the cockatiel and the African grey parrot.)

Cheap! Cheap! And fun, too

Toys can really break your budget, especially if you have a very destructive parrot. No matter how much you love your bird, you're bound to mutter under your breath the first time you watch him gleefully and quickly destroy a toy you spent $20 on just a few hours before. Keep in mind, though, that aggression guided toward toys and perches is better than destructiveness directed toward your bird's mental stability, his feathers, or you. Tearing toys up is properly channeled normal behavior for most parrots, and a very good thing. Just keep reminding yourself of that — again, and again, and again.

Fortunately, some alternatives to expensive store-bought toys do exist, but you need to rely on creativity to find them.

The cardboard cores of toilet-paper and paper-towel rolls are perfect for shredding, especially for smaller birds. String those tubes together on a thick leather cord and hang them in your bird's cage for his discovery and play. Other cheapies include ball-point pens with the ink tube removed, ping-pong balls, old plastic measuring cups and spoons, and plastic bottle tops.

Toothbrushes are another bargain toy, sturdy and colorful. You can buy them new or give your pet your worn ones — just be sure to run them through a hot, soapy wash and rinse first. Hard plastic keys on a ring for human youngsters are also a budget-wise buy that birds love, and real keys can be just as fun. Stringing this type of "jewels" onto leather shoelaces and hanging them in the cages provides a *very* low cost, *very* big entertainment thrill for your parrot. Keep your eyes and mind open for playthings — you may surprise yourself with the possibilities

One dusty bird can really reduce the air quality of a room. Several can make it downright unbreathable. (Remember: Feather dust is not a problem when a bird's in his natural environment outside.) It's a matter of personal preference, of course, but if you're living with one or more dusty birds, we recommend an air filter. You and your birds will breathe better for your decision, and you can look forward to a reduction in your home's dusting requirements.

Clean-Ups Made Easy

Birds are messy, we admit. They destroy toys, they fling food, and they spread old feathers and dust wherever they go. Keeping things clean isn't all that hard, though, with a plan and the right tools.

Basic cleaning supplies

For your own sanity and for your bird's health, you need to lay in a stock of basic cleaning supplies. Here's your shopping list:

- **Brushes:** Assemble an array of brushes with plastics bristles to clean fecal matter off perches, toys, dishes, and cage bars. If you use a bottle to water your bird, you also need a bottle brush. Make sure you can run the brushes you buy through the dishwasher.
- **Cleaners and disinfectants:** Plain old soap and water goes a long way here and won't cost you very much. For disinfecting, use one-half cup of ordinary bleach to one gallon of water. Do your cleaning away from your bird, of course, and make sure to rinse and air-dry anything you clean before reintroducing your pet.

  Although scented cleaners may smell good to you, avoid any strongly perfumed products such as those with pine oils. They can damage your bird's delicate respiratory membranes.
- **Dishwasher:** If you don't have one of these kitchen helpers, bringing a bird into your life and home is a great excuse to invest in a dishwasher. Sure, you can hand-wash in hot, soapy water, but running dishes, perches, and toys through the hottest dishwasher cycle gets them cleaner easier. For rope toys, your washing machine is a lifesaver, too.
- **Handheld vacuum:** Great for snarfing up pellets, dust, feathers, shells, seeds . . . and everything else. You gotta have one.

Preventing messes

Whatever lands on something you can throw away or wash out is one more battle with mess you can win easily. Newspapers and towels are your main weapons in this war.

Newspaper can line the cage (see the nearby sidebar "All the news that fits . . . the cage") or cover the floor. (Plastic mats are good floorcoverings around the cage, too). Some people prefer to use small-animal bedding under the bottom cage grate, and that's fine, too. Skip wood shavings and chips, though, and go for bedding made of shredded paper or cardboard. (Care Fresh is one brand we know and recommend.) Wood shavings and chips are dustier and can irritate your bird's airways, especially in the case of aromatic woods such as pine and cedar.

Some bedding comes ready-packaged with fungal spores. When dampened and maintained in a warm and humid environment — poof! You've got fungus among us, which can be a risk to your bird's health. Frequent changing and cleaning keeps the problem at bay.

Towels provide good footing and mess prevention for any areas your bird may explore — and clean-up is as easy as throwing the towels in the wash. Watch for fraying and worn spots that can catch toes, feet, or heads. Towels are also great for covering your clothing when your bird is in a snuggly mood.

All the news that fits . . . the cage

How common are newspapers as poop-catchers? So much so that many cages are designed to fit the standardized size of an American or Canadian newspaper. (The standardization came about because of advertisers, not bird-lovers, of course!)

Newspapers are great cage liners. You're likely to hear some fuss and bother about black ink posing some risks, but we've never seen a problem, and we know of no study to validate that a threat actually exists. Newspaper inks are mostly soy-based, and although they may rub off on your bird (and your hands while you read the paper), they don't present any health issues that we can cite. We recommend plain old black-and-white pages — no color ink, no glossy paper. Colors and gloss add chemicals your bird doesn't need to be dealing with.

With our tongues firmly in cheek, we offer our *Birds For Dummies* exclusive guide to newspapers, factoring in both readability and more bird-related points.

The winner, by far, is *The Wall Street Journal.* Well written, well edited and . . . well, just fantastic. More Pulitzers than you can shake a stick at, lots of pages every day, and almost no color ink. Plus, if you're the gambling type, you can put the stock pages in the cage and play a little Birdy Bingo. You don't have to tell your stockbroker you're choosing companies because your bird poops on them. The only negative: no weekend papers.

We also like the *Los Angeles Times.* A good read and good heft, especially on Sundays. *The New York Times* is a little lean most days, but Sunday more than makes up for it. *The New York Times* gains points for its lack of color, too, at least Monday through Saturday. Can't go wrong with either paper, really, nor with any of the other big-city newspapers with enough advertising to bump up the page count.

Our vote for worst cage-liner: *USA Today.* Too few pages, too much color, and no weekend edition to chew on, poop on, or otherwise wreak havoc with!

Did you know that many parrots can be "potty trained"? A little effort in training, when successful, can help reduce the mess factor, too. We show you how in Chapter 7.

Save your old towels for bird use, and ask friends and relatives to do the same. You can also look for inexpensive cotton terry shop towels in the auto section of any discount store. These hold up well to mess and washings.

Towels are also an important tool to help you restrain your bird for grooming or when he's sick. To learn how to "towel" your bird, see Chapter 7.

The Best of the Rest Accessory-Wise

You always find a couple of things that just don't fit in any category, and this chapter's no exception. People are always coming up with new ideas and inventions to make bird-keeping better and more fun.

One recent invention: Harness and leash getups for larger parrots. With a harness, you can take your parrot along when you're running errands or visiting, without worrying about him getting away. (Even a wing-clipped bird can achieve enough loft to escape — it's just harder.)

We're also really keen on identification, either with a leg band, a microchip, or preferably both. Leg bands (see the sidebar "What's on that leg?") have been used for years to identify birds, but the microchip is a fairly recent addition to tools for identifying pets (dogs and cats get them, too). The chip is about the size of a grain of rice and contains a unique number to help match up a missing pet with her owner. In pet birds, the chip is inserted with a needle into the breast muscle. Once in place, the number on the chip can be read with a handheld scanner.

What's on that leg?

Banding (or ringing) is the traditional way of identifying pet birds — and is still the most common method. Bands can be either open or closed, with a choice of steel or less expensive aluminum. Identifying information is engraved into the metal.

Open bands are put on adult birds with a special tool that crimps the metal around the legs. *Closed bands* are slipped over the feet of baby birds, who then grow into their IDs. Captive-bred birds may have either kind of band; United States rules require open steel bands, complete with a letter and number code for identification, to be put on any imported birds. Make a note of this number — the code is a practical means of identification for your bird.

Either kind of band, open or closed, provides a good means of identification, but open bands require periodic checking to make sure they fit properly, without any gap where the ends meet. A gap poses the potential for the bird to catch a leg, which can result in injury. Closed bands usually aren't the source of problems — if the right size is used to begin with. When in doubt about the safety of any band, ask your veterinarian. Some veterinarians feel that *all* leg bands are inappropriate; others believe they're necessary for the bird's well-being and the owner's peace of mind. We feel that identification, properly and safely applied, is important, and legitimate protection can include microchips, leg bands, or both. Although no form of identification is foolproof, we believe that any means of ID is better than none.

The American Kennel Club — yes, the dog people — run a microchip registration service for all pets. To sign up your pet, call AKC Companion Animal Recovery at 800-252-7894. The service matches up pets with owners 24 hours a day, 365 days a year, and costs $9 to sign up.

While it doesn't really fit in with the "new ideas" theme of this section, we want to mention an "old idea" that's still a great one! You ought to have a basic first-aid kit on hand. For contents and use guidelines, see Chapter 10.

Chapter 5

Starting Your Bird Off Right

In This Chapter

- Pairing pet with cage
- Meeting the family
- Building your bird's trust
- Training for a lifetime
- Setting up a care regimen

The day you bring your bird home is the day the world changes for you both. For you, this is the grand moment when all the research, all the reading, all the theories, all the admiring of birds from afar suddenly becomes quite real. Did you choose the right bird? Was the source you selected a reputable one? Will you really enjoy living with a bird? Are you up to the challenges? The answers to all these questions become clearly evident as you begin to settle in with your new pet.

For your new bird, this momentous day of change can be downright scary. If he has been hand-fed and socialized by a reputable breeder, the breeder's home may have been the only world he has ever known, and trusting as the bird may try to be, his natural instincts suggest caution. Even if your hand-fed baby bird has spent time in a bird shop after weaning and he is accustomed to a constant parade of strangers, your home is something new, and so are you.

Or perhaps you purchased a little budgie or cockatiel whose interactions with humans have been restricted to being netted out of a group of his buddies and shipped to a pet store to wait to be netted again when purchased. Although hand-fed and well-socialized birds have an easier time adjusting to the life of a pet, many people buy mass-produced small bird species such as budgies or cockatiels anyway, because they don't know better or because they're cheaper. Can you help these birds become confident pets?

Maybe you've taken on a real challenge, a bird who has been sold and sold again, passed from owner to owner and perhaps mistreated along the way. This character views the world with cynicism and fear, and he figures you're bound to be another disappointment. Can you really change his outlook?

The trick in all cases is patience, consistency, and knowledge. We help you with the latter, but the first two are up to you. Read on!

Starting the Relationship Right

Getting your bird settled in comfortably and setting up your relationship is a two-part process, with each connected to the other. You have to ensure that your bird's physical environment is satisfactory, and then start working on his attitude toward you. A suitable physical environment helps you work on the gentle training that can turn your bird into a loving pet.

The training exercises in this chapter are for the parrots — budgies and cockatiels as well as those birds more commonly identified as parrots, such as Amazons, cockatoos, and macaws. (They're all parrots, no matter the size!) Finches and canaries don't crave the intense socialization that parrots do, and these look-don't-keep-touching characters are quite content if your only interaction with them is cleaning the cage and maintaining a fresh supply of food and water. If you have a hands-off bird, read the part of this chapter on bringing your pet home safely and setting him up properly. You can skip the rest.

Setting Up the Cage

The cage is your bird's castle, the place where he will spend much of his time — maybe even all, as in the case of birds such as finches. A cage protects your bird, and this home base also shields your stuff from your bird, who is perfectly capable (if he's a parrot) of reducing prize antiques to toothpicks with his powerful beak.

You want your bird to be safe and to feel secure in his cage, and he should also feel included as part of the family, even when he's confined. Assuming you have a proper cage — see Chapter 4 for more on selection — proper placement can achieve all these goals.

Choose a location where your bird can be adjacent to family activities, but not in the center of them. Your bird will feel most comfortable if his cage is against a wall, so he can watch the goings-on without having to worry about anyone sneaking up on his backside. For the same reason, place the cage where your bird won't be surprised — for example, away from large furniture that may block his view of the room and the coming and going of family and friends. Birds don't like to be startled any more than we do!

Position the cage far enough away from a window that direct sun rays don't fall on your bird — and possibly overheat him, since he can't escape them. Putting the cage *near* a window so your bird can see out isn't a bad idea, though, especially if the window overlooks a changing panorama that can help keep your pet entertained.

Although the kitchen may seem like an ideal place for your bird's cage, think again. The potential for your bird to breathe deadly fumes, such as those from burning nonstick cookware — is too high to take a chance. (For more on common household hazards, see Chapter 19.)

A good place to situate your bird's home is the family room or any other place (aside from the kitchen) where the people in your home hang out. (Gina has her parrot set up in her home office, so she's with him all day long. At night, he moves into another room with her as she reads or watches TV.)

After you choose the location, set up the cage. Don't get too enthusiastic about toys — two or three well-chosen ones are good, but more may be overwhelming. Use a variety of natural and store-bought perches, and be sure to position them so they aren't directly over food and water dishes. You don't want to encourage your bird to poop into his dishes.

For more on toys and perches — including using tree branches — see Chapter 4.

Line the cage bottom with newspaper or any other safe product, and you're ready to introduce your bird to his new home.

The shock of new sights

Predators always consider the possibility that something new in their environment may be edible. Prey animals have to figure the addition's something that could eat them. Is it any wonder then that our pet birds, who are considered a tasty mouthful by many creatures in the wild, may not react with enthusiasm to changes in the world around them? Is it any surprise that your pet bird may initially fear new toys, new cages, or new foods?

Even though your bird may be slow to warm up to new things, don't hesitate to introduce him to fresh experiences and variety — just proceed with patience and understanding of *his* perspective, too.

You can help your bird conquer his anxiety by putting the new item close, but not too close. A new cage? Put it next to the old one for a few days so your bird can observe it. Toys, too, are sometimes better accepted if they remain in view on the other side of the cage bars for a while.

When your bird knows and trusts you, you can make use of mimicry to help your bird adapt. Eating meals together may inspire your bird to try different, healthier foods, and chances are good that if you play with a toy, your bird will, too.

Traveling Home Safely and Sanely

Bigger parrots require a couple of accommodations, one for traveling and one to call home. That's not the case with little birds such as finches or budgies; one properly sized cage is plenty. The temptation to buy a bird, buy a cage, stuff the former into the latter, and race for home may be inviting, but let it pass. Large or small, your bird will be more comfortable in a small box or carrier, with a towel draped over it to darken the space and relax your bird. (Make sure to leave a couple of air holes, though.)

Put a towel in the bottom of the box or carrier to provide the bird with secure footing and stop him from sliding around, even if a perch is available.

Place the carrier where it won't move around or fall. You can put it on the passenger-side floorboard or put the seat belt through the handle to secure it in the seat.

Don't put the carrier in the trunk — exhaust fumes can kill your new pet. And don't put your small bird in a small carrying box on the dashboard while you are driving home — it would be a bad experience for both you and the bird.

Settling In

When you get home, put your bird in the cage and *let him be*. He needs time to adjust to his surroundings and sort through a great deal of new information. We don't care how cute he is (very, we know!), how proud you are of him and how you want to show him off (hard to resist, isn't it?), or how much the kids want to have him perch on their fingers (how many times have they asked now, 100?) — *let your bird be.*

Three days. That's all we ask. You'll have the rest of your lives together, so laying off for a mere 72 hours really isn't asking a lot.

We're not saying you can't talk to your bird; in fact, we want you to communicate with your new family member — gently, and with the utmost respect for how frightened he may be. Sing to him. Read the newspaper to him. Make eye contact and tell him he's beautiful and you love him.

As for physical contact, however, hands off for now. You have to change the cage liner, clean and refill food and water receptacles, and add and remove fresh foods, but do so slowly, calmly, and deliberately. Don't be insulted if he chooses to move as far away from you as possible; your day will come.

Managing Introductions

Living in a multi-species household can be a challenge, even if your house has only two species — yours and your bird's. Add dogs and cats to the mix, and the potential for both delight and danger increases. Pay attention to the danger part, and enjoy all the delights you're bound to encounter!

Kids

If you intend for your bird purchase to be a young child's treasured pet, we hope you invested in one of the hands-off varieties, such as finches and canaries. Young children can indeed enjoy the antics and colors of birds, but they may not be capable of handling birds safely (for both child and bird).

From the age of 10 or so (with emphasis on the "or so," because all children are individuals, maturing at their own rates), any bird who fits in your family's lifestyle is an acceptable candidate, although we tend to prefer the smaller ones for kids — budgies, cockatiels, and lovebirds. They're less intimidating, although some kids aren't fazed by even the largest, most raucous macaw!

You can find tips on choosing the perfect feathered friend for your family in Chapter 2.

No matter the age of your child (or children), you need to be sure they respect the three-day settling-in requirement: Leave the new family member unhandled. Do encourage the kids to interact vocally with the bird, though.

When you start handling the bird (more on that later in this chapter), the children can, too, under your supervision and guidance. Some youngsters have a natural affinity with animals, and they do a wonderful job with them. If yours is one of these kids, you can soon let him or her take over if you want, just as long as you're always careful to ensure an adult is checking that the pet's needs — fresh food and water, and frequent cage clean-ups — are always covered.

Cats

Cats catch birds. Cats eat birds. While many pet cats and birds live together in peace, you should never let such scenes of domestic tranquility lull you into ignoring these basic facts of life. Although macaws and other large parrots are usually plenty capable of teaching kitty to steer clear, small pet birds are often killed by household cats. This sad happening occurred in Brian's own family, in fact, when a new finch became a dead finch at the claws of the family cat in no time flat.

Because the teeth and claws of a cat can carry bacteria that's potentially deadly to birds, never give your cat a chance to try out his weapons on your bird. Get a spray bottle, adjust to the narrow stream, and "shoot" your cat when he ventures near your bird's cage. He'll soon decide to keep himself elsewhere.

If your cat (or dog) tangles with your bird, see a veterinarian immediately, even if the bird seems fine at first. Your bird may have internal injuries or be at risk for a deadly infection. Your veterinarian will likely want to start the bird on appropriate antibiotics, just to be on the safe side.

For help with understanding why your cat does what he does, check out *Cats For Dummies,* by Gina Spadafori and Dr. Paul D. Pion (IDG Books Worldwide, Inc.). You'll also find great information on cat care and training.

Dogs

In Gina's house, her three dogs all react to her Senegal parrot in different ways. Her younger retriever, Heather, discovered soon after Patrick arrived that parrots are like toddlers — where they go, food falls. Heather is always available to snap up whatever Patrick drops, and sometimes, Patrick even tosses her tidbits directly — lima beans always get the flip into the dog's mouth!

Retriever Benjamin pays no attention at all to the bird, while the oldest dog, Andy, a Sheltie, put Patrick in the veterinary hospital with a severe bite wound the first week the bird was in Gina's home. It happened in one nightmarish moment: Patrick fell onto Andy, and Andy reacted as a startled old dog sometimes will — with a bite.

No dog can be fully trusted with a bird, as Gina knows. Her gentle retriever Benjamin gives Patrick rides, but even that is with Gina's hand on his collar. Again, it's a matter of hardwiring — dogs instinctively chase and bite potential prey, whether it's a rabbit in the field, a tennis ball in the park, or a parrot on the loose. Don't take chances. Your bird should never be out of the cage around dogs unless you are there to supervise — and sometimes not even then.

Your dogs need to know that the cage is off-limits, and so, too, is the bird. Teach your dog the "Leave it" command, just in case.

1. **With your dog sitting in front of you, make your hand into a fist and position it under your dog's lower jaw.**
2. **Offer a biscuit with the other hand, saying "Leave it" as you do.**
3. **When your dog reaches for the biscuit, bop her under the chin, enough to close her jaw but not enough to hurt her.**
4. **Offer the biscuit again, repeating the "Leave it" command — and the bop correction, if necessary. If she hesitates or turns away before the bop, praise her!**

This command, incidentally, has a million uses, including control of your dog's inclination to snarf up garbage on walks.

Don't offer your bird to your dog to test the "Leave it" command. Instead, watch your dog's eyes. Say "Leave it" when he's contemplating the bird and provide praise when he averts his eyes.

The bop delivered to teach your dog this point has no place in teaching parrots a desired behavior. In the world and minds of pet birds, bopping just is not cool. (For more on training your bird, see Chapter 12.)

Both cats and dogs can be easily trained to avoid the bird's cage — or the room where the bird's cage is, if necessary, through the use of a Scat Mat, a piece of plastic that plugs into a wall outlet and emits a static shock when your dog or cat steps on it. You can put it in front of the cage or across the entryway of the bird room. Scat Mats don't hurt your pet — the correction is akin to a carpet shock, not pleasant certainly, but not harmful either. Just enough to get the message across. Your local pet supply store may stock Scat Mats; if not, check out our list of pet supply catalogs in the Additional Resources appendix at the back of this book.

Although you shouldn't trust any dog with birds, some breeds need to be watched even more carefully. Terriers, for example, were developed to kill rodents, and they can be very fast and efficient at dispatching small pets, including birds. Not surprisingly, bird dogs may also show intense interest in the family parrot — although neither of Gina's retrievers do. For more on dog selection, care, and training, check out *Dogs For Dummies,* by Gina Spadafori (IDG Books Worldwide).

A final warning: Never leave a dog or cat alone with your bird, or you may come home to a knocked-over cage and a terrified bird being drooled on by a very attentive cat or dog. Use baby gates (for most dogs, but not cats, who can leap them easily), or just close the door, but don't let your cat or dog have access to the cage while you're out.

Other birds

For the safety of the pet birds you have already, skip any introductions until your new bird has been examined by a veterinarian who's experienced in avian medicine. Even a seemingly healthy bird needs to be quarantined for about six weeks before meeting any other feathered family members. As heartbreaking as it would be to lose your new pet to an infectious disease you didn't know he was carrying, imagine how you would feel if you lost any or all of the birds you already have because you introduced them to a sick bird. You just can't be too careful!

After the quarantine period is up, you can move your new bird's cage near the others and let everyone get used to each other. Eventually, you can invite them out together (see Figure 5-1), as long as you watch to make sure everyone's getting along. Many birds do become friends — and more, but you have to check out Chapter 13, our breeding chapter, for that information!

Figure 5-1: As long as each bird's health and territory needs are respected, they can live together in harmony.

Building Trust through Training

After a few days of quiet adjustment, your bird is ready to become a part of your life. You first interactions with your new bird are extremely important, because they set the tone for the kind of relationship you'll have for life. You need to assure your new bird that you are a wonderful, kind, and fun person, but you also need to gently but firmly establish that you are also *the boss.*

You become *the boss* through consistent, firm handling and gentle training. Never, ever hit your bird.

The name game

Naming a bird is great fun, a chance to really let your imagination go.

Look in atlases for interesting names of places and literary references for great character names or the names of authors. Or think of names that are related to your profession or great loves — Gina knows a graphic artist who chose the name Pixel for his Amazon, after the name for the smallest dot on a computer screen. Although plenty of name-your-pet books are out there — and they're all fun reading — we find that a name-your-baby book is just as useful. In Brian's practice, he doesn't see a whole lot of "Polly" parrots, but he has more than a few cockatoo patients named "Peaches."

Make naming your bird a family project, and use this opportunity to interest your children in a trip to the library. You don't have that many opportunities in your life to name a family member, so make the most of it!

Rules for you

Sure, we could have called this section "Rules for your bird," but in fact, most of the learning is really yours. You need to know how to become the leader, transmitting firm, gentle authority in all your dealings with your bird. Some guidelines follow:

- **Know when to leave your bird alone.** Birds are emotional and can be quite moody, and sometimes it's best just to let them be. As you come to know your bird better, you'll be able to identify clearly the times when he wants to be with you and when he wants to be left alone. (You can also check out Chapter 7 for a primer on bird body language.)
- **Control your bird's comings and goings.** Instead of opening the cage door to let your pet out, reach in and give the step-up command (see the next section) and bring your bird out. Likewise, give the step-up command when it's time to put your bird back in his cage. This routine may seem like no big deal to you, but you're sending a message of leadership to your bird.
- **Keep training sessions short and upbeat.** Parrots are highly intelligent, but they don't have the longest attention spans. They get bored easily. Several short interactive sessions a day — just a couple minutes at a time — are better than one or two long ones.
- **Don't let your bird ignore a command.** If you say "Step up," persist until your bird complies, or you set yourself up for trouble down the road. Birds are very smart, and if they figure a way around you, they'll take it. When your leadership starts to erode, you'll have a hard time reclaiming your position.

- **Position your bird at a level lower than your head.** In the bird world, higher birds are leader birds. In the beginning, keep your bird's cage and play gyms below the level of your chin. When playing with your bird, keep your arm low, too, and don't let your bird perch on your shoulder. Later in your relationship, you may allow your bird higher perches if he's not too much of a social climber. Some birds, though, always need to be kept "down" to prevent misbehavior and aggression.
- **Talk to your bird.** Make eye contact and say anything or everything that's on your mind. Birds learn by repetition and by mimicry, so start "naming" things for your bird. For example, when you want to pet your bird, ask him if it's okay, saying something like, "Want a pet?" or "Want a tickle?" or even "Tickle, tickle?" When your bird makes the connection, he'll drop his head to ask for petting — or he may even use the phrase you've chosen!

Above all, don't ruin any good habits your breeder instilled in your bird by letting your pet become a demanding brat. Set limits and stick to them.

Teaching the step-up command

"Step up," or just plain "Up," is the most important command you teach your new bird. When you ask your bird to perform this motion, he should step up onto whatever you're offering, be it your finger (for smaller birds), your fist or arm (for larger birds), or a wood dowel or perch. The step-up command establishes you as the leader and is the basis for all other training.

If your new pet was hand-fed and well-socialized, he may already know the step-up command, but even if he doesn't, expect him to pick it up quickly. Teach it to him by following these steps:

1. **Place your hand (if he's friendly) or a T-perch or a dowel (if he's not) gently against his breast, just above the legs, and say "Step up" in a firm but friendly tone.**

   A T-perch is a perch shaped like the letter T. Some trainers don't like using a T-perch or dowel, and recommend putting a towel over your hand instead.

   The pressure triggers an instinctive reaction, and the bird usually steps right onto the perch or hand, as shown in Figure 5-2.

2. **Follow with lots of praise and even a seed treat or two.**

Make "Step up" a normal part of everyday life with your bird; you can use the command many times a day. The request and response are not only convenient in all kinds of situations, but they also constantly reinforce your gentle leadership.

Figure 5-2: Birds learn the step-up command easily when you press your finger against their belly.

Taming the wild ones

If you follow the advice we offer in Chapter 3, you've probably got a hand-fed, socialized parrot, no matter the size. We realize, though, that for largely economic reasons, most budgies and some cockatiels are not really tame when you buy them — their typical sale prices, tailored to meet the expectations of the general public, just don't support the time and effort that goes into raising a well-socialized baby.

Most of these small birds tame readily — like their larger cousins, they're flock animals, and they want to be part of a family. Be patient and gentle, and they'll come around. (But they will likely never be as friendly as a well-socialized baby.)

Make sure your new pet's wings have been trimmed before starting to tame her, because you'll have a hard time capturing her if she escapes in the house. (And in the capture, you may frighten her so much that taming will become an even greater challenge!)

Start by capturing your little bird gently in both hands. She may squawk and nibble, but if you're gentle and calm, she will settle down quickly. Talk to her, and let her head out so you can make eye contact with her. Hold her with one hand while caressing her with your finger; over time, your bird will grow accustomed to the touch and the attention. Go slowly, in short sessions, and don't push too hard in any one session.

To acquaint her with perching on your finger, hold her body with one hand and press the extended index finger of your other hand against the soles of her feet, which usually instinctively grip. Allow her time to develop comfort with the sensation of holding your finger.

Let your bird set the pace. Use lots of short sessions and always remain calm and quiet during them — send the kids and other pets elsewhere so you can concentrate on your bird. A small carpeted area is great for these sessions — your bird has few distractions and will land on something soft if she falls. (To ensure that any falls are short, work with your bird while sitting on the floor.) When your pet is comfortable on your finger, teach her the step-up instruction and continue to acclimate her to more gentle handling. She'll soon come to look forward to your time together.

If you've taken on a really challenging bird, such as a parrot who has been shuttled from home to home and would rather bite first and ask questions later, you need more than getting-to-know-you exercises. See Chapter 12 for dealing with long-term behavior problems.

Keeping Things Clean: A Basic Regimen

You can live like a slob; we won't stop you. In fact, neither one of us is exactly in a position to throw the first stone. Our offices alone are monuments to clutter, and Gina has the amazing ability to ignore drifts of dog hair when her pack is shedding out in the spring.

Tolerance for mess, to a degree, is a good thing when you share your life with a bird. If you're dreadfully uptight about things being out of place, about dust, about food crumbs, and, especially, about bird poop, you're going to have a hard time getting along with your pet.

Dogs are messy. Children are messy. Even cats have been known to leave the odd hair — or hairball — about. But birds . . . oh my, are they slobs! Food, feathers, poop — you name it, they fling it, far and wide. Little birds are quite capable of making a big mess, and big birds are even better at it. Cleaning up after birds is a constant duty, but it isn't such a chore after you get the hang of it.

As we say, tolerance is a good thing, to a point. And the point where you need to become concerned is where your bird's health can be affected. Cleaning isn't just about neatness — it's about health. Clean, fresh food and water are essential to your bird, and so, too, is keeping his environment as free as possible of the growth and proliferation of bacteria, fungus, and molds — all of which can lead to disease.

Don't take cleaning for granted. Your bird can become sick and even die if you ignore her surroundings. A messy cage is an invitation to fungal and bacterial growth, as well as food poisoning.

You need basic cleaning tools, of course. Brushes, newspapers, towels, a handheld vacuum, and bleach for disinfecting — these supplies are basic. We talk more about them in Chapter 4.

Setting up for cleaning

Getting all your ducks in a row, so to speak, is essential to making cleaning up after your bird easier. If you have to dig under the kitchen sink or through three closets just to find your cleaning supplies, you'll be inclined to let a small mess sit. Put together a kit of bird-friendly supplies just for your pet, and keep it handy so that even small messes are no fuss to clean up.

Some cages come with shelving or cupboards underneath, and these spaces are ideal for storing cleaning basics.

Keep these goods near your bird:

- **Newspapers:** Gina has long been in the habit of separating the newspaper as she reads it, sending color pages and inserts to the recycling bin, and black-and-white papers to the bird area. Having a pet bird means going through a lot of newspaper, so if you don't subscribe for your own sake, do so for your bird's!

  In terms of a bird, a good newspaper is one with lots of pages and little color — and great stories for human readers! Take a look at our very tongue-in-cheek evaluation of major newspaper in Chapter 4.

- **Cloth towels:** Make a collection of "bird towels" — faded or worn towels you're cycling out of your own linen closet. The auto section of discount stores is a good source for inexpensive, plain terrycloth towels; thrift stores and garage sales are another. Cloth towels are great for laying over clothing and for providing solid footing on bird-safe exploration areas.

  Gina has a play area set up for her parrot on the huge lateral file cabinet next to his cage. He has a play gym (more on those in Chapter 4) and toys there, and a clean towel covers the cabinet to keep him from sliding on the slippery surface. Patrick spends his day exploring his open cage and his play area while Gina works.

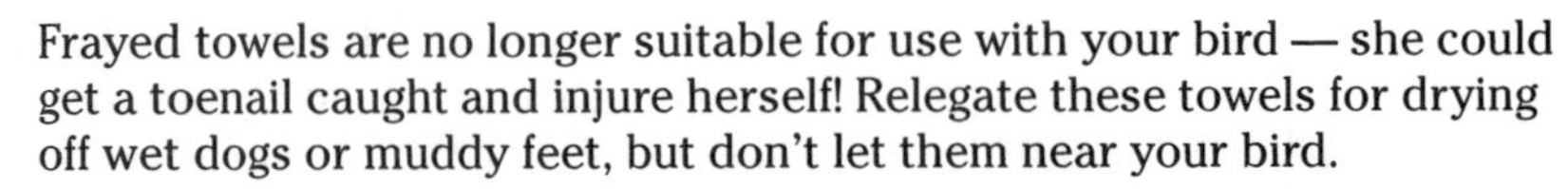

Frayed towels are no longer suitable for use with your bird — she could get a toenail caught and injure herself! Relegate these towels for drying off wet dogs or muddy feet, but don't let them near your bird.

- **Paper towels:** Keep a roll handy at all times, and consider installing a hanger or using one of those vertical towel-holders. Buying in bulk is a good idea with paper towels, because you'll go through them, trust us!
- **Spray bottle with cleaning solution:** Because birds are sensitive to so many fumes, skip the ammonia, pine cleaners, or any other strong cleaners. Simple soap and water will do for everyday touch-ups.

Mark the soap-and-water spray bottle clearly so you don't confuse it with the plain-water sprayer you use to mist your bird.

- **Handheld vacuum:** Buy one just for your bird's room, and mount it close to the cage so you can always find it.

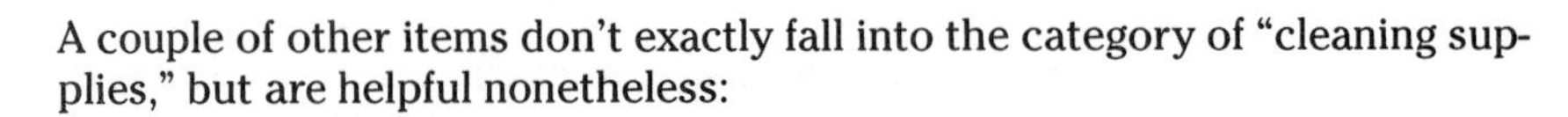

A couple of other items don't exactly fall into the category of "cleaning supplies," but are helpful nonetheless:

- **Mat for under the cage:** The heavy, clear plastic mats intended for use under desk chairs and sold at office-supply stores keep the gunk off your floor. Especially important if your flooring is carpet.
- **Hamper:** We like to keep the bird towels separate from the others in the household, and a great way to do this is by using a hamper to hold them in one place until you have a load for the washer. Put the hamper near the cage for maximum convenience. (Between bird towels and dog beds, Gina swears more she does more loads of pet laundry than people laundry!)
- **Trash bin:** Again, place it right by the cage. Every time you change papers, you won't have to carry them around — just lean over and put them in the trash!
- **Old T-shirts:** Parrots love to nip little holes in cloth, even if the cloth is part of the shirt on your back. Plus, even if you're careful to keep a towel over your clothes when playing with your bird, we have to tell you that poop happens, and you're going to get it on your clothes eventually. Wearing clothes you don't mind getting dirty is a good idea.

Finally, you also need brushes for scrubbing and bleach for disinfecting — more on both in our section, "The big clean," later in this chapter.

Everyday cleanups

Good hygiene is a matter of habit, if you think about it. You're probably in the habit of washing your hands after playing with your pets or before preparing food. Every morning, you get up and brush your teeth, and you do it again before turning in for the night. Do you write these little chores on your calendar so you won't forget them? Of course not: They're part of your routine.

Caring for your bird needs to become part of your daily routine, too. Morning and night, you need to perform some basic cleaning regimen — and keep an eye out for other cleanups throughout the day.

In the morning and evening you should:

- **Remove and replace soiled cage liners.** You may find it easier to do this chore after you've been awake for a while, so your bird has a chance to get her big morning poop out of the way. Putting newspapers both above and below the grid at the bottom of the cage makes cleaning as you go easier. Put a few layers at the bottom of the cage and remove them layer by layer throughout the day, whenever droppings appear.

  Some people insist on keeping cage liners below the bottom grid, in the dropping drawer at the base of the cage, so that their birds don't come in contact with newspaper. Such contact is fine for your bird, but if you want to avoid it — because the ink rubs off, for example — lightly coat the bottom grid with some nonstick cooking spray to keep droppings from pasting onto the bars. (Don't spray with your bird in the cage, though!)

  You can teach your bird to "go" on command, making cleanups even easier! We tell you how in Chapter 7.

- **Clean and replace food bowls and water bowls or bottles.** Some birds get food in their water or even droppings in one bowl or another, and you need to constantly check for bowls that need cleaning. If your bird drinks from a water bottle, check every morning to ensure that it's not clogged by pressing the ball with your finger. (Birds can become seriously dehydrated very quickly.)

- **Feed your bird.** Birds usually prefer to eat after dawn and near dusk, so these are great times to introduce fresh fruits and vegetables — just be sure to remove the leftovers before you go to work or bed. Discard leftover pelleted foods every morning and replace with fresh. Birds don't like stale or old food any better than you do!

  For more on avian nutrition, see Chapter 6

- **Do a quick cleanup:** Finish off your routine by using your cleaning solution, paper towels, and the handheld vacuum to clean up any other messes in the vicinity.

This routine may seem like a lot of work, but it takes only a few minutes each morning and night.

On an as-needed basis, pull out soiled perches and toys. Wood and plastic perches and toys can go right into the dishwasher, as can stiffened rope perches or coils. Throw flexible rope perches in the washing machine along with a load of bird towels.

The big clean

You need to scrub the whole set-up — walls, floors, cage, and all its contents — on a fairly regular basis. How often? Depends on your bird. Big birds are generally messier, if for no other reason than sheer volume of droppings. Some species are real mess-makers, such as the lories and lorikeets.

The mess problem makes lories and lorikeets a poor choice as a pet for some people. Find out more about these birds in Chapter 2.

If your bird's really good at mess-making, you need to do the big clean on a weekly basis. Neater (and usually smaller) species can usually get by on a monthly scrub-down — provided, of course, you're religious about your daily routines, and you remove, clean, and replace dirty toys on an ongoing basis.

For the big clean, take the cage outside and scrub it with soap and water and then rinse it well in plain water. Soak everything you can — perches, dropping tray, and so on — in a solution of one-half cup bleach to a gallon of water (a bathtub's a good place for soaking) and then leave everything out to air-dry in the sun before setting it in place and putting your bird back in it.

High-pressure nozzles for your hose really help knock the mess off your cage. You can also take the cage to a do-it-yourself car wash, as long as you rinse it well with clear water after sudsing.

Cleaning is part of life with birds. Dirty surroundings are more than an eyesore — they're a health-risk for your bird! Get into the habit of cleaning as you go, and you'll find it's not so bad.

Chapter 6

The New Art, Science, and Fun of Feeding Birds Right

In This Chapter

- Bad habits die hard
- Feeding good food for life
- Paying attention to food safety
- Cooking for your bird

If you truly are what you eat, many pet birds would look like turtles, thanks to all the shells they crack off the seeds we insist on giving them.

If you're chuckling in recognition of our little joke, chances are you're one of those bird-owners who needs this chapter the most. If you take away nothing else from our talk of proteins, carbohydrates, fats, and more, note the following, because your bird's very life depends on it:

Seeds alone are not a proper diet for pet birds.

We don't care what you've heard. We don't care who told you. If your pet bird's diet consists solely of seeds, we can assure you that if he isn't sick now, he will be with time.

But if that seed mix you found on the shelf of the grocery or pet store isn't the be-all and end-all when it comes to avian nutrition, what is?

In a word, nothing. No one food is currently all your pet bird needs to thrive, not even the wide array of commercially prepared food pellets that should make up the largest portion of a typical pet bird's healthy diet. Variety is the name of the game when it comes to feeding your pet bird, and in this chapter you find everything you need to select the right combination of foods.

Raising Generations of Junk-Food Junkies

The idea that birds should be fed all-seed diets likely has its roots in two facts. First, birds are uniquely adapted to eat seeds and nuts, able to effortlessly crack even the hardest shells and extract the tender insides. Second, birds *love* seeds.

If birds love seeds and are engineered to eat them, doesn't it follow that the bulk of a pet bird's diet should be seeds? You have to remember that the nutritional needs of our birds' counterparts in the wild may well be quite different than those of our own pet birds, living in luxury in our homes. They're living very different lives! Experts say with certainty that all-seed diets make most pet birds sick over time, because seeds deny them the nutrients they need for longer-term survival and weaken them to the point where other diseases find it easy to take hold. The fact that pet birds can survive at all on such diets is testament to the toughness of birds.

An all-seed diet contributes both directly (through malnutrition) and indirectly (by weakening the bird, making it easier for infectious diseases to take hold) to a serious reduction in the possible life span of any pet bird — by half or more in many situations, in fact.

Birds ought to know what's good for them, right? After all, parrots are very intelligent. Well, so are you, but we bet that fact hasn't stopped you from enjoying tasty treats that you know aren't good for you.

In the case of birds, seeds are the equivalent of a greasy burger. Junk food. And too many pet birds (and people!) are junk-food junkies.

Sunflower seeds are so popular with birds that widespread — and incorrect — opinion suggests that they have in them a substance that's addictive to pet birds. Nope. They're just yummy, so much so that some pet birds act as if they're addicted.

Enter the Pelleted Diet

The trend in recent years has been toward pelleted diets (see Figure 6-1), and pet birds are healthier than ever before as a result. Pelleted diets are readily available from many reputable manufacturers and can be purchased from any decent pet store or from many veterinarians who work with birds.

Figure 6-1: Feeding a bird correctly is easier than ever, thanks to commercial diets that serve as a foundation for healthy eating.

Photo by Dr. Brian L. Speer

Any pet store or veterinarian recommending an *exclusive* seed diet over a pelleted diet should be avoided; they're far behind current thinking. While Brian occasionally tells clients to feed more seeds in special cases (birds who need a quick infusion of calories, for example), these diets are always temporary in nature, and the long-term goal is to graduate the bird to a healthier and more completely balanced bill of fare.

For more indicators of a reputable pet store, see Chapter 3. For more on choosing the right veterinarian for your pet bird, see Chapter 9.

Pelleted food is a blend of foods, such as grains, seeds, vegetables, fruits, and various protein sources. Manufacturers mix the ingredients and then either bake and crumble it or shape it — ending up with pellets of a proper size for any given species (large pellets for large birds, small pellets for small birds).

Too much of a good thing

Pet birds are typically less active than their wild counterparts, and the lack of exercise, coupled with foods such as seeds that are too fatty and amounts of good food that are just plain too much, has contributed to an epidemic of obesity. Just as with humans, extra weight brings with it the risk of many health problems and shortens life spans. Budgies, cockatiels, and Amazon parrots seem particularly prone to putting on weight.

If you think your budgie is pudgy, talk to your veterinarian about dietary changes that may help. Exercise is also important. One of the better toys for a perch potato, especially a larger parrot such as an Amazon, is a stiff rope coil perch, which forces the bird to work to stay in time with the swings and bounces. Good for fighting boredom, too! For more on the problems with obesity, see Chapter 11.

This process produces a food that has a definite and huge overall advantage to the "smorgasbord" way of feeding — the bird can't pick out his favorite foods and ignore the rest. Pellets also are convenient for bird-owners: These commercially prepared diets are easy to buy, relatively inexpensive to feed (definitely so when you consider the veterinary trips they prevent), and store nicely in a cool, dry place.

Pelleted foods are a solid basis for your pet bird's diet, but we strongly caution you that even pellets, wonderful as they are, probably need to be supplemented with some of the foods we talk about later in this chapter — vegetables, fruits, and other such "people food" as bread and pasta. Some birds may even appreciate the addition of a juicy bug now and then — see our sidebar in this chapter, "A bug's (short) life."

Chicken feed? It isn't that easy!

Pelleted food, a poultry industry mainstay for decades, is a relatively new kid within the pet bird industry. Part of the problem manufacturers discovered when developing these foods is the nature of parrots. While chickens aren't the brightest of beings — not even close, really — parrots are very smart. Smart enough to ignore any food they don't like, and most definitely smart enough to manipulate many of their concerned owners to bring them, on command, the food they do like!

Producing a pellet that's good for a pet bird requires knowledge of nutrition and insight into mass appeal. Manufacturers know that they have to create a foodstuff that is actually inviting to a pet bird, so owners have a chance to convert their pets to a healthier diet. Now that food-makers have figured out a way to keep both birds and their owners happy, many pet birds are cheerfully munching their way to good health — and diets continue to improve.

The revolution moves slowly

Old habits die hard, and that adage is certainly true when it comes to avian nutrition. Even today, on the high-tech medium of the Internet, you can find the most old-fashioned of ideas — including some from people who insist that pellets are bad for your bird. Beware! Too many birds are dying young because of such outdated advice.

If you're looking for a bird, make sure you deal with a source who understands the importance of feeding pellets and whose birds have never been allowed to pick up bad eating habits. A lot can be said for starting out with a new bird with no bad eating habits.

For more tips on finding a reputable bird-seller, see Chapter 3. Our list of questions to ask when buying a bird is in Chapter 16.

If you already have a junk-food junkie, hang on — we dig into converting him to a good diet later in this chapter.

Nutrition — the Short Course

When it comes to their eating requirements, most pet birds are more like we are than the other two most popular pets, cats and dogs. Birds are omnivorous, meaning that they can survive on many different kinds of foods — as long as those foods combine to provide them with the balance of nutrients they need.

Don't fall into the trap of believing that if a little bit of (whatever) is good, a lot must be better. Too much of any nutrient may be just as bad as too little. As always, the goal is balanced nutrition. Malnutrition can indicate either too much or too little of specific nutrients — even though we all usually think of deficiencies.

We could write a whole book on avian nutrition, but we don't have to — veterinarian Petra M. Burgmann already has. Her book, *Feeding Your Pet Bird* (Barron's Educational Series), is a super in-depth work for bird-lovers, the best you're going to find without buying a veterinary text. Dr. Burgmann's easy-to-read book includes plenty of pictures of what happens to birds who aren't fed right. Talk about hard to stomach!

The big challenge with her book — with any book, really, even this one — is that what we know about avian nutrition is always evolving. Working with a veterinarian who specializes in birds is the best way we know to advise you to stay current on avian nutrition.

Protein

Proteins, or rather, the amino acids that combine to create them, are justly called the "building blocks of life." Amino acids are in every part of your bird, from the skeleton to the skin to the organs, and they allow your pet to produce those parts that need to be replaced from time to time, such as feathers.

Your bird's own body produces some amino acids, while others have to be acquired from an outside food source. The former are called *nonessential.* (Don't be fooled: Even though the body provides them, they are anything but nonessential!) *Essential* amino acids are those your bird has to eat to get.

You may think of protein as meat, dairy, or eggs, but in fact, protein is found in many other foods, including beans and other vegetables. The difference is that meat, dairy, or eggs are *complete* proteins, which means they typically have all the essential amino acids. An incomplete protein, such as beans or corn, is missing one or more of the essential amino acids. As any vegetarian knows, you can get a complete protein by eating special combinations of incomplete proteins — eating beans with corn is a classic example of combining proteins.

Pelleted foods come with complete or combined proteins already in the mix. You can also give your bird vegetable combinations that offer a complete protein. We recommend you provide complete proteins from time to time — lean poultry, for example, or cooked eggs. Although you may think that munching on a relative is strange bird behavior, we promise your pet won't give it a second thought.

Egg substitutes are wonderful for your bird, for the same reason they are recommended for human heart patients — they're low in cholesterol. Scramble up a dish for yourself and offer your pet bird a spoonful.

Carbohydrates

Carbohydrates are necessary for the production of energy and heat. You find them in rice, pasta, breads, sugar, and starchy vegetables, such as potatoes. Foods with processed sugar may be a carbohydrate, but they shouldn't be showing up in your bird's diet very often. The natural sugars found in fruit are far better for the bird who has a sweet tooth.

Carbohydrates form the largest part of commercial animal feeds, whether they're designed for carnivores, such as dogs and cats, or omnivores, such as birds. In the food pyramid dietary model for human, they also play a large part.

Many carbohydrates are also a source of fiber. While fiber is trumpeted as a good thing in human diets, experts aren't so sure about its usefulness in a pet bird's diet. More research in this area is ongoing — and sure to point to further refinements in commercial diets.

Concerns over fat preservatives

In the last few years, a lot of controversy has been generated over the use of preservatives — primarily BHT, BHA, and ethoxyquin (eh-THOX-ee-quin) — to keep the necessary fats in pet foods from going rancid. These synthetic preservatives have been made the scapegoat for just about every pet health problem you can name.

Many manufacturers have adopted the "If you can't beat 'em, join 'em" approach, which is why some products are now "ethoxyquin free" or "naturally preserved," usually with vitamins C and E.

No good scientific evidence exists to support the decision to avoid synthetic preservatives, either by manufacturers or consumers. If the issue worries you, choose a pelleted food that doesn't have these preservatives. But be aware that you have likely fallen prey to marketing strategies and fear rather than scientific fact in that buying decision.

Fats

In our society, we worry endlessly about the amount of fat in our own diets. But the proper amount of fat is an essential part of a good diet — for people and birds both.

Fat is needed for the absorption and movement around the body of certain vitamins, and it serves as a high-octane source of energy and heat, more than triple the value of carbohydrates in that regard.

Water

Do you think of nutrition as being about what your bird eats? Don't forget that what your bird drinks is just as important to her well-being. Water — clean, fresh, and in ample supplies — is essential to nearly every process of your pet bird's body, which is mostly water.

The tiniest cells of living beings can't survive without water. Nutrients are carried and wastes removed by water. A bird can go longer without food than water.

Always make sure that you supply your bird with water and encourage her to drink by keeping the dish clean and the water fresh. Check the dish frequently to make sure the water hasn't been fouled by food or droppings.

Water bottles are fine, but make sure regularly that they haven't clogged. (Some birds think it's fun to stuff food in the spouts of their water bottles.)

Some bird-owners are absolutely adamant that their pets have only bottled or filtered water. If you want to take that extra step (and expense), that's fine, but realize that the investment may be unnecessary. If your tap water is okay for you to drink, it's likely okay for your bird to drink.

Vitamins

Vitamins, which are found in varying degrees in foods, perform several roles in the everyday functioning of your bird's body. They are divided into two categories — *water-soluble* and *fat-soluble*. Both are important to your bird's health, and too little or too much of any of them in your pet's diet can have dire effects.

Water-soluble vitamins include the B vitamins, as well as niacin, panthothenic acid, folic acid, biotin, choline, and vitamin C. Fat-soluble vitamins are vitamins A, D, E, and K.

Although birds appreciate a juicy slice of orange as much as we do, they don't need it for the vitamin C — it's the one vitamin they produce on their own!

Minerals

Mineral nutrients your bird needs are potassium, magnesium, zinc, calcium, iron, phosphorus, sodium, chloride, and others. Like vitamins, they make up a small part of your bird's diet, but in the correct amounts, they're essential for good health. Also like vitamins, minerals aren't something to play with — too much can be as dangerous as too little.

What Your Bird Should Be Eating

So how do you make sure your bird manages to take in all the nutrition he needs? By offering a variety of healthy foods to maximize the possibility that every one of those nutrients is a regular part of his diet.

Pellet diets

For all the reasons we explain earlier in this chapter, a pelleted diet is an ideal choice for about 80 percent of your bird's diet. A properly formulated modern pelleted diet is only bad if your bird won't eat it — and that can be a common problem in pet birds who've been fed improperly in the past or allowed to become "addicted" to an unsatisfactory diet.

Choose the brand your bird likes best. After you figure out which one that is, you have no reason to switch around. If your bird has been raised on a pelleted diet — and he should have been — the seller can tell you the brand name, so you can continue to feed it. If you have to choose, consider availability; certain brands are hard or nearly impossible to find in certain areas. Other considerations are palatability (does the bird really want to eat it?) and cost (you can expect quite a range of costs in the varying products out there on the shelves).

Always make fresh pellets available to your pet bird. Not only are they the mainstay of his diet, but eating them also gives him something to do when you can't be with him and toys aren't appealing.

Fruits and vegetables

Fruits and vegetables are a good source of carbohydrates, vitamins, minerals, and, in some cases, protein. They are a poor source of fat.

Because some people have in their heads that fruit and vegetables are "good for you," they figure that adding them occasionally balances out a seed diet. Not so. Fruits and vegetables are indeed important, but they can't by themselves correct the nutritional problems caused by an all-seed diet.

Give your pet bird a wide range of fruits and vegetables, including beans, corn, and such green leafies as spinach or broccoli. Because these foods also help combat boredom, leave them in as much of an original state as you can — corn on the cob is much more fun to eat than kernels in a dish, as any kid or parrot knows (see Figure 6-2). Besides, each cut you make into a piece of fruit or vegetable shortens the time before it starts to spoil.

Another thing to remember: Be sure to thoroughly wash anything you offer your bird, just as you do for foods you're going to eat yourself.

Fruits and vegetables are high in water content, which is why they frequently get blamed for causing diarrhea. You can expect an increase in the urine component of the droppings, which is normal for birds who consume a high amount of water. (For more on droppings, see Chapter 8.)

A garden for you all

Even the biggest pet birds aren't really that large compared with any human, which means that providing fruits, vegetables, and other healthy foods isn't going to break your budget. Gina attended an avian nutrition lecture where the speaker described shopping for her bird: one green bean, one small carrot, a dozen grapes, broccoli leaves — her shopping cart really raised eyebrows at checkout!

Still, you can save some money and provide fresh food for your whole family by maintaining a garden, including some fruit trees. Invest in a food dehydrator, and you can really go to town, stocking up a year's supply of healthy treats. Best of all, when you grow your own food, you can be sure it's free of pesticides.

What to plant? Try peppers of all kinds (even jalapeños!), squash, and corn in the summertime, and broccoli and cauliflower in cooler weather. As far as fruits go, you can't go wrong with apples, pears, or oranges. Almonds are good, too. A bonus: The branches of these trees make great perches. (For more on do-it-yourself perches, see Chapter 4.)

Figure 6-2: Making birds work at getting their food, such as leaving corn on the cob, helps keep them busy and entertained.

Fruits and vegetables can "turn" very quickly, especially in more hot and humid environments. Spoiled food can be as dangerous for your pet bird as it is for you, so be careful to remove uneaten portions before they go bad. A rule of thumb: If you wouldn't feel comfortable eating the fruits and vegetables you have put before your pet, you should be offering something fresher.

Naturally pigmented red or yellow plant material plays an important role in making canaries colorful. When eaten as new feathers are coming in, these foods help to produce the vibrant colors much admired in these birds. Nothing can help to change the color of a feather that's already grown, though.

Food for people and other pets

You can offer your pet bird almost any healthy food that you fix for yourself — pasta, rice, casseroles, meats, and cereal. Try to keep fatty and sugary foods out of the mix, along with dairy products. Birds just don't have the ability to digest regular or large amounts of dairy products, because they're not mammals.

Sharing your meal with your pet bird helps your relationship, too. So knock yourself out fixing fabulous meals you both can enjoy. Just keep your portions separate. Your bird shouldn't eat food that has been in your mouth and vice versa.

Another cross-species surprise — you can *occasionally* add dog kibble and monkey food to your bird's diet. Both are edible and entertaining.

Foods and drinks to avoid

You know what healthy food is in human terms — fruits and vegetables, beans, rice, pastas, eggs, lower-fat meats such as chicken, and whole-grain breads. These are the foods you can share with your budgie, cockatiel, or any of the parrots. The food you know that you really shouldn't be eating — high-fat, high-sugar junk food — is a bad choice for you and your bird, so just knock it off.

Some foods that are perfectly fine for you (in moderation, of course) are absolutely off-limits to your pet bird. Top of the list: avocado, which of course means not only plain avocado but anything with avocado in it, from guacamole to a California roll at the sushi bar. Another potentially deadly treat is chocolate (true for dogs, too, by the way). Also, don't share alcoholic or caffeinated beverages with your pet bird.

Nuts

Nuts are a wonderful treat for bird. Not only are they a good source of protein (although high in fat), but they're also an important source of recreation. Feed nuts to your parrots in their shells, so your bird has to work to get the goodies inside.

Many bird toys are designed to keep birds busy trying to figure out how to reach the nuts inside. These puzzles are wonderful for engaging curious beaks and minds. For more on the importance of toys, see Chapter 4.

Seeds

We're so devoted to trashing seeds that you're probably convinced your bird will fall over dead if you offer one. Not true. Seeds are okay as a small part of your bird's diet. They're a good source of carbohydrates and a little too good a source of fat.

Consider seeds a treat, rather than a dietary mainstay. So it's fine to treat your bird now and then, as long as you don't go overboard.

Seeds make wonderful tools for training. Because birds are so nutty about seeds, these treats make great rewards for proper behavior, such as stepping onto your hand (see Chapter 5).

What about vitamin and mineral supplements?

Some pet stores seem to move a lot of unnecessary junk, and most vitamin and mineral supplements fall into this category. If your bird isn't getting all the vitamins and minerals he requires, you need to convert him to a diet that can provide him with the true balance of what he needs. Supplementing an already adequate diet can lead to health problems, some of them severe. And adding supplements to a poor diet will do nothing good except perhaps ensure that your bird will die younger than he should, but with prettier feathers.

If you think your bird needs a supplement, discuss your concerns with a veterinarian experienced in treating birds. If you're right, your veterinarian will likely recommend a product that you can add to the soft food component of your bird's diet — at least until you can coax your pet on to a more balanced diet.

Bird bread and other delights

We wonder if baking industry people have any idea how much of their corn muffin mix is purchased to provide nutritious treats for pet birds? Seems every bird-club newsletter, bird Web site, or bird book has a recipe that lists a box of corn muffin mix as its first ingredient.

The basic recipe, perfect for experimenting: One box of corn muffin mix and one more egg than the box calls for. Prepare the mixture as recommended, adding the extra egg and any or all of the following: a cup of mixed vegetables (fresh, canned, or frozen) or a 4-ounce jar of vegetable baby food, some hulled seeds, some pellets, and the shell of one egg (zap it in the blender to pulverize). Bake in either a greased muffin or cake pan as directed on the box.

Bird bread is a great way to convince a confirmed seed-eater that maybe other food isn't so bad after all. You can break off pieces of bird bread every day or save it as a special treat (it freezes well). Use 1-inch chunks for small birds and relatively larger chunks for big ones.

Another treat is rice and veggie mix. Cook a cup of brown rice. Thaw a cup of frozen corn, peas, and carrot mix (a minute in the microwave will do the job). Mix the rice and vegetables together and add a couple of finely chopped hard-boiled eggs. What could be easier than that?

You can also can "birdify" French toast by sprinkling the egg-drenched bread with hulled seeds and cooking it as usual. Pancakes can be made better from a bird's point of view with the addition of some hulled seeds, too.

Practical Plans for Converting Your Bird's Diet

We recommend choosing a bird who's already eating a healthy diet of pellets and a wide variety of other foods. But we realize you may already have a bird who's a junk-food junkie, or you may have fallen in love with a bird who's a dietary "fixer-upper."

Don't despair. With patience, you can reform even the most stubborn seed-eater. The following are some tips:

- **Confirm good health.** Before messing with your pet's diet, make sure he's in good health by having your veterinarian go over him thoroughly. Birds are adept at hiding illness, and the stress of a diet change may be too much for a bird who's sick.
- **Combine the old and the new.** Mix what your bird has been eating with the pellets and other foods he should be eating. Remember to feed your bird this mixture out of a single food bowl. Never offer enough seed to fill your bird up, and hold off treats for a while.

- **Gradually reduce seeds.** Start with a 50/50 blend of seeds and pellets for two to four weeks and then reduce the percentage of seeds slowly over time. Vary the amounts of pellets, fruit, veggies, and seed you offer each day. Be inconsistent in what your bird can expect to see in that food bowl the next day — your bird will stay busy checking for the jackpot of food he likes. Even if the offerings aren't all he dreams of, he's at the food bowl, so he may as well eat.
- **Feed new foods in the morning.** Birds are the most hungry when they first wake up, so offer pellets and vegetables exclusively at the start of the day before adding seed to the mix later in the day.
- **Monkey see, monkey do.** Birds learn by watching. If you have one bird who is on a healthy diet, let your other bird watch. Another option: Eat in front of your bird. He'll try most anything you're eating, and by that we mean fruits and veggies — we're not suggesting you eat pellets. (But if you really loved your bird. . . .)

Birds can and do starve themselves to death, just like people can. During the dietary conversion process, make sure you observe your bird eating, make sure that he is passing feces in his droppings of adequate volume and consistency, and check the muscle on both sides of his keel bone (which runs right down the middle of his chest) periodically to be sure he's maintaining weight. Don't be in a hurry to change your pet's diet — follow his lead in determining how fast to reduce the amount of seed in his diet.

The nitty-gritty on grit

The idea that all pet birds need grit is another myth that seems to be taking a long time to die. Some pet birds, such a finches and canaries, can make use of an occasional small amount of grit — and most budgies, cockatiels, and other parrots don't need grit at all.

Why do pet stores persist in pushing ground rock on bird-lovers? As with those people who push an all-seed diet, the answer is ignorance. Folks used to believe that grit helps in the grinding organ of the *gizzard,* assisting in the breakdown of foods. But birds do fine without grit — and grit has been shown to remove vitamins A, K, and B_2 from the digestive system.

A tiny amount — as in a couple of grains of grit every couple of months — may be okay for finches and canaries, keeping in mind that no pet bird needs to have access to all the grit they want. For parrots, skip grit entirely. Over-consumption of the stuff has led to many life-threatening problems — grit impaction — in pet parrots, especially young and smaller bird species, such as budgies or cockatiels.

A bug's (short) life

In Brian's and Gina's part of the world — beautiful Northern California — the media always turn up for the annual bug buffet that a local college professor puts together in an effort to educate people on the nutritional benefits of insects. Entertaining as the good professor is as he scarfs down a cricket or grub, his pitch is a hard sell that isn't likely to be turning up in restaurants any time soon.

But his message is on the money: Insects can be good eating, which is why so many nonhuman animals find them tasty as all get-out. (The early bird gets the worm, remember?) A good pet store is likely to have crickets, mealworms, fruit flies, fly larvae (isn't that a better term than maggots?), and other bugs. You can also raise these taste treats on your own. Mealworms are the easiest, and your pet-supply store can provide you with larvae and instructions on how to cultivate them. When your critters start reproducing, it's easy to select out plump, white larvae to add to the diet of your finches and canaries. Yum!

A final note on bugs — if you haven't raised them yourself or purchased them from a reputable source, don't feed them to your bird. Backyard bug-hunting may seem like a great idea, until you consider that you have no clue about what pesticides the pests you pick may have been exposed to, or what parasites they may be carrying.

Birds of a (Slightly) Different Feather

Although most pet birds commonly kept as pets will do splendidly with the dietary guidelines we put into this chapter, you need to be aware of one notable exception — the diet of the nectar-eaters, the lories and lorikeets. These birds do best on a diet of liquids and fruits. Several manufacturers make mixes for lories and lorikeets, so all you have to add is water. The liquid doesn't stay fresh long, however, and needs to be changed a couple of times a day.

Pelleted diets for lories and lorikeets are evolving. In the future, these birds are likely to have diets available that are easier for us humans to handle.

Chapter 7

Beyond Food and Water: Bird Basics

In This Chapter

- Reading bird body language
- Handling birds properly
- Sprucing up appearances
- Planning for boarding and travel

Infatuation can provide a wonderful rush, but the thrill doesn't contribute much toward a lasting relationship. Respect, kindness, consistency, and trust — these are the qualities that can see you through the years.

Do you think we're talking about your relationship with your human life partner? Silly you! We're referring to your relationship with your bird.

Because many pet birds are intelligent and can enjoy long lives, your relationship with your bird may well resemble your connection to other humans, especially with a young child (albeit a child who never grows up). Your bird can become a valued companion, but you are always the one who must provide structure for your pet's life, set limits, and make sure he eats properly and sees the doctor when he's sick.

If all that caretaking sounds like a tall order, it is — but you can handle it, in time. If you've ever dealt with a human infant, just remember your nervous awkwardness as you changed that first diaper. Bet it wasn't long before you were changing diapers without a second thought. All it takes is practice and familiarity.

The same anxiety may accompany your initial experiences with most pet birds. The first time you handle a bird or clip wings or nails, you can expect a little uncertainty. But you learn, both from your successes and your mistakes.

No one is born knowing how to care for a child or a bird. But most everyone can develop some comfort and confidence with the responsibility. In either case, the payoff is wonderful.

Translating Bird Body Language

Because birds aren't born speaking English or knowing how to figure out what we ask of them, the caretaker role revolves around understanding your pet's nature. It's not always difficult. The parrots, highly intelligent creatures that they are, can seem quite human, although this trait may not always seem desirable. (It's no surprise that many bird-lovers compare their companions to 2-year-old humans!)

From the tiniest budgie or parrotlet to the largest macaw, pet birds can be loving, cuddly, playful, or contemplative one minute and demanding, aloof, manic, or peevish the next. Unlike dogs, who are always glad to see you, birds can be moody. Sometimes they want nothing more than to be left alone — in your company, but not in your face.

Some of these moods are pretty obvious — an Amazon in a rowdy state or a cockatoo who wants to be cuddled isn't hard to figure out. Other times, though, behavior signs may be more subtle, and the failure to heed these clues may earn you a nip. Sharing space with a bird is like living with a mate, or family, or roommate — sometimes you just have to pick your moments and know when to back off.

Although some of the body language we talk about in this section applies to all pet birds, we focus primarily on those birds who are routinely handled — the parrots, a broad classification that includes budgies, cockatiels, and lovebirds, all the way up to the giants of the macaw family. Canaries and other finches also can be manic or moody, but because they're primarily hands-off pets, careful observations of their body language isn't quite as urgent.

The eyes have it

Birds have keen eyesight and often stare at something that fascinates or frightens them, using one eye and tipping the head, or using both eyes for a head-on look. When you see your bird fixated on something, follow that line of vision to see what he's looking at, but also look at your bird's body. A relaxed body posture accompanies a calm, curious bird's staring, and a more defensive or aggressive body language demonstrates fright. Most often, a locked-on look is a sign of fascination — like the youngest children, birds can become attracted by something colorful in their environments.

Birds are able to control their irises, shrinking and enlarging their pupils rapidly in a display that's called *flashing* or *pinning*. In the same way you have to translate the meaning of staring, you have to read the whole bird to put the flashing in its proper context. Birds may flash when they're excited or when they're angry. Flashing accompanied by aggressive posturing, such as tail-fanning, signifies a bird who's bound to escalate his warnings — and maybe even bite — if not left alone.

Consider flashing to be the physical display of strong emotion — anything from the "I wanna kill you" vibes of an angry or aggressive bird to the "Hey there, cutie" of an infatuated bird. Pinning may even signify intense curiosity directed toward a person or another bird — "Hi ya! Whatcha doin'?"

If you could look through the eyes of your bird, what would you see? Do birds see in color? How good is their peripheral vision? You know we're going to tell you. Check out Chapter 8 for more.

Say what?

Even if your bird doesn't talk, she may be trying to tell you something. Most birds are highly vocal, using sounds in the wild to establish and protect territory, attract mates, warn of danger, and maintain social connections. Although screeching is the vocalization that bird-owners seem to worry about most, you can figure out a lot about your bird by listening for other sounds.

If you're wishing your screeching bird would just shut up, don't despair — we offer some suggestions in Chapter 12 that may help quiet the clamor.

Here are some of the sounds you may hear coming from your bird:

- **Talking, singing, whistling:** Any of these sounds may be a sign of a happy, contented bird. With good talkers, speaking can be more than a matter of parroting words and phrases; your bird is truly capable of having a conversation with you! (See our sidebar in this chapter for tips on teaching your bird to talk.)

  Amazon and African grey parrots are widely thought to be the best talkers, but they tend to have totally different personalities when it comes to speaking up or speaking out. Amazons love an audience — these born performers often become more active and vocal when a crowd is watching. African greys often "clam up" in such circumstances. When they're settled in more secure surroundings, however, the greys really pipe up.

- **Purring:** This lightweight, growly noise can be about contentment, but you really need to consider the whole context; the sound can have a broad meaning that also encompasses displeasure.

- **Tongue-clicking:** This sound resembles the noise you might make to get a horse to move. When parrots click their tongues against their beaks, they're often asking to be picked up or petted. African grey parrots may click or "pop" as a means of self entertainment, too — completely independent of your presence.

- **Growling:** No ambivalence here: A growling bird is not a happy camper. Growling is most often heard in African parrots, the Congo and Timneh greys, and the Senegal, Meyer's, and other members of the poicephalus club. Brian hears a lot of growling from these guys when they don't want to be examined or handled in his exam rooms. The sound is intermittent, not continuous — growl, inhale, growl, inhale, and so on.
- **Chattering, muttering, and barking:** Often heard at dusk when birds are settling down for sleep, these sounds are about connecting with other birds, touching base with other flock members. Barking can be a mimicking of the sound your dog makes (yes, a parrot can pick that up, too) or may be a louder version of the "Hey, I'm here" chatter. Soft chatter can also be a sign of contentment or the practice exercise of a bird who's learning to talk and practicing (or mumbling) words — just like a toddler getting a feel for words by repeating interesting sounds.

Beak bulletins

Your bird's beak functions as her own multifunctional Swiss Army knife (and we talk about it more in Chapter 8), but the beak can also be part of your pet's body language.

Here are some beak behaviors you may notice:

- **Grinding:** Characterized by the side-to-side sliding of one jaw, or *mandible,* over the other, this sound may remind you of teeth-grinding in humans. Usually this sound attests to a satisfied and secure bird. You're most likely to hear grinding after your pet has a big meal (in which case the expression is comparable to the belt-loosening utterance — or a less attractive venting of fullness — that some humans share following a big feed). Birds also make grinding noises when they're sort of half-asleep.
- **Clicking:** Most often seen in cockatoos and cockatiels, the forward-and-back rubbing of one beak tip over the other is kind of like flipping one fingernail over the other. This motion is a bird's way of staying busy and amused.
- **Beaking:** Young humans like to put things in their mouths, and so do young birds. In humans (and other animals), we call this tendency *teething,* so *beaking* seems as good a term for the action as any when it comes to birds. The young bird who gently presses his tongue against your finger and puts his jaw around it isn't biting — he's just trying to get an idea of what you feel and taste like.
- **Biting:** Fear, anger, or territoriality is behind biting, and you need to factor in both the situation and the rest of the body language to figure out what's going on. But observe from a distance, because bites can be nasty.

Teaching your bird to talk

Not all parrots talk, not even those from the species known best for their mimicry — the double-yellow-headed and yellow-naped Amazons and the African greys. If you're absolutely set on owning a talking bird, buy one who talks already — and make sure you hear the conversation before you plunk down payment.

We suggest that you consider talking a bonus rather than a requisite characteristic of your pet. Choose a young, well-socialized bird and love her for her many fine qualities, whether or not talking is among them. Nothing is at all wrong with trying to teach your pet to talk, though. Some birds do end up with incredible vocabularies — not just the larger parrots. Little parrots, such as budgies, can be great conversationalists.

You can teach your parrot to talk by repeating words clearly or even by using tapes or computer programs that say the same language over and over. You can nurture communication further by using the words in their proper context and setting up an association your bird can grasp.

For example, every time your bird lowers his head to request a scratch, ask him, "Wanna scratch?" and then scratch him. When you give him foods or other toys, call them by name out loud. Play naming games with him — say "Keys" and then tell him "Good bird!" for taking them from you, and then repeat the exercise.

You may have an easier time if yours is a one-bird household. Two birds may be more interested in talking their own language with each other than figuring out your expressions. Some experts also suggest not attempting to teach your bird to whistle, at least not until he has picked up speech. Whistling birds seem to show a reluctance to use words.

What about the words or sounds you *don't* want mimicked? The best you can do is ignore them, providing neither positive nor negative reinforcement. And be fair: If you think it's funny for your bird to swear in private, you have to live with the behavior when the minister's over for dinner.

What your bird says can tell people a great deal about your private life, so much so that you may rue the day you dreamed of enjoying the company of a talking bird. Gina has a friend who house-sat for some people with a cockatoo. Every time the microwave timer went off, the bird yelled, "Hey boys, time for dinner." And the alarm clock's wake-up call was met with a string of four-letter words. Be careful what you say! As children do (ask any parent!), your bird is likely to pick up words and phrases that you'd prefer to keep to yourself, especially if you say them often and with contagious enthusiasm.

Living with a biter is no fun, that's for sure. If your bird seems determined to take a piece out of you, check out our behavior tips in Chapter 12.

- **Yawning and sneezing:** No big surprises here. Birds yawn and sneeze for exactly the same reasons we do — because they're tired or bored, or because something's irritating their nasal passages. If your bird's snorting up mucus or is really uncomfortable, though, call your veterinarian. Your pet needs to be looked at.

- **Regurgitating:** Isn't that a much nicer word than vomiting? When birds bring up half-digested food, they usually don't have a tummy ache — they're expressing their affection. (We're not making this up, really!) Like many animals, birds feed their young by bringing up food. Bonded breeding pairs do this to each other as well, as a sign of closeness. When your bird brings up food when you're near enough to pet him, he's showing that he considers you a mate or companion and wants you to eat well. Birds bob their heads to bring the food up, and when the behavior is performed between birds, the food is put directly into the other's mouth. Don't try this at home.
- **Wiping:** You don't like food on your mouth, and neither does your bird. Deprived of napkins, birds wipe their beaks on perches, on the sides of their food dishes, or on your shirt sleeve. Gina's bird, Patrick, who occasionally catches a ride on the back of Gina's extremely mellow retriever, Benjamin (but only under Gina's close supervision), thanks the dog by smearing food on his ears. Benjamin isn't amused but is tolerant, nonetheless.

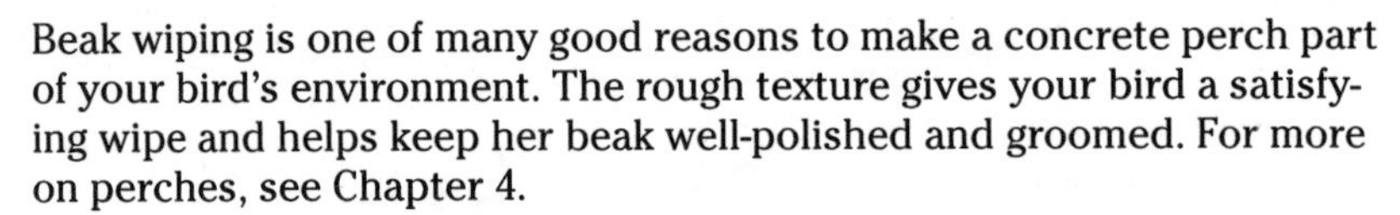

Beak wiping is one of many good reasons to make a concrete perch part of your bird's environment. The rough texture gives your bird a satisfying wipe and helps keep her beak well-polished and groomed. For more on perches, see Chapter 4.

- **Jousting:** Birds play with other birds by slapping or grabbing each other's beaks. This frisky behavior is nothing more than playfulness — usually. Sometimes, though, birds injure each other when playing, especially if there's a big difference in size and strength. Keep an eye on jousting; it's usually harmless, but call your veterinarian if any beak injuries occur.

Wing things

Wings are for flying, of course, but that's not all. Here's how to interpret what else you may see your bird doing with his wings:

- **Shoulder hunching/wing flipping:** The bird baby who attracts his parents' attention gets fed first and often fed most. They do this by flipping wings and hunching their shoulders, accompanied by vocalization and head bobbing. When done for your benefit, you can figure this for attention-getting behavior — usually associated with the need for food or the desire to be fed, especially in a young bird. In a mature bird, however, these juvenile-type movements may mean something's physically or emotionally amiss. Just the wing flips alone, singly or with both wings, can indicate mild annoyance — or an effort to line up the feathers just right.
- **Drooping:** Baby birds need to learn how to fold and tuck in their wings, so drooping in a young bird is nothing to worry about. In an older bird,

drooping wings may indicate illness. If you notice the posture right after the bird exerts herself, consider sheer exhaustion as the cause, especially if your pet's a perch potato. Birds who have just been misted or bathed may also let their wings droop as they dry.

Although not a pet species, the anhinga is one bird who knows how to droop wings with style. This waterbird sits in the sun and holds his wings out to let them dry, a behavior that makes the glossy black bird appear like some kind of mystic icon. A great place to see the anhinga (along with more than 100 other species of birds, and quite a few alligators) is Wakulla Springs State Park, near Tallahassee, Florida. The springs are remarkable for their clearness (when conditions are right), their ancient history (mastodon bones were found there), and their less ancient history (*The Creature From the Black Lagoon* was filmed at the site). For us, though, the birds are by far the biggest draw.

- **Flapping:** Honestly now, if you had wings, wouldn't you flap them? Birds often engage in massive flap-a-thons when they're first released from their cages. Getting some exercise just feels good! They aren't necessarily interested in going anywhere; even birds with unclipped wings can hold on tight to the top of their cage and just flap like crazy. They can even do it upside down!

Tail tales

Even your bird's tail feathers have a tale to tell, if you're watching:

- **Wagging:** Some birds wag their tail feathers for the same reason dogs wag their tails: They're glad to see you! The motion is usually not a continuous back-and-forth wag as with a dog, but more like a quick sideways flip and back. Fast back-and-forth flipping can have another meaning, especially in cockatoos: After some wagging, they'll often take a step back and let fly with an impressive dropping. Other parrots do the wag-step-and-poop dance, too, but usually not with the flair of a cockatoo. Watching for this behavior is a step in potty-training your parrot (see the nearby sidebar).
- **Bobbing:** If your perch potato has just exercised, he's likely breathing hard just to get his wind back, and tail-bobbing's part of the package. If your bird's tail is bobbing and he hasn't been active, he may have a breathing problem or infection. See your veterinarian.
- **Fanning:** Spreading out the tail feathers is one of a collection of behaviors that go along with anger or aggression — and we cover others in the upcoming sections. This showy action is quite common in Amazons who want to impress you with how very tough they are, and the wagging is often accompanied by flashing eyes and an erect body posture — not a bird you want to tangle with at that moment!

Can you potty-train your bird? Yes!

One of the less-pleasant aspects of sharing your life with a bird is dealing with the droppings. When the droppings land on the paper at the bottom of the cage, that's fine, but nobody likes cleaning droppings off the floor (especially if carpeted) or off your shirt if you've been holding your bird when he lets one fly.

With patience and consistency, you can teach your bird to relieve himself on command, in a place of your choosing. Young birds seem to pick up the skill most quickly and reliably, but you can teach an older bird new tricks, too.

Start by observing your bird — the times of day he's most likely to relieve himself and the body language he uses just before, such as tail wagging or stepping back. Pick your desired command — "Go potty" or "Hurry up" will do, as will anything, just as long as you're consistent. (Gina uses "Do the big poop," on her bird Patrick. Hardly elegant, but it gets the job done.)

When you see your bird getting ready to go or you know it's the usual time he does (such as first thing in the morning), ask him onto your hand (or finger, if he's a small bird) and hold him over a wastebasket, newspaper, toilet, or other "poop zone" (some people use paper plates). Give your potty command and praise him when he obeys — even though the response is just a coincidence at first, of course. Praise and stroking are the rewards for correct behavior.

The larger the bird, the longer the time he can "hold it." Budgies and cockatiels aren't good for much more than 15 to 20 minutes, tops, while large parrots can wait for several hours or more.

With training, some birds can hold it for a long, long time. A colleague of Brian's had a potty-trained patient whose owners left him with a pet-sitter, without sharing the "Go" command with the sitter. The bird went a couple of days before the owners were reached on vacation. The sitter held the phone to the bird's ear, the owners gave the command, and the bird bombed away to a very impressive degree!

Most birds aren't that reliable, so keep paper towels and other cleaning supplies at hand.

Posture primer

Approaching bird language in bits and pieces is better than not trying to figure out what your pet's attempting to communicate, but you really have to look at the whole bird to get the message right. Some posturing to watch for:

- **Crouching, head tipped downward:** We can sum this position up in two words: Pet me! The bird who lowers his body and tips his head forward to offer his neck is angling for a good scratch. Indulge him!
- **Crouching, head down, intense stare, eyes pinning or flashing:** This stance is bird talk for "Make my day." This bird is looking for a reason to nail you, and it won't take much. The body is rigid, with feathers raised at the hackles, tail feathers flared, and eyes flashing. This early warning

is sometimes accompanied by a purposeful walk forward, if the bird's on the ground. Know that you're in the company of a tough customer you definitely need to avoid, at least for the moment.

- **Crouching, head down, relaxed body, wings raised or fluttering:** This appearance is another solid statement about a desire for attention. "Hey, babe, I think you're cute. And don't I look cute, too?" In bird lingo, these commonly combined postures attract attention and send a come-hither signal.
- **Body up, head up, relaxed:** The bird's being friendly, especially if she's moving toward you.
- **Body up and rigid, head up, feathers ruffled and flared:** You're seeing a show of territoriality.
- **Quivering:** Your bird may be frightened, intimidated, or cold, the latter common after a good drenching. He may also be a Quaker parakeet, so named because of the tendency to "quake" often.
- **Stretching:** Birds stretch for the same reason we do: It feels good. *Manteling* is one kind of stretch you can see in both birds of prey and pet birds. The manteling bird stretches out a wing and leg on the same side in an impressive show of balance.
- **Preening:** Birds keep their feathers in fine form by drawing them through their beaks, cleaning and coating them with oil they draw from a gland at the base of their tails. They also pull off the sheaths on new feathers. Preening is very much a social behavior, too; birds enjoy preening each other and their favorite people.

Don't confuse preening with the destruction of feathers, a willful act commonly known as *feather-picking*. See Chapter 12 for more on the vexing problem of birds biting off or plucking out their own feathers.

- **Belly up:** When combined with flashing, open beak, general rigidity, and feet up, this display is a sad, sad sight: a bird who is convinced the danger to his life is so great he's prepared to fight to the end (and take a piece or two of his enemy with him). We hasten to add that sometimes birds, especially baby ones, sleep on their backs, but we know you can tell the difference.

- **One final species-specific oddity — head shaking in African greys:** Brian has looked down the ears of lots of African greys whose owners were certain something was hiding inside, because of all the head-shaking. He hasn't found anything — yet. Greys also sometimes put their heads down and against something and dig with their feet. Like the head-shaking, this behavior usually occurs in young birds only.

Getting a Handle on Your Bird

No matter how well you and your bird get along, you occasionally need to do things to him he doesn't particularly appreciate — among them, wing trimming and nail clipping. Because your bird won't always sit still for a procedure he doesn't necessarily like, and because he may decide to bite you in protest, you have to figure out how to safely and securely restrain your pet.

With the hands-off types of birds — canaries and other finches — your first order of business is catching them. A net works fine, but you may be able to catch your bird with your hand, if you darken the room first to "freeze" him. Hold the bird gently but firmly — you can expect some vocal protests, some nipping, and a lot of squirming, but once you get a secure grip on these little ones, they usually settle down.

Parrots — we're talking about everything from little budgies to big macaws — can be asked up onto your hand first, which saves both of you the stress of capture.

Every pet bird, except the hands-off ones, should know the step-up command, a basic tool for instilling good manners in your pet. If you have a young, well-socialized bird, see Chapter 5 for tips on teaching the step-up. If you're blessed with an avian delinquent, see Chapter 12 for techniques to reestablish a good relationship with your bird through step-up and other training tools.

When working with your pet bird, be firm but gentle, and move decisively. Your bird can sense any tentativeness on your part, which is likely to inspire more struggling and invite a possible bite.

Restraining by hand: The "parrot popsicle"

The "parrot popsicle" is a good hold to use if you want to examine your bird closely, but because the technique requires two hands, maintenance care like wing trimming or nail clipping calls for the assistance of a helper.

Some birds become accustomed to wing and nail grooming and will even present a wing or foot, when asked, for you to groom. This scenario, in our eyes, is ideal. However, if you need to use restraint, wing clips and nail trims are almost always easier with a helper — one person restrains, one person does the grooming. Although an experienced handler may be able to restrain and groom a bird with no additional help, the typical pet bird-owner isn't equipped to manage these multiple tasks.

To restrain your bird in the popsicle hold:

1. **Gently place your palm on your bird's back, spreading your fingers with the pinkie toward the tail.**
2. **Bring your thumb to the front and position it underneath the bird's lower jaw.**
3. **Spread your index finger out and up to the back of the bird's head.**

   Your bird should be wrapped in your fingers, and you should be holding him gently but firmly, facing you.
4. **Position your other hand beneath his feet and allow him to grasp your hand to feel more secure.**

   If needed, the hand that the bird's feet are grasping on can also catch the tips of the wings and tail.
5. **Hold your bird upright, and if he fusses, make eye contact and speak to him, or blow gently on his face to get his attention.**

Done correctly, this hold provides a nonstressful manner of restraint — merely an extension of the many ways you probably pet and handle your bird daily. This form of restraint is an excellent way to gain your bird's attention, eye contact, and respect at a moment when it's crucial. Performed incorrectly, at the wrong time, aggressively, or without experience, care, or compassion, this approach can be destructive to your relationship, so make sure you understand this tool well before trying it.

Be careful when releasing your bird from this hold. A contentious character may take the opportunity to deliver a parting shot with his beak. Put the bird down beak-first, making sure he grips something, such as a perch, and then slide your hand backward and off, as the bird steps up onto the perch. Immediately talk to your bird and ask him to step up on your hand and reacquaint himself with you. You have a chance to strengthen the respect you want in your relationship, so don't just walk away without this important last step.

Be very careful to position your thumb under your bird's jaw with *upward, not inward* pressure. You can potentially cut off your bird's supply of oxygen if you put pressure on the windpipe, or *trachea.*

Meet "Mr. Towel"

For a secure way to restrain your bird that allows you the flexibility to clip wings or trim nails, use a towel. A hand towel is fine for small parrots, such as cockatiels and budgies, while a larger bath towel is better for large parrots, such as cockatoos and macaws.

Hold the towel with the ends draped over each hand, as shown in Figure 7-1, make eye contact with your bird, and approach her from the front. Show her "Mr. Towel" and then gently wrap the towel around the bird, usually from the front. When using a towel to restrain your bird, you may not need to keep direct hold of her head, but do expect a few new holes chewed in the towel!

Figure 7-1: To restrain your bird, approach her calmly with a towel and wrap it around her securely — but leave her room to breathe!

When your bird is gently wrapped up like a mummy (be careful not to inhibit her breathing), *you* are in control and can take care of business. Always remember to handle your bird with respect, but also with authority. Keep in mind that Mr. Towel is supposed to be your bird's friend, not a source of dread, doom, or fear.

Wrap the towel tightly enough to control wriggling, but not so tight as to restrict breathing. Pet bird species breathe by moving their breast bones forward and back like a bellows, not to the side as we do with our ribs. You must leave the towel wrap loose enough for your bird to draw breath normally.

With your bird secure, you can pull out a wing or a foot for trimming — possible for one person with a towel wrap, but still easier for two.

A matter of respect

When Brian sees a patient at the hospital, he introduces himself to the bird as a pediatrician would meet a child, with eye contact, a smile, and a friendly verbal greeting. As he's talking to the owner, he's constantly watching the bird, getting a feel for the personality and looking for signs of illness or behavior problems. Mr. Towel doesn't come out until he's needed — if he's needed at all.

Sound reasonable? You'd think so, but too many veterinarians or bird handlers, such as groomers, tend to restrain first and get to know the bird later or not at all. That's the way they were taught, and that's the way they still behave.

Times are changing, and so are veterinarians and other bird handlers — but not necessarily fast enough or consistently enough. Your chosen veterinarian, groomer, or other professional should be comfortable with birds. Yes, restraint is part of the package, but so, too, is respect.

For more on choosing the right veterinarian for your pet bird, see Chapter 9.

Toweling doesn't have to be an ordeal for your bird. Play "towel games" with your pet, such as hide-and-seek, and she'll regard Mr. Towel as her friend. To play: Cover your bird with the towel, then flip it off and say "Peek-a-boo" in an animated voice. And repeat. Birds love to play and will soon look forward to this game. And when she enjoys the interaction, she won't mind so much being restrained by Mr. Towel from time to time.

Practicing Good Grooming

A healthy bird will do a good job of keeping her feathers in fine shape by preening them frequently — pulling them through her beak to distribute oils and keep everything neatly aligned. As accomplished as they are, though, pet birds need human help with other necessary grooming tasks.

Trimming nails

In the wild, birds keep their nail tips blunted by perching on a wide variety of surfaces, some of them quite rough. Few pet birds have such a variety of perching opportunities, so regular pedicures become the owner's responsibility.

You can use either of two techniques in keeping nails short, and which one you choose depends on your personal preference and what your bird deals with best.

The tried-and-true method involves cutting the nails. You can use a human nail trimmer for the task if your bird is small, or the scissors- or guillotine-type tool made for trimming dog nails. Before you start, make sure you also have a supply of *styptic powder,* available at pet stores, to stop bleeding just in case you nick the vein inside the nail.

With your bird restrained, position the cutter to nip off the tip of the nail. Don't go farther back than the tip at first; you can always clip off more later, in tiny increments. If you draw blood, press the powder into the end of the nail until the blood coagulates.

Some bird-owners manage nail trims without any restraint at all. Instead of making a big hairy deal out of the process, they clip one nail a night for a week every month (well, eight days actually, a day for each nail). You can trim while playing or watching TV with your bird. A quick clip, and back to the fun and games.

The other method of nail trimming involves the use of a rotary grinding device, such as the electric Dremmel tool sold for woodworking and other craft work. The rechargeable version is lightweight and quiet and works well for this purpose.

Grinding nails is a two-person job, though. One person restrains the bird, while the other grinds off the nail tip. (Use a medium-coarse head on the tool.)

To extend the time between nail trims and improve your bird's foot health and emotional outlook, provide a wide variety of perches for him. Make one a cement perch, with its great texture for wearing down nails. (Skip those sandpaper-covered perches, though.) For more on perches, see Chapter 4.

The proper length of your bird's nails depends on the size of your bird — larger birds generally need longer nails. One way to get a handle on nail trims is to have your veterinarian or a bird groomer trim the nails the first couple of times; you can then see the correct length for your pet.

Clipping wings

Before you set out on a dreadful guilt trip, understand one Very Important Point: It's perfectly normal to feel ambivalent about wing-clipping. After all, if you could fly, you wouldn't want someone taking away your ability to soar, would you? Certainly not, but to allow your pet bird flight is to put his life at risk.

The hands-off caged birds such as canaries and other finches don't need to have their wings trimmed — they get their exercise flitting about their cage. Any of the more social birds must be kept trimmed, however.

Flighted birds can escape (see the nearby sidebar), and they get injured in more ways than you can imagine (and Brian has seen more unfortunate examples than he could imagine). Birds fly into windows, pots of boiling water, ceiling fans . . . the list goes on and on.

When we choose to bring birds into our homes, we must take responsibility for protecting them from the hazards of our lives. And that usually means keeping their wings trimmed.

We suggest you observe your veterinarian or bird groomer handling the wing-clip a few times before you try it yourself. Some people always have a professional handle the wing trims, and that's fine, too.

A proper wing trim allows a bird to exercise his wing-flapping muscles, the *pectorals,* which is especially important in young, developing birds. A good trim also gives a bird some coasting ability, so he doesn't fall like a rock when attempting to fly. Birds with no flight ability can injure themselves badly, from beak-tip and chest damage to tail-base, cloacal/vent, and wing-tip damage. Excessively short wing trims can also create psychological issues in your pet — it's scary to think you'll fall like a rock! Properly trimmed, your bird should have no ability to gain altitude, but he should be able to fly horizontally to a safe, easy landing.

With your bird restrained in a towel, pull the wing out and look at the primary flight feathers, the last ten — and longest — feathers on the wing. Using sharp scissors, take the ends off the outer six or seven, as indicated by the dotted line in the inset of Figure 7-2. Don't get carried away — you can always trim the feathers more, but you can't put feathers back on! As long as you're not cutting *blood,* or *pin*, feathers (see our sidebar, "The feathers that bleed"), you're not hurting your bird.

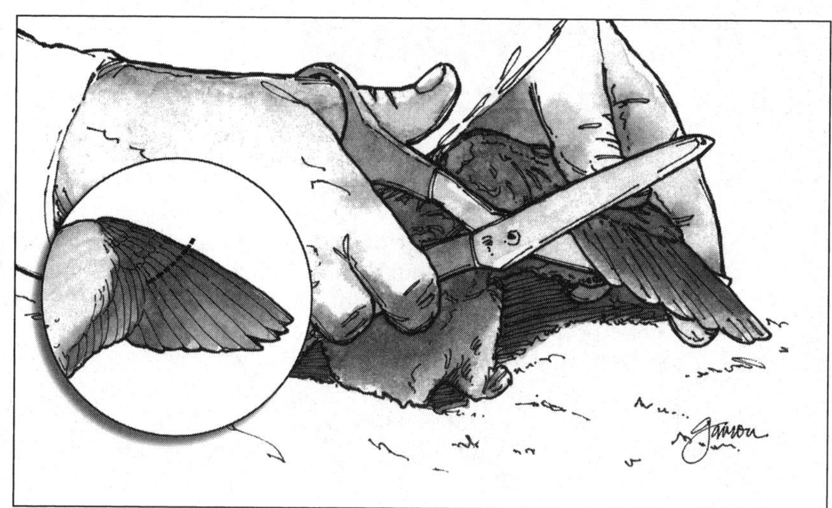

Figure 7-2: Clipping the flight feathers at the end of your bird's wings keeps him safely grounded.

The feathers that bleed

Blood feathers, or *pin feathers,* are new feathers that are starting to grow out, covered with their waxy sheaths, and very well endowed with blood supply for growth. If one of these feathers gets accidentally broken, it usually clots on its own, and that's all there is to that.

Sometimes, though, these feathers may be continually re-injured, causing a recurrence of bleeding, but these scenarios are comparatively less common than simple clotting. A broken pin feather is usually not a life-threatening emergency in an otherwise healthy bird, contrary to popular opinion. Many birds with internal health problems — usually involving the liver — may have some clotting problems, and these birds may be more predisposed to bleeding problems.

Blood feathers are sensitive and seem to itch as they develop, so many birds love to have their incoming feathers scratched or preened by their owners. However, your pet may jump or complain if you kink or hurt one of these pin feathers.

Some people prefer to leave the outermost two or three feathers untrimmed for the sake of appearance and clip the rest of the primary flight feathers. Although this clip may look better, the feathers that remain may be enough to give your bird all the lift she needs to get into trouble, especially if she's a lightweight, such as a cockatiel.

Get in the habit of examining your bird's feathers monthly, clipping any that need it. It's a good idea to mark "Wing Check Day" on the calendar so you don't forget.

Raining down with showers, baths, and misting

Birds like to get wet. Water makes them feel good and stimulates normal preening behavior. And if you compare our homes' dry atmospheres to the moist environs of many birds' rainforest habitats, you can imagine how lovely a nice spritz feels.

You may think that dampening your bird isn't necessary if you live in a humid or rainy place. Remember, though, that it's not the outside environment your bird's dealing with — it's the environment inside your house. Central heat and air conditioning remove moisture from the air, and the indoor environment can be as dry as a desert, especially in winter.

Probably the easiest way to dampen your bird is to use a squirt bottle set to "mist," not "spray." If your bird doesn't like being misted directly, spray up so the water fails like rain.

Some people shower with their pets, and that's fine, too, as is temporarily adding a shallow bathing dish with an inch or so of water to the cage of the hands-off birds, such as canaries and other finches.

A warning for men only. If you choose to shower with your bird, be sure your pet has a secure perch to stand on. Trust us, you don't want your bird to be choosing his own perches when you're naked.

Although your bird won't "catch cold" if he's wet, avoid misting if your pet isn't in good health, because it can add to his stress level and detract from needed energy to deal with his illness.

No rules exist for how often to mist, shower, or bath your bird. Some birds are misted daily and enjoy it immensely, while others are hardly ever dampened and do just fine. Follow your bird's lead.

Escape! What to do if your bird gets loose

Wings are clipped for safety in the home, but they also need to be kept trimmed to prevent an all-too-often disaster — the fly-away bird. Birds are lost every day by people who didn't think twice about opening a window on a fine spring day or who were caught by surprise at just how fast a bird can make it though an open door.

The time to prepare for such a tragedy is before it happens. In addition to keeping wings trimmed, make sure your bird has identification — a leg band, a microchip, or both. Take pictures of your bird and note any unique identifying features. Identification can help reunite you with your bird if someone finds him or help you prove he's yours if the finder is reluctant to give him up, because of real or perceived value or because the finder found your pet as charming as you do. (For inexplicable reasons, people who wouldn't dream of keeping a dog that clearly belongs to someone else have a "finders keepers" attitude when it comes to birds!)

If your bird escapes, immediately put his cage out in the yard with the door open and a big bowl of his favorite foods on top. Once the thrill of being out a day or two wears off, your bird may decide his cage and food dish isn't so boring after all. Keep an eye on the cage to reclaim your wanderer if he reappears.

Let people know you've lost your bird. Make flyers with your bird's picture and post them throughout your neighborhood. Don't forget to leave some with nearby veterinarians and with avian veterinarians, pet shops, and shelters in the region. Take out a classified ad in your local newspaper and post information about your bird on Web sites, such as `www.birdhotline.com`, which has more than 1,000 volunteers signed up to spot loose pet birds worldwide.

Don't give up! Although many birds who are reunited with their owners are gone only a couple of days, some birds have been found after months "on the wing."

Adding a tablespoon of human-grade drinkable aloe vera juice (available in health food stores) to an 8-ounce spray bottle can help an itchy bird. Another old trick: Try adding regular Listerine to bring out the gloss in feathers — a tablespoon in the spray bottle is plenty.

Should you blow-dry your pet? That depends on whether your bird likes the warm rush of air — some really do. If yours doesn't enjoy the sensation, skip it. If you do use a blow-dryer, though, set it on low and don't concentrate the flow on any one spot for more than a split second so you don't risk burning your bird.

Some birds absolutely don't like getting wet, and if yours is among them — or if you're struggling with low humidity in your home — a humidifier is a good investment in your bird's comfort. Another option is to set up a "shower cage" in a sheltered area outside and provide an automatic mister (like those you see at the vegetable counter at the grocery store) that delivers a fine mist periodically as your bird enjoys the sights and sounds of the outdoors. Make sure your bird is supervised constantly so you can intervene if any predator decides to visit.

Bird Care When You Can't

Before you know it, you and your new pet will be like lovebirds, totally infatuated, one with the other and vice versa. You quickly become comfortable in a routine that suits you both. Don't get too comfortable, though, because now is the time to plan for those occasions when you can't be with your pet — when you're called away on business or enjoying a vacation. You may be able to take your pet with you, but make sure you consider what's best for you and your pet.

Pet-sitters

The general title of *pet-sitter* encompasses a wide range of services, everything from a reciprocal agreement between friends to care for each other's pets to paying a neighbor kid to look in or even house-sit to hiring a professional pet-sitting service.

The benefits of having your pet stay in your own home is that he's familiar with the surroundings, which is a very important consideration where birds are concerned. And pet-sitters can do more than just look in on your pet: They can take in your mail and newspaper, water your houseplants, and turn lights on and off. The best ones are lifesavers and practically become family members.

Make sure that you discuss services and prices beforehand, and, if you're dealing with a service, make sure that the business is bonded and insured.

The biggest drawback to pet-sitters is that your pet is left alone a great deal of the time, because most pet-sitters probably can't spend their days or nights giving your pet individual attention. They drop in once or twice a day, make sure everything's in order, and move on to their next client. An arrangement with a young person (especially when school's out) or a house-sitter to stay in your home while you're gone may give your pet more opportunities for companionship. If your pet becomes ill or manages to escape, a pet-sitter may not come back to notice before some time has passed. And, finally, some people just aren't comfortable allowing people access to their homes while they're gone.

Informal arrangements for house-sitting (actually having the person move in while you're gone) or pet-sitting (having the person just drop in once or twice a day to check on your pet) can be even trickier than hiring a professional service. Just ask the friend of Gina's who left her house and pets in the care of a friend's college-age daughter, only to find out that the young woman had been anything but a quiet resident. She hosted guests and even a wild party. The house was a bit worse for wear, but at least the pets were fine. If you're going to go with a young person — and many people do, with no regrets — make sure that parental oversight is part of the picture.

We think that one of the better approaches to reliable pet care is to *trade* pet-sitting. Most animal lovers have friends who also have pets, and making a deal with one of your friends to cover each other whenever you're gone can work out very well. Trading care is a solution that's both reassuring — if you have friends who love animals as much as you do, that is — and inexpensive. All the arrangement requires is your own time in return.

No matter who cares for your bird, make sure they are comfortable with handling your pet, and that your pet is likewise comfortable with the pet-sitter. Some people who may be perfectly happy around dogs or cats may find birds intimidating, especially the big parrots.

Boarding

Boarding isn't as popular an option for birds as it is for dogs or even cats. Birds are happier in familiar surroundings, and putting your pet in the company of strange birds may expose him to heaven-knows-what diseases.

Some veterinarians offer bird boarding, and so, too, do some bird shops. These services are worth checking into, especially if you're already familiar with the provider — for example, if the veterinarian is your own, or if you know the shop is a reputable one, perhaps because it's where you bought your bird. Most boarding facilities control the amount of exposure birds have with one another, and they have requirements regarding the health of the birds they accept as guests. A facility with health requirements prior to entry is better than one that welcomes any and all birds.

Don't leave any boarding decisions to the last minute, if you can possibly avoid it. Check out your choices in advance: See the premises, talk to the staff. You can sense the quality of the overall operation. If you don't feel confident and comfortable with the surroundings, don't leave your bird, under any circumstances.

Can your bird go with you?

While canaries and other finches are often best left at home, other birds may enjoy accompanying you on trips or to work (if you can have your pet at work). The gregarious Amazons may especially relish the chance to show off for strangers, but any healthy parrot — from budgies to macaws — can warm to travel in time.

Make sure your bird has a secure carrier with a perch — see Chapter 4 for more details on choosing your travel cage — and be particularly mindful of where you open the carrier door to help prevent escapes. Pay careful attention to wing trims, and remember always that even a trimmed bird can sometimes gain enough loft to escape.

Home-alone bird

Few of us are able (or willing) to stay home with our pets all the time. Fortunately, birds are quite capable of entertaining themselves while you're off earning the bird food.

When you're away for a few hours, your bird should be left in his cage, of course, but make sure to keep toys rotating through for variety, and leave some music on. Gina's bird seems especially fond of bluegrass music, for some reason, especially the CD with her late friend Rick Abrams and the Piney Creek Weasels. Rick was a world-champion claw-hammer banjo player, so she knows her Senegal has good taste!

Although it's fine to leave your bird while you're at work, it's *not* okay to leave him alone while you skip out for a few days. How would you like to be left with food growing more stale by the minute, water forming a skin (or worse, if your bird poops in the water dish), and a toilet you can't flush?

Alone overnight is probably fine, but anything more than that, arrange for boarding or call a pet-sitter.

Many manufacturers offer harnesses and light leashes for birds, and if you're going to be out and about with your pet, we recommend you look into these accessories. Also be certain that your bird has an ID, in the form of a microchip, leg band, or both. For more on microchips, leg bands, carriers, and harnesses, see Chapter 4.

You can even fly with your bird! Although some airlines allow no pets at all, those that do usually let you bring small pets into the cabin, a much better deal than putting your bird in the cargo area. In any case, you need an airline-approved carrier; if it fits under the seat, you'll be able to board with your bird. Each airline has slightly different rules for pets — some limit the number of animals in the cabin, for example — so call well in advance to make arrangements.

Part III

Keeping Your Bird Healthy

"It's Feathers; I think she's taking steroids."

In this part . . .

Bird health was a mystery even to veterinarians not all that long ago, but things are changing — and fast. In this part, we tell you how your bird functions, what's normal, and what's not. Finding and working with an experienced avian veterinarian is essential to keeping your pet bird healthy, and we tell you not only how to find one, but how to team up with your veterinarian to the best advantage of your pet and your pocketbook. We cover emergency care, too, along with guidelines for when to see your veterinarian immediately, what can wait, and what you needn't worry about. With all the good new information available, more birds are living longer lives — and we tell you how to deal with the special needs of the senior set. When it comes time to say good-bye, we help you through that difficult time, too.

Chapter 8

How Birds Work: The Short Course

In This Chapter

- Understanding the drive behind the design
- Looking at the outer bird
- Making sense of the senses
- Figuring out what's going on inside

When you think about what's unique to birds, chances are you think of their ability to fly. Okay, so maybe some birds don't fly anymore — by design, such as the ostrich and emu, or by human interference, such as with the clipped wings of pet birds. But the goal of flight is still the basic blueprint of every bird born, and the evolutionary choices made to achieve it have dictated the form of the birds you see today, both your pets and the birds you see in the wild.

Don't count the penguin on the list of flightless birds. Although it's true the adorable tuxedo-clad birds can't become airborne, they fly through the water in much the same way as their relatives fly through the air.

What flying demands in real terms is *lightness.* Every detail of a bird must be strong enough to do the job and light enough to allow flight. Flight, after all, is more than a nifty way of getting around: It's the ultimate survival skill for birds, many of which are looked on as tasty hors d'oeuvres by their predatory neighbors. Flying allows for a hasty escape from trouble, and it's a way to easily go where the food supply and climate are more conducive to comfortable living. Would you give up your teeth and a few bones to fly? We would, in a flash.

The change didn't happen that quickly for birds, of course. In 1861, workers splitting slate in a Bavarian quarry came across a fossil that proved the link between reptiles and birds. Named Archeopteryx, the Jurassic-period creature was decidedly reptilian, with teeth, a long tail, and hands with fingers. But outlined in the slate were structures that foretold of the beautiful birds that would eventually fill countless environmental niches around the world: Archeopteryx had feathers!

More than 150 million years ago, an animal that would become the modern-day bird already demonstrated one of the basic facts of avian survival: A bird's gotta fly, because he doesn't want to become someone else's dinner. The flip side is true for predatory birds, such as eagles, owls, and hawks — without flight, they can't hunt. Understand these basic requirements, and you're already halfway to understanding why your bird's put together as he is and what makes him tick. For the other half — read on!

Check out our color section in the center of this book for a visual representation of the bird. You'll never say *nostril* instead of *nare* again!

The Outside: More than Just Beautiful

To see a macaw in flight is to admire a model of aerodynamics. Embodying one clean, straight, and colorful line from his beak to an elegantly long tail, the macaw, like all flighted birds, has a design that early would-be aviators, from Leonardo da Vinci on, couldn't help but admire and emulate. Look at any plane from the earliest fabric-covered creations to the *Spirit of St. Louis,* from the latest jet off the assembly line to the space shuttle, and you can still see where the designers got their inspiration.

We may think we've conquered the air, with an estimated 60,000 people airborne at any given time, but we've still got nothing on the bird. Make reservations? Struggle through crowded airports? Sit in unbearably close proximity to people you wouldn't get within a half-mile of in circumstances of your own choosing? That's *flying?* Ha! In numbers uncountable, birds still rule the skies, and will continue to, until we mere humans can spread our own strong, feather-lined wings and be among the treetops with just a few powerful flaps.

All birds, from the tiny vervian hummingbird (2.4 grams/0.08 ounces in weight) to the imposing but not overly bright ostrich (125 kilograms/275 pounds), belong to a taxonomic class scientists call *Aves.* We honor the bird every time we use the words we've chosen to represent our own efforts at flight: *aviation, aviator, avionics.*

Although every feature of the bird has to be compatible with flight, the way these features have developed is pretty interesting, from beaks to toes.

Built for versatility: The beak

The beak of a bird is a tool with many features. It's a weapon that can put a serious dent in any enemy and damage the relationship with a friend. It can be a delicate tool for feeding a newly hatched chick in the nest or for grooming and adjusting a bird's feathers so that they are "just right." With their beaks, some birds can pick a lock, crush a walnut, or peel the skin off a grape.

At its most basic, the beak on our parrot pets consists of two hard structures, the upper and lower *mandibles,* and an amazingly agile and strong tongue.

A bird's beak is quite the anatomical marvel — and it's also the reason you should know how to restrain your bird comfortably and properly, in case you need to (unless you like being bitten). Check out Chapter 7 for tips on when and how to restrain your bird, either by hand or with the aid of a towel.

A tool for all seasons

Beak shapes and sizes vary widely, depending mostly on the kind of food a certain species eats. The short, straight bill of canaries and other finches is ideal for plucking out seeds, grubs, and other edibles. Birds of the parrot family, including budgies, cockatiels, and the larger parrots, are known as *hookbills* because of the shape and function of their beaks.

The beaks of most parrots are remarkably well-designed for one of their most important tasks: cracking, crushing, prying, or otherwise destroying the protective coatings around many of the foods they like to eat. Like everything else on a creature designed for flight, the beak is surprisingly lightweight considering its strength — a hard shell of constantly growing material (keratin) similar to that found on antlers, over a hollow bony structure. (If the beak were made of solid bone, the weight would probably force a bird to spend his life on the ground, and on his nose!)

Lightweight it may be, but the hookbill's beak is also very strong. Although you would need a hammer or nutcracker to get through hard shells to the nut meat, a bird needs only his ridged beak — and perhaps a foot to hold the nut. With smaller seeds as well as the larger nuts, it's a hand-free operation: Rotate the seed with the tongue to find the seam, apply pressure to crack it at this weak spot, and then rotate it again to slide the meat from the now-helpless pod.

A parrot has such strength in his beak that owners are often surprised to see even the bars of a metal cage fall victim to a chewing bird. Birds have been known to pick off the welds holding bars together (and get lead or zinc poisoning as a result) and even snap the bars themselves. That's why it's so important to choose the best cage you can, one appropriate for the size and strength of your bird. For tips on choosing a safe cage, see Chapter 4.

Parrots also use their beaks as a third foot — they climb with their beaks. You need to remember the third-foot function if your bird grasps your finger with his beak when stepping up onto your hand. Chances are he's not biting — he's climbing. You'll know when he's biting! Baby birds do more *beaking* than older ones. Beaking is the bird equivalent of a human toddler wanting to touch and put everything in his mouth.

Getting bitten is a daily risk or potential fact of life for an avian veterinarian, who handles unfamiliar birds constantly. Fear of bites may be why some veterinarians insist on towel-restraints for every bird before examination, which is the equivalent in many ways to muzzling every dog or cat who comes in. Other arguments for the use of towels for restraint during the physical examination are to help control the bird better and to provide less risk to the bird, as well as to the examiner in some settings.

This approach, however, is not necessarily fair for all birds, and it certainly can lessen a veterinarian's ability to observe the bird. Brian prefers to give each bird the benefit of the doubt, and he assesses the temperament of each patient before reaching for a towel. Tough characters reveal themselves pretty quickly and can be dealt with accordingly. Brian has been bitten plenty of times — it goes with the territory — but not as often as you may imagine. He watches the body language — we've put the basics in Chapter 7 — and offers the back of his hand instead of his finger, to lessen any damage that may occur.

Is your bird's beak healthy?

Although beaks are constantly growing at a rate of 1 to 3 inches per year, depending on the species, the beak of a normal pet bird does not need to be trimmed. Your bird keeps her beak at the proper length through her normal chewing activities. (Chewing is essential both for physical and emotional health of the typical parrot.)

Overgrowth of the beak is frequently a sign of illness, such as liver disease or malnutrition. In many situations, there may be a *malocclusion,* or misalignment of the upper and lower mandibles, not allowing normal wear to occur — and resulting in beak overgrowth. Contrary to what some bird books still preach, don't accept beak trims as a routine healthcare measure — they're not. A bird who gets routine beak trims instead of proper medical attention may get an attractive beak, but the bird is likely to die of the primary disease that is causing the abnormal growth of the beak in the first place. Many of these malocclusions, nutritional issues, or liver problems can be corrected if diagnosed and addressed early and accurately.

Strong as they are, beaks sometimes break. Common causes of beak fractures include fighting between birds of different sizes (with the smaller one usually getting the worst of it) and excessively short wing trims that offer no gliding ability so a falling bird lands hard on his beak (or on his fanny, which can also be injured). In some species, such as the cockatoos, *mate aggression* is unfortunately a fairly common and unpleasant event — with the males beating up on their mates, often tearing off their beaks or severely injuring them.

For optimum beak health, provide your pet bird with lots of things to chew on. Even finches and canaries will often have better beak health if you provide *cuttlebone* (the shell of *cuttlefishes,* a type of mollusk) or another hard material to work with their beaks in their cage. If you see a beak problem, don't try to deal with it on your own. Your bird probably needs the help of an experienced avian veterinarian to properly diagnose and treat any problem.

Say "ahhhhhh"

A pretty obvious anatomical difference between humans and birds is apparent when a bird opens her mouth — she doesn't have any teeth. The experts believe teeth were sacrificed on the altar of flight, just another piece of excess baggage whose function could be managed another way. The cutting, grinding, and tearing abilities were taken up by the bird's hard beak, and some of the digestive functions by the *crop,* a space at the base of the neck that expands to allow for food storage. (Heavy-duty grinding happens a little farther along, in the *gizzard.*)

Right in the middle of the mouth is an organ that we can recognize, because we have one, too — the tongue. Like our own, a bird's tongue is a model of dexterity and sensitivity, but a few differences exist.

The tongue of most pet birds — the hookbill species — is dry and muscular, made even stronger and more useful by an assembly of supportive bones — yes, bones! — running the length of the organ. The color varies depending on the species: It's black in some, pink in some, or a combination of colors in still others.

At the back and base of the tongue, just below the food canal, or *esophagus,* is the *glottis,* or air passage, the first step on the road to the lungs. At the roof of the mouth is the *choanal slit,* which connects to the nasal cavities. By elevating the base of the tongue and glottis to the choanal slit, a bird can effectively close off the opening of the esophagus and pass air directly from the nares (nostrils), through the choana, through the glottis, and directly into the trachea. When food or water is being swallowed, the glottis closes reflexively at the same time the tongue drops to the floor of the mouth, preventing accidental inhalation of food or water into the windpipe, and opening up the esophagus for food to pass through. A bird can breathe through an open mouth, too, by simply opening his mouth and his glottis, and inhaling.

The closeness of the glottis, esophagus, and choanal slit can sometimes be a real challenge to those just learning to hand-feed baby birds — they can inadvertently get the food down the wrong "pipe," with potentially disastrous results. For tips on feeding babies and other bird-breeding challenges, see Chapter 13.

At one time, birds were thought to have only a primitive sense of taste, but that view has changed. Birds are sensitive to the same tastes we are: sweet, salty, sour, and bitter. Sensitivity varies by species, and, as any bird-owner will vouch, some birds show a sweet tooth that rivals any human's.

In most birds, the taste buds are located at the tip of the tongue. Ducks, however, carry some of their taste buds in their beaks, more commonly called a *bill.*

A bird's eye view

Birds have a great sense of vision, as you may imagine for any creature who needs to be able to see what's safe to land on, find what may be good to eat, or spot a predator before it's too late.

Birds can and do see in color, and they have vision that's good in both the close-up and long-distance categories.

How do we know what birds see? Part of the answer is simple deduction, Watson. What good would all those vibrant feather colors be if birds couldn't see them? Some experts insist that birds see even more colors than we do, which may explain why mating continues unhindered in species in which we can't see any difference between male and female — what looks the same to us may not look the same to birds. Good color vision may even be helpful when it comes to finding food. The ability to see some ultraviolet wavelengths allows birds to pick out fruits and flowers, which reflect this light better than do the surrounding leaves.

The eyes in most birds are positioned on either side of the head, not side-by-side as in humans, dogs, or cats. Although this means birds haven't as much range of *binocular vision* — objects seen simultaneously with both eyes — their range of monocular vision approaches 360 degrees — and full monocular vision can be achieved with a simple twist of the neck. The owl, on the other hand, has his eyes positioned more in the front of the head — allowing for better binocular vision and accuracy for successful hunting — but also making it more important to really turn the head around in order to see the full 360-degree spectrum. And, no, they can't turn their heads around all the way!

When a bird wants to get a really good look at something, he cocks his head and focuses one of his eyes. In some birds, the eyes can move independently of each other — most clearly seen in toucans, but also in parrots, to a lesser degree.

Like dogs and cats, birds have a third eyelid, a semitransparent sheet that helps to protect the eye and keep it moist — it's even thought to function as a "windshield" while birds are in flight. Another interesting avian feature is the bird's ability to voluntarily adjust the size of her pupils, usually in a moment of excitement, in a display called *pinning* or *flashing.*

The better to ear you with

You can't see the ears on your bird — birds have no external ear, as humans do — but they certainly do have ears, and they work very well. Protected by a soft swirl of feathers, the avian ear, like the human one, has three sections: outer, middle, and inner.

The outer ear is a short funnel that directs sound toward the eardrum. The middle ear is where sound vibrations are picked up, amplified, and transmitted to the inner ear. The inner ear transmits the impulses to the brain for decoding and also handles balance, with the aid of semicircular canals.

All birds don't hear high- and low-pitched noises as well as we do, but within the range they do hear, they are able to discern more details. The song of a finch would have to be played ten times more slowly for us to be able to hear the richness and detail of sound a bird can.

Many parrots, especially cockatoos, cockatiels, macaws, and the African parrot species, love to have the area around their ear canal scratched. Most also flip for a scratching of their soft facial areas and their armpits, too. (Or should we call them *wingpits*?)

Beautiful, functional feathers

The crowning glory of any bird — and a contributor to extinction for a few species — are the feathers. These gloriously modified reptilian scales protect birds from the elements, keep them warm, attract mates, help put on impressive displays of territoriality, and, in most species, make flight possible.

It's hard to say which of these unique avian characteristics we, as humans, have appreciated more — flight or beauty. Every single feather is the embodiment of both, which is perhaps why humankind has coveted, collected, and worn feathers for as long as birds have had them.

Although less-technological cultures may have made do with found feathers or feathers from the birds used for food, in the last couple of centuries society raised the pursuit of feathers to a brutal level, killing birds by the millions so ladies could have decorative feathers on their hats.

Fashionable feathers were big business at the turn of the century. We found one vintage advertisement for a Southern California farm selling ostrich plumes for $2 to $5. By comparison, for only two cents the farm would send you a souvenir brochure. Incidentally, the molted feathers of ostriches and parrots still find buyers, who use them in crafts and artwork. And the price is about the same as, or even a little less than, it was 90 years ago. Native Americans still covet the feathers of many birds, including those of birds of prey and macaws, for use in their fans, dances, and other cultural events.

Variety

The feather is one of nature's most stupendous feats of engineering. Not only are feathers strong and lightweight, but they are also constantly being replaced. Imagine a modern aircraft with an automatic maintenance and part-replacement system — that's the only way to fully appreciate the seemingly effortless cycle of replacing worn or damaged feathers with new ones. Quite an incredible system, isn't it?

Although feathers vary from species to species — compare the feathers of a penguin with the plumes of an ostrich to see how much — the birds we keep as pets have three basic feather types (see Figure 8-1). They are

- **Down feathers:** The soft, short down feathers, usually closest to a bird's skin, serve to keep the bird warm. Down feathers are the first feathers a baby bird has, and they keep him warm as he grows. That down feathers keep birds warm should come as no surprise: Humans have used the down feathers of birds, especially geese, in any number of stay-warm products, from comforters to jackets. On some species, a few of the down feathers are made to crumble: These *powderdown* feathers break into fine dust to aid in the bird's grooming.
- **Contour feathers:** These feathers have down "puffs" at their base and are stiffer toward the end. Contour feathers cover most of the body, including the down feathers. Dr. T. J. Lafeber, a pioneering avian veterinarian, describes the relationship of the down feathers to the contours as similar to a lined windbreaker: The down feathers keep warmth in, while the contours keep wind and rain at bay.

  Unlike the fur of mammals, which grows pretty evenly over the entire body, contour feathers are arranged in tracts, called *pterylae.* Between these tracts are areas of bare skin called *apteria.*
- **Flight feathers:** The longest and stiffest feathers are those used for flight, and they are found both on the wings (where they are called *remiges*) and on the tail *(rectrices).* The flight feathers are really modified contour feathers — specifically evolved to get the bird up into the air and help keep him there. These feathers have little or no down at the base, and the wing feathers are shaped unevenly, with longer crosspieces, called *barbs,* on the backward edge, called the *inner vane.* (The forward-facing side is called the *outer vane.*) The tail feathers, for the most part, have even lengths of their barbs on the right or left side of the vane. If you look at a flight feather closely, you'll notice threads (called *barbules*) protruding from the barbs. On each barb, the barbules on the upper edge have *hooklets,* and the ones on the lower edge have ridges for catching the hooklets. The result is a strong, smooth, interwoven surface perfect for supporting flight.

A feather may contain up to a million tiny barbules. When you watch your bird grooming his feathers, you see him rearranging the location of the feather as well as pulling the feathers through his beak gently, to help relock hooklets that may have popped loose — kind of like Velcro that came unattached and that needs attention.

Figure 8-1: Different feathers have different jobs: Some provide insulation, while others provide protection or the ability to fly.

The number of flight feathers a bird has depends on the species, as does the number and shape of the tail feathers. A macaw, for example, has 22 flight feathers on each wing (10 primary, as counted from the end of the wing inward, and 12 secondary), along with an even dozen long tail feathers. Compare those long feathers with the short, square tail of the African grey, which would be nearly obscured when his wings are folded if it weren't for the bright red color contrasting with the gray plumage of the rest of the bird.

Maintenance

The gift of flight doesn't come without a price, and for birds that means a large part of their time is spent keeping feathers in fine shape, a behavior called *preening.* Birds are so dedicated to keeping every one of the couple of thousand feathers they have in good order that they make even the neatest human seem like a slob by comparison. Preening is such a large part of a bird's life that it's even part of their socializing — when they're done with their own feathers, they work on those of their mates, often in a most loving fashion.

Birds use their beaks to tend their feathers, but they also get help from an oil gland, called the *preen gland,* and from a specialized feather called a *wick feather,* which helps bring out the gland's oils to an accessible location for grooming and preening purposes. The preen gland is located at the base of the tail in most birds but is absent in the hyacinth macaw and the Amazon parrots. The grooming and preening behavior produces powder and dust, too — as they groom and preen their powderdown feathers, the ends of those feathers crumble into chalk-like white powder, which is distributed over the body. The *powderdown* feathers are typically located on the flanks and over the hips of most birds. The oils from the preen gland and the powder produced from the down feathers help to keep all of the bird's feathers well-groomed and clean.

Birds from the more arid environments — such as some parts of Africa and central Australia — are "dustier" than rain forest birds such as the Amazons, conures, and macaws. Some cockatoos are so dusty that snuggling them for a couple of minutes against your chest can turn a dark shirt nearly white with powder residue. This fine dust is the reason people with allergies (especially to feather dust and dander) or asthma may be wise to think twice about acquiring these species as household residents.

Finally, it's not enough to merely go over every feather individually — it's also important that each feather be nudged into its proper place, to ensure the smooth lines needed for flight.

No matter how fastidiously a bird cares for his feathers, they do eventually become worn or damaged. The bird's body then switches into replacement mode, and the damaged feathers drop, or *molt.* Molting happens typically once or twice a year, generally in the spring and fall, when the rapid lengthening or shortening of the days triggers the change.

The words "sitting duck" apply perfectly to a bird who has lost all his flight feathers at once — which is why nature doesn't work it that way. Flight feathers are usually molted only one or two at a time. Feathers are even molted in many species symmetrically; that is, the same one or two flight feathers that are missing on one wing will be missing on the other, to keep the bird on an even keel when flying. You can often see this when you look up at a turkey vulture flying overhead. Pretty nifty design, if you ask us!

Feather-picking, a bird's destruction of his own feathers, isn't a disease, but a symptom. This vexing problem could be caused by poor health or diet, or by stress or other psychological triggers. For the latest on feather-picking, see Chapter 12.

Up, up, and away

Birds are able to fly for the same reason planes do, and that should come as no surprise, since plane designers have always drawn inspiration from birds. Wings are shaped in what's called an *airfoil,* with the surface more curved on the top edge than the bottom. Air flows faster over the top than under the bottom, and the difference is what creates *lift* and draws the wings (and the bird or plane) upward. By adjusting their wings as planes adjust wing flaps, birds are able to control the amount of lift, and so move higher or lower as they need to.

A leg to stand on, times two

As magnificent a gift as flight is, it's kinda easy to overlook the interesting and well-developed structures supporting a grounded bird — legs and feet. And that's a mistake, because those limbs and their appendages are especially interesting and useful in many birds.

Members of the parrot family — and that includes both the tiniest budgie or parrotlet and the largest macaws — have not one but two pairs of opposable toes, a setup called *zygodactyl.* Bird toes are numbered from the inner to outer, and parrots have numbers 1 and 4 pointing backwards, and numbers 2 and 3 pointing forward. This design is ideal for climbing and grasping, allowing parrots use their feet like a hand. Because so much is made of the opposable thumb of our species, maybe we should be wondering why such smart birds as the zygodactyl parrots aren't making pets out of us! (Truthfully, this does seem to occur in many households, where the parrot truly has successfully "trained" his owner exactly how, when, where, and why to obey his every desire.)

Canaries and other finches have a foot designed strictly for perching and walking. Called a *anisodactyl* foot, their number 1 toe is pointed backward, with the other three pointing forward.

With no feathers on their feet, wouldn't birds like a nice pair of slippers? Not really, because they would interfere with another of the many functions of the feet — temperature control. In cold weather, birds decrease the amount of blood circulation to their legs and feet to preserve body heat. In warm weather, they increase blood circulation to their feet and legs (and beaks, too), making them feel quite warm to our touch and allowing the excess heat to be released. The body temperature of most birds ranges from 103 degrees F to as high as 105 degrees F or more — so it's not surprising that the beak and feet of our birds feel hot or warm to us from time to time.

The nails of pet birds are more like a dog's than a cat's — designed for traction and gripping, not for defense.

Nails wear down naturally in the wild because of the variety of perches and high levels of activity — neither of which are part of most pet birds' lives. Concrete — not sandpaper-covered — perches help to blunt the nails of pet birds, but most still need to have nails shortened from time to time. For more on perches, see Chapter 4; nail-trimming details are in Chapter 7.

Finding Your Inner Bird

To the casual observer, the outer bird most clearly reflects changes made to enable flight — smooth lines, strong, lightweight feathers, and a beak to replace the heavy teeth of mammals. But inside, just as many adjustments have evolved to meet the unique demands of the avian lifestyle.

Them bones, them bones

Perhaps no part of the amazing creatures we call birds has adapted more rigidly to the demands of flight than the skeleton and the bones that form it. So restrictive are the anatomical requirements of flight that the structure of birds is pretty much the same, from the smallest flit-about finches to the largest flightless ostrich.

Strangely enough, it's that rigid adherence to the demands of flight that led to the diversity of birds — with flight, birds could (and did) end up everywhere, continents and isolated islands alike. And after they were there, they changed to better fit the niche in which they found themselves. Beaks show perhaps the greatest diversity, with each species adapting over time to develop a beak that made eating what was available easier. Some birds adapted to their new homes so much that they gave up flying entirely, such as the ostrich, emu, and cassowary, while the penguins adapted the movements of flight to swim through water. Fascinating bunch, the birds!

A tiny bit of history

The original design for birds came from the Archeopteryx, a reptile with teeth, a long tail, a short spinal column, hands at the end of the wings, and the feathers that would remain as standard issue on all the birds to follow. The creature already featured some skeletal developments — a wishbone on which to center wings and a foot for perching, with the opposable toe seen in many birds today, such as canaries and other finches.

Time improved on the design, with key changes that would reduce weight and increase maneuverability. Gone were the teeth, the tail, and the hand (although their skeletal reminders would remain). The age of the modern bird had begun.

Modern improvements

Two main skeletal improvements can be seen in the modern bird's bones — there are fewer of them, and they're lighter in weight.

The old song that goes, "The hip bone's connected to the thigh bone . . ." would have to be modified if you were singing it about birds. That's because in many places the bones aren't connected so much as fused together. Although the hip bone is still connected to the thigh bone of birds, you can find single bones where two or more bones once were in the legs, as well as in the spinal column and pelvis, producing new arrangements that had to be given new names.

One example of this fusing is in the legs, where the *tibia* (lower leg) bone has fused with the upper collection of ankle, or *tarsal,* bones. The name for the resulting assembly: the *tibiotarsus.* Farther down the leg, the lower layer of *tarsal* bones (two horizontal rows of bones in human ankles) have been fused with the *metatarsal,* producing the *tarsometatarsus.* The bird's ankle joint, tecnically, would be called the tibiotarsal-tarsometatarsal joint. Is that a mouthful, or what?

The fusing of some bones may have been just to decrease weight, but the combined bones of the spinal column have another purpose as well. Although the spine of the bird isn't as flexible as ours — you won't see birds bending at the waist to do lateral toe-touches — what they lost in movement they more than made up for in strength. Their modified shoulders and spine are perfect for withstanding the strains of flying.

The strength of the bird's skeleton is even more remarkable when you realize that many of the bones are air-filled, or *pneumatized.* This adaptation lightens the weight of the skeleton, increasing the mobility and flight potential of the bird — without sacrificing strength.

The skeletons of baby birds grow rapidly, another necessary adaptation in a creature that must become mobile quickly. A typical blue-and-gold macaw hatches weighing between 20 and 24 grams (less than an ounce), and in about ten weeks weighs in excess of 1,000 grams, or close to 2 pounds. This incredible increase in weight (a 50-fold growth) is supported in part because of the rapid growth of the skeleton. Talk about growing like a weed!

Live and breathe: The cardiopulmonary system

The breathing and circulatory system of the bird is another model of ultra-light efficiency — one so good at what it does that it can sometimes get a bird into trouble (more on that in a minute).

The respiratory tract starts with the nostrils, called *nares,* and sinus cavities, and proceeds deeper into the bird with the windpipe *(trachea),* lungs, and air sacs. Whereas human lungs have dead-end areas in the lungs for passing oxygen into the blood *(alveoli),* birds have evolved to allow a continual circuit of air flow through their respiratory tracts.

Birds have a four-chambered heart — very similar to the human heart — but it beats a heck of a lot faster, which is why taking a pulse isn't typically part of a bird's physical exam at the veterinarian's. The heart rate of birds can reach as high as 1,000 beats per minute, with the typical heart rate of the budgerigar at 675 beats per minute and the Amazon parrot at about 390 beats per minute. Their arterial blood pressure is also much higher than what we may wish for ourselves — two to four times the human norm. Compared to our own, the respiratory and circulatory systems of the bird are strong, efficient, and supercharged — and it's all an adaptation to allow for maximal absorption and delivery of oxygen to meet the demands of flight.

The mechanisms that allow birds to collect oxygen so efficiently can also put them at risk in the environments we put them in. Fumes from such common household products as nonstick cookware or cleaning supplies can kill the bird who inhales them — and death can come very quickly. For more on fumes and other household hazards, see Chapter 19.

Ya gotta eat: The gastrointestinal system

Like everything else having to do with the bird, the digestive system is lightweight, highly efficient, and designed for maximum mobility.

The first difference you notice is the lack of teeth. Birds don't have time to chew food, nor do they need the extra weight that teeth represent. They swallow their food rapidly, just in case danger requires a quick exit from the feeding site.

From the beak, the food moves down a tube called the *esophagus* and into an organ at the base of the throat called the *crop.* Crops are particularly obvious in babies that are being hand-fed (because they have fewer feathers to hide them and because crops are larger on baby birds than on adults, relatively speaking) or in birds that have really pigged out on a big meal.

The crop functions as a temporary storage organ, and also is the place where the initial phases of digestion begin. When your bird regurgitates food for you to share — because he loves you so — this is where the food comes from.

Not all birds have crops. Some of the ones who don't include the *ratites* (ostriches and emus), penguins, and gulls. All parrots, from budgies and cockatiels through macaws, have crops, as do canaries and other finches. However, the crop may not be so obvious on the small birds in the latter group.

The crop empties slowly, sending food to the stomach, or *proventriculus.* Right behind the proventriculus is the gizzard, or *ventriculus,* which does the grinding work teeth would do — if birds had them. The small and large intestines are where digestion is completed and nutrients are absorbed, in pretty much the same way as the human system works.

One long-lived myth is that birds need to be fed *grit* — particles of rock or minerals — to help their gizzards do the grinding. Not so! In fact, grit can cause problems in birds who ingest too much of it. For the nitty-gritty details, see Chapter 6.

Most birds prefer to eat a bit at a time, although some (like some people) would rather eat a ton at one sitting, or just eat all the time. (And yes, like people, birds get fat, as we discuss in Chapter 11.) A condor, on the other hand, will set down on a yummy carcass, gorge until he can barely fly, and may not eat again for a few days. The difference is that most birds have a constant supply of food, whereas scavengers like the condors have to eat when they can.

The end result of the digestive system is the part that bird-lovers like least — the elimination of waste, or droppings, which are released (as are eggs in female birds) from a single organ called the *cloaca,* or *vent.* (The cloaca is another example of design efficiency — why have two or three openings when one will do?)

Not surprisingly for a creature who needs to stay light, waste products are constantly dumped without regard to where they fall (as anyone familiar with seagulls will vouch). A bird's capacity varies according to size — a budgie may pass dozens of small droppings a day, whereas the largest birds hold it longer, producing larger droppings less frequently.

Their wild cousins may not care where or when the bombs fall, but pet birds can be rather choosy about where they go. Especially in the larger parrots (with their increased holding capacity), you can actually train them to go on command in a place of your choosing, such as in a wastebasket or on a paper plate. For training tips, see Chapter 7.

Bird droppings may look like a mixed-up mess to us, but they have three distinct components: feces (from the gastrointestinal tract), urine (clear liquid from the kidneys), and the white *urates* (concentrated uric acid from the kidneys), as shown in Figure 8-2. Birds can and do urinate without defecating and can defecate without urinating.

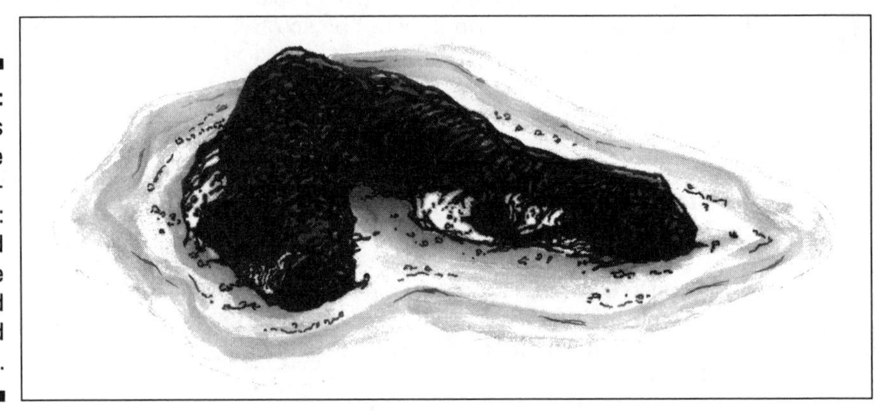

Figure 8-2: Droppings usually have three components: Dark, solid feces; white semisolid urates; and liquid urine.

Many times, what bird-lovers interpret as diarrhea is really just droppings with a high volume of urine in the mix — the result, perhaps, of eating a food with high water content, such as fruit. On the other hand, excessive urinary output can also be seen in birds with diabetes or kidney disease. If your bird is truly urinating in excessive amounts, he needs to see a veterinarian. True diarrhea warrants a veterinarian visit, too.

Is anything bugging your bird?

Worms, mites, lice — how much should you worry about the effect of parasites on your pet bird? The answer: Not too much, overall. Parasites are not only a lot less common a problem than most people think, but the actions some bird-lovers take to get rid of pests that don't exist in their birds in the first place can also put their pets at risk.

Birds who come from reputable sources — see Chapter 3 for more on that topic — are very unlikely to arrive in your hands with parasites, either internal (like worms) or external (like mites and lice).

For the most part, as long as your healthy bird isn't exposed to other birds whose health is unknown, he realistically shouldn't be picking up parasites. Mites, lice, and worms don't just materialize out of thin air.

Regular deworming, using lice sprays, or exposing your pet birds to inhaled toxins for their "protection" from mites can be bad news for your bird. Brian sees more pet birds with problems caused from over-the-counter parasite treatments than he sees birds who actually have or had parasite infestations.

Yes, birds can and do get parasites on occasion. If you suspect your bird has them, don't scattershot a "fix" with some over-the-counter concoction. See your veterinarian for proper diagnosis and treatment, as well as advice on how to prevent reinfestations. There are different types of lice, different types of mites, and different types of intestinal parasites — and there are different types of treatments for these problems, too. An accurate diagnosis, combined with accurate treatment and accurate prevention, should not only safely eliminate the problem but also prevent a reappearance of the pests.

Chapter 9

A Preventive Care Approach to Your Bird's Health

In This Chapter

- Understanding why preventive care matters
- Making your plans: A preventive care strategy
- Choosing the right veterinarian for your bird
- Looking at the role of diagnostic tests in preventive care

In recent years, the emphasis in human health care has increasingly moved toward preventive care — starting healthy, getting healthy, and staying healthy. Eating right, being fit, and taking care of little problems before they become big ones. This approach is universally recognized as the better way to go, enhancing quality of life and saving time, misery, and money along the way.

Veterinarians also know the value of preventive care. In dogs and cats, vaccinations against infectious disease have long been standard, and procedures such as neutering and teeth cleaning are increasingly recognized by pet-lovers for their long-term health benefits to pets.

Very well, you say, but what about *birds?* In the avian world, preventive health care is also a priority: It's just basic good medicine and good old common sense, asked for by savvy bird-lovers and practiced by the veterinarians who share their clients' love of these special pets. Preventive care is proper care, for all the reasons named for humans, dogs, and cats, and for some reasons that pertain to birds alone.

In this chapter, you discover the basic rules of preventive medicine for your pet bird as well as your role and your veterinarian's role in preventive health care. An ounce of prevention truly is worth a pound of cure — and then some.

Preventive care sometimes requires a change of mindset, what may for you be a new healthcare focus. If you're one of those people who gets help only when you notice your pet is ill — or even worse, one of those who waits a day or two to "see if he gets better" — we strongly encourage you to review the basic tenets in this chapter and take them to heart. Over the course of your bird's lifetime — a longer one, most likely, with preventive care — you'll enjoy your bird more, improve his quality of life, and probably save money. Is this a deal, or what?

Although this chapter focuses primarily on preventive medicine, a preventive care approach to keeping a bird physically and mentally sound reaches into every page of this book. We touch on some of the most basic strategies in this chapter, such as nutrition, but we urge you to also look at specific chapters for more detailed information. More nutrition information, for example, is in Chapter 6. Getting the right bird from the right source is the most basic of preventive care measures, and we cover that topic in Chapters 2 and 3. Watch for this icon throughout the chapter; we use it to refer more specifically to related preventive care help.

Preventive Care Is the Best Care

Preventive care is important for us all, humans and animals alike, but for pet birds, it's downright essential. Intelligent as they are, human as they may seem to us, pet birds are different from us in some very important ways — not only are they *not* human, they're not even mammals, like many of our other pets. Then, too, they're prey animals, as opposed to predators. And prey animals act differently.

These differences in the way birds are put together and in the way they behave have a critical influence on the way we should care for them.

How do birds fly? How do they eat? What can they see, hear, and taste? Why don't they have teeth? You want to know more about how your bird's body operates. Check out Chapter 8 for a quick-and-easy guide to the basic bird.

What your bird won't tell you — and why

"I don't know what happened — he was fine yesterday" is one of the saddest comments Brian hears in his practice, usually said over a pet bird who's dead — or soon will be. Death or deadly illness is plenty sad, but many of these tragedies are often made even worse because they could have been prevented. The crucial point we need to impress on you is that a bird who's dead or dying today probably *wasn't* fine yesterday. Yesterday, he was most likely trying desperately to hide the signs of illness and succeeding in the eyes of his owner.

Hiding signs of illness isn't something human beings think is too important. Any parent can tell in an instant when a child is starting to get sick, and many of us live with mates for whom even an ingrown toenail is the reason for much moaning. Dogs don't see much need to hide how they feel, either: Whining is a trait known to both canine and human sufferers alike.

Whining is fine when you're a social animal at the top of the food chain. When you're closer to the bottom, though, whining can draw attention you surely don't want.

Yes, this is a bird book, but we can hear the more curious among you wondering where cats fit in. Cats can also be adept at hiding their illnesses, for the same reason birds are: Although cats are predators, they're also small enough to be prey. For more on cats and dogs, you can't go wrong with *Cats For Dummies* and *Dogs For Dummies* — both are award-winning, critically acclaimed, and published by IDG Books Worldwide, Inc.

If you're a prey animal, showing signs of illness is sure to capture the keen-eyed attention of something with big teeth and a hearty appetite. In some social groups of prey animals — such as herd animals — signs of illness will also get you kicked out of your peer group. Your friends and family know you're destined to be someone's dinner, and they don't want any part of *that.* Been nice to know you. *Hasta la vista,* baby. Survival of the fittest? Don't you doubt it for a second.

Sure, it makes more sense for pet birds to communicate their health problems to their largely clueless human caretakers, but that's not the way the world works. Most pet birds are only a few generations removed from the wild — often not even that — and their survival instincts can't be rewired just because they're now living in a cozy home with humans.

Birds will do anything to hide their illness. They can't help it — such secrecy has been a key survival skill for eons, and we humans can't change it. This "prey factor" is one of the reasons preventive care is so important for birds. Too often when a bird finally seems sick to his owner, she is *very* ill — so much so that she can't hide it anymore, and it's going to be a hard, expensive fight to save her, if she can be saved at all.

More arguments for preventive care

Your bird's instincts to avoid any sign of weakness is one of the most important arguments for preventive care, but it's surely not the only one. Let us list a few more, just in case you're not yet convinced:

- **Scarcity of urgent care:** A veterinarian with more than the most basic knowledge of avian medicine is not always available. Emergency clinics are mostly geared for dog and cat care, and if you happen upon a veterinarian in an emergency clinic who's well qualified to handle an avian medical crisis, you can count yourself very lucky, because it's surely not the norm. Even if you develop an excellent relationship with an avian-savvy veterinarian, she will not always be available for emergency response. And trust us, if you let a health problem simmer, Murphy's Law dictates that it will come to a boiling point at night, on a holiday, on a weekend, or when your veterinarian is on vacation.

- **Cost savings:** Preventive care costs both time and money, we'll grant you that. Although it costs no more to feed a bird properly than to feed him poorly, other aspects of preventive care can ding your bank account. Proper husbandry, from the start-up costs of a safe cage to the time or money spent keeping your bird's environment clean, isn't cheap, nor are annual well-bird exams with necessary diagnostic or screening laboratory tests. Still, a good veterinarian can, in some ways, share the same motto as a car mechanic: "You can pay me a little now or pay me more later." Heading off illness is less expensive in the long run than trying to save the life of a bird in crisis. And besides, would you rather pay to keep your bird healthy and happy — and confirm that he is — or wait to pay to manage a medical crisis that may kill him (and your budget)?

Cause of death: Unknown

The Information Age has souped up the good old rumor mill. Not a day goes by when we don't hear about the latest "bird-toxic" product. Although plenty of items in common household use, from cleaning supplies to cookware, can do your bird in (we cover the most common in Chapter 19), many times what a pet owner thinks has killed a bird is merely a coincidence. Nonetheless, the incorrect cause of death is too often reported as fact — and spread and spread — on the Internet.

This misinformation often starts when a pet owner doesn't realize she has a sick bird on her hands, because the pet is doing his best to behave "normally" in a survival strategy as old as birds themselves. Something new is introduced to the household, and the bird is found dead. "Aha!" thinks the owner, "My bird was fine yesterday, and now he's gone. It must have been that new thing."

But what seems like a closed case is still a mystery, and detective work is the only way to solve it. Some people don't want to know why their birds are gone, others wish to know, and some — like breeders or those with many birds — have to know to protect the rest of their flock.

If you want to know or have to know what killed your bird (and we strongly advise this), you need your veterinarian's help. A *necropsy* is an examination of the bird's body, an attempt to figure out what happened and why. Gruesome as it may seem, the procedure, also called an *autopsy* or *postmortem examination,* is an important educational tool for you (you don't want to lose another bird in the same way) and possibly even an important new finding for the future of avian medicine.

If you don't want to know what happened, that's fine. But if you don't know, don't spread your assumptions — you could be wrong.

- **Bottom-line pragmatism:** Yes, this is also about cost, but in a different way. Birds can be very expensive pets to acquire, especially the larger parrots, with prices that can range into the thousands of dollars. If you've paid a couple grand for a Moluccan cockatoo or ten times that for a palm cockatoo, the cost of preventive care is relatively cheap insurance protecting your investment. Of course, the purchase cost of many of our pet birds pales when compared to the value of these birds to our family and our hearts. Considering the outstanding companionship even an inexpensive-to-buy budgie can provide, we'd like to think you wouldn't place your emphasis solely on the bottom line. But some people do — especially those for whom birds are a livelihood, who must be pragmatic to stay in business — and we thought we should fit them in here, too.
- **Quality of life:** If you have a chronic illness or deal with constant pain, you're well aware how those conditions can take the joy out of life. Just because a bird is hiding his illness doesn't mean he isn't feeling dreadful. It may be days, weeks, months or even years before your bird finally gets so sick that he stops caring what happens to him and reveals the more obvious symptoms of illness. Misery has been his companion for a long time at that point — and we can think of no stronger argument for early medical recognition and intervention.

A Three-Part Plan for Preventive Care

Here's some great news: Preventive care is easy, or should we say easier than the alternative — treating the effects of a full-blown illness. After you learn the basics, your bird is set — for life! Starting birds off right and keeping them healthy may seem a little boring, but it's far easier than fixing what's broken.

How easy? Real easy. In fact, we've boiled preventive care down to three easy-to-remember basic areas, outlined in the following sections.

Although the last part — "Working with the pros" — does entail seeking outside help, the first two parts are pretty much do-it-yourself. Learn what's right, set up a routine, and stick to it.

Because we're telling you what preventive care is, we'd like to put in a word or two about what it's *not.* Good preventive care does not include any attempts to treat or prevent illnesses that your bird may or may not have. A couple of examples: The all-too-common practice of adding vitamins, antibiotics, or pest-control products willy-nilly to your pet's daily rations or environment. Vitamins are no substitute for balanced and proper nutrition, and the indiscriminate use of antibiotics is never a good idea. As for pest-control products, breathing in toxins isn't a healthy way to live. Talk to your veterinarian about the concerns that made you consider such measures, and work to get your bird on the right track to health.

Starting with a healthy bird

Birds that are sold with price tags at the low end of the normal range for their species or free-to-a-good-home “fixer-upper” birds are rarely the bargain they seem to be. That doesn’t necessarily mean you should avoid them, but it does mean that if you go forward with a purchase, do so with your eyes wide open. Ask yourself: Why is this bird a “bargain”?

Maybe because the breeder or seller cut too many corners.

Breeding and selling healthy birds is no small feat — it takes knowledge, proper facilities, attention to detail, and plenty of time, all of which are reflected in the price tag.

Healthy birds come from breeding facilities that practice good flock management, including strict adherence to the *closed aviary concept* (CAC). Briefly stated, the CAC dictates that no birds of unknown health status be introduced to healthy birds. New birds must be quarantined, and they must be screened for health problems — as the others birds already have been. It makes good, simple sense — if you have a group of birds of known, sound health and only bring in others just as healthy, the risks of infectious disease are significantly less.

When birds are transferred from the breeder to the retailer, it falls to the pet store to ensure no new health challenges are introduced. All birds for sale should come from known, traceable, and reputable sources, and the birds should not be exposed to others who may be sick, such as those brought in for grooming or boarding (these birds must be kept separately from birds for sale). This procedure is easiest to accomplish in those stores that acquire birds for resale from a controlled and limited number of sources — not just any person who wants to sell them a bird.

Birds who do not come from such health-oriented, controlled, and documented higher-quality sources are much more likely to be ill (physically or mentally), even if they do not look it at the time of purchase. Many of these will be mass-produced pet birds of the more inexpensive species — budgies, finches, and cockatiels. Maybe you’re figuring you can just replace a cheap bird who dies. You may even have bought from a store that encourages that practice — for them, replacing a sick or dead bird may be less expensive than the effort and costs required to sell healthy birds in the first place. We think it particularly sad to consider that many of these little birds are purchased as children’s pets and will die long before their wonderful potential as companions is recognized.

Because birds are so good at concealing any sign of illness, your best bet for getting a healthy bird to start with is to buy from a store or person who has healthy birds, is committed to keeping it that way, and is willing to back up what she sells. Save yourself (or your child) the heartbreak by insisting on a healthy and higher-quality bird from the get-go. Be prepared to pay more for this bird — realistically, he’ll be a bargain in the long run.

Health isn't the only issue in bird-buying

Another reason to deal with the most reputable sources you can find is for the birds themselves. Bird-breeding establishments comparable to the much maligned puppy mills most certainly exist. In these puppy mill equivalents, progressive health practices may be virtually nonexistent, leaving birds appearing healthy but primed for illness after being subjected to the stresses of shipping and handling. We have no quarrel with reputable commercial breeders producing birds for the pet trade, as long as the birds are treated with proper care and respect.

And we encourage the pet stores who have done so much to promote the responsible breeding, adoption, and care of dogs and cats to extend their concern to other pets they sell — birds, of course, but also reptiles, ferrets, and other small pets.

Remember that as a consumer, money talks. Deal only with those who share your love of pets by selling healthy, well-cared-for animals. The others will have to change to remain in business.

More on buying a healthy bird — including tips on getting one who's also well-socialized and friendly — is in Chapter 3. You can find our buyer's checklist of questions to ask when buying a bird in Chapter 16.

Proper care and nutrition

Good routine care and proper nutrition are what helps a healthy bird stay that way. And it's not hard to provide your bird with either one.

Good care is what the experts call *husbandry,* a funny word in Gina's opinion since she doesn't know all that many husbands who don't have to be reminded by their wives to take care of anything. (Maybe *wifeandry* would be a better word, but we'll stop here before we get ourselves in real trouble or spark co-author disagreements!)

Husbandry involves setting up a safe and secure environment for your bird, one enriched by toys, food, and other materials to keep his mind and body busy. It also involves keeping everything clean — changing cage papers or bedding material, scrubbing perches regularly, and keeping food and water containers clean. Good husbandry involves good food and good, commonsense care. Cleanliness is important, just like mom always taught you!

Everything you need to know about what to buy for your bird — what you need and what you don't — is covered in Chapter 4. How often and how to clean is covered in Chapter 5.

Feeding your typical pet bird properly is another essential part of proper husbandry, and it's one that is finally getting better, with more people every day getting the message about the best way to feed their birds. We can sum it up for you and for most of our pet parrot species: To a basic diet of primarily pellets from a reputable manufacturer, add fresh fruits and vegetable. Seeds are a treat, not a dietary staple.

The myth that seeds are the best diets for birds is one we debunk in Chapter 14. You'll want to read the other nine common bird myths, too — check your knowledge! And for a thorough look at avian nutrition, don't forget to visit Chapter 6.

Working with the pros

Too many times a veterinarian sees a pet only when the animal is sick. We can't stress enough that a reactive approach to medicine serves your bird very poorly.

Developing a relationship with your veterinarian entails an initial well-bird examination (see Figure 9-1), which will likely include the use of some diagnostic tests. Such screening is intended to catch health or behavioral problems that can't be seen — but that can more easily be treated if diagnosed early.

Your veterinarian is more than a "bird mechanic" — or he should be. He should also be a consultant on setting up and maintaining your bird's environment and on proper nutrition. He should be the person you start with when you need basic behavior advice. And he should also be right on the spot to tell you the good things that you are doing, too, and to compliment and celebrate the health of your bird with you.

As you no doubt have guessed, Brian's a true believer in preventive care. With every client, he goes over a mental checklist of items to cover, involving not only obvious signs of good or poor health, but also nutrition, behavior, and general husbandry. His preventive care checklist forms the foundation for Chapter 15.

A veterinarian experienced and up-to-date in avian care is one of the most important professionals in your bird's life, but there are others. An *avian behaviorist* — a person who works with you to fix your bird's behavior problems — can really help to mend a damaged relationship and help you and your bird get along better. We talk about these professionals in Chapter 12. For those who aren't interested in wing clipping and toenail trimming, the services of a groomer can be a godsend. Where to find one? We tell you in Chapter 7, along with tips for you do-it-yourselfers. And finally, don't forget about pet-sitters! Advice on finding the right one for your bird is also in Chapter 7.

Hi There!

Green-cheeked Amazon.

Photo by Dr. Brian L. Speer

Welcome to the color section of *Birds For Dummies.* Considering the beauty of pet birds, their vibrant colors, and their intricate markings, you really need color to fully appreciate what we talk about throughout the book.

The first part shows you the anatomy of a bird, both at rest and in flight.

Then, because cages, for better or for worse, end up being where pet birds spend a great deal — and sometimes all — of their lives, we thought it important to compare and contrast a "basic cage" with a "better one" in the second part. Let our illustrations guide you in choosing the cage that will offer your bird the most features and keep him safe and sane.

After looking at cages, we feature some of the most popular pet birds, along with some of the most under-appreciated.

Finally, we close with a picture to make you smile. Birds have a wonderful sense of humor, and you need one, too, if you're going to share your life with one. So turn the page and enjoy!

Peach-faced lovebird.

Photo by Dr. Brian L. Speer

The Anatomy of Flight

From the strong yet lightweight beak to the tail feathers, every inch of a bird's anatomy reveals the evolutionary process that went into the creation of this ultimate flying machine. Sleek and aerodynamic, the bird is inspiration for humankind's airborne inventions.

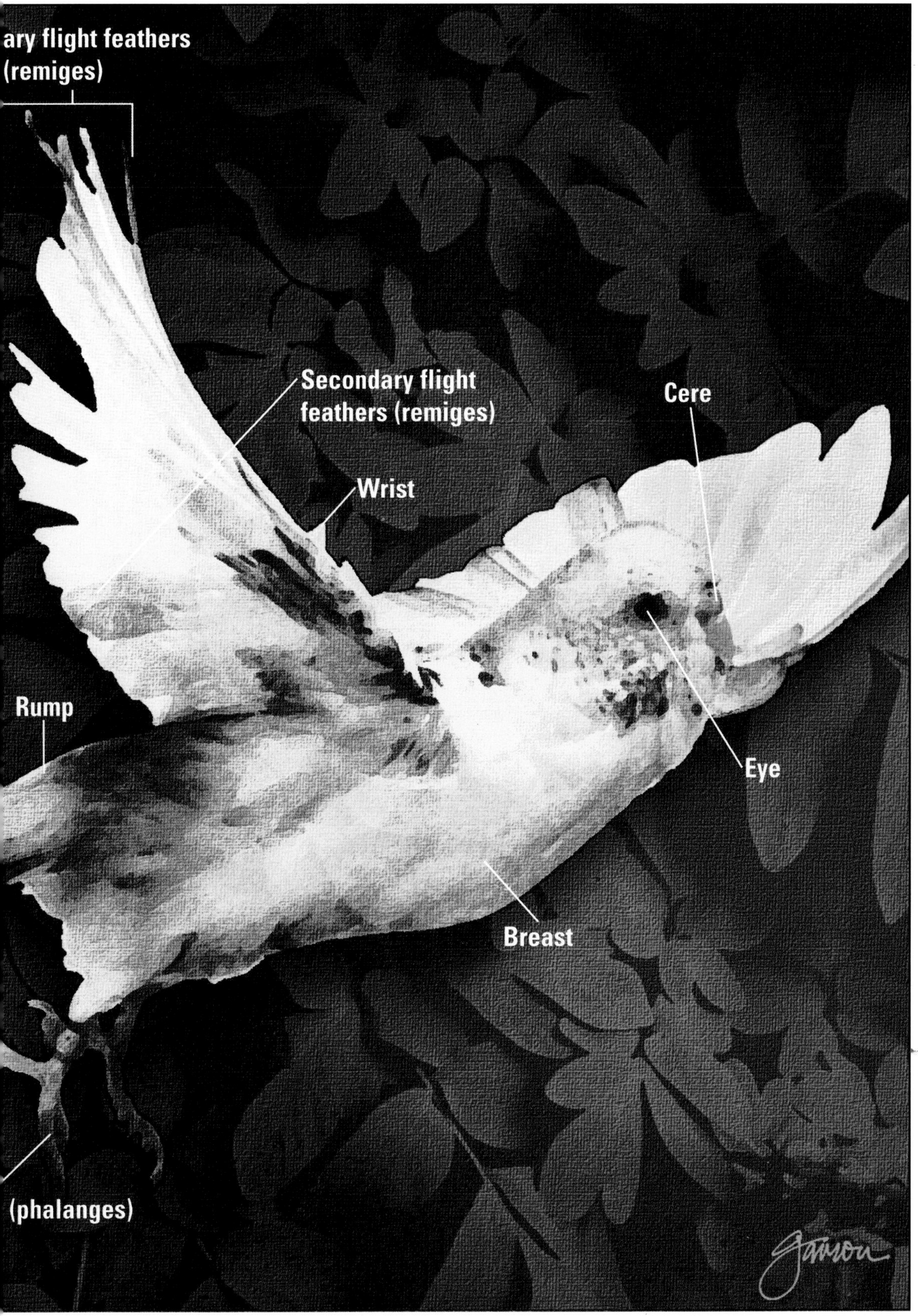

ary flight feathers
(remiges)

Secondary flight
feathers (remiges)

Cere

Wrist

Rump

Eye

Breast

(phalanges)

Basic? Boring!

Too many birds live in cages like this one — secure perhaps, but with little to offer in terms of physical and emotional health. What's wrong with this cage? Quite a lot, really. Because birds aren't helicopters, its vertical design offers little room for movement, and the plain wood perches are hard on the feet. The addition of a sandpaper perch (top inset) can cause even more foot problems, and the "preventive" addition of an anti-pest product (lower inset) is another no-no — birds don't need to breathe in toxic fumes. And the all-seed diet (middle inset)? Awful! A bad place to spend a lifetime, all in all.

Cage, Sweet Cage

Good design and plenty of environmental enrichment makes this cage a better place to be. Start with a sturdy, well-designed cage and add a variety of perches (top inset) — rope, mineral, hard woods like manzanita, and soft woods like pine or citrus. Toss in plenty of toys (bottom inset) to keep mind and body busy — lots to chew on, lots to fuss with, lots to destroy. Someone who knows enough to set up this cage so well is surely also providing a diet with high-quality commercial pellets as its base, augmented by an ever-changing variety of fresh fruits and vegetables (middle inset).

Canaries and Other Finches

Long popular for their color, sounds, and lively antics, canaries and other finches have been successfully bred for centuries.

Photo by Dr. Michael J. Murray

Canaries are judged for their appearance at shows, as well as for their singing ability. This one's a prize-winner.

Photo by Dr. Michael J. Murray

Fancy feathers can be found on many kinds of canaries. Some have crests, like this one, while others have feathers with frills.

Yellow canaries are among the most popular, but they come in many colors and shades. If you want a singer, though, buy a male bird — and listen to the song before paying!

Photo by Dr. Michael J. Murray

Like other finches, these of the star variety enjoy the company of another bird or birds.

Photo by Dr. Michael J. Murray

Society finches like these nesters are one of two species highly recommended for first-time bird-keepers. Zebra finches are the other.

Photo by Dr. Michael J. Murray

Finches come in an astonishing array of patterns and colors, including many striking ones such as these Gouldians.

Photo by Dr. Michael J. Murray

Three Popular Pet Birds

Budgerigars (commonly called parakeets), cockatiels, and lovebirds are among the most popular of all pet birds — and with good reason. Relatively inexpensive to acquire and care for, these charmers may be small, but they're packed with personality.

Photo by Dr. Brian L. Speer

This slate variety of peach-faced lovebird is one of many available as pets. Lovebirds don't need to be paired to be happy, and they enjoy snuggling under your shirt collar, hair, or into pockets, as you can see from the picture on the first page of this color section.

People who dismiss the budgie as a bird just for children are really missing out. Available in many colors and marking varieties and in two body types, budgerigars can be very sweet as well as talented talkers.

Photo by Dr. Brian L. Speer

Photo by Dr. Brian L. Speer

Aw, c'mon, don't you just want to say "awwwwww"? Healthy, hand-raised babies like these young cockatiels will become your best pet bet. Bigger than the budgerigar but still a very manageable size, cockatiels also come in many different color varieties. Not the best talkers but good whistlers, especially the males.

A Tale of Two Conures

Beauty shouldn't be the only criteria when it comes to choosing a bird. Your own tolerance for mess, noise, and activity levels are probably more important in the long run. And yes, too many times birds that might be better pets are overlooked in favor of those who are flashier in appearance. The two birds on this page provide a good example of what you need to consider.

The sun conure is arguably one of the most beautiful of all pet birds, and a clownish and active companion. For the right person, a wonderful choice. But the wrong person is someone who isn't prepared for the sun's outsized personality — and his extremely loud and constant vocalizing. Sun conures are classified as aratinga conures, a grouping that also includes other species such as the jenday, golden-capped, mitred, red-fronted, dusky, and white-eyed conures.

Photo by Dr. Brian L. Speer

The green-cheeked is an example of the "other" group of conures — the ones with less flash, perhaps, but also much less noise and potentially more easy-going personalities. Green-cheeks, maroon-bellies, and black-caps are classified as pyrrhura conures. They're usually smaller and less expensive than the sun, jenday, and the other aratinga conures, which make the plainer green-cheeked and his relations a real find and an excellent pet prospect.

Photo by Dr. Brian L. Speer

Pick a Pint-Sized Parrot

You don't need a room-eating cage and an inheritance to share your life with an intelligent, playful, and loving parrot. Many pet parrot species are small, certainly when compared to the largest macaws and cockatoos. But that doesn't mean they aren't every bit as much a parrot as their bigger relations. We've featured a few of these pint-size powerhouses on these two pages, but many more species are also worth considering.

Photo by Dr. Brian L. Speer

If you think only of little blue budgies when you hear the word "parakeet," you're missing out on a world of wonderful pet potential, such as this canary-winged parakeet, a member of the brotogeris grouping, which also includes the more popular grey-cheeked parakeet.

Photo by Cerise Duran

Hardly bigger than some canaries, parrotlets have a big-bird attitude that may surprise you — they're tiny but tough.

Photo by Dr. Brian L. Speer

Monk, or Quaker, parakeets are popular pets but can become a bit of a problem when they go wild. These parrots adapt so easily to living free that colonies of them have been spotted all over the world, and some states and countries have banned the keeping or breeding of them. As pets, though, they offer plenty of great companion bird features that can't be denied.

The Senegal is the most popular of a grouping collectively known as the poicephalus parrots, which also include the Meyer's and Jardine. All of them are well worth seeking out and make affectionate, relatively quiet pets.

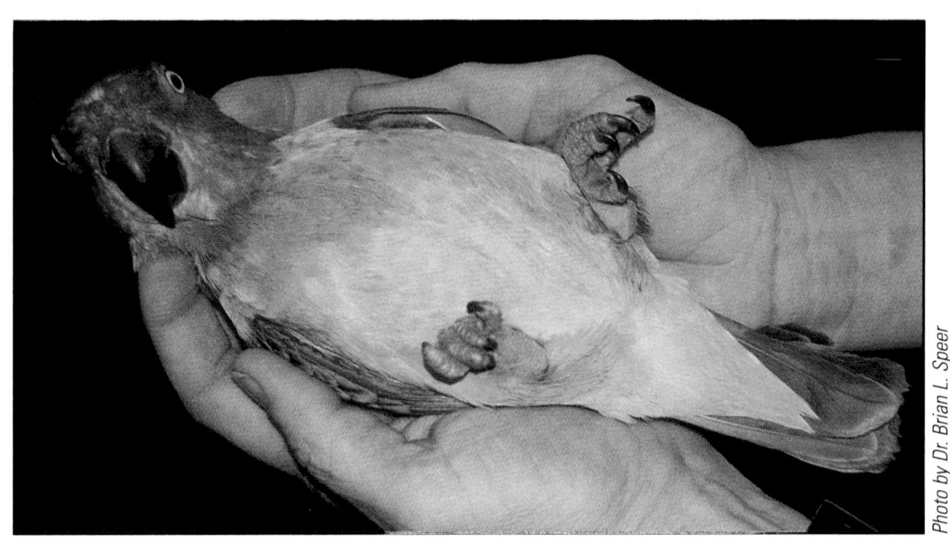

Photo by Dr. Brian L. Speer

The Indian ring-necked parakeet is one of several colorful Asiatic species available as pets. They're a little on the noisy side, but the bright colors of these birds have nonetheless won them many followers.

Photo by Dr. Brian L. Speer

Another of the Asiatic parakeets, the markings of the mustached variety just have to make you smile. This small parrot has a winning personality to go along with his unique appearance, and some can talk quite well.

Photo by Dr. Brian L. Speer

We're Talking Chatty

While many species of parrots can talk, a few show a real talent for it. One of them is the diminutive budgerigar, some of which have picked up vocabularies of more than 300 words. Among the larger parrots, the Congo African grey and the yellow-naped and double-yellow-headed Amazons are renowned for their talking ability.

The Congo African grey parrot is one of the most intelligent of birds, and many pick up words and phrases quickly — too quickly for some owners! The smaller Timneh African grey is also a good talker and is growing in popularity and price.

Photo by Dr. Brian L. Speer

Photo by Dr. Brian L. Speer

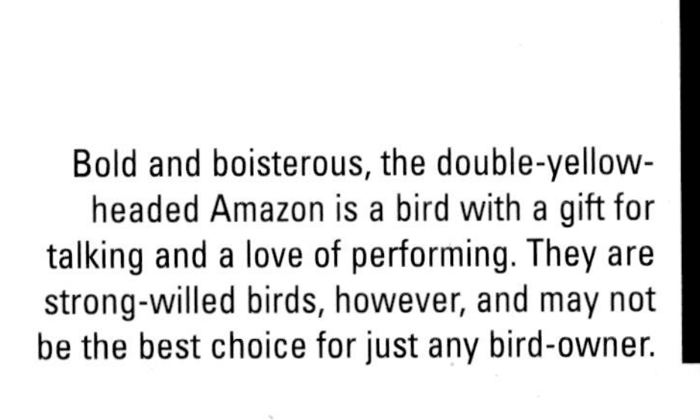

Bold and boisterous, the double-yellow-headed Amazon is a bird with a gift for talking and a love of performing. They are strong-willed birds, however, and may not be the best choice for just any bird-owner.

The Overshadowed Amazons

While the double-yellow-headed and yellow-naped Amazons have justifiably earned their reputations as good talkers, as pets they can be a handful for an inexperienced owner. We like to recommend some of the other Amazon species, such as the two on this page, or any of the relaxed pionus parrots.

Add the orange-winged Amazon to your list of under-appreciated Amazons. Along with the lilac-crowned Amazon, the orange-winged has great pet potential.

Photo by Dr. Brian L. Speer

Photo by Dr. Brian L. Speer

The blue-fronted Amazon is a better choice for most first-time bird-owners, because he may be more easygoing than the more popular species.

Big and Beautiful Birds

Show-stoppers: That's what the birds on these pages are. Some of the largest and most dramatic of pet birds are also very popular, despite the cost of acquiring and caring for them.

Cockatoos have long enjoyed a great deal of exposure and the resulting popularity, but not all species are the "love sponges" the birds are widely thought to be. This Moluccan represents a species that usually loves to cuddle, but other cockatoos, such as the Goffin's, are active birds and resourceful escape artists.

Photo by Dr. Brian L. Speer

The male and female eclectus (this pair is the Solomon Island species) are so different in appearance that they were once thought to be different species. We now know that the lovely purple and red is the female of the pair, although the bright green male is hardly homely, either.

Photo by Laurella Desborough

Photo by Nora Feller

Fans call the hyacinth macaw "the gentle blue giant," and with good reason. The largest of the macaws, the hyacinth is a real softie, and what gorgeous plumage! (Photo courtesy of The Gabriel Foundation)

Photo by Dr. Brian L. Speer

The blue-and-gold is probably the most common of all pet macaws, prized for his good nature and striking appearance.

Turnabout Is Fair Play

Yes, it's a mellow cat who puts up with this little bit of nonsense, but the bird got a kick out of it, and we did, too. We hope it makes you smile.

We included this photo not just for fun but also because it reminds us that you need a good sense of humor if you're going to share your life with a bird — or two, or several. Parrots, from the tiniest budgie or parrotlet to the largest hyacinth macaw, have been growing in popularity in recent years, and while their beauty is surely part of the reason, their intelligence and charm is just as important.

Birds can be messy. Birds can be loud. Birds can be bossy. You need to know these things going in, but you also need to know that you'll never lack for a reason to smile or to laugh when your companion is a bird.

Learn about your bird. Play with your bird. And most of all, love your bird. We promise you'll come out far ahead for the experience.

Now will someone please let the cat out of the cage?

Photo by Dr. Christine Sellers-Stalie

Finding the Right Veterinarian

Choosing the right veterinarian for a dog or cat can be a challenge, but selecting one for your bird will probably be even more difficult. Avian medicine is in many ways still in its youth, shooting up like a teenager. The body of information available is both growing and evolving, and what was considered standard practice even a few years ago may be outdated tomorrow.

Birds are vastly different from dogs and cats, and their health needs are, too. They need a veterinarian who stays current and who is dedicated to providing the very best in care for the birds she sees — and the very best in advice for the owner. To do so requires time — always in short supply — and commitment. You need a veterinarian who has dedicated a good portion of her time and energy to increasing her knowledge of avian medicine — and who knows that education is a process that never ends.

Figure 9-1: Examinations and health screenings by a veterinarian are an essential part of preventive care for your bird.

Why "any veterinarian" may not be right for your bird

Think of veterinary school as a buffet line — a lot of courses on the menu, from which you choose enough dishes to get a well-rounded meal. On that buffet, canine and feline medicine are, in many ways, the meat and potatoes.

Students interested in companion animal species need to know a great deal about dogs and cats, because for most veterinarians, the majority of the patients they see either bark or meow. An in-depth understanding of specialties like cardiology, dermatology, or avian medicine are side dishes, really. The pursuit of more knowledge in these areas is usually done after a student earns a veterinary degree. Your basic veterinary graduates come out of school knowing a decent amount about dogs and cats (or horses, if they went the large animal route), but they usually don't have more than beginners' knowledge of how to treat birds, reptiles, or other small pets, unless they have specifically pushed hard for additional exposure beyond what's normally offered.

This limited education is not itself a problem — you can only fit so much into four years of veterinary schooling, after all. And good veterinarians soon realize that their schooling is only the beginning of a lifetime of learning. A sound basic education is the foundation upon which veterinarians can build their specialty practice, if desired.

After graduation, veterinarians may choose to work with more experienced practitioners and also expand their learning with continuing education courses. Some opt to continue their formal education, seeking to become what's called a *board-certified* or a *boarded* specialist in a particular area of veterinary medicine (more on this in a bit). An informal way to improve knowledge: Many veterinarians discuss cases with more experienced or board-certified colleagues, including those well-known for their expertise, some of whom may teach at veterinary schools or colleges. All these choices build on the basic knowledge a veterinarian learns in school.

Despite the efforts of a good veterinarian to "keep up" with everything, even the most dedicated veterinarians haven't the time to learn it all. They have to pick and choose, and if they don't see a lot of birds in their practice, avian medicine may be one of the areas in which they're less well-versed.

The situation is changing, fortunately.

Because of the increasing popularity of birds and other so-called "exotic pets," such as reptiles, ferrets, rabbits, and rodents, more veterinarians are becoming interested in providing the most up-to-date care possible for these pets.

For the bird-owner, though, the situation can be very hard to figure out — how do you really know what they know? Is the veterinarian who says he treats birds keeping up on current trends? Is he interested in keeping up?

A successful relationship with your veterinarian isn't the same for everyone. We like to measure it in a veterinarian's ability to engender confidence, to engage in open discussion, and to be willing to consult with other colleagues or to refer elsewhere for special treatment if necessary. Combined, these are the basics to building a very powerful relationship between you and your bird's veterinarian.

eVets: Is yours one?

An increasing amount of the advanced learning your veterinarian is doing these days is online, such as that offered by the Veterinary Information Network (VIN), at www.vin.com. VIN is the first and still the largest online service for veterinary professionals, offering its subscribers searches of journal articles, electronic continuing education, and access to specialists and other colleagues who can help with tough cases. Brian serves as an avian medicine consultant for VIN. We admit to being proud of VIN (which was co-founded by Gina's *Cats For Dummies* writing partner, Dr. Paul D. Pion); we think the 6,000 veterinarians who subscribe show an understanding of the importance of keeping current with advances in their profession. The Veterinary Information Network offers a searchable database of more than 25,000 veterinarians worldwide at www.vetquest.com — with VIN subscribers and avian specialists specially marked.

The limitations of the human mind being what they are, Brian stopped seeing dogs and cats years ago because he felt he couldn't do right by them — he'd become a "featherbrain." The condition is serious, in his case: He once couldn't remember off the top of his head how long dogs are pregnant, and when he did remember, he called it an "incubation period," as if dogs came from eggs. Brian's a great doctor for birds, but to help assure the best for his clients who also have dogs, he encourages them to see a colleague with day-to-day experience in good canine medicine.

Special care for a special pet

The body of knowledge in avian medicine is sufficiently large and different enough from canine and feline medicine that we believe you must seek out a veterinarian who has made the commitment to care for his avian patients properly, in a way that meshes best with your own ideas.

No consensus exists on what makes a "good" veterinarian, as far as pet owners are concerned. Some people choose a veterinarian based only on price and convenience, preferring the very least in medical care for their pets. Other pet owners want their animals to be treated as they want themselves to be cared for, using all that modern medicine has available — no matter what the cost. And, of course, many other people are somewhere in between — they want to know all the options, even those they may reluctantly choose not to pursue.

No matter what you're looking for in a veterinarian, we encourage you to find one who'll be willing to look beyond the symptoms — what veterinarians call *clinical signs,* or those that can be observed — and offer to help you to get to the bottom of your bird's health problems so an accurate course of treatment can be found. This kind of medicine is especially important with birds because symptoms can sometimes be misleading. A scattershot treatment of symptoms may not be the best thing for your bird in the long run, and we encourage you to find a veterinarian who understands this and advises you of the same.

Does it seem as if we're pushing diagnostic tests? Perhaps, but given the nature of birds, these tests are sometimes all you can count on to figure out what's going on inside. Do all birds need all diagnostic tests, both for the diagnosis and the prevention of illness? Not necessarily. Good avian medical care is about common sense, judging relative risk factors, and, perhaps most importantly, tailoring care to best serve both you and your bird.

What we're trying to emphasize: *Birds are not like dogs and cats.* You need a different mindset toward avian medicine than you may have when it comes to care for your dog or cat. We're talking *proactive,* not *reactive,* and understanding the lengths to which birds will go to appear healthy until it may be too late.

And we want to point out that proper care isn't just for top-dollar parrots: Less expensive birds, such as the Gouldian finch shown in Figure 9-2, are sometimes considered second-class citizens when it comes to proper veterinary care, but we believe even cheaper birds deserve appropriate medical attention.

Figure 9-2: This Gouldian finch needs the same kind of preventive medical care as a more costly bird.

Photo by Dr. Michael J. Murray

Time and convenience are important, and money, especially, is always a factor in veterinary care, which is still largely unsupported by any form of health insurance. But many times preventive care from a knowledgeable and thorough veterinarian turns out to be a better bargain in the long run, and that's especially true when it comes to pet birds.

Tests? Aw, do we have to?

What is all this diagnostic testing we keep mentioning? It's a revolution in the avian medicine. Diagnostic tests include blood analyses and bacteria- or virus-identifying tests. They are essential in helping a veterinarian find out what a bird will do his best not to reveal — that he's sick with an illness that may, in time, kill him.

As part of a preventive care regimen, laboratory diagnostic tests are constantly being refined and expanded, to improve their ability to catch diseases that cause so many problems among birds — and that are currently the focus of intense, ongoing research.

As important as diagnostic tests are to avian medicine — and to preventive medicine, in particular — they are just one part of the puzzle. He who does the most tests doesn't necessarily win: Preventive care for any pet has never been as simple as a vaccine or a test result. Your part in providing proper daily care and good nutrition, and your veterinarian's part in providing you with expertise, guidance, and "fine-tuning" of what you're doing to care for your bird is the heart and soul of preventive care.

Who's out there, and what are they offering?

If you accept the not-so-radical idea that the veterinarian caring for your bird should know more than the rock-bottom basics of avian medicine, then you're going to be looking for one of two types of practitioners — the person who sees a lot of birds and cares for them well, and the person who does all that and has extra certification to show for his time spent learning about birds.

Here's a shortcut for narrowing your list of possible candidates: Seek the advice and recommendations of the person you got your bird from, assuming he or she is a reputable and knowledgeable breeder or retailer. These folks know very well who practices good avian medicine and are happy to steer you in the right direction.

Board-certified specialists

Board-certified specialists of any kind are comparatively rare birds indeed, especially if you don't live in a large urban area or near a college of veterinary medicine. Even more rare are board-certified *avian* specialists, especially those like Brian who limit their practice exclusively to the care of birds — no dogs and cats allowed!

To become a specialist and to be entitled to add letters behind the DVM (Doctor of Veterinary Medicine), VMD (Veterinary Medical Doctor), or the comparable titles in use around the world, a veterinarian must do more than what was required to graduate from a veterinary college. Specialists are called *board-certified* because testing for specialty knowledge is handled and those extra letters given out by what are called *review boards,* such as the American Board of Veterinary Practitioners (ABVP) or the American College of Veterinary Internal Medical Practitioners (ACVIM).

In the case of a board-certified avian specialist in the United States, the managing entity is the ABVP, which grants titles in Avian Practice along with comparable ones in Companion Animal Practice, Feline Practice, and other areas of expertise.

To become board-certified by the ABVP, a veterinarian must have been in practice five years and must pass a rigorous credentialing process and then study for and pass a test on a species specialty area. "System" specialists, such as *cardiologists* (heart specialists) or *oncologists* (cancer specialists), work with all species, and earn their ACVIM letters after serving residencies and then passing their test. Only veterinarians who have been board-certified are allowed to call themselves "specialists."

Brian is one of those specialists, and he has the extra letters after his name to prove it: Brian L. Speer, DVM, Diplomat, ABVP (Avian Practice), ECAMS. What does all that mean? Board-certified individuals are awarded *Diplomat* status by whatever credentialing body is identified after the word — in this case, the American Board of Veterinary Practitioners (in the Avian Practice category), and also the European College of Avian Medicine and Surgery.

Other practitioners of avian medicine

If you can find a board-certified avian practitioner, is that the best choice for your bird? Not necessarily. Brian knows a great many non-boarded veterinarians who are marvelous with birds, up-to-date on their knowledge, and completely enamored of them as patients. And he knows a specialist or two whose "book-learning" may be top-notch, but who aren't necessarily all that hot with the hands-on work.

So how can you find the right veterinarian? Referrals from other bird-lovers, breeders, or pet stores are grand, but even if you're just thumbing through the phone book, you can start your search — veterinarians who see birds usually mention it in their advertisements. If they're board-certified specialists, you'll see the letters after their name; if not, they can express a special interest in birds but should not claim to be a "specialist."

Occasionally, you may come across an ad that seems to suggest credentials a veterinarian may or may not possess. "Special interest in the treatment of birds" doesn't say "specialist," but gives that impression, doesn't it? The way to figure out what you're dealing with? Ask! There may be nothing at all sneaky intended — the veterinarian may be wonderful with birds whether or not he's a board-certified avian specialist.

Call up a prospective animal hospital and ask how many birds are treated there and whether the veterinarian is a member of the Association of Avian

Veterinarians (AAV). Membership in the AAV at least conveys a professional interest in keeping current on avian medicine. If a veterinarian is not an AAV member, does this mean that they don't know their stuff? Not necessarily, but it's sure an indication.

The Association of Avian Veterinarians is one of our featured Web sites in Chapter 17, but you don't need Web access to track down this group: We've also put its address and phone number in our Additional Resources appendix at the back of the book.

The veterinarian you choose should be comfortable with handling birds in a way that won't stress them unduly (see Figure 9-3), should see them routinely enough to be well-versed in their needs, and should be interested in keeping current on developments in avian medicine. One more trait we feel is very important: He should be willing to discuss the difficult cases with more experienced avian veterinarians.

Figure 9-3: Say ahhh! An experienced avian veterinarian knows tricks to make a bird more relaxed.

Photo by Dr. Brian L. Speer

The cooperative approach: Vet to vet

In a perfect world, every local area would have at least one board-certified avian specialist, but that day will never come. In place of such a dream has sprung up a cooperative approach to avian medicine, where specialists like Brian spend a great deal of their time as consultants, helping other colleagues with their tough cases. It's a way of spreading the knowledge, and it saves a lot of feathered lives.

Some of Brian's workdays consist of nothing but telephone consultations with other veterinarians or with breeders or retailers — he may see only one patient "in the feathers." Although he's based in the San Francisco Bay area of Northern California, his clients and patients live all over the world.

Because of the rapid pace of growth and change in avian medicine, perhaps the most important feature of the veterinarian you choose is that she be willing to reach out for help when she needs it. The help is out there — online veterinary services, board-certified specialists, and more. Get a sense from any veterinarian you're considering as to whether she is willing to do the legwork for the sake of your bird's health.

Chapter 10

Your Bird in Sickness — and Back to Health

In This Chapter

- Recognizing emergencies
- Getting urgent care for ailing birds
- Nursing sick birds at home

Although veterinarians have always done their best for pet birds — relieving suffering is their job and their passion, after all — only in recent years has the body of knowledge of avian medicine grown large enough to start being available and useful for the average pet bird-owner out there. What a difference it's making in the lives of birds and those who love them!

Aviculturists — people who breed and sometimes show pet birds — used to say, "A sick bird is a dead bird." Now, that saying is one of the myths we're happy to debunk in Chapter 14. Veterinarians knowledgeable about and experienced in bird care are saving birds who wouldn't have had a chance even a few years ago. And the revolution has just begun! Advancements in our knowledge of avian medicine, nutrition, and behavior continue to grow, promising an ever-brighter future for our avian companions.

Although all practicing veterinarians are qualified to treat birds by virtue of the degrees granted to them by their alma maters and their governmental licenses, many — if not most — in general practice really don't have enough experience or detailed avian medical knowledge to provide the best medical care available for your bird. You need a veterinarian who is truly experienced and interested in avian care to ensure your bird gets the benefit of the advanced knowledge that's available. We explain who these bird veterinarians are and how to find one in Chapter 9.

Preventing illness is the best way to go — and you can find plenty about that in Chapter 9 — but illness and accidents happen even to the best-cared-for birds and the most vigilant of bird-keepers. To give your bird a fighting chance, you must know a few first aid basics and have a decent knowledge of the signs of illness. You find most of the basics in this chapter, along with an idea of where avian medicine is heading.

We've put other health problems in the chapters that seem to fit them best. Older-bird maladies such as arthritis and chronic malnutrition are in Chapter 11. Feather-picking has both medical and behavioral components, and we put our discussion of its causes and treatments in Chapter 12.

Birds Are Birds — Not People, Not Dogs

Even though the keeping of animals as companions has gone on for countless generations before ours, the focus on the medical needs of *pets* is, to a certain extent, a modern development. Our priorities in centuries past were keeping ourselves alive and healthy, and then caring for those animals who "served" us. Few had the luxury of worrying about animals whose job was to keep us company — we needed to care for those animals whose job was to keep us alive.

Our farming ancestors worried about the horse who pulled the plow and took the family to town or to church; or the dog who hunted, herded, or protected; or large livestock such as cows, sheep, or pigs who provided food, wool, and leather. The history of medical care for these animals — especially horses and dogs — is a long one.

Today many animals are kept as companions and are valued as family members. The change in our perceptions of animals is reflected in veterinary medicine.

When Gina was researching *Cats For Dummies* (which she co-authored with top veterinary cardiologist Dr. Paul D. Pion), she discovered that cats had been given short shrift by the veterinary establishment. The animals had an important job in catching vermin, but they reproduced quickly, and one cat was considered pretty much the same as another. (Some people still hold this view, dumping cats with health or behavior problems in favor of a fuzzy kitten face.)

When cats came into their own as cherished companions, not much was really known about their medical needs — they were treated like "little dogs," without much regard to their distinctiveness. Cat-lovers and veterinarians demanded better, and now a great deal of research is conducted into improving the health of our feline companions. A small but growing number of veterinarians study further to become certified feline specialists, and no competent veterinarian these days would make the mistake of treating a cat like a dog.

This same scenario is playing out now in avian medicine. Although the veterinary community — along with behaviorists, retailers, manufacturers of supplies and food, and, of course, bird-owners — are busy keeping up (or

Traditional versus alternative medicine

Call it anything you like — including "Eastern" or "holistic" — alternative medicine is very hot in human medicine and, not surprisingly, in veterinary medicine as well. The growth of alternative medicine is in part a backlash against high-tech, impersonal (and expensive) care that sometimes seems more interested in the disease than in the patient, but it's also about getting back to the basics of sound preventive care. Alternative medicine includes a wide range of treatment options, from acupuncture to chiropractic to homeopathy to magnetic therapy.

In holistic medicine, the whole patient is the focus, rather than the specific disease. "Western" medicine tends to do better with acute illness, such as a bacterial infection, or with trauma, such as a broken leg. "Eastern" medicine's strength is in dealing with more chronic conditions, such as arthritis.

Some traditionally trained veterinarians now embrace alternative care exclusively, but a great many others accept elements of alternative care as a complement to traditional medicine. Brian is one of those who believes a healthy mix of both kinds of medicine is the best. He's a firm believer in good nutrition, "whole-bird" preventive care, and behavioral counseling, but he's also quite capable with a scalpel or appropriate antibiotic when it's called for.

The American Holistic Veterinary Medical Association is perhaps the best place to start finding out more about alternative veterinary medicine. You can access the AHVMA on the AltVetMed Web site (`www.altvetmed.com`) or contact the organization directly at 2218 Old Emmorton Road, Bel Air, MD 21015; phone 410-569-0795.

catching up) with the changing information about bird care, some folks just aren't hearing the news.

As a bird-owner and as a consumer of veterinary care and bird-related products and services, you must bear in mind one very important concept. We put it large at the beginning of this section, but it bears repeating: Birds are birds, not people, not dogs (or cats, or iguanas, or any other creature you care to name). They react differently than other creatures do, both emotionally and physically. You have to think about them differently, too.

What does this mean in real terms? Don't expect illness to be the same in birds as it is in yourself or your other pets. Don't treat symptoms with medicines meant for people or other pets — you could be reading the symptoms entirely wrong, and even if you guess right, the medicine may not react in the way you hope it will.

Seek out the latest knowledge from experienced and up-to-date veterinarians, behaviorists, aviculturists, and even some specialized retailers. And keep learning!

Home Care Fallacies

We hope we've prepared you for the "bad news" of this chapter: We're not going to present a list of symptoms and their "cures." To do so would be irresponsible on our part. The correct diagnosis and treatment of disease is a job for someone who knows what he or she is doing, and that person is a veterinarian experienced in avian medicine. As a bird-owner you should be informed, and you should demand the best care for your bird and have all your questions answered. But you can't diagnose and treat avian illness from a book, from a phone call to your local pet shop, or even from a Web site you found on the Internet.

The home first aid kit

The role of first aid is to stabilize your bird enough to get help, and to do that, you need to keep some basic supplies on hand. Many different containers will do to hold your supplies, including an old sewing kit or small tackle box. Just make sure whatever you choose is easily portable — a handle is convenient, too.

The first thing to put in the kit is a first aid book. We like to recommend *First Aid for Birds: An Owner's Guide to a Happy, Healthy Pet* (Howell Book House) by Julie Ann Rach and Dr. Gary A. Gallerstein. It's a small, inexpensive book that's easy to navigate and understand.

Tape the name and phone number of your veterinarian and of the emergency clinic inside the lid of your first aid box. Here's what else to keep inside:

- **An old towel:** Use this for catching and restraining your bird (even well-mannered birds can become unmanageable when hurt).
- **Basic bandaging supplies:** Include in these supplies an assortment of gauze pads and rolls. Instead of regular first aid tape (which sticks to feathers), use paper tape or masking tape.
- **Cornstarch or styptic powder:** Use this to stop minor bleeding.
- **Needle-nosed pliers, square-tipped tweezers, scissors:** Use the needle-nosed pliers to pull broken blood feathers (more on blood feathers in Chapter 8). Tweezers come in handy for all sorts of problems.
- **Cotton swabs and cotton balls**
- **Betadine:** This is both a soap and a disinfectant. Use it for cleaning and treating wounds.
- **Hydrogen peroxide:** Use this for cleaning wounds.
- **Heating pad**
- **Syringes with the needles removed and an eye dropper:** You can get syringes without needles from your veterinarian. Use both of these for irrigating wounds or administering fluids or medication.
- **High-energy liquid:** Try Pedialyte or ready-to-mix glucose solution for feeding and restoring fluids.

You also need a carrier or travel cage for transporting your bird to the veterinarian. For more on cages and carriers, see Chapter 4.

The role of home care — your role — is to recognize not only that your bird is ill but also how ill, and to act with appropriate speed. And after your bird has seen your veterinarian, you need to provide supportive care to help your pet regain his health.

We're not trying to drum up business for veterinarians. But any person who dedicates years to studying how to identify disease and treat avian patients is going to be better at it than someone who was hired to ring up dog toys, cat food, and bird cages at a pet store, or even someone who has bred birds for years and has picked up a body of knowledge that may well be out of date. Your bird's health relies on a partnership between you and the right veterinarian.

First Aid Basics

First aid is about saving a life, reacting in such a way as to remove the patient from immediate danger, and then getting more experienced help — a doctor, in the case of a human patient; a veterinarian, in the case of an animal one.

That old scout motto, "Be prepared," is the most important concept in first aid. Here are the basics of preparedness:

- Keep the supplies you need on hand (see our sidebar elsewhere in this chapter on the contents of an avian first aid kit).
- Know what's life-threatening and what's not.
- Know whom to call, where to go, and how to get your bird there safely.
- Know how to help stabilize your bird.

Seem like a lot to remember? It's not, really. If you find out what you need to know before you're called to act — and review it from time to time — you can react instinctively when you need to, and you may well be the difference between life and death for your bird.

So what's an emergency?

One of Gina's veterinarian friends works in an emergency care clinic, and he's constantly amazed at the non-emergencies he's asked to treat at 2 a.m. He's even more astounded by the people who call about a genuine medical crisis and decide to see how their pet is doing in the morning rather than taking the time or spending the extra money for emergency care. Although it may — or may not! — be okay to wait a few hours on a dog or cat who "just doesn't seem right," waiting is probably not a good idea when your pet is a bird: If a bird is sick enough to look sick, he's probably very, very sick indeed.

The rule is: ***When in doubt, call.***

Call your regular avian veterinarian or, if she's not available, an emergency clinic with experience in handling birds. (Be sure you've done your homework and have the numbers to call before you need to. We offer guidance in the section, "Whom to call, where to go" later in this chapter.)

That said, we have some general guidelines on what constitutes a life-threatening emergency, an urgent situation, or one that can wait until your regular avian veterinarian is available.

- **Life-threatening emergencies** need to be dealt with immediately by a veterinarian. They include bites or deep cuts, bleeding that can't be stopped, burns, poisoning, difficulty breathing, collapse, blood in droppings, or straining to defecate or pass an egg. In these situations, you usually can't get help fast enough.
- **Urgent situations** that should be seen by a veterinarian within a few hours of your noticing them include an eye injury or a lack of interest in eating, especially if your bird also seems "puffed up." Sudden swellings also demand relatively fast care, as may broken bones and diarrhea. Direct contact with dog or cat saliva, regardless of whether the skin was broken, is also an urgent matter — your bird will likely need to be started on antibiotics.

  Watery droppings are not necessarily diarrhea. True diarrhea is droppings with poorly formed or loose feces in them. Watery droppings that aren't diarrheal are often the result of increased urine production, which can happen for perfectly healthy reasons such as eating foods with high water content, like fruit. High urine output can also be a sign of disease, such as diabetes or kidney problems. If your bird's droppings always seem to have a high amount of urine in them, your bird needs to be checked out.

  For the lowdown on droppings — what goes into them, what's normal, and what's not — see Chapter 8.
- **Not-so-urgent situations** can wait until the next day or the end of the weekend. Remember, though, to watch your bird carefully. Because birds are so adept at hiding the signs of illness, your bird may well be quite ill by the time you notice. If any of the more urgent symptoms we note earlier in this list pop up, get help. No matter what, bear in mind that a "wait and see" attitude is not appropriate for a sick bird. Call your veterinarian for guidance, at the very least.

Whom to call, where to go

The wrong time to try to find veterinary care is when your bird is seriously sick or injured. After you have a veterinarian experienced in regular avian care — see Chapter 9 for tips in finding one — you need to find out what arrangements are available with that veterinarian for emergency care.

Some veterinarians take after-hours calls, some don't. Some trade coverage with colleagues the way many human doctors do — this week and weekend Dr. A is on call, next week it's Dr. B.

Ask your veterinarian what arrangements he recommends, and if he — or a colleague — will not be available for after-hours care, ask him where you should go to find it.

Although emergency clinics are prepared to do their best for whatever furred, feathered, or scaly creature comes in, wild or tame, some are quite upfront about the fact that they prefer to stick to dogs and cats. Finding this out in advance is obviously a very good idea.

So call. Call your regular veterinarian and discuss the situation, and if you need to choose an emergency clinic for a backup, call around if more than one exists in your area to find out how they feel about treating birds — and working with your regular veterinarian.

Brian is, of course, the veterinarian for Gina's Senegal parrot, Patrick, but he doesn't do her much good in the case of an emergency, since he lives more than an hour's drive from her house. Fortunately, the veterinarian who cares for Gina's dogs is part of a group whose ranks include a veterinarian with a special interest in avian care — and the practice is also open 24 hours for emergencies. Gina's "dog veterinarians" work hand-in-hand with Brian in a bird emergency, as happened when one of Gina's dogs bit Patrick. The teamwork was admirable, with excellent care at the emergency hospital augmented by Brian's specialized expertise on the phone. And Patrick is alive and healthy today to show how well the system works!

When you know who'll be able to treat your bird in an emergency, make sure you know how to get where you're going. The route to your regular veterinarian you surely know well, but how about to the emergency clinic? A dry run probably isn't necessary — unless you're new to the area and don't know your way around — but it's a good idea to know what streets will get you there quickly and without getting lost.

What to do, in what order

When a pet is injured or ill, the first thing to do is take a very deep breath. This is no time to panic!

Using the guidelines in this chapter, figure out the severity of the problem — whether it's immediately life-threatening. If you're by yourself, you need to attend to first aid and then call your veterinarian to let her know what you're dealing with and that you're on your way. If you're not alone, you can handle the first aid while the other person calls the veterinarian.

Tell the receptionist that you have an emergency and explain as calmly and clearly as you can manage what the problem is — what the symptoms are, what the source of the problem is (such as swallowing a lead weight or flying into a pot of boiling water). Calling ahead ensures that the veterinarian will be ready to see you — bumping you ahead of patients who aren't in as much danger as your pet — and will be prepared to deal with the specific problem that's endangering your bird's life.

We suggest stabilizing your bird before calling or having someone else call as you do so, but this is just a basic guideline. You know what you can and can't handle and should adjust your response accordingly. If you don't know what you're doing in handling a sick or injured bird or aren't comfortable doing it — if you pass out at the sight of blood, for example — call your veterinarian *first.* She — or one of her staff — can help talk you through what you need to do.

Before treating or evaluating a sick or injured bird, you need to be able to properly restrain her in a towel. Become familiar with the steps for catching and restraining your bird now by reviewing them in Chapter 7 and practicing a time or two. You simply can't count on your bird's cooperation when she's sick and scared.

In general, you need to get your bird restrained, offer first aid, put her in her carrier with as little handling as possible, and keep her warm as you head for the veterinarian's.

Every bird should have a travel cage or carrier for emergencies. For help in choosing one, see Chapter 4. In a pinch, however, a cardboard box with a few air holes will do, as will a paper grocery bag for small birds. Brian has seen all of these "carriers" — and a few more. Whatever you use, remove the perches and put a towel on the bottom to give your bird firm footing and a degree of cushion and warmth. Put another towel over the cage or carrier — the darkness helps to keep the bird calm.

The following is the basic first aid regimen for various emergencies. Do what you can — as long as you're not making matters worse, of course — and get your bird the help he needs right away.

- **Bites:** Bite or claw wounds by the family cat or dog are always a potentially deadly situation, even if it doesn't seem so at first. Dogs and cats are able predators, and their jaws are quite capable not only of piercing the skin of a bird but also of crushing internal organs and breaking bones. Even a bird who seems to have escaped an attack with "only" a small bite or scratch can fall victim to infection, as can birds with no visible signs of injury at all. If your bird is attacked, attempt to control the bleeding, and contact your veterinarian. Your bird may need to be treated for shock, infection, or internal injuries, and very likely should be started on antibiotics as soon as possible.

- **Bleeding:** Restrain your bird and attempt to figure out the source of the bleeding. Apply direct pressure with a cool towel or your finger (wash your hands first, of course). For bleeding from a toenail you've clipped too short, apply a *styptic,* or blood-stop powder, or cornstarch to help with the clotting. For bleeding from a *blood feather* (a budding feather still in its clear protective sheath), get your needle-nosed pliers and grip the feather as close to the base as possible, pulling it out smoothly. Apply pressure to the place where the feather was. (Again, if you don't feel comfortable pulling the feather yourself, get your pet to your veterinarian right away and allow him to handle it.)

  Although we don't feel that a healthy bird is likely to bleed to death from an injured blood feather, you can stop the bleeding faster in most cases by pulling the broken feather and washing the wound with peroxide. We do not recommend the use of a styptic powder on pin feathers — only on beak tips and toenails.

- **Breathing difficulty:** A life-threatening emergency. Restrain your bird as gently and calmly as you can and place him in his travel carrier, with a towel over it to keep him as sedate as possible. Call the veterinarian and get going. Causes for breathing difficulties can be the inhaling of deadly fumes — such as from cleaning products or burning nonstick cookware — or symptoms of respiratory tract, reproductive tract, or even heart problems. In any case, time is of the essence.

- **Broken bones:** Although usually not immediately life-threatening, a bird with "just" a broken bone is in enough pain to warrant urgent treatment. Another problem with a broken bone: Any accident severe enough to break a bone could also have caused internal damage. Call right away and ask for guidance.

- **Burns:** First aid depends on what substance burned your bird. For boiling water burns, cool water, whether in a mist, a flood, or immersion (for a wing or leg) calms the situation. If grease has caused a burn, flour or cornstarch helps to absorb the still-dangerous material. Household chemicals can burn, too, and they fall into two categories, both of which must be treated differently. Drain cleaner, an example of an acid, should be treated with lots of cool water to dilute the chemical, followed by the application of a baking soda and water paste to neutralize the chemical. Treat a burn with an alkali chemical, such as ammonia, by diluting with cool water and neutralizing with household vinegar. Let the veterinarian take matters from there.

  Don't use topical cortisone products to treat burns or any injury in your bird.

- **Eye injury:** Not usually immediately life-threatening, but still urgent. Restrain your bird and place in the carrier with a towel over it to keep your pet calm — and get to the veterinarian.

- **Eating or drinking problems:** A bird who's not eating or drinking can go downhill in a hurry. Don't wait to see whether he "gets better" in a day or so — call to see whether your bird can get in right away for proper diagnosis and treatment.

- **Fanny problems:** Any tissue sticking out from your bird's fanny, or *vent,* suggests a serious problem that needs to be dealt with fairly quickly. A veterinarian needs to determine the cause of the protrusion and treat accordingly. Call your veterinarian for guidance and keep your pet warm and calm until he can be seen.

- **Head injury:** Flighted birds can get into so much trouble! Flying into a pot of boiling water is one kind of trouble, flying into a window, ceiling fan, or wall is another. You can't do much at home for your bird besides restrain, settle into a carrier, and head for your veterinarian's office.

Keeping your bird's wings trimmed is essential to your pet's well-being. Free flight may seem romantic, but too many hazards exist in the human environment for it to be safe (not to mention the danger of your bird escaping). For help with keeping wings trimmed, see Chapter 7.

- **Heatstroke:** An overheated bird holds his wings down and pants, and may be listless, weak, or unable to keep his balance. Cool — not cold — water from a misting bottle helps bring your bird's temperature down, as does moving him to a cooler part of the house. Offer a little water or electrolyte solution and contact your veterinarian for guidance.

Overweight birds are particularly prone to overheating. For more on obesity and other forms of chronic malnutrition, see Chapter 10.

- **Poisoning:** Birds like to get their beaks on things that aren't good for them — including many that are poisonous. Some common poisons include lead (from paint, welds on poor-quality cages, or even fishing weights), zinc (from galvanized items that have been chewed and swallowed), houseplants, medications meant for humans or other pets, and even good food gone bad. Bloody droppings, vomiting or regurgitation, diarrhea, convulsions or paralysis, or irritated skin around the mouth are some signs of possible poisoning. Call your veterinarian and hit the road. Your veterinarian needs to know what your bird got into — bring the suspect along, if you can.

- **Seizures:** A bird who's having a seizure needs immediate attention to figure out and treat the underlying cause. Call your veterinarian and hit the road.

- **Swallowing or breathing in a dangerous object:** Birds enjoy destroying things, but some of the items they dig their beaks into can elicit a measure of revenge (see Figure 10-1). Toys that are flimsy or not sized properly for your bird can be a source of danger — see Chapter 4 for more on choosing toys — but others are in your home, too. Supervise your bird! Sometimes pieces go down the throat; other times they go up or down the nostrils. If you see or suspect your bird has a problem with any foreign object, call an experienced avian veterinarian for guidance. The problem needs to be evaluated and may require surgery.

Common sense dictates that the best way to deal with emergencies is by working to prevent them whenever possible. Check out Chapter 19 for some dangers you can help your pet avoid.

Figure 10-1: Popcorn can be a real problem if your bird inhales it down his windpipe.

Photo by Dr. Brian L. Speer

No number of pages in a book can make up for years of study and hands-on experience. Birds can and do die from any number of specific diseases and injuries, including infectious ones that can be typically prevented by keeping your healthy bird away from others of questionable health status — but generally not cured. Cancers, heart disease, and diabetes often can be treated, as in human medicine, and catching illness early gives your bird the best shot at survival.

Emergency! The veterinarian's role

If you get on the phone with your veterinarian or an emergency clinic to discuss your bird — and we recommend you do call first — the staff is as prepared as possible for the kind of care your bird needs.

That doesn't necessarily mean your bird gets treated first, especially at an emergency clinic. When you arrive, the staff determines the level of emergency and ranks your bird against other pets, with the most seriously ill or injured pets being treated first. The veterinarian may choose to stabilize your bird with warmth and extra oxygen before proceeding, either because other cases are more urgent or because your bird needs to be settled before being further stressed.

Diagnostic tests are an important part of figuring out what's going on with your pet, and chances are your veterinarian needs to conduct some of these before determining the best course of treatment. Asking what the tests are meant to accomplish is reasonable, as is expecting thorough answers to your questions — although not when a pet's life is hanging by a thread. Your veterinarian should be busy with your bird!

Although the staff of the hospital or clinic does their best to keep you informed, their priority in the case of an emergency is helping your pet. Be patient and cooperative, answering their questions and giving them time and space to do their jobs. You can expect them to discuss testing and treatment options with you along the way, as well as give you an idea of the expense involved.

A life-threatening emergency is just that — an illness or injury that puts your bird's life at risk. Sometimes, despite the best efforts of everyone involved, a pet doesn't make it. You may even be asked to make the decision to end your pet's suffering. For more information on euthanasia and resources to help you cope with the loss of your pet, see Chapter 11.

Infectious Diseases That Panic Parrot-Lovers

The diseases that give parrot-lovers nightmares have big names — mostly starting with the letter "P" for no reason in particular. You need to know they're out there, and how serious they are, so you can understand how very important it is to do your very best to prevent them.

We don't want you to read this section and come away with an idea that your bird is doomed to catch some dreadful, incurable disease — we're not trying to turn you into a *birdochondriac.* Your bird's best protection against any infectious diseases is preventive health care, good nutrition, cleanliness, and keeping clear of birds who may be sick. Review our chapters on basic husbandry (5), nutrition (6), preventive health (9), and multi-bird households (13) — there you find the sections that help you keep disease at bay.

The art and science of accurate diagnosis, prevention, and treatment of infectious diseases of birds is one area of avian medicine that's getting attention and shows lots of promise now and in the future.

Tiny beings, big problems

Some of the deadliest things in our environment are so small you need a powerful microscope to see what they look like. Infectious agents or germs — veterinarians call them *pathogens* — are everywhere. These troublemakers can be put in three categories:

- **Bacteria:** These one-celled life forms can be found inside and outside your bird, and most live in happy coexistence. Some bacteria, called *normal bacterial flora,* are beneficial to your bird, serving as "squatters" that keep dangerous bacteria from settling. Bacteria that are no challenge to some creatures can be dangerous to others, which is why we caution against sharing food that has been in your mouth with your bird — the normal bacteria in your mouth can be bad news to your bird. The sharing of bacteria is also why dog and cat bites are so dangerous — even if the injury is minor, a resulting infection may not be. When properly diagnosed, bacterial infections can usually be fought with antibiotics.

Another thing to understand about bacteria is that they are capable of multiplying both inside a living thing and on surfaces of things such as food and water dishes, countertops, and toys. An example of a disorder caused by bacterial contamination is food poisoning.

- **Viruses:** Viruses are only "sort of" alive, and they rely on the cells of their bird hosts to reproduce — most cannot survive for long exposed to open air. Antibiotics have no effect on viruses, as do few other medications — although the scene is changing, thanks to research into viral diseases that affect other species, such as HIV in humans and feline leukemia in cats. The fight against viruses is basically a preventive one: Some can be thwarted by vaccination, while others are best fought by preventive care — a bird in good health is more likely to withstand an assault by a virus.
- **Fungi:** Primitive plant-like life forms, fungi flourish in moist, warm environments and shed spores that can be inhaled. Fungi are opportunists: They prey typically on those already weakened by disease or with less than normal immune function. Long-term or inappropriate antibiotic treatment also gives them an edge, by killing healthy normal bacteria that can keep fungal infections out. Antifungal medications, not antibiotics, are designed to fight fungal infections.

We provide information on a handful of the more worrisome infectious diseases in the following sections.

Psittacine Beak and Feather Disease

Tell-tale signs of this viral disease include abnormalities in the feathers or beak, hence the name *Psittacine Beak and Feather Disease*. Although the disease is often thought of as one affecting cockatoos, in fact other parrot species and more have been diagnosed with the illness. In young birds, PBFD is usually rapidly fatal; in older parrots, the disease can take up to several years after infection for symptoms to develop — and the bird may succumb to other infections in its weakened state.

Your veterinarian will diagnose PBFD based on his observations as well as a laboratory test and will caution you against "doom and gloom" if your otherwise healthy-appearing bird tests positive for the presence of the virus on a single pass. Not all birds who become infected are destined to develop the disease. Currently no cure or vaccine exists for PBFD, and individual pet birds with the disease should be isolated from other parrots for the rest of their lives to prevent the further spread of the disease.

Can your bird make you sick?

Every animal we share our lives with has the potential to pass on infectious diseases to us, whether it's rabies, parasites, or salmonella. Illnesses that can be passed from animals to humans are called *zoonotic.*

Like any companion animal, pet birds can share illness with their human keepers. *Chlamydia psittaci,* the organism which causes avian chlamydiosis (also known as *psittacosis*), is probably the best-known, and offers arguably the highest degree of risk to some individuals from an infected bird. People in higher risk groups should be especially careful when choosing an avian companion, dealing only with those breeders and shops that maintain the highest level of disease-prevention strategies and working with their veterinarian to best assure the health of their bird. Some experts go further, and suggest avoiding birds (and other pets, such as reptiles and even cats) altogether. Considering the importance of companionship, especially to someone who's struggling with chronic illness, we wouldn't go that far, but we do recommend good education, good husbandry, good veterinary preventive health measures, and plenty of basic common sense when it comes to hygiene.

Allergies are another human health problem in relation to birds. If you have allergies or asthma, especially if you are allergic to feathers and feather dust, you probably should consider avoiding certain species of pet birds. We tell you which ones in Chapter 2.

Can you make your bird sick? Although it's commonly thought that birds can get sick from human colds, that's one of the myths we debunk in Chapter 14.

Pacheco's parrot disease

First documented in parrots in the 1930s, *Pacheco's disease* is caused by a herpes virus. While some species and individuals seem able to fight off the disease, all parrots are capable of being infected.

Pacheco's is brutal to its victims, with death often the first symptom a bird-owner notices. Disease can develop in as little as two days from the time of exposure, with death coming in as quickly as five days or as long as several weeks. Sadly, most diagnoses are made at the examination of the infected bird's dead body. Although a vaccine is available, it's usually given to birds deemed to be in comparatively high-risk environments only, such as those birds that are constantly exposed to new birds or those of unknown health status. If caught early enough, some antiviral medications may help.

Pacheco's disease is best handled preventively, through proper cleanliness, vaccination, and rapid action if the disease pops up in a household or aviary. Sick, dying, or dead birds must be quickly removed, and your bird's living areas disinfected.

Avian polyomavirus

Young budgies were the first diagnosed victims of *polyomavirus,* which was once called *budgerigar fledgling disease*. The virus has been found in adult parrots but primarily remains a problem with all young pet birds, including canaries and other finches.

Symptoms may include depression, bleeding, loss of appetite, weight loss, regurgitation, diarrhea, dehydration, and difficulty breathing. Polyomavirus can kill young birds quickly — within 12 to 48 hours after the first symptoms are noticed. Virtually nothing can be done for infected birds to help rid them of this viral infection.

The good news is a vaccine does exist that can, in cooperation with good husbandry and the isolation of new birds, virtually eliminate infection and the disease from the birds of a home or aviary. The vaccine series starts at the minimum age of 21 days, with the second shot at the minimum age of 35 days. Breeding birds and adult pet birds can also be vaccinated — two shots 14 days apart, and then booster shots annually.

Proventricular dilation disease

"Wasting away" is the classic sign of *proventricular dilation disease,* which was once known as the *macaw wasting syndrome* or *macaw fading syndrome*. Since first discovered, PDD has been diagnosed in many species of birds, not just macaws. The suspected culprit in the spread of PDD is viral — but much remains unknown.

PDD often affects the *proventriculus,* which is the first section of the bird's stomach. Unable to perform its "job," the proventriculus becomes a place where food just rots, sometimes resulting in bacterial infections that can be fatal, as well as simply failing to move food normally to allow digestion to properly occur.

No cure or vaccine currently exists for PDD, although dietary changes and other supportive care may prolong and improve what time the bird has left.

Psittacosis

Enough with the viruses! *Psittacosis* — also known as *chlamydiosis* — is caused by a bacteria. This bacteria causes a disease something like a really serious flu, affecting the breathing or digestive systems.

The antibiotic shotgun and other disasters

Antibiotics are one of the outstanding contributions of modern medicine and have saved countless lives of both the human and animal variety. But we have become so comfortable with these medicines and their frequent usage that we sometimes forget they are powerful drugs that should be used with care.

And yet, many pet-owners respond to any sign of illness by dosing — and often, overdosing — their pets with the couple of antibiotics commonly available at pet-supply stores (and often labeled for other pets, such as fish). This sort of treatment for your sick bird is a spectacularly bad idea, for a couple of reasons.

First, if your bird has a viral or fungal infection, an antibiotic doesn't help — and, particularly in the case of a fungal infection, may even worsen your bird's condition.

Second, all antibiotics are not the same — they each have their target bacteria and may have little effect on bacteria that they're not designed to combat, as well as bacteria that are resistant to their effects.

Finally, regular use of antibiotics may affect both your bird's immune system and the bacteria trying to beat it, leading to the development of antibiotic-resistant strains of bacteria that are hard to stamp out even with the "right" medication.

When you buy an antibiotic at a pet-supply store, you're often wasting your money, and you're certainly losing time — time that should be spent taking your bird to your veterinarian for an accurate diagnosis and targeted treatment.

Psittacosis is a serious killer of pet birds, but it doesn't have to be. If diagnosed early and appropriately treated with the right course of antibiotics, psittacosis can be beaten. Read those key words again: *If* diagnosed early and appropriately treated. They could save your bird's life.

Veterinarians find the disease to be often devilish, hard to diagnose because of the wide range of symptoms. A wide variety of tests are available to support or confirm their suspicions.

Aspergillosis and candidiasis

Fungi and their relatives, the molds, are a significant threat to pet birds. They're not contagious — one bird can't catch a fungal disease from another. Instead, they're the result of poor hygiene and overall weak or poor health — a healthy bird is usually able to fight off a fungal infection.

Although countless kinds of fungus and molds exist, the two that worry parrot-keepers most cause *aspergillosis* and *candidiasis.* Both are more of a concern to bird-lovers in warm, humid places, such as Florida or Hawaii.

Fungal diseases comes in many forms, affecting the nose, the *trachea* (windpipe), lungs, or air sacs. Your veterinarian makes her tentative diagnosis based on the symptoms she sees and backs up her hunch with laboratory tests.

Antifungal medications and supportive care can be effective against aspergillus infections, but they often take a while to work and involve periodic rechecks to assess progress.

Because fungal spores are everywhere, good hygiene is the only way to help prevent the disease — keeping your bird's living area clean to minimize the amount of infectious elements.

Supportive Care

Your bird may not be out of the woods for a while even after your veterinarian treats him. During the recuperation time, you and your veterinarian need to weigh many factors in determining what's best for your bird. Your bird's condition is an important consideration, of course, but so, too, is your skill and comfort in dealing with a sick pet, as well as your ability to monitor your bird closely.

The hospital stay

A severely ill bird usually needs to be hospitalized. He may need tube-feeding or injectable fluids to keep him fed and hydrated, and the warmth and oxygen a "birdy intensive care unit (ICU)" can provide. Perhaps most important, because a sick bird's status can change rapidly, he needs to be under observation by people who can evaluate his status regularly and react quickly to give him the care he needs.

At what point your bird can go home is something you need to discuss with your veterinarian. Some questions she may ask include the following:

- **Will anyone be keeping an eye on your bird?** Even though recuperating birds need plenty of rest and should, for the most part, be left alone, checking on your bird from time to time is a good idea. If you're working long hours away from home, that may not be possible.
- **How comfortable are you with restraining and medicating your bird? Will your schedule allow you to give your bird medications as scheduled?** If you're not proficient at toweling your bird or if injecting medicine (see the section, "Giving medication" in this chapter) leaves you cold, your bird may be better off with a longer hospital stay. If you have vast experience, on the other hand, your bird may be able to go home even if he needs to be hand-fed.

Be honest about what you can and can't do for your bird — honest with yourself and honest with your veterinarian. Some people just aren't comfortable with nursing sick family members, whether two-legged or four-legged. If you're upfront with your veterinarian, you can work out a solution that is good for you and your bird.

Many veterinary hospitals don't have staff on-site 24 hours a day. Your veterinarian should discuss with you his plans for your bird after-hours. In Brian's practice, critically ill birds may come home with him or his staff so they can be monitored. In other cases, a calm night in the hospital is often just what the doctor ordered. Although transporting your pet to a 24-hour clinic may be possible, doing so may not necessarily be the best course of action because of stress considerations.

Home care

If you're able to care for your bird at home, you have to make some adjustments to provide him with as quiet and stress-free an environment as possible.

- **Use a smaller cage, if you can.** If your bird has a travel cage, use it while he's healing. The smaller space keeps him less active and feeling more secure.
- **Lower or remove perches.** Folded towels made excellent "beds" for sick birds, providing a degree of insulation, softness, and a good texture for secure footing. Plus, they can be changed and laundered when soiled. Low perches — 1 one inch off the towel — can make a big difference for your bird, making him feel better but not having to work too hard to get up onto.
- **Keep food and water close by.** If your bird's food and water bowls are attached to higher parts of the cage, take them out of their holders and put them on the floor of the cage. Feed your bird his favorite foods to keep him eating, especially those with high water content, such as fruits (within reason, of course). For the short term, don't worry about complete and balanced nutrition.
- **Maintain a warm environment.** You can choose among several ways to provide extra heat. Heating pads, wrapped in towels and with the cord safely hidden, are fine when kept on a low temperature. Microwaveable "hot packs" are fine, too, as long as they're not too hot to begin with. You can also use a heat lamp or drape an electric blanket over the cage. Whatever source you choose, check frequently on the heat level — warm, not hot! Generally, around 75 to 85 degrees F is a target to shoot for.

- **Strive for peace and quiet.** Try to keep the household as low-key as possible, and place your bird's cage in a spot removed from family activities. Because birds relax in low light conditions, partially covering the cage or dimming room lights helps. Don't turn the lights completely out, though! When your bird decides he wants to eat, make sure that whenever that time is, he can see and find the food you have available for him.
- **Keep handling to a minimum.** Your bird needs to rest. Don't be a worrier and check on him constantly, or stress him with frequent handling. Have you ever been in the hospital and been annoyed at how often you're bothered for medications, blood draws, or blood pressure checks? Wouldn't resting be nice? You bet! So leave your bird alone!

Giving medication

For anyone who has ever struggled with getting a pill down the throat of a dog or cat, the good news is that you can't practically or easily pill a parrot or canary, so you aren't expected to do so. The bad news is it isn't really any easier to get medication in them. You can get medicine inside pet birds in four basic ways. They each have their pros and cons, although the last two, shown in Figure 10-2, are usually what your veterinarian recommends:

- **Water-soluble medications in drinking water:** A lot of the over-the-counter medications we discourage you from wasting your money on are added to drinking water. Adding medication to water is easiest, but it has its drawbacks. You have little control over dosage because you can't count on your bird to drink any set amount of water. Some species drink little water at all, and other birds may not feel up to drinking when they're ill. For these reasons, putting medicine in drinking water is probably not the route your veterinarian recommends, except in some very specific circumstances.
- **Medicated feeds:** The same pros and cons as with medicated water. It's easy to offer medicated feed, but you have no way of making sure any of it gets inside your bird. Brian says that many medicated feeds taste awful, so even if your bird feels like eating he may not touch the stuff with medicine in it.
- **Oral dosage:** Accuracy of dosage is a benefit of giving your bird medication orally — assuming you get the stuff in him instead of dribbling it everywhere but down his throat. You get the appropriate amount in an eyedropper or a syringe with the needle removed and slide the tip into the side of your bird's mouth. The downside you've probably already guessed: Your bird isn't likely to sit still for this procedure, so you have to restrain him with a towel. After he's restrained, a bird who has been hand-fed as a baby will usually go along — the sight of a plastic tip nearing his mouth often causes him to open up in hopes of a meal.

- **Injections:** High marks for accuracy, and after you're used to injecting your bird, high marks for ease as well. As with oral medications, though, you'll likely need to restrain your bird with a towel to inject his medication. Some people get really good at injecting their bird, even after initial reluctance. Those with diabetic birds, for example, may need to inject their birds every day — and it's no big deal for either bird or person.

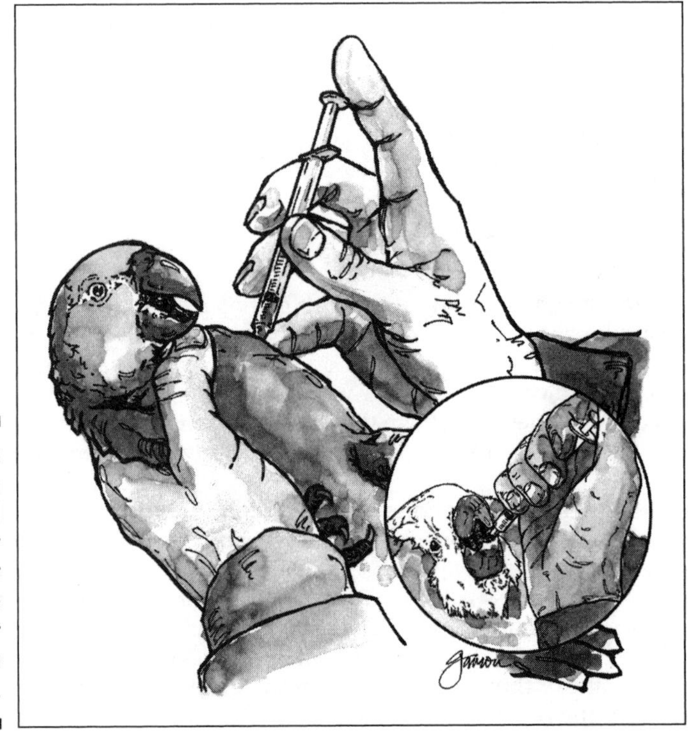

Figure 10-2: Medicating your bird with either injectable or oral dosage is easy after you get the hang of it.

Discuss with your veterinarian which method of medicating your bird is right for you both — and for your bird — and make sure you're comfortable with whatever method you choose. Medication won't do your bird any good if little or none of it gets in him. Ask all the questions you need to, watch your veterinarian demonstrate, and then practice under his tutelage before you go. And if you run into problems at home, call.

Whatever you do, don't skip any medication sent home with your bird, and don't stop giving it because your bird seems to feel better. Administer the medication exactly as prescribed, and call your veterinarian if you have any problems.

Chapter 11

Lifelong Care for Your Bird

In This Chapter

- A companion for life
- Some common older-bird problems
- Coping with the loss of your bird
- Providing for your pet when you're gone

Many of the bird species we keep as pets, such as the large parrots, have the potential to live nearly as long as we can — up to 70 years or more. Even the smaller parrots, such as cockatiels, are capable of outliving almost any dog or cat, a reality that is dramatically changing our ideas of planning for a lifetime of care.

And yet, until recently, relatively few pet birds achieved the life span of which they were capable, many dying in a fraction of the potential time they should have enjoyed on this earth. We just didn't know enough to provide them with what they needed to achieve a long and healthy life.

Oh, but mark our words: Things are different now, and they're getting better by the day.

In just the last decade, great advances in our knowledge of bird care and medicine have started to percolate through the entire avian world — through veterinarians, through breeders, through pet stores, and, finally, through to the average bird-owner (as if such a thing really does exist — we think all bird-owners are anything but average!). The result: healthier, happier birds who can be our companions for years (see Figure 11-1).

These changes can't come soon enough, given the growing appreciation of birds as companions. The next decade and beyond promises even more for those who love sharing their lives with birds.

Figure 11-1: With proper care and attention, your bird can be a wonderful companion for decades.

In this chapter, we share the latest on health concerns for aging birds, along with the help you need to cope if your bird dies. Because basic good care and preventive medicine have no age limits, we strongly encourage you to review the information on those topics in Chapters 5 and 9, along with proper nutrition in Chapter 6.

Why Birds Are Living Longer

So what's behind the life span increases among pet birds? The same forces that contribute to our own healthier lives make a notable difference in the bird world — the knowledge of how a life lived well can be a life lived long. In the case of pet birds, though, serendipity (or just plain luck) has also played a role.

Domestically raised versus wild-caught

More pet birds are domestically raised than ever before, in response to large-scale bans by many countries (including the United States) on importing wild-caught birds for the pet trade. Laws that were introduced to protect birds in the wild — and to fight the cruelty that was, at times, involved in their capture and transportation — ended up creating demand for domestically bred and raised pet birds.

The best of these breeders have changed the very nature of the birds available as pets. Healthier, better socialized, and comfortable in a human environment, these birds are solid citizens from the start, spared the stresses of capture and the exposure to infectious disease that was so common in wild-caught birds.

Although the growth and refinement of bird breeding, or *aviculture,* has been a boon to the pet bird trade, not all breeders do their part to ensure that the birds they produce are healthy, well-socialized pets. And they sell to retailers who are likewise sometimes in the dark about the right way to do things. The bird-supply business is full of opinions, as are most other things in our lives. We worry what you may hear may not be what's right for your bird. We can't stress enough the importance of getting a healthy bird to begin with. For the ins and outs of bird-buying, see Chapters 3 and 16.

New views on nutrition

When pressed for one — and only one — reason for the increased health and longevity of birds, Brian starts out by saying he honestly can't choose one. And then he picks nutrition.

And then he backtracks into bird breeding because of the aviculturist's massively important role in getting baby birds started on good foods, which comes back to . . . nutrition. Good nutrition is another area with a strong parallel to what we know in our own lives. When you're young, you can get away with a junk food diet — or, at least, it seems as if you can. High-fat foods, few fruits and veggies, and an emphasis on some food groups over others are all things we seem to muddle through when we're young, but bad habits catch up to us as we age. The same truth applies to birds. High-fat, seed-only diets may seem to be fine for young birds, even for years, but they do take a toll in the end.

The advent of nutritionally balanced, pelleted foods has been perhaps the greatest single leap forward in bird care. The selection of high-quality commercial diets that are available is truly astonishing, especially when compared with what was available just a decade ago. Even more promising is the continued education of the pet-owning public about feeding these foods, along with fresh, healthy "people-food."

For a thorough overview of what your bird should and shouldn't be eating, check out Chapter 6.

The importance of research

Because avian medicine is still evolving, we encourage all bird-lovers to support continued research into bird health. The contributions can be monetary — we offer a couple of worthy funds in our Additional Resources appendix at the back of this book — but you can give an even more personal gift.

When you lose a bird, talk to your veterinarian about allowing her to perform a postmortem examination, which is the only way to determine an accurate cause of death — and perhaps find a key that can help other birds survive. This knowledge can have direct value for you and other birds you have or may have in the future. *Morti vivos docent* — the dead teach the living — is as true in avian medicine as it has always been in human medicine.

Even living birds can help to advance medical knowledge. Brian likes to share the stories of birds afflicted with a deadly disease who ultimately became critical to understanding how their disease was acquired and spread to others. Owners of these birds donated them to a qualified university researcher, who figured out and then disseminated information that has since saved the lives of countless birds.

Making such a selfless decision can, of course, be difficult, but we also believe that for some, the realization of helping to save lives can help with a loss.

The veterinary contribution

When Brian was studying to be a veterinarian, "avian medicine" — what little there was of it — was primarily dedicated to keeping poultry alive and healthy long enough to become somebody's dinner. Very few veterinary schools taught students the basics of pet bird medicine and surgery. Veterinarians in practice weren't well-equipped with the knowledge they needed to care for pet birds — little information was actually available for sharing — and so pet birds pretty much lived or died. Even the best veterinarians had limited ability to make a positive difference in the pet bird population.

In the last 20 years or so, and especially in the last decade, the body of medical knowledge about pet birds has grown.

The advent of focused avian health care specialists like Brian and groups like the Association of Avian Veterinarians signifies these changes. More is known today about how pet birds should be cared for, how they get sick, and how they can be made well. And while the need for new and insightful information is ongoing, more veterinarians than ever are interested in exploring the subject of pet bird care — and that means an even brighter future for our avian companions.

Health and the Older Bird

The problems of "older birds" don't necessarily start at an advanced age. For the purpose of this chapter, we define a bird as "older" when it's past the age of sexual maturity, which differs from one species to another. Many behavior problems present themselves at this stage — we cover those challenges in Chapter 12. This is also the point in your bird's life when bad health habits start coming home to roost.

Although we put the most common problems in this section, keep in mind that the information you find here can't be all-encompassing. A good relationship with a well-qualified veterinarian is key to keeping your pet bird healthy as he ages.

Chronic malnutrition

In medical terms, a *chronic* condition is one that happens over time, as opposed to an *acute* condition, which can come up quickly. An acute condition — a bite, say, or poisoning — can put your bird's life at risk immediately. A chronic condition can be just as deadly, though, stealing life away in little chunks over time. Chronic malnutrition, which simply means continued bad eating habits, is one of the more insidious problems shortening the lives of birds. And it comes in at least two varieties — too much and too little.

Obesity

Fat birds are everywhere, and the problems they suffer because they're overweight are fairly similar to those caused by excess weight in our own lives. Obesity puts stress on bones, joints, and internal organ systems. The list of health problems associated with obesity is a long one, and it includes liver problems, heart and lung problems, diabetes and other pancreatic disorders, fatty tumors, thyroid problems, and added stress to the skeletal system, especially the feet. Overweight birds are also at higher risk during surgery or stressful handling.

Seed-heavy diets (which are high in fat) are often to blame for obesity, but some birds (like some people) eat such large quantities of even a perfectly balanced diet that they put on weight. Add in boredom, lack of exercise, and even overfeeding as a chick, and you can figure out why veterinarians see a lot of pudgy birds like the one in Figure 11-2.

Figure 11-2: This cockatiel suffers from obesity, which can severely affect the quality and length of her life.

Photo by Dr. Brian L. Speer

Genetics does play a role in determining a predisposition to obesity in pet birds. Amazon parrots, large cockatoos, cockatiels, and budgies seem to pork up much more frequently than other pet birds. Elderly birds and breeding hens of all pet species are also at a higher risk.

Because those nifty height/weight charts for humans don't exist for birds, you need to rely on your powers of observation — and those of your veterinarian — to determine whether your bird is overweight. Some of the signs include

- Rolls of fat around the abdomen and hip areas, along with cleavage on the abdomen or breast area.
- Visible fat under the skin, which Brian calls the "broiler chicken look." The skin of most normal pet birds is typically very thin and quite transparent. When the skin is wet with rubbing alcohol, you should be able to see dark pink or red muscle underneath. In overweight birds, you see yellowish fat under the skin instead.
- Breathing difficulty, such as labored breathing, especially after physical exertion.
- Heat intolerance, shown by excessive wing drooping or open-mouthed breathing in a hot environment.
- Overgrown upper beaks. Some birds grow their upper beaks excessively long if they have underlying obesity and fatty liver disease problems. This is particularly true in Amazon parrots and budgies.

If you suspect your bird is fat — and especially if you *know* your bird is fat — see your veterinarian right away for nutritional counseling and other ways to attack the problem.

Because lack of activity is one of the factors contributing to obesity, look for ways to motivate your bird to move around more. A great bird toy that inspires exercise is a stiff rope coil perch, which requires a bird to stay constantly active to remain aboard. They're great fun, and they really burn the calories. For more on outfitting your bird, see Chapter 4.

Undernutrition

The lack of critical nutrients in a bird's diet — undernutrition — can make birds seem old and fragile before their time. The most common nutrients missing in poor diets are vitamins A and D and calcium.

Vitamin A has an important role in maintaining healthy vision, helps maintain the integrity of the skin and mucus membranes, plays a part in the function of the immune system, contributes to normal reproduction and the proper growth of bones, and likely has a role in the maintenance of healthy cells.

Vitamin D deficiencies can mean trouble, too. This nutrient helps to absorb calcium from the gut and to regulate blood calcium levels in the body. Without vitamin D, bones grow weak and fragile, prone to easy breaking.

Calcium nutritional deficiencies may appear similarly to vitamin D deficiencies but are linked directly to the dietary calcium levels and the calcium-phosphorus balance of the diet.

Calcium nutritional deficiencies can also lead to osteoporosis in female birds, the result of chronic egg-laying that forces the birds to pull calcium reserves from their very bones, weakening them as a result. We talk about reproductive health concerns in Chapter 13.

A proper diet of commercial pellets supplemented by fruits, vegetables, and other healthy people-food is the best way to treat these deficiencies before they become health problems.

Although you may entertain thoughts of throwing vitamins at your bird to make sure he gets enough A, D, and calcium, we urge you to forget any such idea. Balanced nutrition comes from a balanced diet, and by adding what you think your bird may be lacking, you may end up substituting one problem for another — or adding one problem on top of another. Your veterinarian is your most reliable source of knowledge about whether your bird needs vitamin supplements, in the short or long term.

Can a bird be both overnourished and undernourished at the same time? However unfair, the answer is *yes*. Improper diets can cause both obesity and nutritional deficiencies, resulting in a fat bird who's still starving for the vitamin, mineral, or protein components of a healthy diet.

Cataracts

Weakening vision is a problem in aging birds just as it is in aging humans and other animals, and one of the main problems is cataracts. This condition is an increased density of the lens of the eye, and while it's often an old-age problem, it isn't always. The cause needs to be sorted out, and surgical options do exist that can restore vision in some of our older birds.

In Brian's experience, however, blind birds who are otherwise healthy can get along just fine — as long as you don't rearrange the furniture on them, and you take extra care to let them know when you're approaching them so they don't bite out of fear.

Arthritis

Old bones and joints become a little less functional with age, as many of us have come to find out with our own bodies. Arthritis is defined as any inflammatory problem within a joint, and the condition may have several causes. If you notice your bird is consistently lame or see swelling at the joints, have your veterinarian check out the problem. Caught early and properly diagnosed, arthritis may be treatable, sparing your bird years of misery. Another reason to see your veterinarian: Some forms of arthritis, such as gout or infection in the joints, can even be life-threatening.

Heart disease

Birds, especially sedentary ones on high-fat diets, can fall prey to many cardiovascular problems, such as thickening arteries. Although early heart disease is now more manageable than ever before, the best recommendation is still diet, exercise, and early diagnosis and treatment of any problems that do erupt. Signs of heart disease may include a shortness of breath, fainting spells, enlargement of the abdomen — or sudden death, with no warning signs whatsoever. Another good argument for preventive care, wouldn't you say?

Knowing When It's "Time"

Euthanasia, the technical term for "putting a pet to sleep," is one of the hardest decisions you must ever make, and the choice doesn't get any easier, no matter how many times over the years you face it. Your veterinarian can offer you advice and your friends can offer you support, but no one can make the decision for you. If you live with an elderly or terminally ill bird, you look in her eyes every morning and ask yourself: Is this the day I help my friend to the other side?

To know *for sure* that you're making the right decision is impossible. Asking guidance from your friends, family, and veterinarian is appropriate, but only you can make the final decision. After others share their empathetic "If it were my companion" advice, they need to respect your decision without question.

Some owners choose euthanasia before their bird's discomfort becomes pain, which is sooner than many people are able to come to grips with their pet's condition. Some owners use a pet's appetite as the guide — if an old or ill bird is no longer interested in eating, they reason, he's not interested in anything. Other owners wait until no doubt remains that the time is at hand and they know their bird is hurting.

Each guideline is the right one for some birds and some owners at some times. You do the best you can, and then you try to put the decision behind you and deal with the grief.

Ironically, the incredible advances in veterinary medicine in the past couple of decades have made the decisions even more difficult for many people. Not too long ago, the best you could do for a seriously ill pet was to make her comfortable until that wasn't possible anymore. Improvements in avian medicine — and more are on the way — keep alive birds who wouldn't have had a chance even a few years ago.

If you have a realistic expectation that veterinary care can improve your aged or chronically ill bird's life — instead of simply prolonging that life, sometimes in misery — then treatment is a reasonable option. But don't allow guilt or wishful thinking to push you into making a decision that doesn't feel right to you.

Euthanasia is a kindness extended to a treasured bird, a decision we make at a great cost to ourselves. It's a final act of love, nothing less.

Amazing as it seems to us, you can find books and other references that provide a how-to approach to euthanasia at home. Frankly, the suffering such approaches inflict makes our stomachs turn, and they suggest that birds are somehow less deserving of a peaceful death than are dogs and cats. They're not. The gentle easing from life a veterinarian can offer is your final gift to your bird. Please make compassion the last act your bird knows, if euthanasia is necessary.

Euthanasia options

Should you be with your pet at the end? What should you do with the remains? The questions are all difficult, but no answers are wrong.

As performed by a veterinarian, euthanasia is a quick and peaceful process. The animal is unconscious within seconds and dead within less than a minute; the euphemism "put to sleep" is a perfect description. Those who attend the procedure come away reassured that their pets felt no fear or pain.

If you're bringing your bird in — as opposed to making the decision for a sick bird already in the veterinarian's care — call ahead to set the appointment and make clear to the receptionist what you're coming for. That way, the staff can ensure that you won't sit in the waiting room — you, your bird, and your grief. Your veterinarian is going to do his best to make sure that all your questions are answered and that you're comfortable with everything before proceeding. Brian discourages bird-lovers from staying with their pets at the end, but if you feel strongly, discuss the issue beforehand with your veterinarian. If you do stay, your veterinarian can prepare you for what you will see.

Remember: Crying is normal, and your veterinarian understands. So, too, we believe, does your bird.

You may want to spend a few minutes with your pet afterward, and your veterinarian understands that, as well, and is going to give you all the time you need alone to begin the process of dealing with your loss. (If your pet dies while in the veterinarian's care, you may also choose to view the body to give yourself closure and let the healing begin. Discuss this decision with your veterinarian.)

You may be more comfortable with having your pet euthanized at home. If so, discuss the matter with your veterinarian directly. Many vets extend this special service to long-time clients. If yours doesn't, you may alternatively ask your veterinarian to recommend a colleague who offers house calls. Perhaps more importantly, however, we want to make sure that the veterinarian you choose is familiar with proper technique in birds, in order to make the process as stress-free as possible for you and your bird.

After your pet's death, most veterinarians will discuss the value of having a postmortem examination done, to confirm the diagnosis and to make sure that you or your other birds at home are not potentially at risk of any infection that may have been present. The postmortem is a much more common event in birds than in dogs and cats, and it is important to consider the potential value in the event of the death or euthanasia of your bird.

You can handle your pet's remains in many ways, and doing so is easier on you overall if you make this decision beforehand. Your veterinarian has the information you need on your choices, which may include having your local animal control department pick up the body, burying the pet in your backyard or at another site (where it's legal and with the landowner's permission, of course), arranging for cremation, or contracting with a pet cemetery for full services and burial. Again, no choice is "wrong." Whatever feels right to you and comforts you best is what you should do.

Several manufacturers offer tasteful and attractive markers for your yard to memorialize your pet; these items are often advertised in the back of such magazines as *Bird Talk*. Other choices include large rocks or slabs of stone or a tree or rose bush. Even if you choose not to have your bird's body or ashes returned, placing a memorial in a special spot may soothe you.

Another way to celebrate the memory of your bird is to make a donation to your local humane society, regional school of veterinary medicine, bird health or rescue foundation, or other favorite animal charity. (A donation in a beloved companion's name is a wonderful thing to do for a friend who has lost a pet as well.)

The major greeting card companies now market pet sentiments, and among the items available are some elegant sympathy cards. We see these cards as further proof that society is recognizing the strength of the bond we share with our pets. Don't be surprised to receive a card from your veterinarian, friends, and family, and know, too, that a card, call, or note is always appreciated when you know someone who is dealing with the loss of a pet.

Dealing with loss

Many people are surprised at the powerful emotions that erupt after a pet's death, and they're embarrassed by their grief. Remembering that pets have meaning in our lives beyond the love we feel for the animal alone may help. Often, we don't realize that we're grieving not only for the pet we loved, but also for the special time and the ties to other people the animal represented in our lives. Considering the potentially long life span of many pet birds, you may be dealing with the loss of a companion you've known longer than any other. Is it any surprise that you're grieving?

Adding to the sadness of loss is the fact that for some bird-owners, the pet they lose may have been in the family for a generation — or more! Not that longevity is the key to a bird's value: Brian has helped many clients through the loss of charming budgie companions, who have passed on after a life span that was a fraction of what a macaw may enjoy.

Taking care of yourself is important at this difficult time. Some people — the "It's just a pet" crowd — don't understand your feelings and may shrug off your grief as foolish. Even those who may understand the emotion over the loss of a dog may not be so empathetic when a bird is gone — a lot of people just don't "get" the "bird thing" like we do. The company of other pet-lovers is very important. Seek them out to share your feelings. The Internet is a great place to post memorials and share memories with others who understand.

A difficult time, no doubt, but remember: In time, the memories become a source of pleasure, not pain. You're not on any set timetable, but healing happens. We promise.

A handful of books and one really fine video may help you help your child with the loss of a pet. From Fred Rogers (yes, Mister Rogers of Neighborhood fame) comes the book *When a Pet Dies* (Putnam) and the video *Death of a Goldfish*. Rachel Biale's *My Pet Died* (Tricycle Press) not only provides pages that children can fill in, but also offers special pages of advice that parents can tear out. Finally, Judith Viorst's *The Tenth Good Thing About Barney* (Aladdin) is a book that experts in pet loss have recommended for many years. While not specifically about birds, these resources can still help.

You're not alone

You may find comfort in talking to others about your bird's death. Ask your veterinarian about pet loss support groups. Almost unheard of a couple decades of ago, these groups now exist in many communities. You may also want to see a counselor; this, too, can be helpful.

Veterinary schools and colleges are among the leaders in creating programs to help pet-lovers deal with loss. A handful now operate pet loss hotlines staffed by veterinary students trained to answer questions, offer materials that may help you (including guidelines for helping children with loss), and just plain listen. These are wonderful programs, and they're free for the cost of the call. (If you call during off hours, they call you back, collect, during their normal hours of operation.)

Locations, operating hours, and phone numbers of pet loss hotlines are as follows:

University of California
School of Veterinary Medicine
Davis, California
Hours of operation: 6:30 to 9:30 p.m. Pacific time
Mondays through Fridays; Tuesdays through Thursdays during summer
530-752-4200

Cornell University
College of Veterinary Medicine
Ithaca, New York
Hours of operation: 6 to 9 p.m. Eastern time
Tuesdays through Thursdays
607-253-3932

Washington State University
College of Veterinary Medicine
Pullman, Washington
Hours of operation: 6:30 to 9 p.m. Pacific time
Mondays through Thursdays; 1 to 3 p.m. Saturdays
509-335-5704

University of Florida
College of Veterinary Medicine
Gainesville, Florida
Hours of operation: 7 to 9 p.m. Eastern time
Mondays through Fridays
352-392-4700, Ext. 4080

Michigan State University
College of Veterinary Medicine
East Lansing, Michigan
Hours of operation: 6:30 to 9:30 p.m. Eastern time
Tuesdays, Wednesdays, and Thursdays
517-432-2696

Ohio State University
College of Veterinary Medicine
Columbus, Ohio
Hours of operation: 6:30 to 9:30 p.m. Eastern time
Mondays, Wednesdays, and Fridays
614-292-1823

Tufts University
School of Veterinary Medicine
North Grafton, Massachusetts
Hours of operation: 6 to 9 p.m. Eastern time
Mondays though Fridays
508-839-7966

Virginia-Maryland Regional College of Veterinary Medicine
Blacksburg, Virginia
Hours of operation: 6 to 9 p.m. Eastern time
Tuesdays and Thursdays; calls referred to Ohio State when school is out
540-231-8038

University of Illinois at Urbana-Champaign
College of Veterinary Medicine
Urbana, Illinois
Hours of operation: 7 to 9 p.m. Central Time
217-244-2273

Iowa State University
College of Veterinary Medicine
Ames, Iowa
Hours of operation: 6 to 9 p.m. Central Time
Mondays through Fridays
888-478-7574

What If You Go First?

First things first: You can't leave your estate to your bird because in the eyes of the law, a pet is an "it," with little more legal status than a chair. Nor can you set up a trust for your pet for the same reason. The beneficiary of a trust must be a bona fide human being, and the fact that you think of your bird as a person doesn't really matter, because the courts don't share that perspective.

Although you, of course, need to consult with your attorney about the legalities of providing for your pet in the event of your death, talking the subject over with your friends and family is even more important, because you have to identify one of them as a potential caretaker. You must leave your avian "property" to that person, along with enough money to provide for the bird's care for life. You have no real control over the outcome, which is why you need to choose someone you trust and then hope for your bird's sake that things turn out okay.

No one likes to think about dying. But you have a responsibility to those you leave behind, and that includes your pets, especially when you're talking about a bird who may potentially outlive you for decades. Talk to your friends, family, and even your veterinarian. Call an attorney. Just don't rely on the kindness of strangers to care for your pets if something happens to you. Your bird deserves better than that.

The Association of the Bar of New York City offers a low-cost pamphlet on providing for your pet if you can't. To order "Providing for Your Pets in the Event of Your Death or Hospitalization," send a $2 money order or check made out to the Association of the Bar and a self-addressed, stamped, legal-sized envelope to the association's Office of Communications, 42 W. 44th Street, New York, NY 10036.

Part IV
Living Happily with Your Bird

"Listen McKenzie – those are my sheep in your living room! Now, either you do something about keeping your Border canary locked up, or I WILL!!"

In this part . . .

Despite the best intentions of bird-lovers, behavior problems are commonplace — and often tragically mishandled. In this part, we look at the behaviors that drive bird-owners crazy and suggest practical solutions for turning around a bad situation. And then we take up the matter of multiple-bird households. Are you really prepared to add to your flock of pets or try your hand at bird-breeding? We help you decide and walk you through everything you need to know, from breeding to baby-raising.

Chapter 12

Getting to "Good Bird!": Dealing with Behavior Problems

In This Chapter

- Being "bad": It's only natural
- Setting up a framework for good behavior
- Dealing with specific problems

Perfection is overrated, in our experience. We don't expect it in our families. We don't expect it in our friends. And we certainly don't expect it in our pets. After all, if we have a hard time getting along — or even communicating well — with our own kind, how can we expect to have an easy time of it with another species?

If, in the popular vernacular, men are from one planet and women from another, many a frustrated pet owner must sometimes feel that birds are from another galaxy entirely. Or are they? From the smallest budgie or lovebird to the largest macaw or cockatoo, the parrots (the birds we talk about in this chapter) are intelligent, generous, territorial, sometimes sex-crazed, affectionate, distant, talkative, uncommunicative . . . we could go on, but we bet you're getting the picture. Birds are a lot like humans! And you have to admit: We're no standard-bearer for good behavior as a species.

Human as they may seem, though, birds are still birds. And you have to be understanding both of their needs and of their motivation for doing the things they do. What you see as "bad" behavior may well be perfectly normal for a bird, and you have to think like a bird to alter the behavior you don't want — if you can.

Ah, and there's the rub. With some birds, "bad" — really, normal — behavior can't be changed, and for others, the road to change is a long one. The quick fix isn't all that common when it comes to behavior, and we want to emphasize that fact going in. Still, if you're ready and willing to work with your bird, chances are you'll end up with a pet who's easier to live with.

Behavior resources worth tracking down

People can most certainly have a lot of problems with their birds, so you can expect to find a lot of advice on the market. We like to single out three resources produced by top behaviorists for special praise — a book, a video, and a magazine.

The book is Mattie Sue Athan's *Guide to a Well-Behaved Parrot* (Barron's Educational Series), which provides a good book-length treatment of the points we make in this chapter, with some good stories to really heighten the interest.

Brian uses Chris Davis's video, *Demystifying Pet Bird Behavior* (Bird Lady Productions; check the Additional Resources appendix for ordering information) in his practice. Davis is excellent at showing and explaining bird body language and offering good advice on correcting problems. The video closes with the heartwarming story of a scarlet macaw who'd been abused for years and still was able to blossom into a loving pet when someone gave him patient, gentle handling.

Sally Blanchard's *Pet Bird Report* magazine comes out a half-dozen times a year. The PBR offers information you won't find anywhere else, geared to improving every aspect of your bird's life, and especially his behavior. (We feature the *Pet Bird Report* Web site in Chapter 17. You can subscribe to the magazine online, or check the Additional Resources appendix for ordering information.)

Don't be discouraged by the prospect of working on a bird who's making you crazy. Seemingly miraculous turnarounds are possible with pet birds. Hard work, patience, understanding, and commitment can make almost any relationship work.

No matter what else you take out of this chapter, remember this concept: The first step in dealing with a behavior problem is to make sure it doesn't have its primary roots in an underlying health problem.

Take a look at nutrition in Chapter 6 and basic bird health problems in Chapter 10. You also need a veterinarian skilled in avian medicine to help your bird regain health — we help you find one of those in Chapter 9.

A Framework for Good Behavior

Fixing a behavior problem in a pet is rarely a matter of reacting only to the problem, be it biting, screaming, or feather-picking. Good behavior builds from within, and that's especially true with creatures as intelligent as birds. Show us a bird who's a well-behaved member of the family, and chances are we're looking at a bird who gets plenty of positive attention, eats properly, is in good health, is well-trained, and gets a good amount of exercise.

Preventing a problem is always easier than fixing one, which is why we stress prevention in this book. Chapter 5, with its emphasis on starting a bird out right, complements this chapter, which focuses on getting a bird back on track.

Yes, we know your bird is driving you crazy, and maybe it doesn't make sense to you to worry about, say, your pet's diet when his screaming is damaging your eardrum. But a relationship is kind of like a house, in that a sturdy one always starts with a good foundation. With your bird, the time is right to bolster the groundwork.

Ensure Your Bird's Health

You are doomed before you start if you try to work on the bad behaviors of a bird who's sick, for two primary reasons:

- A bird who's sick — and remember, a bird can be very sick indeed without showing any symptoms — is hardly interested in you and what you want from her. She's fighting for her life, and that's where her energies must be focused.
- Whatever is wrong with your bird may be causing the behavior problem. Feather-picking or even self-mutilation, for example, can be an outward symptom of any number of internal medical conditions. Another possibility: Your bird may be in pain. Consider how unhappy a bird with an undiagnosed arthritic leg — yes, it happens! — is going to be about being asked to step up on your hand. Wouldn't you bite if it meant you'd be left alone?

If you have a bird with a behavior problem, the veterinary hospital is your first stop. Your veterinarian can not only work to restore your pet to good health or document that baseline health is sound, but she can also offer some basic, solid behavior advice or help you find someone who can.

Getting a bird healthy before working on behavior issues is so important that most *avian behaviorists* (see our sidebar, "Calling for help," in this chapter for information on these professionals) will not even take a case unless and until the pet has been thoroughly examined by a veterinarian who has experience with birds.

Be Fair to Your Bird

Look around your home — does it bear any resemblance that you can see to an Amazon rain forest, an African jungle, or the Australian outback? Likely not. And yet, these environs are your bird's natural habitat. When your bird is falling asleep at night, is he dreaming of some jungle he may never have known (see Figure 12-1)? Pet birds are wild at heart — a fact you need to keep in mind when trying to deal with behavior problems in your pet. Even a bird born into domestication and lovingly raised by human hands is still not more than a few generations — and sometimes far less — from the wild life.

Figure 12-1: Birds may not dream of the jungle, but their wild instincts are still part of who they are.

Domestic life is a trade-off for birds — a bargain, we must point out, they had no say about making. Sure, their lives may be longer in captivity, and maybe they don't have to worry so much about food (it's provided) and predators (they're discouraged). But they also don't have the pleasure of living in a huge flock of their kind, of flying for miles a day, of landing on anything they fancy and tearing it apart just for the sheer joy of it. (And then pooping all over it before they fly to somewhere clean and new.)

To put it bluntly: No wild bird lives in a cage.

You can't turn your home into a rain forest or other natural environment, but you can manage some substitutions that help make up for what your bird is missing.

Create a suitable environment

Although many of today's zoos go to great effort to keep animals happy, this situation wasn't always the norm. With little more than bare enclosures and food, many zoo animals in years past slowly went mad or got sick and died from the stress of captivity. Compare that existence to the rich environments the better zoos provide for their animals today — as close to wild as you can get. Even when building a massive, natural-like habitat isn't possible, good zookeepers today do their best to enrich the environment of their charges. Toys, training, food that's more challenging to find and eat — all these and more are part of a good zoo today, and the animals are better for it.

We encourage you to consider following the example of these zoos and improve the space your bird calls home. While zoo birds aren't pets — they're generally not handled, and they don't have to be a human companion — you can still learn from the zoos and their tricks of the trade.

If you're looking for a well-researched, engrossing, and sometimes eye-opening book on how zoos work today, pick up a copy of Vicki Crock's *The Modern Ark: The Story of Zoos, Past, Present and Future* (Bard Trade Paperbacks). The way zoos deal with the issues of captivity help you gain a new perspective on the challenges that face you and your bird.

Not all zoos hear the message of better care for their captive creatures — and many birds and other animals suffer as a result. We encourage you to make your voice heard and support the efforts of zoos to modernize for the sake of the animals. And vote with your feet on the second-raters that show no interest in improving: Don't patronize them!

A cage may be an unnatural home, but it doesn't have to be an unhappy one. Make sure your bird has room to move, a variety of places to perch, and toys to keep both mind and body busy.

Check out Chapter 4 for information on buying a cage and accessories, and Chapter 5 for tips on setting up your bird's home. In our color section, you can find an illustration of the basic, boring cage that too many birds call home — and the souped-up environment you should be providing for your bird.

Spend time in positive interaction

Have you ever had a teacher or boss who never had anything nice to say about anything you did but came down hard on you if you made a mistake? Did you find that person likable? Did you enjoy being around that person, or were you stressed out waiting for the boom to fall?

We're not sure why so many people are so quick to criticize and so slow to praise, but we do know this all-too-human tendency can have a negative effect on your bird. Instead of waiting to catch your bird doing something wrong, look for opportunities to praise your pet. A few sweet words, a favorite treat, or a neck scratch — your bird deserves these signs of respect for being the kind of companion you want him to be, however briefly he's managing to pull it off.

Is he playing quietly with a toy? Staying on his play gym? Show him you approve! Spend time with your bird every day, working on good behaviors such as the step-up command (more on this later in this chapter), playing with toys together, and just plain hanging out. Talk to your bird, snuggle your bird, if he likes that sort of thing (not all do), and take time to figure out your bird's favorite places to be scratched.

If the only time you deal with your bird is to (occasionally) clean up the cage, change the food and water, and to yell at him for screaming, you're not holding up your end of the deal. Your pet bird should be a member of your family. Make him one, and always keep an eye out for opportunities to let your bird know he's appreciated. He'll appreciate you back!

Get that bird a job!

Find something for your bird to do, or you can count on him finding something on his own. Give him lots of things to destroy, puzzle toys to figure out, and treats that take some effort to eat — like an occasional almond or other nut in the shell, or corn on the cob.

Be creative! Try using tree branches as perches — we list the safe kinds in Chapter 4 — and recycle old ball-point pens into chew toys (with the ink cartridge removed). Celebrate when your bird makes mincemeat of something you've provided him for just that purpose. Bird can be seriously destructive, and providing an outlet for those tendencies is a wonderful way to give your bird a "job."

Be Firm with Your Bird — but Gently

Children may fuss about the house rules, but it's pretty well accepted by parenting experts that children like the security of having limits set for them and knowing those restrictions are consistently and fairly enforced.

Birds like being treated the same way, and perhaps that's not very surprising, considering how many bird-lovers say their parrots are like 2-year-olds.

Another human-bird parallel: Like some people, some birds are opportunists — if you're not going to be boss, they're happy to take on the job, whether you want them to or not. Not all birds are bucking for a promotion to boss, but even the most easygoing pet birds enjoy the security of knowing there's someone in charge.

Being a leader doesn't mean being a dictator. To borrow a phrase from renowned dog trainer Carol Lea Benjamin, you need to be a *benevolent alpha* — top dog . . . er, bird, but in a kind and respectful way.

Becoming top bird

You can't sit your bird down and explain to him that you're in charge, and you can't write the house rules and post them on your refrigerator. You have to explain your expectations in a way your bird understands. You have to show him who's boss, in some ways that may seem very subtle to you but speak volumes to any parrot. Here are the rules you need to introduce to your problem bird so that he can start accepting you as boss:

- **Your heart, his head:** Altitude is where it's at for birds, even in their social interactions. Dominant members of the flock settle on the higher branches of trees, while the lower-ranking birds perch underneath. If your bird has an attitude problem, he needs to be lowered a peg or two — situated so his head is never higher than your heart.

  Achieving this goal may mean removing the roof-top play gym your bird's cage may have come with if it offers your bird too high a vantage point, as well as lowering portable play gyms and perches. Cancel shoulder rides; carry your bird on your hand and keep your arm down. When your bird stops showing an attitude problem, he may be able to get some height added to his liberties — as long as his behavior does not change accordingly.

- **You're grounded, buddy!** Another aid to keeping your bird's expectations grounded in reality: wing trims. Birds whose wings are trimmed for safety can't cop the attitude a flighted pet can. (Of course, even the best-behaved bird should have his wings kept trimmed — for safety!)

- **Follow the leader:** Teach your bird the step-up command — we explain how in Chapter 5 — and practice, practice, practice. Use a towel over your hand for nip-prevention if you have to, but make sure your bird is stepping up on command, as demonstrated in Figure 12-2, during several short sessions a day.

Figure 12-2: A well-mannered parrot like this Amazon will raise his leg eagerly to step up when asked.

Photo by Dr. Brian L. Speer

- **Go where I tell you; stay where I put you:** Your bird needs lots of time out of his cage, and letting him out is another opportunity to reinforce your role as boss. Don't let your bird come out of the cage on his own or at his convenience — ask him to step up onto your hand and place him on his day perch or play gym. If he gets down, don't make a big deal about it — just ask him to step up and put him back in place, again and again and again if need be. He'll get the point soon enough.

Calling for help

When you're dealing with a problem bird — especially if the situation is long-standing, and even more if it's causing strife in the family — you can easily get sidetracked by the frustration and anger you feel. A one-on-one consultation with an avian behaviorist can really help put you and your pet back on track.

Finding someone qualified to solve bird behavior problems calls for attention to experience and expertise, and credentials are a tricky business. Some behaviorists are veterinarians with extra study in the field of animal behavior; others are people with degrees in animal behavior, psychology, or something similar. Some of the more well-respected animal behaviorists around, however, got their "degrees" from the School of Hard Knocks — and they've been doing great work for years.

A veterinarian experienced in avian medicine is the best place to start when your bird has a behavior problem. Many, such as Brian, are pretty good with the behavior advice, while others prefer to make sure your bird is healthy and then refer you to someone else for help.

Some behaviorists make home visits. Others do telephone consultations, in part because many clients are too far away to visit. Usually, a consultation with a follow-up or two can bring you relief and deliver enough information to keep you headed in a positive direction. Rates vary widely but can range to $100 per consultation — expensive, perhaps, but not when compared with the price of living with a bird you find intolerable.

Why punishment doesn't work

Yelling at your bird doesn't solve a problem — if anything, your shouts are usually a negative reinforcement of a behavior like screaming. Your bird wanted attention, any kind of attention, and he got it. He won.

Beyond not solving a problem, hitting almost always makes the problem worse. ***You should never, ever strike your bird.***

Physical punishment doesn't work because your bird has no frame of reference for understanding it. You can train a dog through punishment — although it's certainly not the best way to do so — because dogs receive physical discipline from the day they're born. Their mothers knock them over, hold them down, and breathe threats in their puppy ears when their behavior warrants it. Puppies physically dominate their littermates in ritual displays you can see at work anywhere two dogs meet — posturing that sometimes becomes a fight if one dog isn't getting the respect he thinks he deserves from the other.

Birds aren't hardwired to understand physical discipline the way dogs are. Punishing your bird makes him think you're an unpredictable jerk at best and a dangerous lunatic or predator at worst. If you were a parrot living with someone who popped you for reasons you didn't understand, wouldn't you be inclined to protect yourself by biting?

Striking a bird can do more than injure your relationship. Physical violence can injure his body. Even the largest birds are much smaller than humans, and they can be hurt easily by a physical correction.

You can distract a bird from a problem behavior and redirect the behavior, but you can't punish him for it. If your bird is chewing the edge of a piece of furniture, you can slap your hand on a nearby table to startle him into stopping and then approach him, ask him to step up, and find him something more appropriate to destroy. But don't hit him, yell at him, or even (as is sometimes suggested) shoot him with water. These strategies flat-out won't help, and usually are going to make the problems much worse in the long run.

Problem-Solving Troublesome Behaviors

If your bird is healthy, and if you've fussed with his environment and your attitude to help him see you as the boss, you can start to work with the individual behaviors you can't stand.

Sometimes, returning your bird to good health and fixing his attitude takes care of the problem. Sometimes, adjustments take a little more work. And sometimes, what bothers you can't be fixed. Sorry, but it's the truth. Doesn't mean you should stop learning and trying, though.

Feather-picking

If we had to pick one problem that has bird-lovers, behaviorists, and veterinarians alike pulling their hair out in frustration, we'd have to choose *feather-picking,* a bird's willful destruction of his own plumage.

The first thing you need to know about this problem: Feather-picking is a symptom of something else that's wrong with your bird. The only hope you have of "curing" feather-picking is finding out and treating what's behind the behavior.

Feather-picking relates to a staggering variety of problems; any one or any combination of the following scenarios can be at the bottom of your bird's plucking:

- **Health problems:** Medical conditions behind feather-picking include allergies, parasitic infections, bacterial infections, abnormal growths (cysts) in the feather follicle, internal health problems, vitamin deficiencies, and hormone-associated problems. And that's the short list!
- **Low humidity:** Many birds come from extremely humid environments, and our houses can't hope to duplicate the conditions of a rain forest (we'd be miserable). The dry air of most houses can be a factor in feather-picking and can also set the stage for some secondary medical problems.
- **Boredom and pent-up energy:** Birds are active and intelligent, and they don't always handle the strain of being forced to sit around in a cage all day. Without things to play with and stuff to destroy, and without being able to get out of the cage and exercise, birds may direct all their energy toward self-mutilation.
- **Psychological problems:** Although birds need to have their wings trimmed for safety, a bad wing trim — too short, with no allowance for an "easy landing" — can upset a bird so badly that she starts tearing at herself. True phobias can and do exist in parrots, as well as other obsessive-compulsive behavioral disorders — all of which can result in feather-damaging behavior.
- **Attention-seeking:** You love how your bird looks. He starts tugging at feathers and you freak, imagining your beautiful bird with the broiler-chicken look. Every time he touches his feathers — even for normal preening behavior — you rush over. See how this works? "Aha!" thinks your bird. "All I have to do to get attention is pull a feather!"

So what can be done with the feather-picker?

Call your veterinarian, as *soon as the problem appears*. You need to rule out — and possibly fix — the medical problems before you can proceed. Make sooner, rather than later, your emphasis: In general, the longer your bird has been picking, the greater the probability of a habit or unresolvable pattern of behavior being set. Don't wait a few years before addressing a picking problem — when it starts, you need to start looking for a solution.

After your bird receives a clean bill of physical health, you can start making environmental adjustments to see whether you can ward off the picking. Prepare for the project to be a long one! Start a diary to record your changes and any effects they may have on your bird's behavior.

Start shaking things up, in small increments. A daily misting with a spray bottle and the addition of a room humidifier may be part of the solution. Also consider different toys, a smaller cage or a larger one, a new cage location, keeping a radio playing during the day, covering the cage to ensure your bird 12 solid hours of sleep, and more interaction and play with you as possibilities in the war against feather-picking.

We know: You want a definitive answer. Alas, one doesn't exist. The best we can suggest is to be patient, work with your veterinarian, and be prepared to love your bird no matter what he looks like. In some cases, feather-picking is for life. In others, the problem is only occasional. Yes, some birds do become full-feathered again, but not every pet bird is bound for complete redress in the plumage department.

The strategies that *don't work* for feather-picking include all manner of over-the-counter sprays and pesticide treatments for mites that probably don't exist on your bird. In general, you're wasting your money to try these concoctions, and you may be risking your bird's life.

Biting and other forms of aggression

Any parrot is capable of delivering a pretty powerful punch with his sharp, strong beak, and nobody likes to be bitten. Birds bite for any number of reasons, including

Prozac for birdy?

With dogs on Prozac and other drugs for behavior problems, you may naturally wonder: Can a medication stop my bird from ripping himself to pieces?

Believe us, Brian would like nothing better than to say yes and to write a prescription for a medication to cure the frustration of feather-picking.

Unfortunately, many medications, from mood-adjusters like Prozac to tranquilizers like Valium, have been tried on feather-pickers — with discouraging or extremely variable results. Research continues, of course, but you can expect to wait a long time for that "miracle drug," if it ever comes at all. Any drug that's intended to help has the best chance of working when it's directed to the underlying problem — again, feather-picking isn't a disease, but rather a symptom.

- **Fear**
- **Territorial protection**
- **Redirected aggression:** They can't bite what they want to, so they bite who's at hand.
- **Dominance:** Your bird may just be showing you who's boss.

Swallow your anger and remind yourself that striking back at a biting bird makes matters worse. Your bird needs the security of understanding who's the boss and what's expected of him. Read the section "A Framework for Good Behavior" in this chapter and put the regimen in place in your home. These changes are key to developing a trustworthy bird from the inside out.

Even the sweetest bird can have an off day. Learn to read your bird's body language — we cover the topic in Chapter 7 — and give your bird space when he needs it.

One simple correction for biting is the *earthquake*. With your bird on your hand, watch for the beginning of a bite — timing is everything — and wobble and drop your hand slightly (think *minor* earthquake). The correction is more distraction than punishment, but it gets the point across to your bird.

Screaming

Enduring a certain amount of loud vocalizing goes with living with a parrot. Some species are worse than others — some bird-lovers have kiddingly said that if you really don't like someone, give him a nanday conure, a world-class screamer if there ever was one.

Even relatively quiet birds pipe up at dawn and dusk — the time in nature when they'd be using their voices to "touch base" with the rest of their flock. Birds also scream for some of the reasons they feather-pick: They're bored, they're stressed, and they want attention.

To quell the noise, put in place the "framework for good behavior" (see the section by the same name elsewhere in this chapter). Avoid positive or negative reinforcement of screaming; don't rush to pick up your bird every time he pipes up, and don't go over to yell at him.

You can "adjust" sunrise and sunset by covering your bird's cage, but be fair — you can't keep your bird in the dark all the time. Use the cover maneuver for those times when you just have to sleep in or when you think your head will explode if you hear one more scream. Cover the cage and get a couple of aspirin — you're having one of those days, and the best thing you can do is just get through it. Covering your bird is *not* a permanent solution to screaming, however.

Covering your bird's cage to help with a behavior problem is really the only reason you need a cage cover at all, in most indoor settings. Contrary to popular belief, your bird doesn't need his cage routinely covered at night, either to get enough sleep or to stay warm. He's perfectly capable of managing both without a cover.

And no, you can't have your bird devocalized surgically — the alteration doesn't work with their anatomy. Success in the screaming category comes from behavior modification, not from the surgeon's scalpel.

What If You Can't Fix the Problem?

Some relationships just aren't meant to be, no matter how hard you try to make them work. Although we do not believe you should "get rid of" — oh, how we *hate* that phrase — your bird at the first, second, or even third sign

Sex and the single bird

Bees may do it, and even educated fleas do it, but when your bird wants to do it, you may find it a little disturbing. Small parrots like budgies come into sexual maturity under a year of age, while bigger parrots, such as the large macaws, may not reach maturity until they're 7 or older.

When those hormones surge, though, you'll know it; particularly in birds such as Amazon parrots or some cockatoos. A lot of behavior problems can surface when birds become sexually active — and we talk about them in this chapter, feather-picking, biting, screaming — but one of the behaviors caused by sexual maturity is . . . sex.

Some birds go in for self-pleasuring, using perches or toys to rub against. Some birds start eyeing their owners as prospective mates, putting on grand "come hither" displays by lifting their tails and screaming for their owners to pet them . . . just so. Your bird may lay eggs, which settles the question of gender once and for all (she's a she!). The eggs won't hatch — without a male, they can't be fertile — so you just put them in the trash, after she's finished laying her clutch. (Some birds simply won't quit laying, and for those, you need hormonal or even surgical help from your veterinarian.)

Good food, safe surroundings, and the long days of spring and summer shift the hormones into high gear, but the excitement doesn't last forever. You can wait for the days to shorten again, or you can find the "Off" switch by using a cage cover to make dusk arrive earlier (or dawn later). In the meantime, keep up your daily handling routines, such as practicing the step-up, and be aware that your bird isn't exactly going to be emotionally stable during this exciting time.

Can you spay or neuter your bird to avoid hormonal problems? The procedures are done, but not nearly as commonly as in cats and dogs. Surgery is still at a stage that is far from routine, but in some extreme cases of physical or behavioral problems related to hormones, the procedure is an option your veterinarian may want to discuss.

of problems, we do realize that in some cases your bird may be better off in a new home.

By "new home," we do not mean placing an ad in paper — "Parrot and cage, $800" — and handing your bird over to the first person who shows up with the dough. You need to be up-front about your bird's problems and honest with both yourself and any prospective new owners in discussing the difficulties. Someone more experienced than you may well be able to handle a bird who's just too high-powered for your taste.

Ask your veterinarian for help if you need to find a home for a bird. Brian often has a bird or two on the board at his hospital who's looking for a new address — rather than euthanize a bird for behavioral problems or allow it into an unsuitable placement, he'd rather help find the right home for the "problem child."

Rescue and placement groups — we list several in the Additional Resources appendix at the back of this book — are another option.

Pull out all the stops when it comes to working with your bird's behavior problem. But even if you decide to place your bird with someone else, you have a responsibility to your bird to do right by him.

Giving up your bird doesn't necessarily mean you're not meant for an avian companion. You may have chosen the wrong species for the life you lead — a bird too dominant, too loud, and so on, or you may have purchased a bird who was a behavioral train wreck (or at least well on the way to disaster) when you got him.

Before you even consider falling in love with another feathered face, do your homework. We recommend a thorough reading of Chapter 2, on bird species, and of Chapter 3, on choosing a reputable source. If you made mistakes, be sure you learn from them!

Chapter 13

Living in a Multiple-Bird Household

In This Chapter

- Adding more birds: Pets or breeders?
- Ensuring health in your "flock"
- Birds do it, bees do it . . . should you help?
- Raising happy, healthy babies

The joy of having a pet bird does bring with it one small problem. Sorry we didn't bring this up sooner, but we weren't sure you were ready for the tough truth. You see, once you've given your heart to an avian companion, a little seed takes root in your soul, an implanted idea that's likely to spring vigorously to life at the slightest provocation. Then you may do something crazy.

You may already be at risk! Have you ever been to the bird shop for supplies and found yourself looking at a particularly charming bird, wondering if your credit line (or mate) would tolerate the addition of a new pet, along with a cage and other paraphernalia? Have you ever looked at a bird magazine, seen a bird quite different from your own — bigger, smaller, more talkative, more mellow, and always, so beautiful — and thought, "I wonder what it would be like to live with one of those birds?" And finally, have you ever gone so far as to act on these thoughts, bringing home a second, third, or even seventh bird?

If so, congratulations. You have NEB Disease — Never Enough Birds.

You needn't worry your doctor about the situation, though. NEB disease is normal enough and usually poses no health risk to either you or your birds (see the nearby sidebar "How many birds are too many?" for the exceptions).

Whether you're interested in having plenty of feathered pets or you're planning to start breeding, you may find that being a flock parent is a very rewarding experience. We know: We both have NEB, and we're doing great!

How many birds are too many?

We know of many people who happily share their lives with ten or more pet birds. And we know of other people for whom one bird is really more than they should have.

Some well-meaning people get in over their heads with too many cats and dogs, but with birds, the "collector" mentality seems to be an even more common problem. Some people end up with more birds than they can manage. Infectious diseases can overwhelm these households if proper husbandry isn't practiced, especially if corners have been cut on good veterinary care as well.

Multiple-bird households — whether the birds are pets or breeders — are a good thing, in our opinion, but only if the birds are well cared for. If you have one bird, you're familiar with the noise, the mess, and the amount of time it takes to attend to your pet's emotional and physical needs. Ask yourself if you're really in a position to take on more responsibility.

How many birds are too many? Simply put: one more than the number you can care for properly. You owe it to your birds and to yourself to know your limits and to stay within them.

Because you don't want to make any mistakes in choosing additional birds, we recommend you visit our chapters on choosing the right kind of bird and the right place to get him, in Chapters 2 and 3.

Companion Birds or Breeders?

Before you add another bird, ask yourself what relationship you hope to have with the new bird. The answers help you decide the next step to take.

Do you want another pet bird, or are you thinking of a breeding partner for a bird you already have? You usually can't have it both ways. When birds become breeders, they bond tightly to their mates, and you're not of much interest to them anymore. If you can't stand losing the companionship of your pet, you'd better pass on the idea of letting your pet bird become a breeder.

The more the merrier

While statistics don't really exist to support our theory, our experiences tell us that once you're a "birdbrain," one pet bird soon becomes two — or more. And no real reason exists to fight the urge to let your flock grow. As long as you have the desire, time, energy, and money to care for each bird properly, you may discover what many people already know: More birds can bring even more pleasure and beauty to your life.

Birds are natural at living together. In the wild, they live in groups called *flocks,* and their social nature is part of the reason they make such great companions for people — they're able to make us a member of their family, even as we make them a member of ours. As happy as you can be with more than one bird — and as happy as your birds can be with each other — you may hear people cautioning that you can expect to be ignored when birds have each other for company.

Will the pet bird you have now ignore you if you get another? Probably not. Although pair-bonded birds usually only have eyes for each other, birds who aren't "in a family way" can live quite happily and sociably as part of a blended human-bird family, and they won't cut you out of their lives as long as you continue to be part of their lives and give them the attention and handling they crave.

A bird who's not getting enough attention may go nuts when her owner finally has time for her. If this is the kind of relationship you have with your bird, proceed with caution before adding another pet bird. First of all, if you don't have time for one bird, you don't have time for two. And second, your neglected bird will likely glom onto a new bird like a piece of driftwood after a shipwreck — and then who needs you anymore? Two birds who have eyes for each other are the ideal if you're looking to breed them, but if you want companions, you're sure to feel left out.

To avoid the problem of your birds excluding you, make sure you have a solid relationship with the bird or birds you already have before adding any others. Give all your birds — new and old alike — quality time alone with you.

Are you breeder material?

Instead of imagining more pet birds, you may be thinking about adding birds for breeding to your household.

The jump into bird breeding is a pretty large one, and you definitely need to think carefully before making the leap. While cats and dogs seem to do pretty well on their own as parents — handling mating, feeding, and early training quite well — birds are different. You may have a hard time getting them to mate at all, much less produce fertile eggs and hatch babies. Human intervention — that's you — may be required from the earliest stages, as soon as the egg appears.

Although a dog or cat mother happily handles the midnight, 2 a.m., and 4 a.m. feedings, if you plan to hand-feed your baby birds, you should expect to handle these tasks — and more! Hand-fed birds are raised by humans sometimes even from the moment they're hatched — fed around the clock, kept warm, cleaned, and weaned. Because you're not naturally or instinctively equipped for being a bird parent, you need more than just good intentions. You need a great deal of time and dedication. You also need to invest in some pretty pricey equipment, including incubators, brooders, scales, and more.

One good source for breeding supplies is a small company called Petiatric Supply, run by a pleasant pair of bird-lovers, Joe and Carla Freed. We provide information on how to reach them in our Additional Resources appendix at the back of this book.

Although birds can be expensive to purchase, they're surprisingly not very profitable to breed. Raising healthy, well-socialized, hand-fed babies is extremely labor-intensive, as is purchasing, maintaining, and replacing the equipment you need. One survey of aviculturists reveals that only 15 percent of these breeders take away any kind of profit on producing new generations of birds.

Money and time are prerequisites for bird breeding, but you also need a pretty hard heart on occasion, because you're going to lose some babies along the way. What we may see as a tragedy is merely nature's way — some babies aren't meant to make it. And the odds are you will someday have one of those doomed ones. Although losing babies is not a common event, be aware that it does occur with time, and it can be emotionally rough for some folks.

Have we put you off breeding? That's not our intent. Brian has been breeding birds for more than a decade, and although Gina's strictly into companion birds, she admires the work of good breeders. Breeding birds can be incredibly rewarding. Working with bird babies, watching them develop with your help into loving, well-adjusted companions, is very exciting. Bird breeders have helped prevent some species from becoming extinct, and they've created interesting color and feather variations in some of the most common species, such as canaries, cockatiels, and lovebirds.

Breeding birds is a challenging calling, with many rewards for those who can handle the demands. A hobby for some, a profession for others, aviculture requires a fairly awesome investment in time, in emotion, and in money for an array of expensive equipment. The task of raising healthy, well-socialized pets is not for every bird-keeper, but those people who do the job well find raising birds to be a pleasure.

Closed Aviary Concept: Rules to Live By

Whether you're considering adding birds to your household for companionship or for breeding, you need to follow some important rules to ensure the health of both the birds you have and the birds you're going to add to your flock. Aviculturists call these rules the *Closed Aviary Concept (CAC),* and disregarding them puts your birds' health at risk.

At its most basic, the CAC is a strategy for developing a healthy collection of birds — and then keeping them that way. The basic rules are as follows:

- **Ensure that the bird or birds you already have are in good health.** Because of the nature of birds, you can't just eyeball one — nor can a veterinarian — and figure that because he looks healthy, he is healthy. Your bird or birds need to be thoroughly examined by a veterinarian who is experienced in working with avian patients, and the birds may require preventive laboratory work to ensure they're not carrying an infectious disease. (For more on preventive care, see Chapter 9).
- **Never, ever introduce a bird without determining that he's healthy and up to par with the healthy birds you already have.** A bird can look completely normal and still be incubating an infectious disease that may take his life — and the lives of some of the birds you already have if you expose them to him. Have a veterinarian with experience in avian medicine check out your new pet.
- **Quarantine the new bird or birds for at least six weeks away from the others.** The temptation is to go straight from the veterinarian's into the flock — but resist temptation. While screening tests are a help, they're not perfect. A quarantine period will give any diseases a chance to show themselves without putting the rest of your birds at risk. The separation also gives your new bird time to settle in and time for you to get to know her on a one-on-one basis. Be sure that you're not a "link" between a bird in quarantine and the other birds. Don't swap dishes, toys, perches, and so on, and wash your hands before and after handling any new birds.

Don't take the Closed Aviary Concept lightly, and don't cut any corners in implementing it. Imagine your heartbreak if a bird you just brought home harbored a disease that ended up killing a bird you've cherished for years.

Infectious diseases — we cover some of the worst ones in Chapter 10 — can kill your bird. If you're careful about introducing new birds and follow CAC precautions, you can rest assured you're doing the best you can to keep these killers from spreading into your home.

Choosing Compatible Pets

Unless you're planning to house your birds in different rooms, they're going to have to be compatible with each other as well as with your tolerances and lifestyle. Fortunately, ending up with a happy flock is pretty easy. We offer a few guidelines to choosing companions that are likely to get along with each other and with you as well. Exceptions exist to every rule, these included, but following them gives you your best shot at peaceable coexistence.

One way to "psych" birds into becoming better behaved toward one another is to keep their living quarters at the same height — and all of them below your shoulder when standing. In the bird mind, "Height equals might:" Dominant birds get the higher perches. By keeping everyone on the same level, you remove the psychological advantage of any one bird. (For information on how cage and perch height can affect the relationship *you* have with your birds, see Chapter 12.)

Species and gender issues

If you're choosing birds for companionship, not breeding, don't give any of your birds the opportunity for pair-bonding if you can help it. Because you don't always know whether your birds are male or female, you may be adding, say, a female blue-and-gold macaw to a household with a male of the same species. Mixing up the species makes for a much better plan. If you have a macaw and want another large parrot, consider a cockatoo. If you have an Amazon, perhaps a conure would be a good addition.

Pair-bonding exists in male-male and female-female couples — although the combinations produce no offspring, of course. The situation is common enough that when a happy pair of breeding birds aren't producing fertile eggs, an avian veterinarian is likely to suggest confirming that the pair contains one male and one female.

Most birds, both male and female, look the same to us. When we can't tell them apart, we need a little help from science to do so. The gender of birds is generally determined either by DNA testing of a blood sample or by the surgical examination of internal sex organs (which are, of course, the only kind of sex organs the aerodynamically efficient bird has). For companion birds, DNA is probably the more popular way of determining gender. For a breeding bird, though, the surgical option is often preferred, because the procedure not only determines what kind of "equipment" a bird has, but also reveals the stage of maturity and any problems.

Size and temperament issues

Although we know of bird-lovers whose budgies, lovebirds, or parrotlets get along famously with their larger cousins, as a general rule you're probably better off sticking to birds of about the same size, if you expect to allow them contact between each other.

Learn about the temperament of the species you have in mind — we offer insights into many of them in Chapter 2. Although every bird has individual characteristics, some species tend to be more aggressive than others. Birds who can't get along (see the nearby sidebar, "You talkin' to me? You talkin' to *me?*") can injure each other severely — with bites, broken beaks, and more. You may think the damage typically goes only one way, with the bigger birds hurting the little ones. But some little guys really know how to get their licks in — they've even bitten toes off their larger avian companions!

You talkin' to me? You talkin' to *me?*

The wide range of size in pet birds suggests that combining some species is just asking for trouble. The tiny parrotlets, for example, have a full-sized personality that may make some big macaw feel inclined to see them more as a protein treat than a companion, should the smaller bird venture onto the larger's turf.

Perhaps the best example of a little bird with a big attitude is the grey-cheeked parakeet, a bird who's often a real sweetie with people but who simply doesn't like other birds. This is one bird who's always ready to rumble with the bigger boys. These cheeky little guys will march over to the biggest cockatoo, Amazon, or macaw and pick a fight — with easily imagined results.

Brian has patched up a more than a few pugnacious grey-cheeked parakeets in his day. His experience suggests that if you do decide to add another bird to a grey-cheek's household, putting the new bird in another room and always keeping them separate is a good move.

Despite your best planning, if you end up with incompatible birds, they're better off living separate lives, or at least in separate cages or rooms within your home.

The Joy and Challenges of Breeding

When you decide to become a bird breeder, you can look forward to an exciting time ahead of you — and a lot of learning and hard work.

Although we touch on some of the basics here, breeding is one area of bird-keeping that requires you to seek some one-on-one help. A veterinarian with experience in avian care can serve as your mentor, but so, too, can a reputable and experienced breeder. In fact, a reputable breeder may be a better choice as a mentor, because not all avian veterinarians have experienced the "joy" of 2 a.m. hand-feedings for weeks at a time and of wondering hourly whether an egg is developing properly. Breeders have experienced these dubious pleasures, and the best ones are happy to share their expertise with a dedicated novice.

Although Brian is an accomplished avian specialist and breeder now, he learned and continues to learn a great deal about breeding not just from veterinary sources but also from top breeders.

In all phases of breeding birds, we encourage you to find a mentor. Particularly in one aspect, hand-feeding, we can't *in any way* condone a "learn-it-yourself" approach. If you try to figure out hand-feeding baby birds on your own, you are very likely to have sick or dead babies on your hands.

Pet to breeder to pet — a unique concept

Sure, dogs and cats are better pets when spayed or neutered, but even those animals used for breeding can remain people-friendly their whole lives. The same is not usually true for birds. Bonded breeding pairs generally are interested only in each other, not in humans, and they need to be left alone together to produce offspring.

Because birds are now living longer, healthier lives than ever before, we're seeing the concept of "life stages" taking hold with some bird-keepers. Young birds are raised and cherished as pets until sexual maturity or beyond, and then paired for breeding. After their breeding time is past, these birds reclaim their role as part of a human household.

Such an idea may be hard to get your arms around if you're in a dog-and-cat frame of mind, but you have to consider that the potential life span of a parrot is far longer than most of our other common household pets. Many parrots have life spans that are comparable to our own. We go through different stages in our lives, some of them involving children, others not. Is it so hard to imagine a similar life for a long-lived pet bird?

Many of the birds being born today will always know the benefits of preventive care and good nutrition. When these birds are past their reproductive years, they'll be healthy and happy enough to retire to years as a cherished companion.

Spare the babies — and yourself — the misery: Find an experienced veterinarian or breeder who's willing to show you the ropes with this delicate procedure.

Pair bonding: 'Til death do us part

Finding a suitable mate for your bird may not be as easy as you think. Although cats and dogs are perfectly content to engage in "one-night-stands" with partners they'll never see again, parrots must form strong bonds (see Figure 13-1) before they're interested in reproducing. And they just don't fall in love with the first feathered face they see.

Some species, such as the blue-and-gold macaw, are fairly easy to pair up, forming pair bonds with relative ease. Other species are pretty picky. The African grey parrot is one of the more selective birds. You can introduce a pair of greys and get an immediate "Wow, that's the one for me" reaction — or you can have two birds together for a decade, and they'll always stay on opposite ends of the perch!

When they're compatible, parrots mate for life, but the "life" in question is not the birds' lives, but rather the life of the relationship. As long as the two birds remain together, they'll usually remain bonded, but if one dies or disappears, the other will try to form a new pair bond with another bird.

Figure 13-1: Birds form tight bonds with their mates, and they can be very affectionate with one another.

Bonded pairs of parrots are pretty solidly attached to their mates, but straying isn't unheard of. Brian likes to tell of one aviary where two pairs of birds "divorced" their mates and spent their time lusting after the birds next door. After the humans moved the birds around to put compatible couples together, everyone settled down and made babies! Other variations are possible, too. For example, a male canary may happily take two or more mates, flitting back and forth between his families — and the females don't seem to mind.

Setting up your love birds

Even if you have a pair of birds making eyes at each other, don't expect any babies until you establish the right environment. Breeding birds need

- **Proper housing:** Breeding pairs don't get the out-of-cage freedom that pet birds should get because they're usually no longer responsive enough to humans to be let out safely — and because they'd rather be left alone with each other. As a result, they need a cage with plenty of room for two birds to move about comfortably, along with the usual items that are part of every good setup — lots of toys and a variety of healthy perches.

- **Plenty of privacy:** Breeding birds need to be spared the distractions of human life. Set your birds up where they can be alone together — and leave them be, as much as possible.
- **Plenty of food:** An abundance of food is one of the triggers for reproduction in many species. Birds instinctively avoid bringing babies into a world where food supplies are questionable. Regularly feed your birds a high-quality commercial diet, supplemented with lots of fresh fruits and vegetables.
- **A nesting area:** The kind of nesting box depends on the species. Talk to your veterinarian or a breeder experienced with your bird's particular species about an appropriate nesting setup.

Even with seemingly perfect conditions for breeding, you may not have the formula "just right" for your birds. Rely on your veterinarian and other breeders for insight and information. Health problems may be at fault, or maybe your breeding setup needs some fine-tuning. Or maybe you're just expecting too much, too soon. Good things come to those who wait!

Most pet birds mate through a process called the *cloacal kiss.* The female pushes her cloaca partially through her vent, and the male rubs his vent against it to deposit sperm, which the female can store for a few days to fertilize her eggs when she ovulates. Just because birds are actively mating doesn't mean babies are on the way, though. Birds just like to mate!

In some birds, such as the domestic turkey, artificial insemination is used over natural breeding — those tom turkeys are just too big to do the job on their own.

The Awesome Egg

The egg is one of nature's most amazing creations, and the story of how it's produced is even more awesome. The female houses an "assembly line" called the *oviduct,* where in just slightly more than a day, the promise of life is produced, set up with nourishment, and wrapped in protective membranes and, finally, in the hard casing that most of us visualize then we hear the word "egg."

A part of an egg's yolk is what becomes the hatchling, if the egg is fertile and if conditions favorable to incubation remain constant. The yolk starts out as a single cell, which is why the yolk of an ostrich egg is the largest single-celled organism in the world.

Toby and Tilly: A love story

Hello Hollywood! Here's a love story that isn't your usual boy-meets-girl, boy-loses-girl, boy-gets-girl yawner. Try this one on for size: Boy meets bird. Bird falls in love with another bird. Bird cuts boy out of his life.

Well, maybe we won't hold our breath waiting for the contract to write the screenplay, but we like the story of Toby and Tilly anyway.

Toby is Brian's first bird, a blue-and-gold macaw brought into his hospital in a lidded plastic garbage can by a man who wanted some cash to get his "bird problem" off his hands. Love at first sight happened between Brian and Toby, and soon the bird was Brian's constant companion, even riding to and from work on Brian's shoulder.

And then came Tilly.

Tilly was to be a companion for Brian's wife, Denise, but the two birds had eyes for each other only. Brian set up the pair in an aviary and was rewarded with several healthy, happy babies the first year they were together.

More than 15 years have passed since Toby came into Brian's life, and Toby and Tilly are still quite the happy couple. They still raise some fine babies, and they are both clear in their message to Brian: "Leave us alone!"

Natural incubation

Fertilization occurs high in the oviduct of the hen, shortly after the *ovum* (the female's contribution to a new life) is produced. As the yolk (ovum) traverses down the oviduct, yolk membranes, dense *albumen* (the egg white), two shell membranes, and the egg shell are all added on in a period of a little over one day.

At egg-laying time, a fertile egg's embryo is roughly the equivalent of a very early pregnancy in mammals, which makes it easier to understand why some eggs never hatch. Just as many human pregnancies are lost before a woman even knows she's pregnant, many eggs contain defects that prevent their development, even under seemingly perfect conditions.

Eggs don't start their development into hatchlings until the warmth of a parent is applied, and for good reason. If each egg started developing as soon as it left the mother, the babies of a *clutch,* or group of eggs, would hatch at different times, leaving the last babies to hatch at a significant disadvantage when it comes to survival. By having the eggs develop and hatch more or less simultaneously, more hatchlings have a chance at survival.

Artificial incubation

Humans get involved in the incubation of eggs for a couple of reasons. One, because under the artificial conditions of a human-made environment, some pairs of birds are simply not capable of hatching their own eggs. They won't incubate them, and they may even destroy them, refuse to feed their chicks after they hatch, or even kill their young hatchlings.

The other main reason human beings meddle in bird reproduction is because they can use a bird's own species survival mechanisms to produce more babies than would be normal. Eggs are good eating, which is why many predators love to raid bird nests for eggs (and for young birds, too). A suddenly empty nest triggers a bird to produce another clutch of eggs to replace those that are gone. This procedure, called *double-clutching,* enables an aviculturist to incubate one set of eggs while the birds incubate the others.

Artificial incubation involves an *incubator,* a machine that keeps the eggs at optimum temperature and humidity for the species, turning the eggs at regular intervals as the birds themselves would.

The amount of time between when an egg starts to develop and when a chick hatches (the incubation period) depends on the species, just as the gestation period between different species of mammals varies. Budgie eggs, for example, develop for 16 days, cockatiels and lovebirds for 18, and larger parrots, such as Amazons, for about 24 days. Other species of parrots may spend as much as 34 days in the shell.

You can tell whether an egg is fertile and developing by a procedure called *candling.* Shine a bright light — such as a penlight — though the egg from behind. A living, developing egg shows a web of red veins.

Raising the Babies

The moment a baby starts poking his way out of the shell is when the real fun begins.

The babies of the more common pet birds — all parrots, canaries, and other finches — are born with their eyes shut and completely naked (see Figure 13-2), unable to retain heat or moisture without the help of attentive parents — or of humans acting as parents. If you're going to hand-feed your babies, this is the moment you change from one piece of equipment to another — from the incubator, designed for the warming and turning of eggs, to the *brooder,* a place where baby birds (who don't need turning) are maintained at the proper temperature and humidity for their species as they grow.

The naked babies of our common pet bird species are called *altricial,* as opposed to the fully fuzzed, eyes-open, and mobile *precocial* babies of chickens, pheasants, and ostriches.

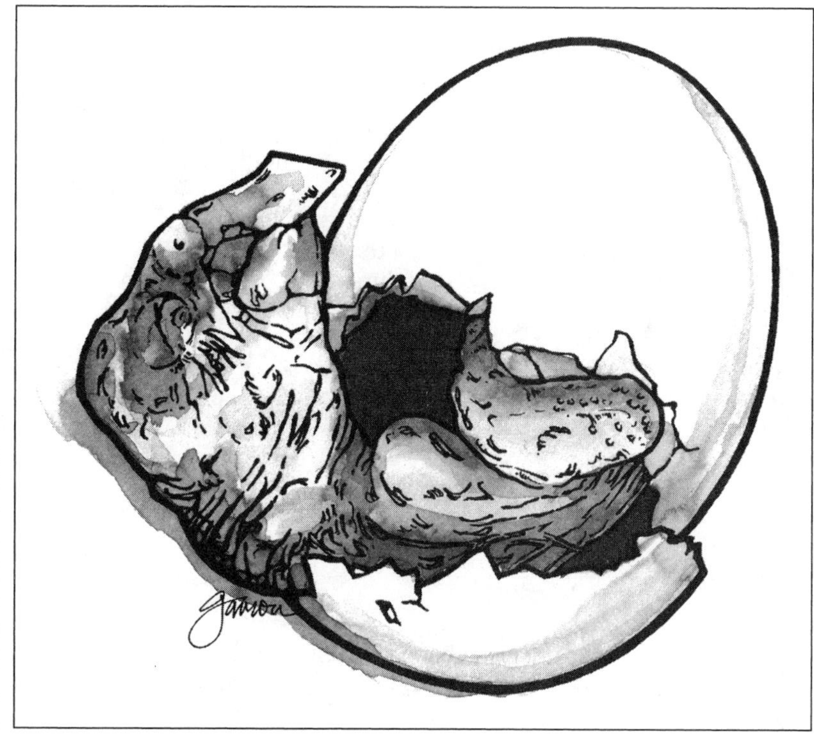

Figure 13-2: Parrots and other common pet-bird species are born naked and helpless.

Hand-feeding and socializing

Bird parents feed their young by regurgitating food from their *crops* (a food storage organ at the base of the neck) directly into the babies' mouths. We're not really equipped to barf for baby birds, so we raise them through hand-feeding.

Hand-feeding is not a learn-as-you-go skill. You need to practice under the watchful eye of an experienced person, working with their help until you can hand-feed as naturally as shifting the gears of a car.

Although different methods exist for getting food into baby birds (we recommend using a commercial preparation for complete nutrition), syringes and spoons, as shown in Figure 13-3, are perhaps the most common methods among small or hobby breeders. To start out, you feed hatchlings around the clock, in two-hour intervals. The length of time spent hand-feeding — weeks, even months — and the intervals between feedings depend on the species.

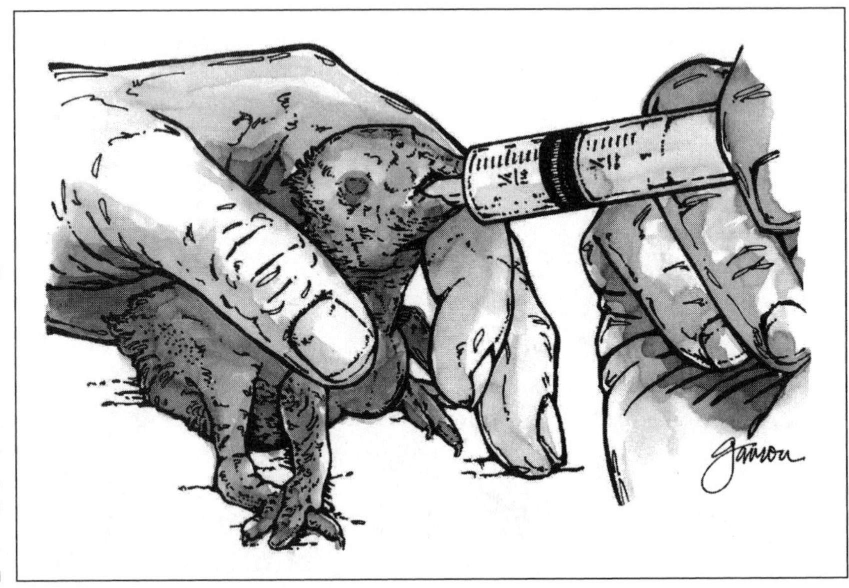

Figure 13-3: An experienced person can help you learn proper hand-feeding of baby birds.

Raising several clutches of babies can be quite stressful and exhausting, and indeed, these all-too-human problems factor into the diseases or even death of babies, especially at the end of a breeding season. Brian has been known to take in an exhausted client's babies at the bird hospital for a day or two so the person can get some sleep — a lifesaver to both the babies and the hand-feeder!

Careful daily record-keeping is as important as proper feeding. You must weigh babies daily and record their weights to ensure that they're developing normally.

You need help to learn how to be a good hand-feeder, but if you've ever raised a human baby, you probably have what it takes. Not surprisingly, most hand-raisers are women who've raised children — and fill their "empty nests" with birds.

The basics to hand-raising are the same as with human infants: Keep them warm, keep them clean, and feed them when they're hungry.

One other important parallel to raising a human infant you need to remember: *The most important ingredient to add is love.*

A baby bird needs to be socialized to human beings. Talk to your babies. Handle your babies gently and lovingly. Sing to them, play the radio, and just be with them. Every touch the baby feels, every sound he hears is making him more comfortable with people, and that makes him a better pet. Raising the body of the baby birds with good and regular food, combined with raising their minds and hearts with love, is a powerful combination.

Weaning and fledging

Weaning is the stage where baby birds go from hand-feeding to free-feeding, eating a healthy diet on their own. The key concept: Weaning isn't something you do *to* a baby bird; it's something a baby bird does on his own. You don't have to train a bird to eat like a "grown-up," and you most certainly don't schedule a set age at which to wean the bird. At whatever time is right for that bird — different species wean at different times, and so, too, do individual birds — he'll start to pick at and play with grown-up food, soft foods such as soaked pellets and bananas to begin with and then harder food, such as commercial pellets and hard vegetables and fruits.

Don't complicate the weaning process by continuing to hand-feed babies without really giving them the opportunity to wean themselves. Let them use their natural instincts and curiosity to teach themselves about new foods.

Instead of offering to hand-feed first, provide your baby with a wide variety of healthy foods, commercial pellets soaked in water plus easy-to-eat fruits and vegetables, such as bananas and corn cut off the cob. Remove toys from the cage, so the baby is inclined to play with and learn to eat the food.

Wait a half-hour or so beyond the regular hand-feeding time and then offer the syringe or spoon with hand-feeding formula. If your baby still wants to be hand-fed, feed him. If your baby is not too interested in the syringe and even turns his head away from you — perhaps busy playing with a banana or some other exciting new thing that is fun to chew up — skip that feeding.

Put the grown-up food in a shallow, wide dish, such as a pie pan, and make sure the container is on the baby's level — they're a little clumsy at this age. A shallow pan gives the baby the opportunity to eyeball everything that's offered and even climb in the pan for play, if desired.

Don't force weaning on a schedule. Continue to offer grown-up foods before hand-feeding, and be patient. Your baby will come around in time. And don't panic if your careful record-keeping reveals weight loss: Typically, most babies lose some weight during their weaning phase, up to 15 percent of their peak weight in some cases. Usually, that's just baby fat disappearing, nothing more.

Along with starting to eat adult food, your baby will begin practicing and learning another grown-up skill, flying. We feel that even though most pet birds spend their lives with their wings trimmed for safety, the babies need to be able to *fledge,* or learn to fly. Let them. They aren't too coordinated at this age, and any help in that area, such as leaving their wings unclipped for a while, is usually much appreciated on their part!

Flying the nest

After you've poured your heart and soul into raising your bird babies, you want them to go to homes where they'll be loved and properly cared for. Some breeders prefer to sell their babies to a reputable bird shop instead of dealing with pet buyers directly. They may sell unweaned babies to the shop and have shop employees continue to feed and then wean the birds, or they may sell the babies weaned and ready to be sold.

No matter how you choose to sell your babies, be sure to pay attention to the same kinds of details we suggest when you're on the other side of the fence as a buyer. Check out Chapter 3 to remind yourself of the hallmarks of a reputable bird shop, and don't let your babies go to any retailer who won't take proper care of them or make sure that they go to an educated buyer.

Expect, if you're selling your babies through a good-quality retailer, to be quizzed and "tested" — they want to know that they're bringing good quality and healthy babies into their store. And not all stores even consider bringing in outside birds for resale — some only sell birds that they have bred and raised themselves.

If you're letting your babies go directly to the public, you need to assume the primary roles of educator as well as seller. With all you know from buying, caring for, and breeding your birds, you're in an excellent position to educate prospective buyers — and to turn away those who won't be good caretakers of your special babies.

Visit Chapter 16, with its questions to ask when buying a bird, and consider how you'd answer those questions as a seller. Above all, remember your babies have value beyond the money you can get for them — they represent countless hours of your time, and they leave your custody with a piece of your heart. Make sure they go with someone who understands how very special they are.

Part V
The Part of Tens

"Of course I'm jittery. I'm here alone, the lights went out, and now I can't find the bird."

In this part . . .

You can find a little bit of everything here, an information-packed part that epitomizes the saying, "Last but not least." We debunk some myths, tell you the coolest bird sites on the Web, and warn you about common household products that could do in your feathered friend. And that's not all! How about tips on preparing for disaster, questions to ask when buying a bird, or the ten best birds for beginners. Just for fun, we also give you a few bird jokes worth repeating — we bet you laugh right out loud at least once, even if you've already heard them!

Chapter 14

Ten Bird Myths — Debunked!

In This Chapter

- Easy keepers — or not?
- Polly want seeds?
- One isn't the loneliest number
- Speak up, will you?

Humans may have kept close company with birds for thousands of years — and admired them from afar for even longer — but only recently have we gained a true understanding of how to help our winged friends be healthy and happy in our households. Even so, we've hardly scratched the surface. Recent advances in health and behavior knowledge will continue, even as our appreciation for birds moves, as they say, to higher levels.

And yet . . . misinformation is everywhere. In books — even new ones — in veterinary, bird-club, or bird-shop handouts, and certainly on the Internet. Most of the information is well-meaning, based on what was thought to be true even a few years ago.

To help you separate the seeds (which your birds don't need, as you can see if you read on) from the hulls (which at least provide exercise for your pet), we've assembled some of the more common myths — and taken them apart, one by one.

Birds Are Low-Maintenance Pets

In a rare departure from a life of writing about pets, Gina once took an assignment to write about a talented interior designer, hoping in some small way to pick up some wisdom regarding her own home — to this day decorated in Early Thrift Store (which is kind of in now!). She met the designer at a house on which he was working and listened eagerly to his (expensive) plans for the place.

"And here," he said, waving his arm at one wall, "I see an aviary. Those blue parrots . . . what do you call them . . . macaws? Perfect colors!"

Even the suggestion that birds are "things" to enhance the decor of a room reveals a great deal of ignorance about the nature of these intelligent pets. Unfortunately, the designer's views are not uncommon. Too many people see birds as little more than a beautiful, colorful addition to a room, a low-maintenance pet you just set on a perch and be done with.

Birds *are* beautiful. They *do* add color to our lives. But if you go into your relationship with one thinking that all you need to do is throw a little seed at your pet now and then, you're going to find out the errors of your ways — and quickly. Plus, you're sure to miss out on the great pleasure of living with what can be an intelligent, affectionate, and challenging companion.

Figure on spending time every day for basic cleaning. Time on the weekends for more of the same, with extra scrubbing and disinfecting thrown in. Time for preparing nutritious meals, with vegetables and fruit. And time, most of all, for enjoying your bird's company, and letting him enjoy yours.

Without effort on your part, you're going to have a sick bird or one who's bored, lonely, and unhappy — a feather-picker (so much for all that beautiful plumage) or even an empty cage.

You want low-maintenance? Get a stuffed animal. Even fish tanks take some effort. But if you're willing to make the personal investment in your relationship with your pet, you can expect to receive wonderful rewards.

Birds Are High-Maintenance Pets

You can't just throw your bird in a cage and forget her, but neither do you have to center your whole life around caring for your bird. And yet, some people do. Some bird-owners disinfect their birds' quarters three times a day — scrubbing cages, cleaning dishes, soaking perches in a bleach solution. Overdoing tidiness isn't necessary, no matter what you may have heard.

Good husbandry requires cleanliness, make no mistake. But the work some bird-lovers put into keeping their birds squeaky-clean borders on obsessive.

You don't have to pick up every food crumb as it falls. Sterilization is not necessary on a daily basis, as long as you make fresh food and water available in clean dishes and change cage papers once or twice a day.

Make life easier on yourself: Invest in a handheld vacuum, a seed-catching bib for the cage, and anything else that can help keep things neater.

Beyond those basics, relax. Use the time you have for your bird for togetherness, snuggling, training, and play. You'll both get more out of the experience.

So how much cleaning is too much and how much is not enough? Check out Chapters 5 and 7. For tips on what you need to buy to make your life easier, see Chapter 4.

Birds Are Fragile

Some folks in this world — and you may be among them — believe that birds are so delicate that a cold breeze is enough to do them in. In fact, birds are among the hardiest and most successful creatures on earth, adapted to many different ecological niches — including the one that brings them into our homes as pets. With bodies designed for the rigors of flight, birds are very tough — so much so that were we possessed of their powers, we might seem like superheroes.

Birds fight illness with tenacity, endure temperature variations with no effect, and live for years on the equivalent of junk food that many owners insist on giving them. They are survivors! With proper husbandry, nutrition, and medical attention that focuses on disease-prevention, your bird may well outlive you.

Because of the potentially long life span of some birds — up to 70 years or more for large parrots such as macaws — planning for care if something happens to you is very important. For information on how to ensure that your bird's long-term care is covered, see Chapter 11.

A Hand-Fed Bird Makes a Better Pet

Among the feathered pet population, improvements in the breeding of birds is one of the bigger developments over the last couple of decades. The advancements are good news for birds in the wild — whose numbers have been decimated by the pet trade — and a positive move for people who want to share their lives with an avian companion. Captive-bred birds make the best pets.

Captive-bred doesn't necessarily mean hand-fed, however, although in many cases, birds come from both backgrounds. The key is not the feeding of baby birds but the socializing. Natural parents can do a decent job of feeding, and as long as human caretakers ensure that the babies are handled and exposed to loving human care, captive-bred birds benefit from the best of both worlds.

Hand-feeding is fine, and we most certainly don't want to knock those breeders who do it. No matter how they're fed — by their parents or by human hands — gentle, patient socialization is the way to build the trust in humans so essential in a good pet.

We share some tips for building trust in your birds — along with a strong bond between you and your pet — in Chapter 5.

Seed Is the Best Diet for Birds

How pervasive is this myth? You can find out by asking any child: "What do birds eat?" The answer you're likely to hear: "Seeds!"

Wrong, wrong, wrong. Pet birds fed a diet of only seeds eventually become malnourished and may develop serious illnesses or even die. So why does this "Birds eat seed" idea stick with us?

The myth is perpetuated by so-called experts who have kept birds for years but who haven't kept up with the current research trends, as well as by pet product manufacturers and retailers who want to keep less useful or antiquated merchandise selling, either because they don't know any better or because they don't care.

Although we talk about specific nutrition in Chapter 6, know before you turn there that for most pet birds — and certainly for the parrots — seeds are the equivalent of birdy junk food, high in fat and low in balanced nutrition.

You can find the foundation of proper nutrition for your pet bird in a box or bag of nutritionally complete pelleted diets available from high-quality pet-supply retailers or veterinarians. Add healthy "people food," and even some seed, to this basic diet, and your bird is on the way to healthy eating for life.

Unfortunately, some birds (just like some people) vastly prefer junk food to a well-balanced diet and will resist their owners' efforts to switch them. If your bird is a seed-junkie, check out Chapter 6 for help in converting her to healthier habits.

Birds Get Mites Easily

Here we have another bit of nonsense that sells a lot of useless junk at pet stores. People are appalled when their pets start chewing off their own feathers, and they seek help, preferably something easy. They are far too happy to hear (incorrectly) that their pet most probably has mites, and they buy a pesticide to eliminate what isn't really there.

In truth, Brian rarely sees mites in his practice — but he does see a whole lot of feather-pickers. The problem is a complicated one and usually suggests something is wrong with the bird's mental health as much as his physical health.

The best way to have your bird's maladies correctly diagnosed and treated is by having a good relationship with an avian veterinarian. Otherwise, you may be throwing money away on useless products — and endangering your bird's life.

Birds Catch Colds from People

Although birds may become infected with human influenza type viruses, those bugs rarely make a bird ill. Human colds and flues come and go, and so it's easy to imagine people thinking what looks the same in people and bird is, in fact, the same illness, but it's usually not.

If your bird is sick with what appears to be cold- or flulike symptoms, chances are very high that something else is going on, and you need to call your veterinarian.

Don't blame yourself for passing on your own cold. You couldn't have, realistically.

As with all pets, birds are capable of passing some diseases to humans. These diseases, called *zoonoses*, don't represent much of a concern as long as you're careful to engage in good habits such as hand-washing before and after handling pets, and making sure your bird remains in good health.

A Sick Bird Is a Dead Bird

Before birds earned their just place as welcome and respected pets, medical care wasn't very advanced. The nature of illness in birds was misunderstood, and signs of illness usually missed — by the time a pet bird appeared sick, he was usually too sick to be helped.

The good news is a lot can be done for a sick bird today. Birds are fighters, and given the help they need from modern avian medicine, they can pull through injuries and diseases that once may have done them in.

Don't give up on your bird! Learn to recognize what's normal and what's not and how to get help when you spot changes — we help you with this in Chapter 10. Even a very sick bird may well survive with modern antibiotics and supportive care from a knowledgeable veterinarian.

Lovebirds Will Die of Loneliness If Not Kept in Pairs

If you want to keep a pair of lovebirds, we're not going to stop you. Their affectionate behavior toward one another is inspiring to watch. But don't complain to us when you start feeling like an in-law on a honeymoon: Neither bird will be terribly interested in you, because they have each other.

The lovebird — or rather, a *single* lovebird — is a great bird for beginners. They're not too big, not too loud, not too hard to care for, and very affectionate. If you decide to invite a lovebird into your life, you can expect to share company with a wonderful pet, and one that will not miss the lovebird mate you never bring home.

All Parrots Talk

Most parrots species, from budgies to macaws, are capable of mimicking sounds, words, or phrases, but not all individuals learn to talk. Patient, clear repetition helps your parrot learn to pipe up, but don't be disappointed if your pet never develops this skill.

Male cockatiels are better at talking (whistling, too) than their female counterparts, but most larger parrot species have no obvious difference in talking ability between the genders. Your best chance at finding a talker is to adopt one who has proven ability or to choose from those species best known for talking. Two to consider: the African grey, shown in Figure 14-1, or Amazons, especially the double-yellow-headed or yellow-naped varieties of the latter. These birds are so known for their speech abilities that we don't recommend them to folks who love to swear — the birds can pick up words and phrases that they overhear, and they're not hesitant to pepper their chatter with them gleefully.

Figure 14-1: The African grey is a species especially gifted at picking up words, phrases, and sounds.

Photo by Dr. Brian L. Speer

Chapter 15

Ten Steps to a Healthy Bird

In This Chapter

- Hey, look me over
- Gooooood bird!
- Tests, tests, and more tests
- Vaccinate? For what? Maybe, maybe not

Birds are hardy creatures, capable of living well for years, even decades, when provided with a good diet and proper care and handling. But for them to reach their true pet potential, they have to start out right — and far too many don't. Some pick up infectious disease from less-than-ideal breeding operations, while others may contract illness when exposed to other birds during shipping or when waiting to be sold.

Even when a bird gets off to a great start, the wrong care or handling can turn a situation sour in little time. Screening for infectious disease and practicing proper husbandry is the best preventive-care medicine you can provide for your bird.

In Brian's hospital, preventive care and education go hand-in-hand, in the form of a checklist he uses to ensure that a new patient receives the best treatment from the very beginning. We share the items on his list here, so you can check them off yourself with your own veterinarian. They don't all have to be done in the same visit, but working through the list is a good way to set the stage for continued good care. With luck, every check will confirm good health, but if it doesn't, you can feel good about catching a problem before it becomes potentially deadly.

More detailed information on nutrition is in Chapter 6, and you can find help with equipment in Chapter 4 and behavior in Chapter 12. See Chapter 13 for tips on maintaining more than one bird, and don't forget our other health chapters — Part III is dedicated to the topic!

What better time to ask questions than when you have your veterinarian cornered in an examination room? A good veterinarian never minds taking the time to educate a client — the better educated you are about your bird, the better a client you'll be, and the healthier your bird will become. You and your veterinarian are partners in providing your pet with good health, and you must be comfortable enough with each other to accomplish this goal.

The Physical Examination

An experienced avian veterinarian isn't usually in a hurry to get his hands on your bird. Quiet observation, in fact, should be the first stage of any expert examination, as illustrated in Figure 15-1. Visual observation of the bird in her cage (or travel cage) or on a perch when relaxed can reveal a great deal. Through patient attention, your veterinarian can determine whether the bird's breathing is easy or labored, and he can size up the density and quality of plumage and the ease with which the animal moves. This first stage also allows the veterinarian to start evaluating the relationship you have with your bird and the potential problems — are you tentative or frightened in handling your pet, for example? During this portion of the exam, your doctor speaks to both you and your bird, collects a history, and asks appropriate questions of you about your bird.

Figure 15-1: A veterinarian can learn a great deal just by letting a bird relax, as this toucan is doing.

Photo by Dr. Brian L. Speer

In the second part of the examination, your veterinarian actually handles your bird. A towel wrapped around the bird serves as a safe and comfortable restraint, especially helpful if your pet is expressing anxiety or less-than-the-best temperament. (If you don't already know how to perform the towel trick, now is a good time to ask your veterinarian to demonstrate. We also show you how in Chapter 7.) Restraining makes it possible to do those procedures your bird doesn't like, such as having blood samples drawn or toenails or wing feathers clipped. The hands-on examination should be as short as possible to keep the pet's stress level down — and yours, too!

For information on who's out there to treat your bird and how to find the very best veterinary care, see Chapter 9. You don't necessarily need a certified specialist — many general-care veterinarians do wonderfully by their avian patients — but you do need a veterinarian who likes to treat pet birds and keeps up on the rapid changes in the field of avian medicine.

Caging and Husbandry Review

With a smaller bird, the initial look-see may even reveal problems with the cage and its accessories, since small birds are often brought to the hospital in their everyday environment (not possible with the massive cages designed for their larger relatives).

If you bring the cage, your veterinarian can easily evaluate its appropriateness for your bird. Is the size right? Bar spacing proper? Perches, dishes, and toys safe and placed well? Your veterinarian can offer direction on all these items — and more. If you aren't able to bring your bird's cage along, ask your vet to review caging basics with you to ensure that your pet has safe housing with enough room to shake some tail feathers.

What makes a cage proper? You can find the answers in Chapter 4, as well as in our illustration in the color section of this book.

You don't have to bring the cage with your bird. You may find it easier to bring your bird in a carrier. We review modes of transportation in Chapter 4. With a small bird, even a carrier may not be necessary. Brian sees many small birds arrive safely at the hospital in a brown paper grocery bag — although a carrier is probably a better idea!

After a complete review of caging, your veterinarian should ask you about your cleanliness routine — how often you change cage liners or litter, how often you clean dishes, when (if ever) you scrub the cage and perches, and so on. Your housekeeping's not being questioned — well, maybe a little — rather, the focus is on not giving infectious disease a foothold and on not using cleaning or pest-control products that may be dangerous to your bird. Your veterinarian may have some suggestions for making life easier or may even tell you that you're cleaning too often.

Food for Thought: The Right Nutrition

The recent revolution in avian nutrition has left behind more than a few breeders and pet stores — and a lot of bird-owners, too. Expect a conscientious veterinarian to go over the proper diet for your bird — the main course, limited-quantity treats, and bill-of-fare no-no's.

If your bird is on a diet that should be improved, your veterinarian ought to work with you on a gradual plan to convert your pet to better eating. (It's not just a matter of changing foods one day.)

Although your veterinarian may sell or recommend a line of foods that is perfectly adequate for your pet's nutritional needs, be aware of other products on the market that may be just as good. Ask not only for a recommendation but also for an evaluation of the handful of products that may suit your bird. If your veterinarian emphasizes the house brand, you should be able to ask why without risking offense. It's a fair question, and it should be met with an honest answer — even if the veterinarian admits he just likes the products he recommends better.

Behavioral Check-Up

Your veterinarian can tell a lot about your pet's adjustment to life in your household — and your patience and consistency — by gauging how comfortable you are with your bird. Even the most well-meaning owners fall into some very bad traps when it comes to behaviors. The result can be the conversion of a sweet-natured baby into a difficult, demanding, and possibly even dangerous pet.

Brian tends to spend a great deal of time on behavior issues, handling his patients to see where they draw the line and watching their owners' reactions. When he encounters a bird who won't put up with much handling, he shows the owners how to deal with the pet without putting pet or person at risk and suggests ways to remedy a situation that's going to be heading south quickly.

Even if everything's going well, an attentive veterinarian takes the time to discuss problems that may appear, what to watch for, and how to get through trying situations unscathed. Some birds go through an adolescent period that's not much different from a human one, with hormones raging and fights over control and good manners cropping up on a daily basis. Coping with these difficult stages is key to the survival of your relationship.

Guideline for Multi-Bird Households

Three words to remember: *Closed Aviary Concept.* You can find much more about the concept in Chapter 13, but it can be summed up pretty easily this way: Don't risk the health of the birds you have by introducing a potentially sick one.

How can you keep your birds safe? Preventive health screening, common sense, and quarantine. Your veterinarian should be able to explain safe ways to keep a new bird separate and for how long. And when you get the okay to make it one happy bird family, your veterinarian should also have some tips on how to handle the introduction.

Testing the Blood

The emphasis when it comes to avian health is on preventive care, and one facet of this care is establishing what's normal for your bird. One of the ways your veterinarian determines your pet's personal profile is by drawing blood for a *baseline CBC,* or *Complete Blood Count.* This test, one of the more basic in both human and veterinary medicine, is used both to gauge good health and as a diagnostic tool to help determine the presence and type of illness. In birds, the test measures four or five variables, such as the total white blood cell count. Your veterinarian may also suggest blood chemistries. Results of baseline blood testing help to fill in some of the gaps in your veterinarian's understanding of the overall health of your bird and greatly help him to get a feel for what's going on under those beautiful feathers. (Kind of like checking under the hood of a car.)

Your veterinarian obtains blood samples by nail clipping or by *venipuncture,* the insertion of a small needle into a vein. The latter is rapidly becoming the preferred method, using neck or wing veins for the draw. Would you like to have your blood tested by clipping your nails back until they bleed? We wouldn't, either!

Screening for Bacteria

Your veterinarian may also suggest screening for bacteria, taking a swab across the roof of your bird's mouth, or his eyes, or nose (if discharge is obvious), or getting a sample from his feces or a swab of his fanny, more formally known as the *cloaca.* Your veterinarian can then have one or more tests performed to spot any troublemakers among the normal bacteria, fungi, or viruses that may be present.

Two tests are commonly performed: *Gram's stain* and the *bacterial culture*. Gram's stain is a less-specific test to give the veterinarian an idea of what general kinds of bacteria may be present. The culture, which involves actually growing and identifying bacteria, provides a more precise identification of bacteria present, as well as the ability to test those bacteria for their sensitivity to antibiotics, should treatment be indicated.

A Couple More Diseases — Maybe

Psittacine Beak and Feather Disease, or PBFD, is a serious and contagious ailment affecting so-called "Old World Birds" — species from Africa, Australia, and Indonesia. If your bird is a representative of one of these species, your veterinarian may suggest a blood test to determine whether PBFD is present. A positive result may not be as bad as you think. Some birds who test positive for PBFD may have been exposed to the virus but are on their way to shaking it.

Your veterinarian can advise you as to what the test results mean and how your bird should be retested or treated, if necessary.

Another disease your veterinarian may want to test for is *chlamydiosis,* otherwise known as *psittacosis* — not only for your bird's sake but possibly for your own. Psittacosis can be a problem for some people.

For more on PBFD, psittacosis, and other infectious diseases, see Chapter 10.

For the Record: What and Who Are You?

Although you can guarantee that birds can tell the difference, we humans (even veterinarians) can't easily tell the boys from the girls in a great many species. This ambiguity may have no bearing on how good a pet your bird becomes, but some people can't stand not knowing the gender of their birds. Their reasons may have nothing to do with an interest in breeding. Some people just want to know whether to choose a masculine or feminine name, while others want to know so they can be prepared for problems down the line, such as reproductive problems in females.

When we can't tell them apart, the answer is testing. A veterinarian can use a surgical procedure to determine gender, but more commonly uses a blood sample or any newly formed feather (called a *blood* or *pin* feather) to check a pet bird's DNA. Both of the noninvasive tests take a couple of weeks to process.

The eclectus parrot is one bird even we humans can't confuse when it comes to figuring out which birds are males and which are females. The male eclectus is a bright green with red patches under his wings, while the female is a shimmery purple with red head and tail, one of the more handsome pets around. Each member of the pair is so different that the two genders were once considered different species. For a full-color picture of these vividly marked pets, check out our color section.

After you settle the gender issue, give serious consideration to giving your pet a unique identity with a microchip. Your veterinarian may suggest this safety measure, a device the size of a grain of rice that can be inserted into the bird's breast muscle. A microchip can help you recover your bird if she disappears and prove your ownership if someone steals your pet. For more on microchips and other forms of birdy ID, see Chapter 4.

A Shot for Birdy?

Unlike dogs and cats, birds don't get a series of baby shots — not yet, anyway. One vaccination exists, for a potentially deadly infectious disease called *polyomavirus,* and its use is a topic of much discussion in the avian community, by breeders, retailers, and veterinarians alike. Some professionals advise vaccinations for all birds, while others recommend shots only for breeding birds or for those going to a place with a potentially high level of exposure, such as a pet store. Still others don't recommend inoculation at all.

We ride the fence on the issue. Your veterinarian isn't wrong if his opinion differs, but he should let you know about the vaccine, and why he is or isn't recommending it. If you choose the shot for your pet, your bird needs a booster 14 days later.

For more on polyomavirus, see Chapter 10.

Chapter 16

Ten Questions to Ask When Buying a Bird

In This Chapter

- A little history, please
- Beware the mass-producers
- Let's be sociable
- What's for dinner?

Love at first sight? Slow down a little! When it comes to buying a bird, you need to be a savvy consumer, with your head more in control than your heart and your wallet firmly in your pocket — or better yet, left at home — until you have good answers to some crucial questions.

Restrain your urge to buy until you're certain what kind of bird is the right match for you. If you go to a bird shop or breeder without a solid understanding of the differences between species, you may well end up falling in love with a pretty bird who doesn't really agree with your personality and lifestyle. Check out Chapter 2 for more on how to choose; Chapter 18 lists our picks of good starter birds.

Where Do You Get Your Birds?

Sad to say, the world is full of people selling pets who are better suited for another line of work. To them, a bird (or a puppy or kitten) is nothing more than something to produce as cheaply as possible and sell as profitably as possible. Aside from the philosophical question of whether a living creature should be treated like an object — we certainly don't think so — birds who are produced in a strictly bottom-line manner can be a very bad choice for a pet.

Healthy pet babies come from healthy parents and are raised in healthy environments, on healthy foods, and lovingly socialized by human "godparents." They're not the stressed-out "production units" you may find in the care — and we use the term loosely — of a mass-producer. For a bird to have a chance as a good pet, he needs an idea of what a human being looks, sounds, and smells like, a chance to bond to a species that doesn't look very much like his own.

Because we have seen the sick and unsocialized babies who are the direct result of poor-quality breeding and marketing practices, we think your best bet is dealing with an experienced local breeder or a shop who buys from one. (Brian, for example, sells his macaw babies through reputable bird shops because he doesn't want people dropping in at his home.)

Ideally, you want to deal directly with a seller who either breeds his own birds or buys from locals he is confident in. Most shops are happy to share the source of their birds — after all, an honorable operation is proud of the quality of the pets it has for sale. Other shops prefer not to reveal the names of their breeding sources — sometimes at the request of the breeders — but can assure you that they're local, can provide references (more on that later in this chapter), and will stand behind the quality of the birds they sell.

An individual or shop that cannot or will not tell you the source of its pets — or that makes some vague reference to a large production facility — is probably not your best bet for a healthy bird with good pet potential. "We get our birds from lots of local breeders and from a few large producers" may not be a sign of good quality control; the health of the babies is often only as good as the health of the poorest quality supplier, because of the highly infectious nature of some types of disease. In general, the fewer the number of breeders supplying a store, the better.

Depending on where you live and the type of bird you're hoping to buy, a reputable breeder may not be in the same state as you are. In some areas — Florida and California among them — breeding and selling pet birds is a pretty big industry, with lots of participants, both large and small, professional and hobbyist. Trying to find a breeder in the Midwest, though, may be as hard as finding beach toys there during wintertime — they're around, but not that common. A reputable bird store deals only with good breeders, whether they're in the same city or hundreds of miles away.

How do you know whether you're dealing with a reputable breeder or bird shop? We give you the inside track in Chapter 3.

How Many Birds Do You Sell a Year?

We're still on the same track with this question, trying to ensure that a seller is able to pay attention to birds as individuals. Although a reputable shop may sell 200 to 300 birds or sometimes more a year, all healthy and well-socialized, any retail outlet that moves markedly more than that number ought to set off alarms in your head.

Socialization and health are everything in this game, and our experience shows us that large-scale operations just aren't able or willing to pay as much attention to these factors as quality care requires. And how can a breeder, with his hundreds or thousands of breeding pairs housed in colonies without any concern about who's mating with whom, possibly be in tune with a bird's predisposition to congenital problems or his current state of health? Get 'em hatched, pack 'em up, and ship 'em out by the thousands isn't the way to produce a healthy pet, in our minds.

Even though you're taking a risk with a mass-produced bird — and possibly supporting some questionable businesses — you also have to remember that small isn't necessarily better when it comes to bird breeding. A careless, sloppy, or uninformed breeder can mess up one clutch of baby birds just as surely as a mass-producer can ruin thousands. Some small-scale hobbyists are excellent. Some aren't. Some larger breeding operations are excellent. Some aren't. Health and socializing — those are key elements!

A *clutch* is bird-speak for what you find in a nest — eggs laid at the same time from a particular breeding pair, to be incubated and hatched at one time.

What Are the Terms of the Sales Contract and Post-Purchase Warranty?

A bird who may appear perfectly healthy at the time of sale may in fact be harboring an infectious disease or birth defect that can limit the quality of his life, if not eventually kill him. Such a situation can be heartbreaking, of course, but it can also be financially devastating. Some parrots carry price tags into the thousands — and tens of thousands — of dollars, not to mention the significant expense of cages and other must-have bird equipment for a bird you may not have long and can't afford to replace.

Make sure the sales contract spells out what happens if something goes wrong — if the bird becomes ill or dies, for example. While nothing can make up for the sadness of losing a bird, a contract spelling out terms of replacement or compensation with a decent post-purchase warranty can at least offset some of the financial burden and provide a measure of protection to both the buyer and the seller.

Expect the seller who has the bird's welfare in mind to strongly recommend you to have the bird examined by a qualified veterinarian of your choice within a certain time frame — 48 to 72 hours is a common recommendation.

The veterinary check ensures to your own satisfaction that your new bird is healthy. The seller should lay out the ground rules if the bird is not — full refund, store credit, or whatever.

For more information on protecting your rights in the purchase process, see Chapter 3.

What Are Your References?

Ask the seller for names of recent buyers — within the last year or so. Call a couple of past buyers and ask what they thought of their dealings with the shop or breeder, and ask them what kind of companions their birds have turned out to be. A good sign: Breeders or shops that stay in touch with buyers and are always available to help out with behavior or husbandry recommendations. Satisfied customers continue to patronize a bird shop for boarding, grooming, and supplies.

A veterinary reference is important, too. Ask the bird store owner or breeder for the name of his or her veterinarian, and if the business can't provide one, don't buy. A seller who treats his own birds or who doesn't believe in or practice preventive veterinary care isn't the kind of person from whom you can safely buy. Who knows what illnesses are brewing in birds with such precarious beginnings? The sellers certainly don't, and you're smart to skip the opportunity to find out.

How Old Is This Bird?

Most novice bird-owners are better off with a young bird, one without the "baggage" of past relationships. But because of their real or perceived value, problem parrots are often sold time and time again, with each owner hoping to reclaim at least part of the purchase price while dumping an unmanageable bird on someone else. Although finding older birds who make wonderful pets is within the realm of possibility, the only absolutely sure way to know a bird's history is to buy a *weaned* baby — one capable of eating without assistance — from a reputable source.

A reliable seller knows the age of your bird; ideally, a "hatch date" appears on the paperwork that comes with the bird. If a bird was raised by parents, not by human hands — perfectly acceptable if she has been socialized — an exact hatch date may not be known, but the seller should be able to give you an estimate that's pretty close. Good breeding practices include good recordkeeping: When you see evidence that the paperwork has been taken care of properly, most often so has the bird!

In some species, you can determine approximate age by markings or eye color — both of which change as a bird matures.

Keep in mind that young is good, but unweaned babies often are not. Few new bird-owners have the expertise to hand-feed, wean, and socialize an unweaned baby, like the one shown in Figure 16-1. Don't buy into old-fashioned thinking suggesting your bird is destined to bond better if you buy him unweaned, and don't fall for a lower price for an unweaned baby. Too many novices who buy unweaned babies end up with dead birds, sad to say. Cockatiels and budgies are weaned by 6 to 8 weeks of age; larger parrots range from 14 weeks to up to 6 months.

Figure 16-1: Cute as they are, unweaned babies such as this cockatiel aren't the best pet bet, especially for a first-time buyer.

Photo by Dr. Brian L. Speer

Some nonprofit organizations work not only to rescue birds with problems but also to educate prospective adopters so they have a better chance of making the newly forming relationship work. By requiring classes for adopters, these organizations help to ensure educated bird-owners are prepared to deal with any health or behavior problems in their new pets. We highlight a couple of these groups in our Additional Resources appendix at the back of this book. They deserve your support!

Does This Bird Have Any Medical Problems, Past or Current?

This question may require some tact — you don't want to accuse someone of trying to sell you a sick bird. Still, you have a right to know — and a need to know — any medical history. If you find the bird you fancy is currently under medical care, don't buy until a veterinarian has certified the pet's return to good health. Not all problems are easily remedied, so don't take a chance. If the bird recovers and you still want him, fine.

You want to feel confident that the seller has a history of using a veterinarian — an overreliance on home remedies and guesswork is another warning bell. A tactful way to find out whether the bird's illness has been properly addressed is to ask for a copy of the medical record so your own veterinarian can review it. If there is no medical record because the seller hasn't used a veterinarian for care, beware!

Does This Bird Have Any Behavioral Problems?

A lot of birds end up in new homes because their owners can't deal with behavior problems. In general, a novice bird-keeper is better off avoiding such a problem pet, but if you feel capable of taking on the challenge, be sure to understand what you're likely to face.

Feather-picking is pretty obvious, since the afflicted bird may look more like a plucked chicken than a parrot in full, colorful plumage. Don't fall for that old line, "He's just molting." He may not be. Other potential problems may not be so straightforward. Some birds don't like men; others don't like women. Some are afraid of people with glasses or have no basic training in good behaviors such as stepping onto a hand or perch. Others scream constantly for attention — usually because that's what their previous owners have (inadvertently) taught them.

Go into any such situation with your eyes open and be determined to work on the problem in full knowledge that some sad situations can't be fixed, and others require a great deal of time and patience. Some birds get passed around more than a football, growing more unhappy and insecure with each change of family (wouldn't you?). If you aren't willing to put some time and effort into a problem bird, don't consider taking one on. Parrots are highly intelligent — it's one of the reasons they're so popular. But it's also one of the reasons "recycled" birds are such an iffy proposition. When a bird has had a rough life, he often bears psychological scars that can make him a very challenging pet indeed.

Gina's little Senegal parrot, Patrick, had been in four homes by the age of 2 when he came to live with her. He had a medical file an inch thick and had plucked himself raw. His sweet nature saved him from his previous owner's desire to euthanize him — the veterinarian, Gina's friend Dr. Carla Weinberg, asked to find him a new home instead. Patrick's feather-picking has eased since his adoption, and the finally fuller little fellow could not be happier sharing his life with Gina — and vice versa! His feathers aren't the only improvement: The little guy has learned to trust, to explore, and to play.

Quite a change! To every rule there is an exception, and Patrick is one of them. He ended up in the right place at the right time, with a person willing to take a chance on him.

How Have You Socialized This Bird?

If the answer to this question is "Huh?" consider looking elsewhere when shopping for anything except birds who aren't meant to be handled, such as members of the finch family, canaries included.

Birds don't have to be hand-fed to be socialized — that's a myth we'd like to correct. Parent-raised birds have wonderful pet potential, as long as they're handled, played with, and talked to by humans while they're growing. You don't expect every kitten or puppy to be bottle-fed from birth, do you? Of course not! Mother dogs and cats do a wonderful job of raising their own offspring, and as long as the babies are handled and exposed to people, they have no problem transferring their affection from Mom and littermates to members of their new, human family. The same is true of birds: It's perfectly fine to let a bird's parents do the raising, as long as the babies are socialized by humans.

If the bird you're thinking of buying *has* been hand-raised, that's fine, too, provided you realize that the overall handling, not the hand-feeding, makes the difference.

A dependable breeder or bird shop can explain how the birds have been socialized, how they've been handled, and how much time has been spent with them. You *don't* want to hear, "He's a nice bird, and if you can get him out of the cage, he's yours." (You can find out more about socialization in Chapters 3 and 13.)

Because of the economic realities of hand-feeding the less-expensive birds — the profit margin just isn't there — many budgies and some cockatiels aren't socialized at all. From an economic perspective, nurturing an eclectus parrot or hyacinth macaw (both with price tags in the hundreds to thousands of dollars) makes more sense than to lavish that much attention on a bird who may fetch as little as $10. If you find a socialized budgie or cockatiel, you're in luck! But if you end up with a bird who's largely wild, you can work toward building trust and a good relationship. We explain how in Chapter 5.

What Have You Been Feeding This Bird?

If the seller says "Seed" — run! All-seed diets are not healthy for birds and shorten their lives in the long run. You have to wonder what else could be wrong with a bird whose seller doesn't even know or take the time to make you aware of this basic fact. Some bird folks make their own diets from a nutritious blend of "people food" and seeds. Others feed one of the balanced pelleted diets, supplemented by fresh vegetables and fruit.

Our recommendation is to support a seller who already has the bird on one of these commercial diets and to stick with it when you take your bird home. Research shows that pelleted diets keep birds healthy. They make caring for a pet bird easier, too, since you won't have to figure out your bird's nutrition needs every day and fix meals from scratch. The makers of commercial pellets have already done that job.

Pellets aren't the whole story — you need to supplement commercial foods with a healthy dose of fruits, vegetables, and other foods. Don't worry, though: Avian nutrition isn't that complicated. Check out Chapter 6 for diet tips that can put your bird on the right track.

May I Visit and Get to Know the Bird Before Buying?

We put this question in because it's a good idea to spend some quiet time observing any bird you're considering before the checkbook or credit card comes out. You need to look at a bird as an individual, not just go by what you think is normal for each species. A pionus parrot may indeed have more in common with another pionus parrot than with an African grey, but that doesn't mean personality differences don't exist among individual birds.

One of Brian's favorite stories is from the very first clutch of blue-and-gold macaws he raised — Uno, Dos, and Tres. Dos literally hatched with an attitude problem, and she still pretty much has one, 15 years later. She is with an owner with whom she fits well, fortunately for this girl, but getting her through her "childhood" was a challenge from the first crack in her egg! Although of the same parents, she was very different from her nestmates.

Look beyond the beautiful plumage and try to pick up clues from the bird you plan to share your life with. Observe quietly, and see how the bird responds. Is he interested in your attention? Afraid? Indifferent? If you let him perch on your hand, does he seem to relax? Can you get a sense of the individual bird? Do you like him? Do you think he likes you?

If you've carefully considered all the other questions in this chapter, we give you our permission to fall head over heels in love. In fact, we encourage it!

Chapter 17

Ten Must-See Avian Web Sites

In This Chapter

- Just for kids
- Spotlight on behavior
- Lost and found
- Bird watching — without leaving home

No one can deny the power of the Internet to inform, enflame, and entertain. But honing in on the information you need and want online isn't as easy as some folks may suggest. No quality control exists on the Internet. It's easy to find dreadful information — outdated, misguided, and flat-out dangerous.

We're aware of this fact of contemporary life because we've been on the Information Superhighway since it was a two-lane dirt road. We use it in our work, and we use it when we play. And we know this from experience: Despite the dangers of misinformation, the Internet is an incredible resource for bird-lovers. With a computer and a modem to hook into your phone line, you can shop for your bird, research species and health topics, enjoy some humor, or just hang out and look at bird pictures.

Lots of possibilities exist for bird-lovers on the Internet — and we cover how to connect with them in Chapter 1 — but one of the easier ways for beginners to poke around is to use the graphical part of the Internet, called the World Wide Web.

A list of sites can't begin to hit all the best bird resources on the Web, which is why we've fudged and offered you more than ten. But even a hundred wouldn't do the job, nor would a thousand. If you feed the word *bird* or *parrot* into a search engine, you find that the subject triggers about a million and a half suggested places to look on the Web.

So try out our humble offerings, and don't be shy about exploring on your own. Many pages offer connections, called *links,* which can take you to other bird sites if you click the links with your mouse; in fact, some pages are nothing *but* links. Following some of these links can turn up some real gems. Happy exploring!

For more on surfing avian cyberspace — finding FAQS, newsgroups, e-mail lists, and chats — see Chapter 1. We also think you may enjoy some of the ...*For Dummies* books on the subject, such as *The Internet For Dummies,* 6th Edition, by John R. Levine, Carol Baroudi, and Margaret Levine Young, and *World Wide Web Searching For Dummies,* 2nd Edition, by Brad Hill (IDG Books Worldwide, Inc.).

The Internet changes quickly, and so does its content. We try our very best to keep our listings current, but Web sites move or die every day. If you can't find something we list here, try to locate it through a search engine such as Yahoo! (`www.yahoo.com`) or Excite (`www.excite.com`). Chances are you can find the site in another location.

Fun for Kids — and Adults, Too

Anyone living with an avian companion readily admits you have to have a good sense of humor to deal with the everyday challenges, from the food-flingers to the parrots who pick up people talk you'd prefer they didn't repeat — and who choose to interject those colorful phrases at every inappropriate moment.

A sense of humor is why we really like Enchanted Learning Software's "All About Birds" site (`www.EnchantedLearning.com/subjects/birds/Allaboutbirds.html`), which offers a collection of jokes along with some basically sound bird facts aimed at the grade-school set — all in a very pleasingly designed package. Very colorful!

Sure, you can expect a couple of chicken/road jokes, but how about this for a variation on the theme?

Q. Why did the chicken go to the seance?

A. To get to the other side.

We admit to being easily amused, so much so that we've included a few bird jokes of our own in Chapter 21.

Your kids will be amused, too, as they discover all kinds of neat stuff about bird anatomy, locomotion (some birds swim and run instead of fly), eating habits, and evolution.

Oh, and by the way . . . What's smarter than a talking parrot? A spelling bee!

Behavior Help and Then Some

Parrot behavior consultant Sally Blanchard is a woman of strong will and equally intense opinions, as you discover when you visit her Web site, "The Pet Bird Report" (www.petbirdreport.com). Blanchard's interest is in providing people with the information they need to maximize their pet birds' potential — and she does a great job with this Web site and with her magazine of the same name. (Subscription information for the latter is in the Additional Resources appendix at the back of this book.)

Pet Bird Report (PBR) contributors include some of the more dedicated and forward-thinking veterinarians, behaviorists, and breeders around, and the online offerings are usually well-done, although we quibble some with an overemphasis on anecdotal and "gut-feeling" information in some articles, as opposed to a more scientific-based approach. Still, there's no denying the love and respect for birds that these people embody, and the desire to make life better for both pet and wild birds. The PBR is built on a strong, ethical bedrock that more people in the pet industry should emulate.

The strength of the site is in its behavior articles, where you can find help with all the things that drive bird-lovers nuts. Another thing we like: the advertising policy. From cage- and toy-makers to breeders and food manufacturers, all advertisers need Blanchard's approval before she takes either their ads or their money. This policy makes it less likely to find a product that's either substandard or unnecessary.

As we said, this is one strong-willed woman. And although we may disagree with her on occasion on some details, we can't deny that her heart is in the right place — and the lot of pet birds is better because of her work.

If your bird is suffering from a behavior problem — or if you are! — check out our tips for preventing and fixing bad bird habits in Chapter 12.

Enrapt over Raptors

Birds of prey are cool. The folks at the Raptor Center at the University of Minnesota understand the essential coolness of these birds, and they've got a fabulous Web site to prove it (www.raptor.cvm.umn.edu/).

The center is an internationally known medical facility for birds of prey, with an emphasis on "medical treatment, scientific investigation, education, and management of wild populations." The center's Web site is a great place to find out about these birds and an even better place to adopt one! Adoption really means sponsorship, because the organization relies on donations to keep going. (Staff members report that it costs $40,000 a year just to feed the birds in their care.) Sponsorships start at $20 a year and include information on the bird of your choice as well as a newsletter.

The Web site's not just a marketing pitch, though. The Raptor Center uses it to educate on such topics as what to do with an injured raptor or updates on current cases in the center's veterinary clinic. Look for lots of great links to other raptor programs around the world, too!

Help Us Get Home

If nothing else, the "Bird Hotline: World Wide Bird Lost and Found" Web site (`www.birdhotline.com`) packs the power to convince you of the importance of keeping your bird's wings trimmed. Although some of the birds listed have been stolen, most have simply been lost — through an opened door or a cracked window. The hotline's pages are filled with heartbroken owners who realized in a fraction of a second how easily a flighted bird can . . . well, fly!

The Bird Hotline is an amazing labor of love, an attempt to use the Internet to link bird-lovers worldwide into a "Bird Patrol" looking for lost pets — and they've signed up nearly a thousand! The site lists not only birds who have been lost or stolen but also birds who have been found. The best part, of course, is the collection of stories with happy endings — those birds who are safely reunited with their owners. (Far too few, sadly, in comparison to the number of lost birds listed.)

Education is another goal of the Web site. Its creators note that anyone who finds a dog or cat immediately thinks about locating an owner, but too many folks who find a bird assume the rule is "finders keepers." That notion has a chance of changing as Web site visitors read and share stories about how much these pets are missed.

The site also offers some basic bird-care guidelines, but really, that's secondary to the outstanding work of these bird-lovers. Join the Bird Patrol today!

Reducing the risk of losing your pet isn't the only reason to keep your bird's wings clipped, but it's certainly a good one. We go over some of the others in Chapter 19, and in Chapter 7 you can find what you need to know to keep your bird grounded.

While the cooperative efforts of the Bird Patrol are commendable, don't rely on the kindness of strangers to assure your lost bird's return. Birds are valuable, hard to trace, and easily sold with no questions asked for quick cash, which makes them enticing to burglars. If your bird turns up in someone else's hands, you may have a hard time proving you are your pet's owner. That's why identification such as a microchip is important. For more information on microchips and other forms of ID, see Chapter 4.

Meet Alex, the Star

Alex the African grey may be the most well-known parrot in the world, and that's in no small measure due to more than two decades of work by his owner, Dr. Irene M. Pepperberg, who has helped to revolutionize our understanding of the intelligence of birds.

"Communications with Parrots: The Pepperberg Homepage" (`www.cages.org/research/pepperberg/index.html`) showcases both Alex and Pepperberg, which makes it a must-see for anyone who wants to know more about parrots. Through her research, Pepperberg and her colleagues have shown that birds such as Alex are not just gifted mimics; they actually understand a great deal of what they say.

Alex, at age 20, is the oldest of the three birds Pepperberg works with. He can, according to the Web site, "count, identify objects, shapes, colors, and materials. [He also] knows the concepts of same and different, and bosses around lab assistants in order to modify his environment!" Recent work with phonics suggests that Alex may someday even be able to read.

The Web site contains many of the articles written about Alex and Pepperberg, as well as articles written by Pepperberg herself, including one on how to help your parrot learn to talk. Fascinating stuff, with some scientific links you can't find elsewhere.

It's Academic

Ornithology is the study of birds, and the Web offers a couple of sites with decent scientific credentials. One of them is BIRDNET (`www.nmnh.si.edu/BIRDNET/index.html`), sponsored by the Ornithological Council in the interest of inspiring more people to value birds and the research related to them. The site offers information about current research and legislative issues, a list of experts in the field, help with bird-watching, an online newsletter, and a link to online ornithological discussion.

Birds of a Feather, Flocking Together

A visit to the American Federation of Aviculture's home page (www.afa.birds.org/) can enlighten and make you feel grateful: Without the AFA and other activist groups, the companionship of a bird may be out of reach for all of us. The AFA was formed in 1974 in response to legislation that would have greatly restricted the ability to keep birds, in response to concerns over diseases threatening to damage the poultry industry. Today, the Arizona-based group has more than 5,000 members and 200 clubs and organization under its umbrella, and it still works to improve the lot of pet birds through education, research, and advocacy. The site's a good place to stop to check the pulse of avian issues. Another is the International Aviculturist Society's site (www.funnyfarmexotics.com/IAS/).

Both the U.S. and International societies have plenty of links to other organizations, but if you're looking for a bird club in your area, check out the list at www.poozleanimus.com/clubs.htm.

Aviculture is a fancy word for the breeding and keeping of birds in captivity; the term is also used to represent the entire industry of bird-keeping, from breeders and bird stores to magazines and companies that manufacture cages, food, and equipment.

The Source for Health

In the history of veterinary medicine, the Association of Avian Veterinarians counts as a fairly recent entry, but its growth is indicative both in the number of birds as pets and in bird-owners' interest in keeping them healthy. Founded in 1980, the AAV has more than 3,000 members worldwide today, although relatively few of them are full-time avian practitioners like Brian.

The AAV Web site (www.aav.org), shown in Figure 17-1, reflects the group's goals, with information both for the general public and for member veterinarians, all geared to improving avian health. Through the Web site, you can gather some basic health information, order pamphlets or articles, or search for an AAV member in your area. Among the few featured links is one to keep in mind: the ASPCA/National Animal Poison Control Center site (www.napcc.aspca.org).

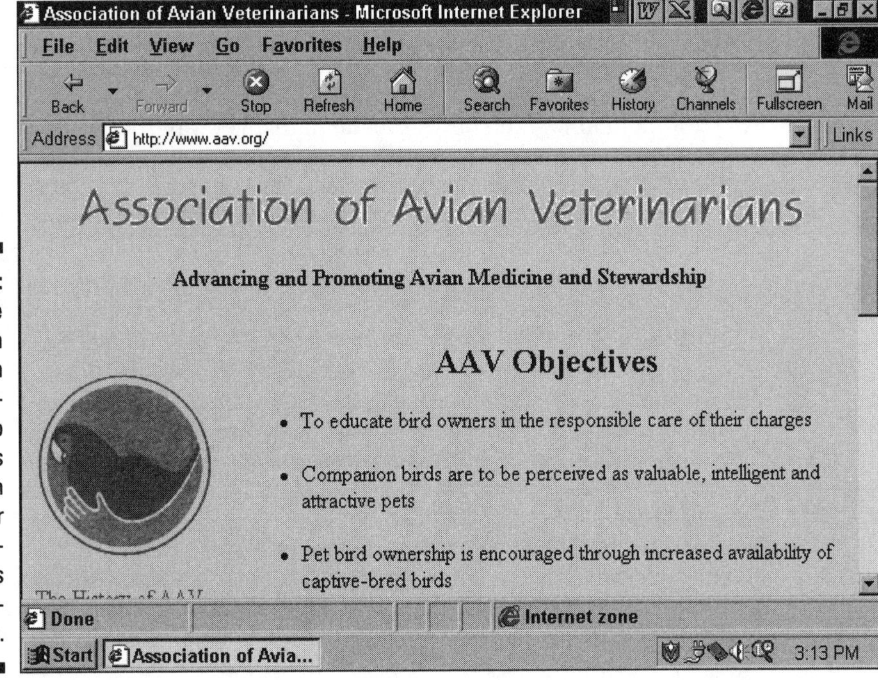

Figure 17-1: The Association of Avian Veterinarians' Web site offers information both for health professionals and the general public.

Another important veterinary site is the Veterinary Information Network (`www.vin.com`), an online service for veterinary professionals. Brian is an avian medicine consultant to the company, which has more than 5,000 member veterinarians worldwide. NetVet's page of bird resources (`netvet.wustl.edu/birds.htm`) is also worth spending time on.

The AAV's search engine leaves a lot to be desired. Although it invites you to search for ZIP code or city, you won't get much from either of those searches because the program doesn't recognize nearby ZIPs or cities. Your best bet is to search for all the AAV members in your state and then scan the list to see which ones are in your area. Another option: VetQuest, offered by the Veterinary Information Network at `www.vetquest.com`. Specify "avian" and the site delivers listings, also by state. One advantage to the VetQuest listings: You can download a map to help direct you to the hospital or clinic.

Remembering Birds in Need

Birds don't always have it so easy, which is why groups spring up to help pet birds and to assist in preserving wild ones and their habitats. We focus on one of each because we support them and because we think their Web sites are useful and entertaining.

The Gabriel Foundation (www.thegabrielfoundation.org) is a Colorado-based charity that works to rescue, rehabilitate, and rehome unwanted pet birds, as well as educate bird-owners about proper care of their pets. Gabriel was the hyacinth macaw of founder Julie Murad, who lost the bird as a result of improper care by the bird's breeder and a veterinarian. The loss shocked Murad into a life dedicated to helping birds, and the foundation now shelters birds waiting for adoption, some with special physical and emotion needs. The birds are listed on the site, along with information on how to adopt and other ways to honor Gabriel's memory by helping out this nonprofit group.

Preserving birds in their ever-more-endangered environment is the focus of the World Parrot Trust USA (www.funnyfarmexotics.com/WPT). The pages include information on conservation projects and articles about why wild birds deserve our concern.

And a Flock of Others

Obviously, we never meant to limit ourselves to ten Web sites — it was just too hard. We tried to lump them into ten categories, at least, but even that turned out to be a challenge. So we've thrown some sites we like into a category of their own. Every one is entertaining and a good place to start exploring.

The Online Books of Parrots (www.ub.tu-clausthal.de/p_welcome.html) is a German site dedicated to helping visitors identify and discover more about the hundreds of parrot species in the world. A ton of information here; take your time to find your way around.

On a decidedly lighter note is the Buba the Bird Web site featured in Figure 17-2 (www.dublclick.com/coconutinfo/buba.html), starring an African grey with a rather remarkable repertoire of words, phrases, and sounds, some of them in Hawaiian. Buba works as a paper-shredder and computer-disk eraser for Coconut Info Software in Hawaii, and his officemates have put together a fitting homage to this clever bird. Be sure to download the sound files of Buba talking, as well as a message to Buba from a staffer at the "Tonight Show" — stardom beckons for this talking wonder!

Finally, we offer a nod of approval to Gillian's Help Desk (www.exoticbird.com/gillian/index.html), a well-organized resource for bird-lovers. You can see the home page for this site in Figure 17-3.

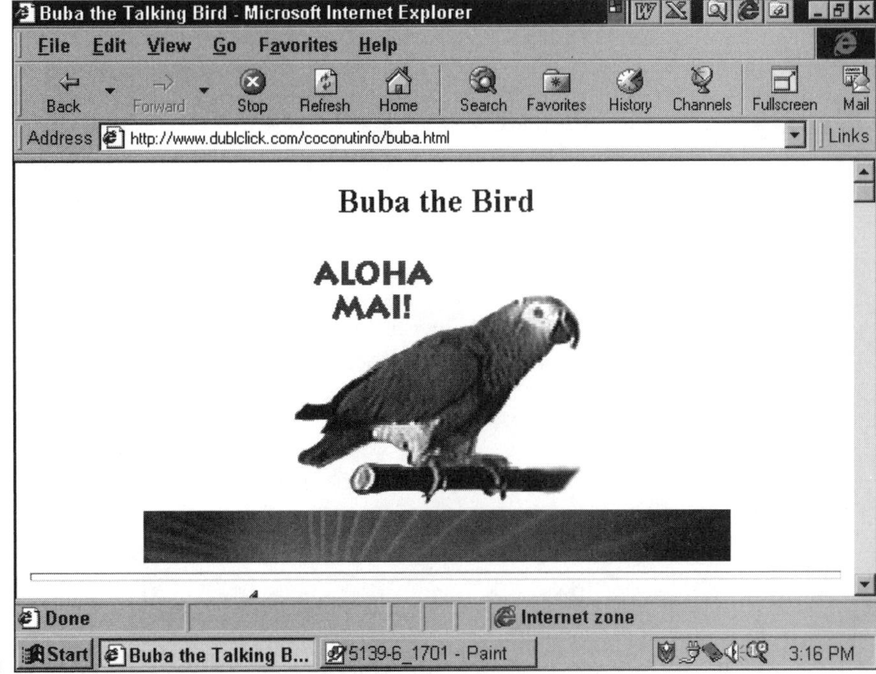

Figure 17-2: African greys are known to be great talkers, but Buba is especially gabby, as his Web page reveals.

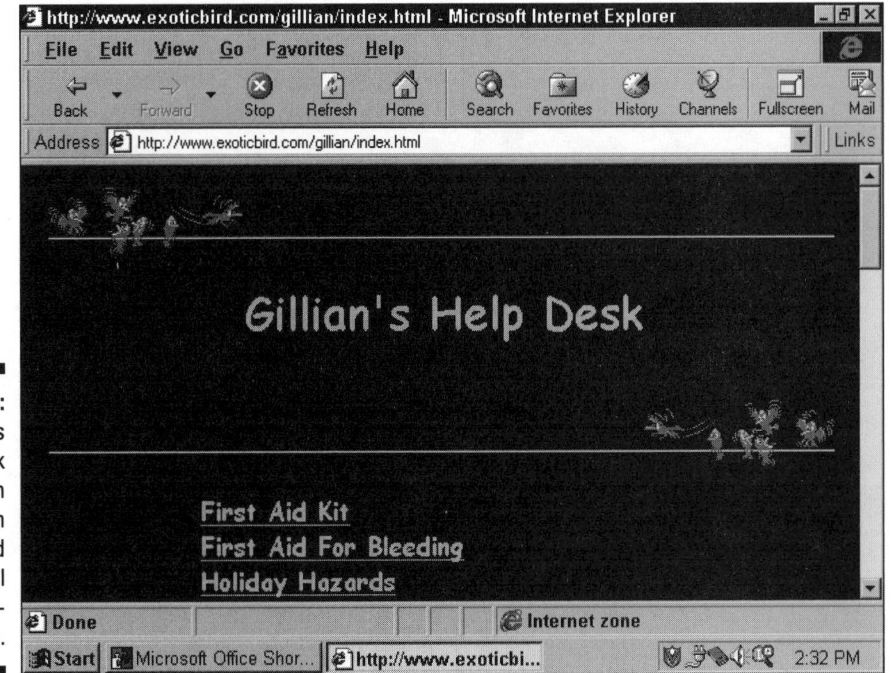

Figure 17-3: Gillian's Help Desk is an information packed site well worth bookmarking.

Chapter 18

Ten Best Birds for Beginners

In This Chapter

- Sing out for canaries
- Finches forever
- Unbeatable budgies
- A world's worth of parrots

When it comes to birds, too many people get in over their heads, choosing a pet who's too large, too loud, too expensive — and ultimately, too much to handle. If your list of must-have birds includes only the largest and most colorful parrots, we think you need to expand your horizons and consider some other birds with great pet potential before you buy.

The world of birds is large, with more than 300 species of parrots alone — although, of course, not all of them are commonly available as pets. Some of these species are perfect for the first-time owner, in different ways. Some are good because they don't need — or want — to be handled, and some for the opposite reason — because they are feathered love sponges. In this chapter, we present an admittedly subjective list of birds, some well-known, some not, that are reasonably priced, reasonably sized, and just plain reasonable to live with. Some birds, such as the blue-and-gold macaw and the cockatoos, can also be excellent first birds, but they are more expensive to buy and maintain, and often more challenging to live with.

You must always deal with a reputable breeder or bird store when shopping for any pet; otherwise, all those wonderful traits we attribute to birds may be nonexistent in the animals you encounter. We're sorry to say, but some pet retailers see birds as goods to be bred, shipped, and sold as quickly and efficiently as possible. Rapid stock turnover may be a great plan for merchandising widgets, but it's not always ideal for pets. Deal with people who sell healthy, well-socialized birds, and you can count on the best start possible.

For more information on choosing a bird and finding a reputable source from which to buy, see Chapters 2 and 3. When you think you have a good seller, Chapter 16 provides the questions you need to ask to help you confirm your instinct. And don't forget to check out the color section of this book, because there we feature some of the birds in this chapter.

Canaries

The canary — among the oldest, most popular, and most varied pet birds in the world — is well-known for his vocal talents and vibrant color. Have a look at two in Figure 18-1. Canaries hail originally from the Canary Islands, which were not named for their most famous residents but for the dogs the Romans found there. (*Canis* is Latin for "dog," and somewhere a nun smiles brightly at finally being proven correct that Gina would one day find her Latin classes useful.)

Figure 18-1: Canaries are delightful pets for beginning and experienced bird-keepers alike.

Photo by Dr. Michael J. Murray

Canaries are actually finches, but because most people think of them as separate, we've followed suit. Wild canaries are green and yellow, but when folks think of them today, they most often conjure up a brilliantly colored yellow bird, thanks, mostly, to the Sylvester-outsmarting cartoon character, Tweety Bird.

In fact, canaries come in many colors and varieties, thanks to centuries of selective breeding. Canaries can be sleek or plump in body type, smooth or puffy when it comes to feathers, with colors from yellow to bright orange to greens and browns. If you want a singer, though, make sure your new bird is a male — female canaries don't sing.

Although still one of the more popular birds in the world, the canary isn't talked about as much for its pet potential as it used to be. And that's a shame, because the bird is perfect for beginners who aren't sure they want as much interaction as some other species require. The canary is happy to hang out in a cage and entertain you with beauty and song. In fact, they'd rather *not* be handled.

Robert Stroud, the famous Bird Man of Alcatraz, was fascinated by canaries and horrified by the poor care they received from most pet-owners. Although his ideas on avian husbandry are woefully out of date, a statement he made in 1940 was ahead of its time: " . . . thousands of owners of pet canaries [are] too lazy to take the trouble to learn how to care for their birds, [and they] imagine that when they keep a cupful of cheap, stale packaged seed, and throw them a leaf of stale, wilted, half-rotten lettuce once in a while [that] they perform their whole duty."

Because they don't require or desire handling, the canary can be a good children's pet, providing song and beauty and allowing youngsters to observe the wonder of birds close-up.

Finches

Another mostly hands-off bird is the finch, a little charmer who embodies the word "vivacious." Finches are flashy, fast-moving, and fun to watch, with a lively, constant twittering that's considerably below the decibel level parrots are capable of attaining. Several species of finches are available as pets, but for beginners the most easily available are the zebra finch and the society finch.

The zebra (so named for striping, especially on the tail and face) is an Australian native who's available in many distinctive varieties that differ in color — more variety than you can find in any other finch species. And anyone can tell the girls from the boys when it comes to the common gray zebras — boys have bright orange cheeks and dark orange flanks, and girls don't.

Society finches are a human creation — one of the few species of pet birds that never existed in the wild. Also called the Bengalese finch, the society comes in many colors and patterns and is an easy keeper who's comfortable in human surroundings, as you may expect from a thoroughly domesticated species.

Finches do better in a social situation, so plan on buying two or more and giving them a cage with plenty of space to exercise their wings — these birds get around by flying, and unlike parrots, they don't climb for exercise.

Because they're perfectly content to live without handling, finches make an excellent aviary bird. They're always a delight to observe. For this reason, the finch is also good for a caged bird in an older child's room.

Because finches are small, some people believe they don't need much in terms of cage size — and that's wrong. Finches need room to fly, and when housed with others of their kind, they need enough space to have a bit of territory to call their own. When they're too crowded, territorial battles between cage-mates are common. For more on cages, see Chapter 4.

Budgies (Parakeets)

At last, a bird in the hand! Because of their small price tag and easy availability, budgerigars (commonly known in the United States as parakeets) are often treated as a throw-away bird — easily purchased, easily disposed of, easily replaced. This deplorable attitude keeps people from valuing these birds for their affectionate personality — some budgies even become very good talkers, albeit with tiny little voices.

Budgies are commonly found in two varieties, differentiated by body type: The narrow American and the huskier English. Colors now reach far beyond the green or blue you may remember from the pet department at the dime store. Because these birds are sold so inexpensively (especially the American), hand-raising doesn't pay, so few breeders invest the time or trouble. Budgies can be tamed by gentle, patient handling and can bond closely to their human companions. Others are more suited to life as a cage-bird, and always prefer to be unhandled.

Hand-raised budgies are worth seeking out for their excellent pet potential. For more on how to find a healthy, happy baby bird, see Chapter 3.

For a child old enough to understand the need for gentle, respectful handling, budgies are ideal pets. But don't let their reputation as a great child's pet keep you from considering one as a companion for an adult. These active, loving, entertaining birds are easy to keep and relatively quiet.

Dealing with a good source is important when buying any pet bird, but finding a reliable seller is even more so with budgies. Mass-produced birds are harder to tame because they haven't been socialized, and they're more prone to life-threatening diseases.

The name *budgerigar* comes from Australia's native humans, the Aborigines. Four syllables is a mouthful, which is probably why some people started calling these brightly colored birds "parakeets." Although the name's not wrong, it's imprecise. While all budgies are parakeets, all parakeets aren't budgies. Many species of parakeets exist, and many of them are available as pets, including the Quaker (see the upcoming description), grey-cheeked, ring-necked, and canary-winged, to name a few.

Cockatiels

Cockatiels are an exceptionally popular bird, and justifiably so. These small parrots are flat-out loving, and they live to snuggle and be petted. If you only recognize the gray bird with orange patches, you may be surprised at how many colors are available these days, thanks to the work of some highly energetic breeders.

Some cockatiels learn to talk, but many are better at whistling. This bird is another who's a good choice for children (see Figure 18-2), as long as the youngsters understand the need for careful handling.

Figure 18-2: The albino cockatiel on the left is a particularly good child's pet.

Photo by Dr. Brian L. Speer

A cockatiel can become whatever you make it. Show your pet love and interact with it often, and you can expect to come up with a real winner here.

Quaker Parakeets

The Quaker didn't acquire its name from any religious leanings. The bird is thought to have earned the descriptive title through one of its native sounds or the shivering of its youngsters when they beg for food.

Green with a silvery front, Quakers are active and upbeat, and they like to vocalize. Some learn to talk, while others love to whistle. All can be loving if socialized when young and given consistent, respectful handling.

We have to admit to little hands-on experience with Quaker, or Monk, parakeets, and the lack of acquaintance isn't because we don't like them. They're illegal in California, where we live; the powers that be consider them a threat to native species and agribusiness because of their ability to adapt to a wild lifestyle. Although we can't really say we agree with the policy, we can say the Quaker is well worth considering if you live in places where they are legal. Other states in the U.S. that ban them include Hawaii, Connecticut, Pennsylvania, Kentucky, Tennessee, Wyoming, Rhode Island, and Georgia. A few other states regulate them in one way or another. (For information on the latest restrictions where you live, check with your nearest Department of Agriculture or fish and game authorities.)

Quaker-lover Kathleen Carr of Florida tracks sighting of feral colonies of Quakers on her Web site, www.monkparakeet.com. She reports feral colonies in more than a dozen states and points out that in Florida the birds thrive in the wild.

Poicephalus Parrots and Parrotlets

The small African parrots known collectively as *poicephalus* are an easy-going bunch. Of the species available as pets, Senegals are probably the most common, a handsome little bird with a gray head, green back and wings, and yellow-orange underside. Other species in the group include the Meyer's, Jardine, cape, red belly, and brown head — all known for their small size (a little bigger than a cockatiel) and affectionate personalities. Not the best talkers here, but some manage verbalization quite well. Their noise level isn't too bad.

Poicephalus can be devoted to their owners, and after they decide you're trustworthy, they are especially fond of having their heads and necks scratched — in fact, they beg for it, tipping their heads and leaning over to expose their necks for a good scratch.

An even smaller parrot to consider: the parrotlet. Don't let their small size fool you; these 5-inch dynamos are all parrot — active, inquisitive, loving, and demanding. Two varieties are commonly available as pets, the Pacific and the green-rumped, but more species are becoming increasingly available. Apple-green or blue in hue, parrotlets are more quiet than some of their larger relatives, and some develop the gift of gab.

Some species are better talkers than others, picking up words, phrases, and household sounds with little or no effort on the part of their owners. Other species are able to mimic a few sounds if their owners work with them patiently. For information on which species are the best talkers, see Chapter 2. For tips on speech training, see Chapter 5.

Pionus Parrots

Pionus are sometimes overlooked because they're just not as flashy as other parrots — their beauty is more subtle. But what they lack in bright colors they make up for with winning personalities.

Several species of pionus are available as pets, including maximillian, blue-heads, dusky, bronze-winged, and white-capped. Pionus are slightly larger than the poicephalus but are still small enough to be easy to keep and handle. Their personalities are considered among the more sedate, and they're not excessively loud. (Nor are they considered fantastic talkers, although they're certainly capable of learning a few phrases.) The word most connected with the pionus is "sweet," and it fits — socialized, well-handled birds are unparalleled as loving companions.

And when you're in love with one, you can appreciate the subtle beauty of these birds — the plumage of a healthy pionus has an almost iridescent quality about it.

Pyrrhura Conures

The conures are one of the larger groups of parrots, with more than 100 species and subspecies. As pets, conures are well-represented, too, with about a dozen available, including such well-known birds as the jenday, dusky, and the sun. These three belong to the aratinga genus, but our best-for-beginners picks belong to another category, the pyrrhura genus. (Does it seem like we always choose the ones that are hard to spell and pronounce?)

If you find it easier, call them either green-cheeked or maroon-bellied, because these are the most commonly available species in the category. Whatever you call them, though, you can look forward to a lovely pet. Both species are much, much quieter than the sun conure (but then, so are some rock bands). Enthusiasts say the pyrrhuras are affectionate and playful. Colors aren't as dramatic as the red-and-gold sun, but the greens of the lesser-known conures still make for an attractive companion. Some may even grace you with a few acquired phrases.

Although aratinga conures such as the sun may not be the best choice for beginners, their colorful appearance and clownish personalities have won them plenty of fans — and a starring role in the movie *Paulie.* (Paulie was a blue-crowned conure.) For more on the aratinga conures, see Chapter 3. We also compare and contrast these two categories in our color section of this book.

Amazon Parrots

The Amazons are a little bigger and more expensive than many of the birds we have described so far, but they're just too darn appealing to leave off the list. Amazons are among the best talkers around, especially the yellow-naped species. Amazons are also beautiful, brilliant, and they love to clown around. When Brian hears a bird entertaining himself and everyone around in the waiting room of his hospital, he knows without looking that it's an Amazon. They love to be in the limelight, and they seem to feed off the attention they attract.

Amazons are mid-sized parrots, very active birds who truly enjoy spending time with the people they love. An Amazon appreciates his toys, too, and is one of the easier birds to train to perform certain behaviors.

Some Amazon species are easier to live with than others. For beginners, we like to recommend the lilac-crowns (shown on the right in Figure 18-2), blue-fronted, red-lored, and white-fronted. These smaller species are less likely to push, are generally quieter, and all around are easy to handle.

The problem for beginners: Amazons can be *too* smart. As with any parrot, you need to be sure you're giving your bird lots of structured socialization, a fair share of toys, and plenty of exercise. See Chapters 5 and 12 for help.

Peach-Faced Lovebirds

Peach-faced lovebirds are beautiful, active, and playful. Talking is possible, but it's not what these small parrots are known for. A well-socialized peach-faced can be your best pal for years, if you don't leave him to waste away alone in a cage. When hand-raised and socialized with humans, these little guys love to be handled, carried around in your shirt pocket or under the hair on your collar. They're very affectionate, not overly loud, and capable of picking up a few phrases.

Lovebird species commonly available as pets include the Fischer's, black-masked, and peach-faced, with the last being the more popular. Peach-faced lovebirds also come in many interesting color mutations, including lutinos, olives, and pieds.

Chapter 19

Ten Common Dangers to Your Bird's Life

In This Chapter

- Predators!
- Lure of the wild blue yonder
- Revenge of the killer houseplant
- Medications that can kill

Birds are hardy creatures in many ways, survivors both in the evolution game — where they boast residency in nearly every ecological niche — and in the challenging role of sharing their lives with us.

Although life in the rain forest or jungle harbors plenty of risks, so, too, does the modern human dwelling. Some of these hazards are obvious, and others manage to sneak up on bird-owners who don't realize what's happening until it's too late. We don't want you to be in that sad latter group.

Your bird's best protection is a safe cage and an observant owner. But you need to know what to look out for to keep your pet safe. To help build your awareness, we share a list of the more common dangers here. Read them all, and give your home the once-over, removing or reducing any risks you find.

Birds can get into all kinds of trouble, and Brian has seen plenty in his practice. One of his favorite stories recalls the time he got a frantic late-night call from some folks who'd been partying a little too heartily. Seems their canary had inhaled a fair amount of marijuana smoke and was acting . . . funny. Singing his heart out, to be precise. After determining that the bird would probably be okay and the owners weren't in any condition to drive, Brian suggested the owners take a quick stroll to the store for something to help manage the effects. "That bird is going to have the munchies," Brian told them. A funny story, to be sure, but of course, you shouldn't expose your bird to any drug your veterinarian hasn't suggested — legal or illegal.

Yum-Yum Little Birdy

First, a joke. A fellow is having trouble with his parrot's swearing, and he tells the bird that if she doesn't knock it off, he's going to put her in the freezer as a punishment. The bird disregards the warning, so the man puts her in the freezer for a few minutes to think things over. He lets the parrot out and asks her if she has learned her lesson.

"Yes, yes!" squawks the parrot. "I'll never swear again. But you gotta tell me one thing."

"What?" says the man.

The parrot says: "What did the chicken do?"

Now, before we go any further, we suppose we have to point out we do *not* endorse putting parrots in the freezer or punishing them in any way for "bad" behavior. (For the real story on correcting behavior problems, see Chapter 12.) It's a *joke,* okay? And the reason we include this story is not only because it's funny but also because we want to make you aware that the distinctions between what we choose to keep as pets and what we choose to eat as dinner are highly arbitrary. Most of us think chickens are good to eat and parrots are great companions. Other predators think they're all fair game. And you really can't blame them. The best you can do to protect your bird is to remember who's sharing your happy home — and who may drop by uninvited.

Some predators are more obvious than others and are especially dangerous to birds kept in outdoor aviaries. Rats, mice, raccoons, and opossums all would relish a taste of your bird, and although they may not pose much of a risk to the bigger pet birds, they can be a formidable danger to smaller ones.

More common, however, are the predators we live with and also call pets: dogs and cats. Aside from the obvious danger from teeth and claws, dogs and cats can also transmit infectious elements in their saliva that can do in your bird.

Don't take a chance. Although some pets seem to get along wonderfully with birds, don't ever discount the power of instinct — never leave birds unattended with dogs and cats.

If your bird is attacked by *any* animal, talk to your veterinarian immediately, even if everything seems fine. Internal damage may otherwise remain undetected past the point of remedy, and the prompt dosing of antibiotics may be necessary to ward off a potentially life-threatening infection. Your bird need not even be bitten — having cat saliva on his feathers is enough to introduce an infection that could kill him.

For more on keeping birds safe from cats and dogs, see Chapter 5. Emergency-care guidelines — what can wait, what can't — are in Chapter 10.

Flying Is for the Birds

Flying is one of those things that adds to the incredible appeal of birds, their mystique, and their wonder. Birds are not the only creatures who fly, of course. A zillion insects manage it, as do mammals such as bats. But birds do it with style, with grace, and, often, a flash of brilliant color. We envy them, because only recently in human experience have we taken to the sky — and let's be honest, blasting place to place inside a jet-propelled metal tube hardly has the same panache.

But when it comes to most pet birds, flying out into the wide, wild world is too dangerous to risk. Unless you intend to never remove your bird from an aviary big enough for him to fly in, you need to keep his wings trimmed. Our homes are not suitable for flighted birds, period. Brian has treated — and lost — birds who slammed into windows or who landed in sizzling frying pans and boiling pots of water. Some birds even fly into open toilets and drown. (Our advice on that danger is easy: Keep the lid down!) Brian has also known birds who've landed in ovens, in fireplaces, and into the open, drooling mouths of dogs.

The bottom line on flying: The risk is way too great for a household pet. With some effort from you, your bird can indeed have a happy, healthy life without ever rising to the heavens.

Not all pet birds need to have their flight feathers kept short — just those who come out of their cages to interact with their owners. Finches and canaries are happier if not handled or allowed out, and their feathers should be left alone so they can fly in their cages for exercise. (Which means they need a cage large enough to do so! See Chapter 4 for cage-selection guidelines.)

Trimming flight feathers isn't difficult; it just takes practice. We show you how to groom your bird properly — clip wings and trim toenails — in Chapter 7. Make sure you watch a wing trim being done first before attempting it on your own; poorly done wing trims can cause as many problems as they prevent.

The best way to enjoy flighted birds is in the wild, and a great way to do that is to take up bird-watching. Find out all about this fast-growing hobby in *Bird Watching For Dummies* by Bill Thompson III (IDG Books Worldwide, Inc.).

Bird on the Loose

Although this danger relates to not keeping flight feathers trimmed, we put it in its own category for emphasis.

Your bird may love you, but that doesn't mean she won't seize the opportunity provided by an open door or window. And even if she's not inclined to consciously attempt an escape, taking flight is an instinctive move for a bird who's spooked or frightened.

The best way to prevent losing your bird in this way is to be zealous about keeping wings trimmed, put screens on your doors and windows, and be careful about opening any route to the great outdoors. If you like to take your bird with you when you go out, use a travel carrier or cage, or consider one of the harness-and-leash get-ups available in bird-supply catalogs or through the ads in the back of bird magazines.

A lost bird is a double tragedy because colonies of escaped pets can be a threat to native birds by displacing them from their habitats. Former pet birds do very well in warm places such as Florida, as you may imagine, but they can do surprisingly well in colder climates, too. One pet species, the Monk or Quaker parakeet, is such a successful colonizer that it has been banned in several states as a danger to native birds and agriculture. Colonies of these birds have been spotted as far north as Chicago.

Look for tips on how to encourage an escaped bird to come home in Chapter 7. You can find a Web site dedicated to reuniting lost birds with their owners in Chapter 17.

Inhalant Dangers

Remember the historical accounts about canaries being put to service in mine shafts? Coal-miners once used birds as an early-warning system for dangerous gases. Because birds are highly sensitive to dangerous fumes, a sick (or dead) canary meant fumes were building up to toxic levels — a clear signal that the miners had to get out to save their own lives.

Although this practice has been replaced by more accurate — and certainly more humane — monitoring equipment, the fact remains that pet birds have sensitive respiratory systems. In our tightly sealed homes, they can be killed quickly by aerosol products and cookware coatings. Remove your bird before using insecticides and cleaning products, even those that seem as benign as air freshener. Be especially careful about insecticides: Read the label and look for ingredients such as pyrethrin, fenoxycarb, and precor, all of which are safe around birds after the application has dried.

Perhaps the most insidious danger is from nonstick cookware, such as Teflon or Silverstone. When overheated, these products emit fumes that can kill your bird quickly — without harming humans or other mammals. You can't smell or see the gases, so the only way to protect your bird from injury is to keep your feathered friend out of the kitchen when you're using such cookware or when setting your oven's self-cleaning feature.

Although many folks recommend simply getting rid of nonstick cookware, such a compromise is impractical for many people. The risk of using a suspect product is greatly reduced if you monitor it closely — not allowing pots and pans to overheat — and ensure that your bird is always safe in another room when you're cooking or baking. Also keep an eye out for nonstick surfaces in other household objects, such as irons and toaster ovens, and for aerosol products that promise protective coatings for your cookware.

Seemingly every new product sparks a rumor of toxicity. Although we agree it's good to be cautious, check with an avian veterinarian to set the record straight on any rumor you hear.

A final inhalant caution: Don't smoke around your bird, and don't leave cigarette butts where your pet can get hold of them. Cigarette smoke is just as bad for your pets as it is for you.

Plants Not for Nibbling

Birds are great chewers, and sometimes that tendency gets them into trouble. They can ingest metals that are toxic — more on that later in this chapter — as well as nibble plants that can do them some damage.

Although we encourage giving your pet bird some plant material to destroy (it's good exercise and fights boredom), a few common plants are worthy of off-limits warnings. Primary among them: the philodendron. Check the nearby sidebar "Toxic plants" and move any suspect ones out of reach. Better yet, don't allow your bird access to any plants at all, except for the branches you put in the cage for perches and chewing material.

You can find more information about using tree branches as perches — including which ones are safe — in Chapter 4.

Toxic plants

Birds can be deadly to plants, but more than a few plants are quite capable of seeking revenge. Here's what the ASPCA/National Animal Poison Control Center, a resource for veterinarians, says are some bad seeds. Most "just" make your pet sick, but a few of them can kill. If your pet tangles with any of these, call your veterinarian. And don't forget: Even "good" plants can cause problems if they've been sprayed with insecticide.

Aloe vera (medicine plant)

Amaryllis

Andromeda japonica

Apple (seeds)

Apricot (pit)

Asparagus fern

Autumn crocus

Avocado (fruit and pit)

Azalea

Baby doll ti

Baby's breath

Bird of paradise

Bittersweet

Branching ivy

Buckeye

Buddhist pine

Caladium

Calla lily

Castor bean

Ceriman

Cherry (wilting leaves and seeds)

China doll

Chinese evergreen

Christmas cactus

Christmas rose

Chrysanthemum

Cineraria

Clematis

Cordatum

Corn plant (all dracaena species)

Crown vetch

Cyclamen

Daffodil

Daisy

Daylily

Devil's ivy

Dieffenbachia (all varieties; commonly called dumb cane)

Dracaena palm

Dragon tree

Elephant ears

Emerald feather

English ivy

Fiddle-leaf fig

Flamingo plant

Foxglove

Fruit salad plant

Geranium

German ivy

Glacier ivy

Gladiola

Glory lily

Hawaiian ti

Heavenly bamboo

Hibiscus

Holly

Hurricane plant

Hyacinth

Hydrangea

Impatiens

Indian laurel

Indian rubber plant

Iris

Japanese yew

Jerusalem cherry

Kalanchoe

Lilium species (includes Easter lily, Japanese show lily, Oriental lily, Tiger lily, and so on)

Lily of the valley

Marble queen

Marijuana

Mexican breadfruit

Miniature croton (and other varieties)

Mistletoe

Morning glory

Mother-in-law's tongue

Narcissus
Needlepoint ivy
Nephthytis
Nightshade (solanum species)
Norfolk pine
Oleander
Onion
Peace lily
Peach (wilting leaves and pit)
Pencil cactus
Philodendron (all varieties)
Plum (wilting leaves and pit)
Plumosa fern
Poinsettia
Pothos (all varieties)
Precatory bean
Primula
Privet
Rhododendron
Ribbon plant
Sago palm (cycas)
Schefflera
Sweet pea
String of pearls/beads
Sweet pea
Taro vine
Tomato plant (green fruit, stem, and leaves)
Tulip
Weeping fig
Yesterday, today, tomorrow plant
Yucca

Foods That Shouldn't Be Shared

Cleaning products aren't the only dangerous items in your home. Although we recommend sharing healthy people-food with your bird, don't hand over even a morsel of avocado, chocolate, or anything with caffeine.

Birds are also sensitive to foods that have spoiled or grown mold. Give your pet fresh food only and remove it from the cage before it has a chance to spoil. Another food caution: Because you don't know what was sprayed on any fruit or vegetable you buy, be sure to wash any produce before offering it to your pet.

We cover healthy food choices for your bird in Chapter 6, along with everything you need to know about proper nutrition.

Metals That Are, Like, Heavy, Man

Although zinc poisoning does turn up from time to time, by far the top danger of heavy metal poisoning is from lead. Lead can be found in weights for fishing and for curtains, bell clappers, solder, some types of putty or plaster, some linoleum, stained glass, costume jewelry, leaded foils from champagne and wine bottles, batteries, some ceramic glazes, the backs of some mirrors, paints, and galvanized wire.

No pet owner is going to feed a fishing weight to a pet, but as always, the inquisitive nature of birds put them at risk. The energetic chewing of a parrot can even reveal lead paint many layers down on the walls of an old house.

You have to keep an eye out for dangerous metals in your bird's environment, but some things you may worry about aren't a problem. Pencil leads, for example, aren't made of lead anymore, and contrary to some long-held beliefs, you have nothing to fear from regular black newspaper ink or "child-safe" paints.

Maybe Some Medicine Will Help?

If you ever consider, even for a second, giving your bird some medication just because you think it may help, we implore you: Stop!

Over the counter human medications, even those as seemingly benign as aspirin, acetaminophen (Tylenol), or vitamins, can poison your bird. Commonly available bird products — such as antibiotics, mite sprays, or feather-picking "remedies" — should likewise be avoided. Always check with your veterinarian before giving *any* health product to your bird. And don't guess on dosages for medications prescribed for your bird, or overdose with the idea that if a little is good, more must be better. Birds are small compared to people, and so the margin of error when it comes to medications is slimmer. Follow your veterinarian's directions precisely on any medication sent home with your bird.

Birds are clever and exceptionally interested in exploring and tasting. Keep not only medications — those pharmacy containers are appealing to play with — but also any questionable household product out of your bird's reach. Some to watch out for: mothballs, rodent poisons, cleaning fluids, deodorants, matches, carpet fresheners, and flea products meant for dogs and cats. Don't leave your bird free to explore in areas where such products may be stored!

Watch Where You Step

With the exception of finches and canaries, birds need and appreciate "out time" — periods of freedom beyond the cage for playing and socializing. Because most birds' wings are properly clipped before the pets are allowed out, their means of locomotion includes the same bipedal type we use — they walk around on their own two feet.

Sometimes that mobility means a lot of exploring on the ground, and that can present some hazards. Being on the ground puts your birds within the reach of dogs and cats, but it also makes them easy to step on. And a human foot — backed up by human weight — can cause some real damage to the delicate avian bones it lands on.

We advise not allowing your bird to wander around on the ground at all, but if you do so, make a habit of looking down before you plant your big feet. Better still: Let your bird hitch a ride on you (see Figure 19-1).

Figure 19-1: Carry your bird to protect him from being stepped on or attacked by other pets.

A Shocking Surprise

You can figure that your puppy, if properly trained, is bound to outgrow his need to chew everything in sight, from furniture legs to your favorite shoes, but you can't make that assumption with a bird. They're lifelong chewers, and one of the things they sometimes encounter is an electrical cord.

Our best advice is to do just as you would with a puppy — keep all cords out of chewing range.

Chapter 20

Ten Disaster-Planning Tips for Bird-Lovers

In This Chapter

- Planning for the worst
- Keeping your bird safe
- Helping others

Tornado, earthquake, hurricane, fire, flood — if you were faced with any of these and had to leave your home, would you know how to help your bird? Disaster-planning experts advise you to take your pets with you when told to evacuate, but that plan's not as easy as it sounds.

Sandwiched between the idea of taking your pets with you and the reality of accomplishing a safe evacuation is a lot of thought and planning. To help you prepare for all sorts of unplanned events, we walk you through the process of being ready for the worst — and hoping for the best.

The good news: When it comes to disasters and pets, consideration for preparedness has changed a great deal in recent years — all for the better. Once left to their own survival instincts in times of calamity, animals today are the focus of much planning, with organizations in place to complement those caring for human victims.

In fact, a model program started by the California Veterinary Medical Association positions a veterinarian in each county to help coordinate animal-relief efforts. Other states are starting to see the light, too, with veterinarians, shelter groups, and specially trained disaster teams from the Sacramento, California-based United Animal Nations Emergency Animal Response Service prepared to do for animals what the Red Cross does for people — on an international basis!

These positive developments are the result of a growing realization that animals need help, too, and that some people choose to put their lives in danger rather than abandon their pets.

Despite all this progress, your bird's chances of surviving any kind of crisis still depend mostly on you. Don't put off preparing for the unexpected. No one likes to think about the possibility of catastrophe, but your pets are counting on you.

Consider the Possibilities

Disaster preparedness starts with a simple question: What if? Ask yourself that question, and then consider not only the kind of crisis you're most likely to face, but also special challenges such as your being away from home when disaster strikes.

People need to rely on each other during emergencies, and this fact is just as true when it comes to your pets. Get to know your neighbors and talk about how you might help each other out. Find out from local shelters and veterinary organizations what their emergency response plans are.

Veterinary connections can be tricky for bird-owners. Because you need someone experienced in avian care, your veterinarian may not be located anywhere near you. Brian's clients, in fact, come to him from all over Northern California, and some drive for hours to bring their birds to him.

In a disaster, you may not have the luxury of relying on a veterinarian who's far away. Make sure you know nearby veterinary hospitals, especially those offering around-the-clock and emergency care. Keep a current list of which local veterinarians are willing to provide care or board for your birds in an emergency situation. Know who is agreeable to consulting by telephone, if needed, with your regular veterinarian to coordinate and possibly enhance the level of care your birds receive. Make note, too, of shops that have a special interest or focus in birds, particularly those that board birds.

A crisis isn't always a community-wide event. When considering your options, think about what would happen if you were suddenly injured or hospitalized, from a car accident, say, or a heart attack.

Make a Contact List

You're not likely to lug your phone book around with you in an emergency. And even if you have one of those nifty personal organizers, you're bound to appreciate the low-tech certainty of a simple sheet of paper that lists all the information you need — especially if you run out of battery power or drop your electronic organizer in a puddle.

So make a contact list. All you really need is a sheet of paper or two, slipped into a plastic page protector you can pick up at any office-supply store very cheaply. Handwrite the info or print it out from your home computer. (If you keep the master list on your computer, you can update it easily and print out a current version every so often. Beats cross-outs and erasures!)

To take the business of an emergency list to its logical conclusion: Your wisest move is to have a list of emergency contacts to cover everything for you and your family. But for the purpose of this book, we're just concerned with your birds.

List the name, location, and phone number of your regular veterinarian, and then the same information for nearby backup hospitals and emergency clinics. Same goes for local humane and animal-control shelters, animal groups, and bird shops. Include friends and neighbors, too, along with your local office of emergency services.

The final step: Put the list where you know you can find it. Better yet, make a few copies — one for the house, one for the car, one for work, and so on.

Make Sure Your Bird Carries an ID

Most animals will survive a disaster. But too many will never see their families again without a way to determine which pet belongs to which family. Although you may be lucky enough to avoid being separated from your pet, you need to be ready for just that possibility. One way to contribute to a continued connection is to make sure your bird has identification. (You also need to make a "Lost Bird" kit, which we cover later in this chapter.)

Your bird may have a leg band already, and if so, be sure you note the identifying letters and numbers. Whether your bird is banded or not, we highly recommend you have your bird microchipped. This simple procedure provides permanent identification for your important pet.

For more information on leg bands and microchips, see Chapter 4.

Make and Trade Bird-Care Files

Prepare a couple of files with up-to-date medical records, your pets' microchip or leg band numbers, your veterinarian's phone number and address, feeding and medication instructions, recent pictures of your pets, and written descriptions noting any unique markings or other physical details.

Talk to other animal-loving friends, ask them to do the same for their pets, and then trade files. The more people who know about your bird and how to care for him, the better.

Collect Food and Supplies

Number 1 on the list of disaster gear is a travel cage or carrier for any bird whose regular lodgings aren't portable — anything bigger than a finch or budgie, in most cases. You probably already make use of a travel cage or carrier for trips to your veterinarian or for any other travel outside the home — we talk about choosing one in Chapter 4. The key, in a time of crisis, is to make sure you know where the cage is and how you can get to it easily — an emergency isn't the time to look for a ladder or dig through junk in the basement or attic.

Also keep a few days supply of food at hand, along with bottled water. Our recommendation for a pelleted diet — see Chapter 6 for more on nutrition — lends itself well to feeding your bird on the run. Pack in some of your bird's favorite dried fruits, nuts, and seeds, too. Don't forget to rotate these disaster supplies on a regular basis, so they're always fresh.

Include any medication your bird is on. If your bird takes any maintenance medication, get an extra supply and put it in rotation — use it after your current medication runs out, and put the refill in the disaster kit. That way, your "disaster" medicine is always current. And finally: Toys! Your bird is going to need to take out his stress on something, and better it be toys than you or his own body.

Keep a First Aid Kit Fully Stocked

Every pet-lover needs basic first aid supplies packed into a neat, portable kit. Make sure the kit includes scissors (for wing trimming), cloth towels (for restraint), and paper towels (for clean-up). And don't forget styptic powder for cauterizing bleeding nails or beak tips, if needed. If your kit doesn't have a first aid booklet, tuck one inside. Consider keeping two kits — one for home, one for the car.

One of the problems with first aid kits is that you're always picking at them in everyday life — a little ointment here, some gauze there, and where did the scissors go? Be sure to replace promptly any supplies you use. Otherwise, when you really need your kit, the cupboard may be bare.

For a complete list of basic first aid supplies for birds — along with help in recognizing an emergency — see Chapter 10.

ResQPet makes nifty emergency kits for all kinds of pets, birds included. Pet-Pak, Inc., manufactures animal first aid kits in five sizes, all neatly packed in plastic containers (the four larger models have handles). Both companies offer top-quality equipment, complete with instructions on how to use it. The ResQPet kit also includes a supply of water and a couple of other items such as a space blanket. For more information, see the Additional Resources appendix at the back of this book.

Plan, Plan, Plan, and Practice

With your research done and your supplies assembled, the next logical step is a real plan for what to do "in case." Design strategies for what to do if you're home, or if you're at work, and make sure everyone in the family knows about them — children included!

Rehearsals are a great idea. If you've been through something once or twice , the act has a better chance of becoming second nature — get the travel cage, get the bird, get the supplies, everything in the car, and let's go! A dry run can also point out any problems with your plan, which you can then remedy.

Keep Your Bird Secure — and Separate

Disasters can bring out the best in people and pets — but they can also bring out the worst. Your bird is bound to be scared, stressed, and disoriented, and he is likely to feed off your uncertainty as well. Keep your bird secure in his travel cage, and keep handling to a minimum. Be alert to your bird's body language — even sweet-natured pets may strike out in fear. Try to maintain as regular a schedule as possible, feeding at normal times if you can.

To help your bird maintain his good health, keep him away from other pets if at all possible, especially other birds who may be carrying heaven-knows-what diseases.

Keep a "Lost Bird" Kit Ready

The onset or aftermath of a disaster isn't the best time to get flyers printed up, so make up some generic ones and keep them with your emergency supplies. In the biggest type size you can manage, center the words "LOST BIRD," along with a clear picture of your pet. Then below, include a description of your pet, including any identifying marks, and a space to add the phone number where you can be reached, as well as any backup contacts, friends, relatives, neighbors, or your veterinarian. Print up a hundred copies and keep them in a safe, dry, and accessible place.

A staple gun enables you to post your notices; keep one loaded and tucked in with a supply of thumbtacks and electrical tape.

If your bird becomes lost, post flyers in your neighborhood and beyond, as well as distributing them at veterinary hospitals and shelters. Relying on the kindness of strangers is nice, but offering a reward may inspire some folks to be just a little bit kinder.

Be Prepared to Help Others

You may be lucky to survive a disaster nearly untouched, but others in your community may not be so fortunate. Contact your local humane society and veterinary organization now to train as a volunteer so you can help out in a pinch. Disaster-relief workers do everything from distributing food to stranded animals to helping reunite pets with their families — and helping find new homes for those who need them.

Volunteering is not only a good thing to do — it's the *right thing* for anyone who cares about animals and people.

Chapter 21

Ten Classic Bird Jokes (Just the Clean Ones)

In This Chapter

- A man walks into a pet store
- Foul-mouthed fowl
- Riddle me this

Take my bird, please! Parrot jokes have been around forever. People just can't resist the appeal of placing a creature who can talk into purely human situations. We waded through a couple dozen bird jokes, including a handful you wouldn't want to repeat in polite company. (Even though some of the off-color ones are pretty cute!)

We picked the best of the clean ones. A pretty silly bunch, to be honest, but your bird won't mind a few laughs at his expense. After all, you should hear what he says about you!

Okay, we know someone out there will complain that parrots don't behave this way, or that pet birds need to have their wings kept clipped so they can't get themselves in trouble flying. To those people we say, very maturely: "Well, duh!"

These are jokes, folks. Lighten up a little.

What Would We Do without the Guy Who Walks into the Pet Store?

So a guy walks into a pet store. He sees a parrot and asks the bird, "Hey, can you talk, stupid?" The bird says, "Yes. Can you fly, moron?"

And then two guys walk into a pet store.

Two (insert your favorite buffoons here) walk into a pet store and buy four budgies. The sales clerk puts them in a box, and the two guys leave. They drive onto the middle of a bridge, and then one guy holds a bird in each hand and jumps. The other man watches the unfortunate result and says to himself, "Gee, budgie jumping doesn't seem like much fun after all!"

Will We Ever Get Out of the Pet Store?

A pet store owner is showing off a parrot to a prospective buyer. "When you pull his left leg," he says, "he sings 'Dixie.' When you pull his right leg, he sings 'The Battle Hymn of the Republic.'"

"What happens if you pull both legs?" asks the customer.

"I fall over, you dope!" says the parrot.

Oh, This One Is Punny

Q. What shape is an empty bird cage?

A. A polygon. (Polly-gone, get it?)

If You Thought That One Was Silly . . .

Q. What do you get when you cross a parrot with a lion?

A. I don't know, but when he talks, you better listen!

And Back to the Pet Store . . .

A fellow walks into a pet store looking for a singing canary. "Got just the thing," says the owner, pointing to a bird cage hanging from the ceiling.

"Not so fast!" says the customer. "I want to hear this bird sing before I buy him."

The store owner puts the bird on the counter, and the bird sings his heart out, a river of lovely song. And then the customer notices the bird is missing a foot. "That's a one-legged bird!" he yells. "What, are you trying to rob me?"

"Absolutely not!" sputters the store owner. "You said you wanted a singer, not a dancer!"

Take a Cruise with Us

A captain's parrot spent a lot of time watching the cruise ship's magician and in time, he figured out all the tricks. Bored, he started shouting out how the tricks were done:

"He's hiding a rabbit under the table!" "All the cards are the same!"

The magician was furious, but he couldn't say much because it was, after all, the captain's parrot.

Then the ship sank, and the parrot and magician found themselves together in a lifeboat. The parrot was silent for days, but at last, he spoke up.

"All right," he said. "I give up. What did you do with the ship?"

It's Always Good to Pray

A woman had a female parrot who wouldn't stop swearing. She tried everything and was constantly embarrassed by her pet's gutter mouth. Her fiancé's parents were coming over to dinner to meet her, and she was desperate to clean up her bird's language.

A friend of hers had two male parrots with perfect company manners. One said the rosary all day, and the other repeated Hail Marys. She thought the pair would be a good influence on her bird, so she made arrangements to bring them over for a visit.

The boy parrots settled in and looked over at the girl parrot. "Okay," says one to the other. "You can knock off the praying now. We got what we asked for."

A Little Respect, Please

A burglar was fumbling around in the house he'd broken into, trying to figure out where the valuables were. In the dark, he heard a voice say, "Jesus is watching."

Unnerved, he turned on his flashlight and pointed it in the direction of the sound. He discovered the speaker was a parrot.

"So you're Jesus," he said to the bird. "Big deal."

"No," corrected the parrot. "My name's Tony. Jesus is the Rottweiler."

Elementary, My Dear Watson

A guy took his bird to the veterinarian. "I have good news and bad news," said the vet. "The bad news is that your bird has chirpees."

"Oh, no!" said the man. "What's the good news?"

"That it's tweetable," said the veterinarian.

Enough Parrots!

You've no doubt heard a million "Why did the chicken cross the road?" jokes, but we're going to close with something a little different.

Q. Why didn't the chicken skeleton cross the road?

A. Because he didn't have the guts.

Please, please forgive us our silliness. But we made you laugh, didn't we?

Appendix

Additional Resources

Throughout this book, we mention products, supplies, groups, and services that can help make things better for you and your bird — or all birds, in the case of some groups. We put a collection of resources together here, so you can find what you need.

Supplies

If you find a great bird shop in your area — Chapter 3 tells you how to know whether you're really in the right place — you can look forward to reliable advice and proper supplies. The following are catalog/Web merchants we know and recommend:

Bird Lady Productions
(Bird health and behavior videotapes)
P.O. Box 540248
North Salt Lake, UT 84054
801-298-9093

Bird Things
(General bird supplies)
1025 Tanklage Road, Unit D
San Carlos, CA 94070
888-297-8833
www.birdthings.com

Hornbeck's
(General bird supplies)
7088 Lyndon Street
Rosemont, IL 60018
www.hornbecks.com

Petiatric Supply
(Incubators, brooders, hand-raising supplies)
3030 Mascot Street
Wichita, KS 67204
316-831-9500 or 888-224-3247
www.petiatric.com

Pet-Pak, Inc.
(First aid kits)
P.O. Box 982
Edison, NJ 08818
800-217-PETS
www.petpak.com

Pet Warehouse
(Scat Mats for dogs and cats, also bird supplies)
800-443-1160
www.petwarehouse.com

ResQPet
(Disaster relief kit)
888-738-7377
www.resqpet.com

Periodicals

We include two magazines here. *Bird Talk/Birds USA* is a good general-interest magazine for all bird-lovers, while the *Pet Bird Report* is geared toward parrots, especially parrot behavior.

Bird Talk/Birds USA
P.O. Box 6050
Mission Viejo, CA 92690
949-855-8822
www.animalnetwork.com

Pet Bird Report
2236 Mariner Square Drive, No. 35
Alameda, CA 94501
510-523-5303
www.petbirdreport.com

Veterinary and Aviculture Groups

These groups are a great resource for bird-lovers, whether you're looking for an avian veterinarian, trying to find information on breeding birds, or wanting to make a donation toward avian health research.

American Federation of Aviculture
(Also has a nonprofit health foundation)
P.O. Box 56218
Phoenix, AZ 85079-6218
602-484-0931
www.afa.birds.org/

Association of Avian Veterinarians
(Also has a nonprofit health foundation)
P.O. Box 811720
Boca Raton, FL 33481-1720
561-393-8901
www.aav.org

Note: You can also find international listings for aviculture groups online at www.upatsix.com/associations/.

Conservation Groups

Many bird species are endangered in the wild, some because of the pet trade, others because of habitat loss. We encourage your support of groups to preserve birds in the wild.

World Parrot Trust
Glanmor House
Hayle, Cornwall TR27 4HY
www.worldparrottrust.org
(Also links to several national offices)

World Parrot Trust Canada
PO Box 29
Mount Hope, Ontario LOR 1WO
905-385-9500
www.worldchat.com/parrot/cwparrot.htm

World Parrot Trust USA
P.O. Box 50733
St. Paul, MN 55150
651-994-2581
www.funnyfarmexotics.com/WPT

Rescue and Adoption Organizations

Regular animal shelters are usually not equipped to handle birds. Many groups have been organized in response to the need, offering education, rescue, and adoption services.

Bird Placement Program
P.O. Box 347392
Parma, OH 44134-7392
330-722-1627 or 216-749-3643
www.avi-sci.com/bpp/

Caged Bird Rescue
911 Thompson Road
Pegram, TN 37143
615-646-3949

Feathered Friends Adoption & Rescue Program
East Coast Headquarters
4751 Ecstasy Circle
Cocoa, FL 32926
407-633-4744
West Coast Branch
941-764-6048

For the Love of Parrots Refuge Society
3450 Interprovincial Highway
Abbotsford, British Columbia
604-854-8180 or 604-854-8381

Foster Parrots Ltd.
P. O.Box 650
Rockland, MA 02370
781-878-3733
www.fosterparrots.com

Foundation Dutch Parrot Refuge
Stichting N.O.P.
Wintelresedijk 51
5507 PP
Veldhoven, Holland
0031-40-2052772
www.iaehv.nl/users/nop/enover.htm

The Gabriel Foundation
P.O. Box 11477
Aspen, CO 81612
877-923-1009 (toll-free)
www.thegabrielfoundation.org

GreyHaven Exotic Bird Sanctuary (British Columbia)
604-584-0916
www.greyhaven.bc.ca

Macaw Landing Foundation
P.O. Box 17364
Portland, OR 97217
www.cnnw.net/~mlf/

Mickaboo Cockatiel Rescue
www.avianrescue.org/mickaboo/

NBARC, Inc.
Northcoast Bird Adoption and Rehabilitation Center
P.O. Box 367
Aurora, OH 44202
330-425-9269 or 330-562-6999
www.adoptabird.com

New England Exotic Bird Sanctuary
P.O. Box 241
Greenfield, MA 01302
www.neebs.org

New Life Parrot Rescue and Helpline Service
P.O. Box 84
St. Neots
Huntingdon, Cambridgeshire PE19 2LB
England
011-441-480-353-948

Oasis Sanctuary Foundation Ltd.
P.O. Box 3104
Scottsdale, AZ 85271
www.the-oasis.org

Parrot Rescue!
Dee Thompson
P.O. Box 645
Savage, MD 20763
301-498-7148
www.charm.net/~huribead/parrotrescue.html

PEAC
Parrot Education and Adoption Center
P.O. Box 34501
San Diego, CA 92163-4501
619-232-2409
www.peac.org

Providence House Avian Rescue and Support Services
P.O. Box 4040
West Richland, Washington 99353-4000
509-967-1103
http://revolution.3-cities.com/~coughlin/

Rescue Me
P.O. Box 33818
District of Columbia 20033-3818
202-332-7434
www.rescueme.org

The Shyne Brown Foundation
19922 Egret Lane
Loxahatchee, FL 33470

TARA
Tucson Avian Rescue and Adoption
520-531-9305 or 520-322-9685
www.found-pets.org/tara.html

The Tropics Exotic Bird Refuge
P.O. Box 686
Kannapolis, NC 28082-0686
704-932-8041 or 704-634-9066
tropics@juno.com

Index

• A •

accessories. *See* pet supplies
acrylic cages, 67
acrylic perches, 73
activity, lack of, 199
adoption organizations. *See* rescue and adoption organizations
African grey parrots, 39, 123
age, as factor in buying, 51–55
aging birds, 54–55
air-cleaners, 77–78
All About Birds, 266
all-seed diets, 100
alternative medicine, 175
altricial babies, 234
Amazon parrots, 39, 281–282
American Federation of Aviculture, 270, 305
American Holistic Veterinary Medical Association, 175
anatomy, 140
  anisodactyl foot, 149
  beak, 140–143
  bones, 150–151
  cardiopulmonary system, 152
  choanal slit, 143
  cloaca, 153
  crop, 143, 152–153
  ears, 144–145
  esophagus, 143, 152
  eyes, 144
  feathers, 145–148
  feet, 149–150
  gastrointestinal system, 152–154
  gizzard, 143
  glottis, 143
  heart, 152
  legs, 149–150
  nails, 150
  respiratory tract, 152
  skeleton, 150–151
  tarsometatarsus, 151
  taste buds, 143
  third eyelid, 144
  tibiotarsus, 151
  tongue, 143
  vent, 153
  wings, 149
  zygodactyl toes, 149
anhinga, 121
animal attacks, 286–287
anisodactyl foot, 149
antibiotics, 188
antique bird cages, 69
apteria, 146
aratinga conures, 37
Archeopteryx, 17, 139, 150–151
arthritis, 200
artificial incubation, 233–234
Asiatic parakeets
  Alexandrian parakeets, 30–31
  cost, 31
  derbian parakeets, 30–31
  life span, 31
  mustached parakeets, 30–31
  plum-headed parakeets, 30–31
  ring-necked parakeets, 30–31
aspergillosis, 188–189
Association of Avian Veterinarians, 170–171, 270–271, 305
attention-seeking as reason for feather-picking, 218

avian, 12
avian behaviorists, 164, 216
avian medicine, 165
  board-certified specialists, 169–170
  clinical signs, 167–168
  diagnostic tests, 168, 169
  postmortem examinations, 196
  practitioners of, 170–171
  research, importance of, 196
aviary, 12
aviculture, 12
aviculturists, 173
avis, 12, 162

• B •

baby birds, 52–53
  hand-feeding, 52
  socialization, 53
  unweaned, 52
  weaned, 52
banding, 81
barbules, 146
barking, 118
baths, 130–132
beak, 140–141
  growth of, 142
  health of, 142
  hookbills, 141
  shapes, 141
  sizes, 141
  strength of, 141
  as tools, 141–142
beak behaviors, body language, 118–120
beaking, 118
beauty, 13–14
beginner birds
  Amazon parrots, 281–282
  budgies (parakeets), 278
  canaries, 276–277
  cockatiels, 278–279
  finches, 277
  Monk parakeets, 279–280
  peach-faced lovebirds, 282
  pionus parrots, 280–281
  poicephalus parrotlets, 280
  poicephalus parrots, 280
  pyrrhura conures, 281
  Quaker parakeets, 279–280
behavior, 209–210
  boss, having bird accept you as the, 215–216
  destructive behavior, creating outlets for, 214
  good behavior, framework for, 210–211
  positive interaction, spending time in, 213–214
  problem. *See* problem behavior
  resources, 210
  restrictions, setting and enforcing, 214–217
belly up, body language, 123
bird bread, recipe, 111
bird cages. *See* cages
Bird Hotline, 21
Bird Hotline: World Wide Bird Lost and Found, 268–269
bird jokes, 299–302
Bird Placement Program, 306
Bird Talk/Birds USA, 304
Bird Things, 303
bird-care files, making and trading, 295–296
bird-keeping
  beauty as reason for, 13–14
  companionship as reason for, 15–16
  cost of, 17–18
  death of owner, 205–206
  generally, 11–12
  high-maintenance aspect of, 16–17
  longevity of birds, 17
  mess due to, 18

noise, 18
pet to breeder to pet cycle, 230
reasons for, 13–16
song as reason for, 14–15
speech as reason for, 14–15
time-consuming nature of, 16–17
BIRDNET, 269
birds
appeal of, 11
and cats, 87–88
and children, 34, 87, 204
companion qualities, ignoring, 11
and dogs, 88–89
domestication of, 13
as food, 13
life span increases, 194–196
naming, 91
other birds, introducing to, 89–90
as sustenance, 12–13
bites, 180
biting, 118–119, 142, 219–220
bleeding, 181
blood feathers, 130
blue-and-gold macaws, 42
blue-headed pionous, 36
board-certified specialists, 165
boarding, 133–134
bobbing, 121
body language, 116
barking, 118
beak behaviors, 118–120
beaking, 118
belly up, 123
biting, 118–119
bobbing, 121
body up, head up, relaxed, 123
body up and rigid, head up, feathers ruffled and flared, 123
chattering, 118
clicking, 118
crouching, head down, intense stare, eyes pinning/flashing, 122–123
crouching, head down, relaxed body, wings raised or fluttering, 123
crouching, head tipped downward, 122
drooping, 120–121
fanning, 121
flashing, 116–117
grinding, 118
growling, 118
jousting, 120
manteling, 123
muttering, 118
pinning, 116–117
posture, 122–123
preening, 123
purring, 117
quivering, 123
regurgitating, 120
shoulder hunching, 120
singing, 117
sneezing, 119
staring, 116
stretching, 123
tail behavior, 121
talking, 117
tongue-clicking, 117
vocalization, 117–118
wagging, 121
whistling, 117
wind behavior, 120–121
wing flipping, 120
wiping, 120
yawning, 119
bookmarks, 21
border canaries, 30
boredom as reason for feather-picking, 218
breathing difficulty, 181
breathing in a dangerous object, 182

breeders, 56, 59
 age of birds, 260–261
 behavioral problems of birds, 262–263
 feeding the birds, 263–264
 how many birds sold a year, 258–259
 medical problems of birds, 261–262
 post-purchase warranties, 259–260
 questions to ask when buying a bird, 257–264
 references, 260
 reputable sources, importance of, 163
 retailers, transferring birds to, 162
 sales contracts, 259–260
 socialization of birds, 263
 visiting before buying birds, 264
 where birds come from, 257–258
breeding, 15, 225–226
 active mating, 232
 babies, raising, 234–237
 cloacal kiss, 232
 eggs, 232–234
 fledglings, 237
 food as condition for, 232
 hand-feeding babies, 235–236
 housing, proper, 231
 mentors, help of, 229–230
 nesting areas, 232
 pair bonding, 230–231
 privacy as condition for, 232
 record-keeping, 236
 socializing babies, 236
 weaning babies, 237
broken bones, 181
brooders, 234
brotogeris parakeets, 32
Buba the Bird, 272, 273
budgies, 25, 32–33
 American style, 32
 as bird for beginner, 278
 body types, 32
 cost, 32–33
 English style, 32
 life span, 33
bugs, feeding to your bird, 113
burns, 181
burying dead birds, 202–203
buying, 47
 age as factor in, 51–55
 avian veterinarians as resource for, 56
 bargains, 60
 from breeders, 59
 captive-raised, 48
 females, 49–50
 health as factor in, 50–51
 home, bringing bird, 86
 males, 49–50
 older birds, 54–55
 from pet stores, 55–58
 price as factor in, 60
 from private parties, 59–60
 questions to ask when, 257–264
 from reputable sources, 55–60
 rights, protecting your, 60–61
 risk, minimizing, 48
 sales contracts, 61
 warranties, 61
 wild-caught versus captive-raised, 48–49

• C •

CAC (closed aviary concept), 162
Caged Bird Rescue, 306
cages, 66
 acrylic cages, 67
 bar-spacing, 66–67
 convenience, 68
 covers, 70
 design, 67–68
 droppings trays, 67–68
 knockdowns, 68–69
 location for, 84–85

metal cages, 67
new items, introducing, 85
placement of, 68
quality of, 67–69
secondhand cages, 66
setting up, 84–85
size of, 66–67
stands for, 68
sturdiness, 68
time-out cages, 69
travel cages, 70
width, 67
wood cages, 67
caiques, 37–38
canaries, 13, 25, 29–30
as bird for beginner, 276–277
color of, 30
life span, 30
roller canaries, 30
song, 14, 30
candidiasis, 188–189
carbohydrates, 104
cardiopulmonary system, 152
Carolina parakeet, 14
carriers, 70
for emergencies, 180
home, bringing bird, 86
cassowaries, 44
cataracts, 200
cats and birds, 87–88
Cats For Dummies (Spadafori and Pion), 88
cement perches, 72
chattering, 118
cheap toys, 78
chickens, 43, 45
children and birds, 34, 87, 204
chlamydiosis, 187–188
choanal slit, 143
choosing a bird, 23–45
criteria for, 23–27
species. *See* species
chronic malnutrition, 197–199
cleaning supplies, 78–79, 96
cleanups
basic regimen, 94–98
bedding used for prevention of, 79
brushes for, 79
cage liners, removing and replacing, 97
cleaning supplies, 78–79
cloth towels, 95–96
dishwashers for, 79
disinfectants for, 79
everyday cleanups, 96–97
feedings, 97
food bowls, cleaning and replacing, 97
hampers, 96
handheld vacuums for, 79, 96
health issues and, 95
mat for under the cage, 96
newspapers used for prevention of, 79, 80, 95
old T-shirts, 96
paper towels, 96
plastic mats used for prevention of, 79
preventing, 79–80
quick cleanups, 97
setting up for cleaning, 95–96
spray bottles with cleaning solution, 96
thorough cleanings, 98
towels used for prevention of, 79–80
trash bins, 96
water bowls, cleaning and replacing, 97
weekly cleaning, 98
clicking, 118
cloaca, 153
Closed Aviary Concept (CAC), 226–227
closed bands, 81

cockatiels, 34–35
  as bird for beginner, 278–279
  color mutations, 50
  cost, 34
  gender, determining, 50
  health problems, 34
  life span, 34
  vocalness, 35
cockatoos, 40–41
colds, 245
Communications with Parrots: The Pepperberg Homepage, 269
companionship, 15–16
complete proteins, 104
concrete perches, 72
conservation groups
  World Parrot Trust, 305
  World Parrot Trust Canada, 305
  World Parrot Trust USA, 305
contact lists, 294–295
contour feathers, 146
conures, 36–37
cost, 26–27
  African greys, 39
  Amazons, 39
  Asiatic parakeets, 31
  brotogeris parakeets, 32
  budgies, 32–33
  caiques, 38
  cockatiels, 34
  cockatoos, 41
  conures, 37
  eclectus, 41
  hawkheads, 38
  lovebirds, 33
  parrotlets, 33
  pionus, 41
  poicephalus, 35
  Quaker (Monk) parakeets, 32
cremation of dead birds, 202–203
criteria for choosing
  cost, 26–27
  interactivity, 24
  messes, 25
  noise, 25–26
  size, 24–25
  talking ability, 26
crop, 52, 143, 152–153
cutting nails, 128

• D •

dangers
  animal attacks, 286–287
  being stepped on, 292–293
  electrical cords, 293
  flying, 287
  foods, 291
  human medications, 292
  inhalants, 288–289
  losing your bird, 288
  medications, 292
  metals, 291–292
  toxic plants, 289–291
death
  autopsy, 160, 202
  burying, 202–203
  child's grief, 204
  cremation, 202–203
  donations, making, 203
  euthanasia, 200–202
  greeting cards for, 203
  grief, 203–204
  loss, dealing with, 203–204
  necropsy, 160
  of owner, 205–206
  pet loss support groups, 204–205
  postmortem examinations, 160, 196, 202
  unknown causes, 160

Demystifying Pet Bird Behavior (Davis), 210
diagnostic tests, 168, 169, 183–184
diarrhea, 154
diet, 99
- alcohol, 109
- avocados, 109
- avoiding certain foods, 109
- bugs, 113
- caffeine, 109
- chocolate, 109
- converting, 111–112
- dairy, 109
- feathers and, 109
- fruits, 107–109
- grit, 112
- meals, sharing, 109
- nutrition, 103–106
- nuts, 110
- obesity, 101
- pellet diets, 100–103, 107
- recipes, 111
- reforming, 111–112
- seeds, 100, 110, 244
- sunflower seeds, 100
- supplements, 110
- vegetables, 107–109

dinosaurs, relation to, 17
disaster planning tips
- bird-care files, making and trading, 295–296
- contact lists, 294–295
- first aid kits, 296–297
- food collection, 296
- helping others, 298
- identification for bird, 295
- lost bird kit, 297–298
- options during a crisis, 294
- plans, creating, 297
- rehearsals, 297
- securing your bird, 297
- separating your bird, 297
- supplies, 296
- disease. *See* infectious diseases

dishes, 74–75
DNA testing for gender, 50
dogs and birds, 88–89
Dogs For Dummies (Spadafori), 89
domestication of birds, 13
dominance as reason for biting, 220
donations made after death of bird, 203
down feathers, 146
drinking problems, 181
drooping, body language, 120–121
droppings, 154
ducks, 43, 45
dust on feathers, 148

• E •

ears, 144–145
eating problems, 181
eclectus parrots, 41, 49, 255
egg-binding, 49
eggs, 232
- artificial incubation, 233–234
- natural incubation, 232–233

electrical cords, 293
e-mail lists, 20
emergencies
- after hours care, 178–179
- basic first aid regimen for, 180–183
- bites, 180
- bleeding, 181
- breathing difficulty, 181
- breathing in a dangerous object, 182
- broken bones, 181
- burns, 181
- carriers for, 180
- determining what are, 177–178

(continued)

emergencies *(continued)*
  diagnostic tests, 183–184
  disaster planning tips. *See* disaster planning tips
  drinking problems, 181
  eating problems, 181
  emergency clinics, 179
  eye injuries, 181
  fanny problems, 182
  head injuries, 182
  heatstroke, 182
  life-threatening emergencies, 178
  not-so-urgent situations, 178
  poisoning, 182
  seizures, 182
  severity of, determining, 179
  stabilization, 180
  swallowing a dangerous object, 182
  towel restraint used during, 180
  urgent situations, 178
  vent problems, 182
  veternarian's role, 183–184
  what to do, 179–183
  where to go, 178–179
  whom to call, 178–179
emergency clinics, 179
emus, 44
escaping birds, 131
esophagus, 143, 152
essential amino acids, 104
ethoxyquin, 105
euthanasia
  deciding on, 200–201
  options for, 201–203
everyday cleanups, 96–97
extinction, 14
eye injuries, 181
eyes, 144

• F •

fanning, body language, 121
fanny problems, 182
FAQs, 19
fats, 105
fat-soluble vitamins, 106
fear as reason for biting, 220
featherdust, 77–78
Feathered Friends Adoption & Rescue Program, 306
feather-picking, 123, 148, 218–219
feathers, 145
  apteria, 146
  barbules, 146
  contour feathers, 146
  diet and, 109
  down feathers, 146
  dust on, 148
  feather-picking, 148
  flight feathers, 146–147
  hooklets, 146
  inner vane, 146
  maintenance of, 147–148
  molting, 148
  outer vane, 146
  powderdown feathers, 146, 148
  preen gland, 148
  preening, 147–148
  pyerylae, 146
  rectrices, 146
  remiges, 146
  variety of, 145–147
  wick feather, 148
feces, 154
Feeding Your Pet Bird (Burgmann), 103
feet, 149–150
fiber, 104

finches, 14–15, 25
as bird for beginner, 277
canaries, 29–30
Fischer's, 28
Gouldians, 28
life span, 29
society finches, 28
zebra finches, 28
first aid basics, 177–184
First Aid for Birds: An Owner's Guide to a Happy, Healthy Pet (Rach & Gallerstein), 176
first aid kits, 176, 296–297
flame wars, 20
flashing, 116–117
flight feathers, 146–147
flying, danger of, 287
food
danger of, 291
as entertainment, 75
new items, introducing, 85
food, pelleted, 101–102
For the Love of Parrots Refuge Society, 306
Foster Parrots Ltd., 306
Foundation Dutch Parrot Refuge, 306
fragility of birds, 243
fungal spores, in bedding, 79
fungi, 185

• G •

Gabriel Foundation, The, 271–272, 307
gardens, 108
gastrointestinal system, 152–154
geese, 43, 45
gender, determining, 49–50
Gillian's Help Desk, 272, 273
gizzard, 143
glottis, 143
good behavior, framework for, 210–211
greenfinches, singing abilities, 14
green-winged macaws, 42
greeting cards for loss of pet, 203
grey-cheeked parakeets, 229
GreyHaven Exotic Bird Sanctuary (British Columbia), 307
grief, 203–204
grinding, body language, 118
grinding nails, 128
grit, 112, 153
grooming, 127
baths, 130–132
blood feathers, 130
cutting nails, 128
grinding nails, 128
misting, 130–132
nails, trimming, 127–128
pin feathers, 130
rotary grinding devices, 128
showers, 130–132
wings, clipping, 128–130
growling, 118
Guide to a Well-Behaved Parrot (Athan), 210
gyms, 74

• H •

hand-fed birds, 243
hand-feeding baby birds, 52
hawkheads, 37–38
head injuries, 182
health
bacteria screening, 253–254
of beak, 142
behavioral check-ups, 252
blood testing, 253
breeding facilities, 162
buying, as factor in, 50–51

(continued)

health *(continued)*
cage review, 251
characteristics of good, 51
chlamydiosis testing, 254
disease testing, 254
gender testing, 254–255
husbandry review, 251
multi-bird households, 253
nutrition, 252
physical examination, 250–251
preventive measures. *See* preventive care
Psittacine Beak and Feather Disease testing, 254
psittacosis testing, 254
quarantine of new birds, 89–90
steps to a healthy bird, 249–255
vaccinations, 255
health problems as reason for feather-picking, 218
hearing, 145
heart, 152
heart disease, 200
heatstroke, 182
helping others during disasters, 298
high-maintenance pets, 242
historical background, 12–13
holding birds, 124
hand, restraining by, 124–125
towel, restraining by, 125–127
holistic medicine, 175
home alone, leaving bird, 134
home care
fallacies, 176–177
first aid basics, 177–184
first aid kit, 176
role of, 177
home first aid kit, 176
hooklets, 146
Hornbeck's, 303
human medications, 292
humans, passing disease to, 186
humidifiers, 77–78
husbandry, 163–164
hyacinth macaws, 43

• I •

identification, 295
escaping birds, 131
leg bands, 81
microchips, 81–82
sexing results, 50
illness. *See also* emergencies
after hours care, 178–179
emergency clinics, 179
infectious diseases, 184–189
medication, 191–192
misunderstanding, 245
older birds, 197–200
recuperation, 189–192
severity of, determining, 179
what to do, 179–183
where to go, 178–179
whom to call, 178–179
infectious diseases, 184
antibiotics, 188
aspergillosis, 188–189
bacteria, 184–185
candidiasis, 188–189
chlamydiosis, 187–188
fungi, 185
humans, passing disease to, 186
Pacheco's disease, 186
polyomavirus, 187
proventricular dilation disease, 187
psittacosis, 187–188
Psittcine Beak and Feather Disease, 185
viruses, 185

inhalants, danger of, 288–289
inner vane, 146
intelligence, 15
Internet
  e-mail lists, 20
  FAQs, 19
  newsgroups, 20–21
  out-of-date information, 19
  rumors, 19
  Web rings, 21
  Web sites. *See* Web sites

• J •

Jardine's parrots, 35
jokes, 299–302
jousting, 120
junk-food junkie, 100
  converting a, 111—112

• K •

knockdown cages, 68–69

• L •

The Large Macaws: Their Care, Breeding and Conservation (Speer), 43
large parrots, 38
  African greys, 39
  Amazons, 39
  cockatoos, 40–41
  eclectus, 41
  macaws, 42–43
  pionus, 41
legs, 149–150
lice, 155
life spans, 17
  Amazons, 39
  Asiatic parakeets, 31
  budgies, 33
  caiques, 38
  canaries, 30
  cockatiels, 34
  cockatoos, 41
  conures, 37
  domestically raised birds, 194–195
  hawkheads, 38
  lovebirds, 33
  macaws, 42
  nutrition and, 195
  parrotlets, 33
  pet to breeder to pet cycle, 230
  pionus, 41
  research, importance of, 196
  veterinary contribution, 196
life-threatening emergencies, 178
lories, 25, 35–36, 113
lorikeets, 25, 35–36, 113
losing your bird, 288
loss, dealing with, 203–204
lost bird kit, 297–298
lovebirds, 25, 33, 246
low humidity as reason for feather-picking, 218
low-maintenance pets, 241–242

• M •

Macaw Landing Foundation, 307
macaws, 42–43
  blue-and-gold macaws, 42
  green-winged macaws, 42
  hyacinth macaws, 43
  military macaws, 42
  mini macaws, 43
  Scarlet macaws, 42
manteling, 123
medication
  danger of, 292
  feather-picking, 219
  feeds, medicated, 191
  injections, 191
  methods, choosing, 191
  oral dosages, 191
  water-soluble, 191

medium-sized parrots, 35–38
  caiques, 37–38
  conures, 36–37
  hawkheads, 37–38
  lories, 35–36
  lorikeets, 35–36
  poicephalus, 35
  Senegal parrot, 35
metal cages, 67
metals, 291–292
Meyer's parrots, 35
Mickaboo Cockatiel Rescue, 307
microchips, 81–82, 255
military macaws, 42
mimicry, mynahs, 43
mineral perches, 72
minerals, 106
mini macaws, 43
misting, 130–132
mites, 155, 244–245
moderators, 20
The Modern Ark: The Story of Zoos, Past, Present and Future (Crock), 213
molting, 148
Moluccan cockatoo, 40
Monk parakeets, as bird for beginner, 279–280
multiple bird households, 223–225
  breeding, 225–226
  Closed Aviary Concept (CAC), 226–227
  compatibility considerations, 227–229
  existing birds, ensuring health of, 227
  gender choices, 228
  living quarters kept at same heights, 227–228
  new birds, ensuring health of, 227
  pair-bonded birds, 225, 228
  quarantining new birds, 227
  size issues, 228–229
  species choices, 228
  temperament issues, 228–229
  too many birds, 224
muttering, 118
mynahs, 43

nails, 150
nails, trimming, 127–128
naming your pet, 91
natural incubation, 233–234
NBARC, Inc., 307
netiquette, 20
New England Exotic Bird Sanctuary, 307
new items, introducing, 85
New Life Parrot Rescue and Helpline Service, 307
newsgroups, 20–21
newspapers as cageliners, 80
normal bacterial flora, 184
not-so-urgent situations, 178
nutrition, 103
  carbohydrates, 104
  complete proteins, 104
  essential amino acids, 104
  fats, 105
  fat-soluble vitamins, 106
  fiber, 104
  minerals, 106
  preservatives, 105
  preventive care, 163–164
  protein, 103–104
  vitamins, 106
  water, 105–106
  water-soluble vitamins, 106

Oasis Sanctuary Foundation Ltd., 307
obesity
  Amazons, 39
  older birds, 197–199

older birds
  activity, lack of, 199
  age as factor in buying, 51–55
  arthritis, 200
  cataracts, 200
  chronic malnutrition, 197–199
  euthanasia, 200–202
  heart disease, 200
  illness, 197–200
  obesity, 197–199
  undernutrition, 199
Online Books of Parrots, 272
open bands, 81
options during a crisis, 294
ostriches, 44
outer vane, 146

• P •

Pacheco's disease, 186
parakeets
  Alexandrian parakeets, 30–31
  Asiatic parakeets, 30–31
  brotogeris parakeets, 32
  derbian parakeets, 30–31
  generally, 30
  Monks, 31–32
  mustached parakeets, 30–31
  plum-headed parakeets, 30–31
  Quakers, 31–32
  ring-necked parakeets, 30–31
parasites, 155
Parrot Rescue!, 307
parrotlets, 25, 33
  cost, 33
  life span, 33
parrots, 26
  African grey parrots, 39, 123
  Amazon parrots, 39, 281–282
  beaks, 141
  budgerigars, 32–33
  caiques, 37–38
  cockatoos, 40–41
  conures, 36–37
  eclectus parrots, 41, 49, 255
  generally, 30
  hawkheads, 37–38
  Jardine's parrots, 35
  large parrots, 38–43
  lories, 35–36
  lorikeets, 35–36
  lovebirds, 33
  macaws, 42–43
  medium-sized parrots, 35–38
  Meyer's parrots, 35
  parakeets, 30–32
  parrotlets, 33
  pionus, 41
  poicephalus, 35
  red-bellied parrots, 35
  Senegal parrot, 35
  small parrots, 30–35
  talking ability, 246
  vocal talents of, 14–15
PEAC, 308
peach-faced lovebirds, as bird for
    beginner, 282
peacocks, 45
peafowl, 45
peahens, 45
pellet diets, 57, 100–102, 107
  appeal to birds, 102
  outdated advice about, 102
pent-up energy as reason for feather-
    picking, 218
Pepperberg Homepage, The, 269
Pepperberg, Irene, 15
perches, 71
  acrylic perches, 73
  cement perches, 72
  concrete perches, 72
  destructibility, 71

(continued)

perches *(continued)*
  mineral perches, 72
  plastic perches, 73
  PVC perches, 73
  rope perches, 72
  safety, 71
  sandpaper-covered perches, 72
  tree branches as, 73
  variety, 71
  wood perches, 71
periodicals
  Bird Talk/Birds USA, 304
  Pet Bird Report, 304
Pet Bird Report, 210, 267, 304
Pet Care Forum, 19
pet loss support groups, 204–205
pet shops
  accessories, 57
  age of birds, 260–261
  attention to pets, 57
  behavioral problems of birds, 262–263
  birds, care of, 58
  cleanliness of, 57
  feeding birds, 263–264
  how many birds sold a year, 258–259
  medical problems of birds, 261–262
  pelleted diets for birds, 57
  post-purchase warranties, 60–61, 259–260
  questions to ask when buying a bird, 257–264
  references, 260
  sales contracts, 60–61, 259–260
  socialization of birds, 263
  staff, 56–57
  visiting before buying birds, 264
  where birds come from, 257–258
pet supplies, 65–66
  air-cleaners, 77–78
  Bird Lady Productions, 303
  Bird Things, 303
  cages, 66–70
  cleaning supplies, 78–79
  dishes, 74–75
  food as entertainment, 75
  gyms, 74
  harnesses, 81
  Hornbeck's, 303
  humidifiers, 77–78
  leashes, 81
  leg bands, 81
  perches, 71–73
  Pet Warehouse, 304
  Petiatric Supply, 304
  Pet-Pak, Inc., 304
  playstands, 74
  ResQPet, 304
  toys, 75–77
  water bottles, 75
  waterers, 74–75
Pet Warehouse, 304
Petiatric Supply, 304
Pet-Pak, Inc., 304
pet-sitters, 132–133
pin feathers, 130
pinning, 116–117
pionus parrots, 41, 280–281
pionus snarfle, 41
plans for disasters, creating, 297
plastic perches, 73
playstands, 74
poicephalus parrotlets
  as bird for beginner, 280
poicephalus parrots, 35
  as bird for beginner, 280
poisoning, 182
polyomavirus, 187
postmortem examinations, 160, 196, 202

posture, 122–123
potty-training, 122
powderdown feathers, 146, 148
precocial babies, 234
preen gland, 148
preening, 123, 147–148
preservatives, 105
preventive care, 157–158
  advice your bird can live without, 161
  arguments for, 159–151
  bottom-line pragmatism as argument for, 161
  cost savings as argument for, 160
  diagnostic tests, 169
  healthy bird, starting with a, 162–163
  husbandry, 163–164
  illness, hiding signs of, 158–159
  nutrition, 163–164
  plan for, 161–164
  professionals, working with, 164
  proper care, 163–164
  quality of life as argument for, 161
  scarcity of urgent care as argument for, 159–160
problem behavior
  avian behaviorists, 216
  biting, 219–220
  environment, creating suitable, 213
  feather-picking, 218–219
  health problems, determining whether roots are in, 210
  height of cage/play gym used to reinforce your role as boss, 215
  lack of flight used to reinforce your role as boss, 215
  letting bird out of cage used to reinforce your role as boss, 216
  new home for bird with, finding, 221–222
  not able to fix, accepting sometimes you are, 217
  physical discipline, 217
  placement groups, 222
  punishment, 217
  rescue groups, 222
  screaming, 220–221
  sexual maturity and, 221
  sick birds, 211
  step-up command used to reinforce your role as boss, 215
  wild life, inclination toward, 211–212
protein, 103–104
proventricular dilation disease, 187
Providence House Avian Rescue and Support Services, 308
psittacine family. *See* parrots
psittacosis, 187–188
Psittcine Beak and Feather Disease, 185
psychological problems as reason for feather-picking, 218
purring, 117
PVC perches, 73
pyerylae, 146
pyrrhura conures, as bird for beginner, 37, 281

Quaker parakeets
  as bird for beginner, 279–280
  cost, 32
  ownership regulations, 31
quarantine, 162, 227
quivering, 123

• R •

Raptor Center at University of
Minnesota, 267–268
recipes, 111
rectrices, 146
recuperation time, 189
food, 190
handling, minimal, 191
home stay, 190–191
hospital stay, 189–190
medication, 191–192
perches, removing, 190
quiet, 191
smaller cages, 190
warm environment, 190
water, 190
red-bellied parrots, 35
redirected aggression as reason for
biting, 220
regurgitating, 120
rehearsals for disasters, 297
relationships
breeders, 27
heavy contact, 27
minimal contact, 27
starting correctly, 84
training as part of. *See* training
remiges, 146
rescue and adoption organizations
Bird Placement Program, 306
Caged Bird Rescue, 306
Feathered Friends Adoption & Rescue
Program, 306
Foster Parrots Ltd., 306
Foundation Dutch Parrot Refuge, 306
Gabriel Foundation, 307
GreyHaven Exotic Bird Sanctuary
(British Columbia), 307
For the Love of Parrots Refuge
Society, 306
Macaw Landing Foundation, 307
Mickaboo Cockatiel Rescue, 307
NBARC, Inc., 307
New England Exotic Bird
Sanctuary, 307
New Life Parrot Rescue and Helpline
Service, 307
Oasis Sanctuary Foundation Ltd., 307
Parrot Rescue!, 307
PEAC, 308
Providence House Avian Rescue and
Support Services, 308
Rescue Me, 308
The Shyne Brown Foundation, 308
TARA, 308
The Tropics Exotic Bird Refuge, 308
Rescue Me, 308
respiratory tract, 152
ResQPet, 304
rope perches, 72
rotary grinding devices, 128

• S •

sales contracts, 61
sandpaper-covered perches, 72
scarlet macaws, 42
Scat Mat, 89
screaming, 220–221
securing your bird, 297
seed, 100, 110, 244
seizures, 182
Senegal parrot, 35
separating your bird, 297
settling in (bringing home), 86
sex, determining, 49–50
sexual dimorphism, 49
shelters, 55
shoulder hunching, 120
showers, 130–132

signs of illness
  bird specific treatment, 174–175
  droppings, high urine output in, 178
  emergency, determining what is an, 177–178
  urine output, high, 178
  where to go, 178–179
  whom to call, 178–179
singing, 117
skeletal improvements, 151
small parrots
  budgerigars, 32–33
  generally, 30
  lovebirds, 33
  parakeets, 30–32
  parrotlets, 33
  snarfle, pionus, 41
sneezing, 119
socialization, 53, 243
species
  cassowaries, 44
  chickens, 43, 45
  ducks, 43, 45
  emus, 44
  finches, 28–30
  geese, 43, 45
  generally, 27–28
  large parrots, 38–43
  medium-sized parrots, 35–38
  mynahs, 43
  ostriches, 44
  parrots, 30–38
  peafowl, 45
  small parrots, 30–35
  toucans, 43
  turkeys, 43, 45
staring, 116
step-up command, 92
stress bars, 51
stretching, 123
styptic powder, 128, 176
sun conures, 13, 37
sunflower seeds, 100
supplies. *See* pet supplies
surgical sexing for gender, 50
survival threats, 49
swallowing a dangerous object, 182
synthetic preservatives, 105

• T •

tail behavior, body language, 121
talking, 117, 119
TARA, 308
tarsometatarsus, 151
taste buds, 143
territorial protection as reason for biting, 220
The Large Macaws: Their Care, Breeding and Conservation (Speer), 43
The Modern Ark: The Story of Zoos, Past, Present and Future (Crock), 213
The Shyne Brown Foundation, 308
The Tropics Exotic Bird Refuge, 308
third eyelid, 144
tibiotarsus, 151
time-out cages, 69
tongue, 143
tongue-clicking, 117
toucans, 43
toxic plants, 289–291
toys, 75–77
  cheap toys, 78
  connectors, 76
  construction of, 76
  destruction of, 78
  fear of, 77
  household items as, 78
  materials, 76
  new items, introducing, 85
  size of, 76

training
  alone, knowing when to leave bird, 91
  control of bird's comings and goings, 91
  ignoring commands, 91
  positioning bird, 91
  potty-training, 122
  rules for, 91–92
  sessions, length of, 91
  step-up command, 92
  talk, teaching bird to, 119
  talking to bird, 91
  taming wild ones, 93–94
  trust built through, 90–94
travel cages, 70
traveling
  boarding your bird, 133–134
  bringing your bird with you, 134–135
  home, bringing bird, 86
  leaving bird home alone, 134
  pet-sitters for your bird, 132–133
tree branches as perches, 73
turkeys, 43, 45

• U •

umbrella cockatoo, 40
undernutrition, 199
Up At Six, 19
urates, 154
urgent situations, 178
urine, 154

• V •

vent, 153, 182
veterinarians
  after hours care, 179
  Association of Avian Veterinarians, 170–171, 305
  bacteria screening, 253–254
  behavioral check-ups, 252
  biting, protecting against, 142
  blood testing, 253
  board-certified specialists, 169–170
  caging review, 251
  chlamydiosis testing, 254
  consultations between, 171–172
  credentials, 170–171
  disease testing, 254
  emergencies, role in, 183–184
  emergency care, 178–179
  gender testing, 254–255
  handling bird, 170–171, 250–251
  husbandry review, 251
  life spans, contributions to increasing birds', 196
  multi-bird households, 253
  nutrition checking, 252
  observation of bird, 250
  physical examination of bird, 250–251
  preventive care, 164
  Psittacine Beak and Feather Disease testing, 254
  psittacosis testing, 254
  referrals to help in finding, 170
  restraint, methods used for, 127
  selecting, 165–168
  vaccinations, 255
  Veterinary Information Network, 167
veterinary examinations, 50
Veterinary Information Network, 167
veterinary visits, after tangle with cat, 88
viruses, 185
vision, 144
vitamins, 106
vocalization, 117–118
Vogelbauer Museum, 69

• W •

wagging, 121
Wakulla Springs, 121
warranties, 61
water, 105–106
water bottles, 75
waterers, 74–75
water-soluble vitamins, 106
Web rings, 21
Web sites, 19–21, 266–273
  All About Birds, 266
  American Federation of Aviculture, 270, 305
  American Holistic Veterinary Medical Association, 175
  Association of Avian Veterinarians, 270–271, 305
  Bird Hotline: World Wide Bird Lost and Found, 268–269
  Bird Placement Program, 306
  Bird Things, 303
  BIRDNET, 269
  bookmarks, 21
  Buba the Bird, 272
  Communications with Parrots: The Pepperberg Homepage, 269
  described, 21
  Foster Parrots Ltd., 306
  Foundation Dutch Parrot Refuge, 306
  Gabriel Foundation, 271–272, 307
  Gillian's Help Desk, 272
  GreyHaven Exotic Bird Sanctuary (British Columbia), 307
  Hornbeck's, 303
  Macaw Landing Foundation, 307
  Mickaboo Cockatiel Rescue, 307
  NBARC, Inc., 307
  New England Exotic Bird Sanctuary, 307
  Oasis Sanctuary Foundation Ltd., 307
  Online Books of Parrots, 272
  Parrot Rescue!, 307
  PEAC, 308
  Pet Bird Report, 267
  Pet Warehouse, 304
  Petiatric Supply, 304
  Pet-Pak, Inc., 304
  Providence House Avian Rescue and Support Services, 308
  Raptor Center at University of Minnesota, 267–268
  Rescue Me, 308
  ResQPet, 304
  TARA, 308
  The Tropics Exotic Bird Refuge, 308
  Up At Six, 19
  Veterinary Information Network, 167
  World Parrot Trust, 305
  World Parrot Trust Canada, 305
  World Parrot Trust USA, 305
weekly cleaning, 98
whistling, 117
wick feather, 148
wind behavior, 120–121
wings, 149
  clipping, 128–130
  flipping, 120
wiping, 120
wood cages, 67
wood perches, 71
World Parrot Trust, 49, 305
World Parrot Trust Canada, 305
World Parrot Trust USA, 305
worms, 155

• Y •

yawning, 119

• Z •

zoonoses, 245
zoos, 213
zygodactyl toes, 149

Notes

Notes

Discover Dummies Online!

The Dummies Web Site is your fun and friendly online resource for the latest information about *...For Dummies®* books and your favorite topics. The Web site is the place to communicate with us, exchange ideas with other *...For Dummies* readers, chat with authors, and have fun!

Ten Fun and Useful Things You Can Do at www.dummies.com

1. Win free *...For Dummies* books and more!
2. Register your book and be entered in a prize drawing.
3. Meet your favorite authors through the IDG Books Author Chat Series.
4. Exchange helpful information with other *...For Dummies* readers.
5. Discover other great *...For Dummies* books you must have!
6. Purchase Dummieswear™ exclusively from our Web site.
7. Buy *...For Dummies* books online.
8. Talk to us. Make comments, ask questions, get answers!
9. Download free software.
10. Find additional useful resources from authors.

Link directly to these ten fun and useful things at **http://www.dummies.com/10useful**

For other technology titles from IDG Books Worldwide, go to **www.idgbooks.com**

Not on the Web yet? It's easy to get started with *Dummies 101®: The Internet For Windows®98* or *The Internet For Dummies®*, 6th Edition, at local retailers everywhere.

Find other *...For Dummies* books on these topics:
Business • Career • Databases • Food & Beverage • Games • Gardening • Graphics • Hardware
Health & Fitness • Internet and the World Wide Web • Networking • Office Suites
Operating Systems • Personal Finance • Pets • Programming • Recreation • Sports
Spreadsheets • Teacher Resources • Test Prep • Word Processing

IDG BOOKS WORLDWIDE BOOK REGISTRATION

We want to hear from you!

Visit **http://my2cents.dummies.com** to register this book and tell us how you liked it!

- Get entered in our monthly prize giveaway.
- Give us feedback about this book — tell us what you like best, what you like least, or maybe what you'd like to ask the author and us to change!
- Let us know any other *...For Dummies*® topics that interest you.

Your feedback helps us determine what books to publish, tells us what coverage to add as we revise our books, and lets us know whether we're meeting your needs as a *...For Dummies* reader. You're our most valuable resource, and what you have to say is important to us!

Not on the Web yet? It's easy to get started with *Dummies 101*®*: The Internet For Windows*® *98* or *The Internet For Dummies*®, 6th Edition, at local retailers everywhere.

Or let us know what you think by sending us a letter at the following address:

...For Dummies Book Registration
Dummies Press
7260 Shadeland Station, Suite 100
Indianapolis, IN 46256-3917
Fax 317-596-5498